NUCLEAR
JIHAD

RELATED TITLES FROM POTOMAC BOOKS

Terror on the Internet: The New Arena, the New Challenges
—Gabriel Weimann

WMD Proliferation: Reforming the Security Sector to Meet the Threat
—Fred Schreier

NUCLEAR JIHAD

A Clear and Present Danger?

TODD M. MASSE

POTOMAC BOOKS
WASHINGTON, D.C.

Library of Congress Cataloging-in-Publication Data
Masse, Todd.
  Nuclear Jihad : a clear and present danger? / Todd M. Masse. — 1st ed.
      p. cm.
  Includes bibliographical references and index.
  ISBN 978-1-59797-528-5 (hardcover : acid-free paper)
  1. Nuclear terrorism—United States. 2. Nuclear terrorism—United
States—Prevention. 3. Jihad. I. Title.
  HV6433.86.M37 2011
  363.325'50973—dc22

                                                      2011002711

Printed in the United States of America on acid-free paper that meets the American
National Standards Institute Z39-48 Standard.

Potomac Books
22841 Quicksilver Drive
Dulles, Virginia 20166

First Edition

10 9 8 7 6 5 4 3 2 1

To my wife, Eileen; my daughter, Alexandra;
and the Masse family,
with love.

We stand on the shoulders of others.

If the Soviets do an excellent job at retaining control over their stockpile of nuclear weapons—let's assume they've got 25,000 to 30,000; that's a ballpark figure—and they are 99 percent successful, that would mean you could still have as many as 250 that they were not able to control.

—(Then) Defense Secretary Richard Cheney,
Meet the Press, December 15, 1991

If we continue along our present course, nuclear terrorism is inevitable. Indeed, if the United States and other governments keep doing what they are doing today, a nuclear attack on American soil is more likely than not in the decade ahead.

—Graham Allison, Douglas Dillon Professor of Government,
Harvard University, 2004

While [such] worst-case scenarios can highlight U.S. weaknesses and lead to more robust plans, they are too often [more] sensational than real, and too frequently disconnected from the goals and capabilities of actual terrorist groups. The result is . . . "a false sense of insecurity."

—Daniel Byman, Director of Security Studies,
Georgetown University, 2008

Terrorism with chemical, biological, or radiological materials is likely to occur in the United States. Nuclear terrorism is unlikely to do so; it is simply too difficult, both to acquire fissile material and to construct a viable weapon.

—Gavin Cameron, Senior Research Associate,
Monterey Institute of International Studies, Spring 2000

The likelihood that a terrorist group will come up with an atomic bomb seems to be vanishingly small—perhaps substantially less than one in a million. Moreover, the degree to which al-Qa'ida—the only terrorist group that has explicitly threatened to strike the United States—has sought, or is capable of obtaining, such a weapon seems to have been substantially exaggerated.

—John Mueller, Department of Political Science,
Ohio State University, 2008

This idea that in order to make a decision you need to focus on the consequences (which you can know) rather than the probability (which you can't know) is the *central* idea of uncertainty.

—Nassim Nicholas Taleb, Professor of Sciences of Uncertainty,
University of Massachusetts at Amherst, 2007

CONTENTS

FIGURES AND TABLES

PREFACE

A nuclear terrorism threat to the United States exists, yet there is no inexorable march to Armageddon. The threat is clear, although not necessarily present. While there may be other groups that have the intent
and operational capability to buy, steal, or construct their own improvised
nuclear device (IND), al Qaeda currently represents the greatest terrorist nuclear threat. Al Qaeda clearly intends to attack the United States with unconventional weapons, as demonstrated by the messages disseminated through
its sophisticated communications network. However, its current capability to
construct, deliver, and detonate a nuclear device in the United States is far
less obvious. The nuclear terrorism threat, then, may be clear insofar as its
consequences are dire and understandable, but it is not necessarily present or
imminent given that no terrorist group, to the best of current public knowledge, has married the intent to harm the United States with the capability to
acquire or otherwise construct a nuclear weapon. Given some of the inherent
difficulties in constructing even a crude nuclear weapon, the substantial (but
incomplete) successes in protecting fissile material, and ongoing counterterrorism efforts to destroy terrorist capability to execute complex catastrophic
attacks, nuclear terrorism is not inevitable. Moreover, while the security of
nuclear weapons and fissile material in Pakistan remains a substantial concern,
U.S. policymakers in a position to know have stated they are confident that
Pakistan's nuclear weapons are secure. There is no place, however, for com-

placency. The international community, led by the United States and Russia and international bodies including the International Atomic Energy Agency (IAEA), must continue to aggressively implement measures to decrease the risks of nuclear terrorism. The nuclear terrorism response must be as dynamic as the threat it faces.

From a policymaker's perspective, nuclear terrorism is a classic case of a high-consequence, low-probability problem. It is imprudent not to take action against such a threat, yet when other lower consequence but much higher probability terrorist attack vectors also need to be detected, prevented, and managed, the optimal mix of nuclear security and counterterrorism resources remains an open question. Some argue that given a $14 trillion economy, dedicating resources to even such a low-probability threat represents another inevitable cost of being a substantial power in the international system. Others argue that the focus on nuclear terrorism and other worst-case scenarios distracts U.S. attention from more likely terrorist attacks, including terrorists' tried-and-true mass-casualty attacks using conventional weapons; engenders an environment in which the populace lives in fear instead of with fear; and does not accurately reflect the history of terrorists' attempts to use unconventional weapons.

There are at least two schools of thought on nuclear terrorism, and while they agree on some issues, their assessments of the nuclear terrorism threat are very different. These two schools of thought, which represent possible extremes in the nuclear terrorism debate, are categorized herein as the "conventionalists" and the "skeptics." The conventionalists tend to view the nuclear terrorism threat as imminent or highly likely over the next five to ten years. Although they concede that nonnuclear tools, such as sound national and international law enforcement and intelligence, are useful in combating nuclear terrorism, their primary focus and policy prescriptions are on nuclear security. Some conventionalists might even argue that nuclear security can be perfect. Conventionalists also believe that if a sophisticated terrorist group acquires fissile material, it will be relatively easy for the group to develop an IND. Skeptics, while recognizing the grave consequences of a terrorist nuclear detonation, tend to discount the nuclear terrorism threat. They argue that there is a long chain of events between a terrorist group's potential acquisition of a nuclear weapon (unlikely) or fissile material (more likely) and a detonation in the United States, and there are many opportunities for a multilayered system of defense to disrupt a terrorist plot. Skeptics view the history of terrorists' uses of weapons of mass destruction (WMD) as unsuccessful and believe that terrorist groups wanting to garner public attention, inflict fear, and bleed the U.S. economy will revert to tried-and-true conventional attacks, which remain capable of inflicting mass casualties.

Given the complexity of nuclear terrorism, invariably any discussion of the issue leads to questions about myriad other national security issues, including broader concepts of nuclear deterrence, the "domino theory" of nuclear proliferation among nation-states (for example, if Iran develops nuclear weapons, so too will Saudi Arabia), the overall effectiveness of U.S. counterterrorism policies, societal resiliency, and the extent to which a nuclear detonation in a major city would cause mass migration away from urban areas in the United States, as well as a host of other important national issues. Given the scope of research for this project, *Nuclear Jihad* touches on each of these issues in only a cursory manner but recognizes their centrality to U.S. national security and the country's standard of living.

This book has eight chapters. Chapter 1 frames and defines the issue of nuclear terrorism. Chapter 2 explains the terrorist pathway to a nuclear detonation. Chapter 3 considers fissile material compromise and the methods and policies in place to detect such compromises. Chapters 4 and 5 "unpack" the issue by summarizing the arguments about the nuclear terrorist threat probability and reviewing the demand- and supply-side dimensions of nuclear terrorism. From the demand-side dimension, what is the narrative associated with terrorist intent, motivations, and capability to acquire and detonate nuclear weapons? From the supply-side dimension, how much fissile material or how many nuclear weapons may be reasonably within reach of terrorists? Chapter 6 provides an assessment of whether terrorists can be deterred and the extent to which nuclear forensics and attribution can serve as deterrence multipliers. Chapter 7 analyzes U.S. and international strategies for preventing nuclear terrorism. Finally, chapter 8 offers some concluding thoughts. A series of appendices also provide further information on nuclear terrorism policy options as well as descriptions of the U.S. government's core nuclear terrorism programs and initiatives.

The purpose of this book is to contribute to a body of research aimed at integrating these two sides of the equation—to illuminate the forces driving supply and demand and to assess policy measures to ensure that the supply and demand curves never meet. The book does not make specific policy recommendations, but it does conclude that the alarmist public and official perceptions of a clear and present nuclear terrorism danger are overemphasized and that nuclear terrorism is not inevitable. A substantial theme of the book is that optimal policies to prevent nuclear terrorism are ones in which very conscious and sustained efforts are made to integrate policies and actions that combine supply- and demand-side reductions. Absolute physical security of fissile material does not exist, nor does a world free of terrorism. Policymakers at the senior-most levels of the U.S. national security bureaucracy, specifically the National Security Council (NSC), must be provided with the coordination and budgetary tools (even if indirectly through influence with the Office of Management and Budget) to aggressively manage all programs designed to decrease the nuclear terrorism risk.

Why, in the twenty years since the fall of the former Soviet Union and the ten years since the terrorist attacks of September 11, 2001, has there not yet been a nuclear terrorist attack? There are numerous complex reasons for this positive development that will be explored in this book, but the facts that building a nuclear weapon is not a trivial effort, fissile material security has improved markedly over time, counterterrorism efforts have been achieving results, and the nuclear nonproliferation regime remains intact (although under stress) are all contributing factors to the absence of nuclear terrorism. History, however, does not unfold in a linear fashion, so the absence of attacks today does not necessarily mean that this benign state of affairs can be projected indefinitely into the future. Nevertheless, claiming nuclear terrorism is inevitable, axiomatic, or plausible discounts the improvements that have been made in physical protection of fissile material and the incomplete yet meaningful successes of U.S. and allied counterterrorism efforts (particularly those designed to undermine core al Qaeda operational capabilities).

ACKNOWLEDGMENTS

The research and analysis conducted for this book were graciously supported by the Johns Hopkins University Applied Physics Laboratory. Specifically, I would like to extend my sincerest appreciation to Duncan Brown, fellow, National Security Analysis Division, and Ronald Luman, special assistant to the director for Strategic Planning, for their support and patience in making this book possible. I would also like to thank Zachary Davis of Lawrence Livermore National Laboratory; Brian Michael Jenkins of RAND Corporation; Caroline Barnes of the Federal Bureau of Investigation (FBI); Alfred Cumming of the Congressional Research Service; John Benedict, Michael Deane, Robert Leonhard, John Nolen, and Stan Puchalla of the Johns Hopkins University Applied Physics Laboratory; Christopher Hamilton (retired FBI); and Professor Friedrich Steinhausler of the University of Salzburg for their constructive and insightful reviews of the research and analysis that resulted in this book. Each of these individuals added significant value to the book, and I am grateful for their efforts. The views expressed in this book are not necessarily those of the Nuclear Regulatory Commission or any other government agency at which I have served. Ultimately, the judgments and conclusions, including any errors, belong solely to me.

ONE

Introduction

Nuclear terrorism is a relatively complex subject.[1] The threat of nuclear terrorism is characterized by multiple uncertainties, unknowns, and competing assessments of risk and probability. The probability of nuclear terrorism and policy responses to it have been debated intensely among scholars, scientists, and national security practitioners.[2] As with all robust debates, there are numerous and sometimes opposing schools of thought regarding the likelihood of nuclear terrorism on U.S. soil and the appropriate mix of policy responses. Each school of thought makes certain implicit and explicit assumptions about the supply and demand sides of this issue and supports those assumptions with plausible arguments. While various experts have attempted to assess it, there are no accurate means of calculating with any high degree of confidence the probability that a terrorist group will be successful in acquiring and detonating a nuclear device in the United States or in any other geographic location. As will be discussed below, what are important are supply and demand issues that interact to affect any upward or downward trends in this probability.

There are at least two schools of thought, and a spectrum of views, on nuclear terrorism. While analysts and policymakers agree that a nuclear weapon in the hands of a terrorist group would represent a clear and present danger, they differ substantially over (1) the probability of nuclear terrorism and (2) whether terrorist groups have the intent *and the capability* to acquire or build an improvised nuclear device (IND), deliver it to U.S. soil, and detonate it.

Those who view with skepticism the probability that a terrorist group could successfully detonate a nuclear weapon in the United States are referred to herein as "skeptics." They believe, in short, that there are many obstacles a terrorist must overcome to be successful and that there are many opportunities for a "defense-in-depth" systems strategy to raise the risks of such an operation for terrorists to perhaps unacceptable levels. They believe that concentrating on worst-case scenarios may not only take the focus off more likely conventional terrorist attacks but also lead to substantial opportunity costs and arguably generate excessive fear and anxiety in the population, thus facilitating a key terrorist goal. Moreover, this group is somewhat skeptical of technical determinism, or the belief that the spread of technology will inexorably lead to terrorists or other nonstate actors acquiring nuclear weapons.

Others believe, however, that the probability that terrorists will be able to successfully execute a nuclear attack is increasing and that the consequences are too high not to address the threat comprehensively. Those who follow this school of thought are referred to throughout the book as "conventionalists." For the purposes of this book, conventionalists are not defined as those making defeatist and fringe arguments that the end of the world is near, nor do they necessarily believe nuclear terrorism is inevitable. However, adherents to this school of thought are inclined to focus on consequences and terrorist intent rather than on the nuclear terrorism supply chain and terrorist capability to acquire or build a nuclear weapon. This school of thought might be reflected in a comment made by former U.S. Central Intelligence Agency (CIA) director Michael Hayden:

> A WMD program fundamentally centers on political intent. By that measure alone, there is no greater national security threat facing the United States than al-Qa'ida and its associates. Bin Ladin has said repeatedly that he considers the acquisition of nuclear weapons as a religious duty. And we know that al-Qa'ida remains determined to attack our country in ways that inflict massive death and destruction. We are fortunate that those with the clearest intent to acquire and use weapons of mass destruction are also the least capable of developing them. But the potential destruction from an improvised nuclear device—no matter how elementary—is so great that all that really matters to the CIA is that we know terrorists are determined to use them.[3]

Individuals in this school of thought believe that simply because we have not seen a nuclear terrorist attack yet does not necessarily mean it cannot happen. They believe that the threat of nuclear terrorism may be perceived by some as a "Black Swan," but it is not. According to Nassim Nicholas Taleb, author of *The Black Swan: The Impact of the Highly Improbable*, a Black Swan is an event with the following three attributes: "First, it is an *outlier*, as it lies outside the realm of regular expectations, because nothing in the past can convincingly point to its possibility. Second, it carries extreme impact. Third, in spite of its outlier status, human nature makes us concoct explanations for its occurrence *after* the fact, making it explainable and predictable."[4] Conventionalists believe that nuclear terrorism is not a Black Swan because, while it may have extreme impact, it is explainable, predictable, and indeed somewhat probable given the world situation today. Many conventionalists likely view themselves as pragmatic because the policies they advocate to prevent nuclear terrorism wager only money—some would say in the overall context of a $14 trillion economy, relatively small amounts of money—on what many view as a classic low-probability, high-consequence national security threat. According to the conventionalists, the psychological and physical effects of even a low-yield nuclear detonation are so devastating that this wager is not only prudent but an obligation for those entrusted with protecting U.S. national security.

While these two schools of thought represent two likely extremes on a spectrum of assessments of nuclear terrorism, they are used herein for illustrative purposes. Most experts in this issue area will (and should) be reluctant to place themselves in either category. By painting the opposing viewpoints, the intention is to allow readers to think anew about the problem by assessing underlying assumptions and how best to integrate supply- and demand-side measures to reduce the risk of nuclear terrorism.

THE STAKES

There is little debate and nearly universal agreement on the catastrophic, if not necessarily existential, physical and psychological effects a nuclear detonation would have on a U.S. city.[5] There are also areas of resounding consensus within the nuclear terrorism debate, such as the supply-side need to secure at its source fissile material—high-enriched uranium (HEU) and plutonium, the necessary precursors for any fission device.[6] As Harvard professor Graham

Allison has posited, if there are no "loose" nuclear weapons (or HEU or plutonium) and no new nascent nuclear weapons states, then there will be no nuclear terrorism.[7] However, some have cautioned compellingly against putting excessive faith in the illusion of a perfect "protect fissile material at the source" defense, arguing that while fissile material protection is one element of an appropriate policy mix, it should not be the sole policy prescription.[8] Substantial progress has been made on nuclear security since the dissolution of the Soviet Union in 1991, yet twenty years have passed since that international relations milestone event, and some argue the threat is increasing. As former senator Sam Nunn has said, the nonproliferation debate is rarely about direction; more often "it is a question about speed, resources, and level of effort."[9] Since the dawn of the nuclear age there have, thankfully, been no incidents of nuclear terrorism.[10] Yet time may not necessarily be on the side of those seeking to prevent nuclear terrorism; national and international urgency on this issue, according to many analysts, must be increased.[11] It is likely imprudent to underestimate or to overestimate adversarial capabilities in this area. With underestimation, one risks strategic surprise and possible catastrophic consequences; with overestimation, one risks opportunity costs, excessive public fear, and a potential lack of focus on more likely terrorist attack scenarios with conventional weapons.

The threat of nuclear terrorism is a global one, and it requires global solutions. While international organizations, such as the International Atomic Energy Agency (IAEA) and the United Nations Security Council (UNSC) have an important role to play, ultimately global nuclear security and counterterrorism fall within the province of nation-states, which must take actions to secure their nuclear materials and to undermine the ability of terrorist groups to acquire or build a nuclear weapon.

In the aftermath of the terrorist attacks of September 11, 2001, the United States became a relatively more hardened target, though it retains the vulnerabilities associated with any open society. While domestic vulnerabilities remain, detonating a nuclear device overseas is likely to be less risky, from a terrorist perspective, and have a higher probability of being successful than detonating a device within the United States. Even though nuclear weapons security within the United States is imperfect, the likelihood that a terrorist group could acquire a U.S. nuclear weapon within the country is very low.[12] It is far more likely that a nuclear weapon or fissile material to build an improvised nuclear device would be acquired by a terrorist overseas. If a terrorist group could construct an improvised nuclear device, it may only have one such device, would value it dearly, and may not wish to assume the detection risk, however small, of transporting the device across international borders into the United States.[13] Moreover, the group might achieve its objectives—instilling fear and anxiety in the Western mind and disrupting international commerce—by exploding a nuclear device anywhere in the world. After a terrorist detonation of a nuclear weapon anywhere, the immediate questions will be whether there are second and third nuclear weapons and where the next detonation will be. In short, a nuclear terrorist attack need not necessarily occur in the United States to be effective insofar as terrorist goals are concerned. Indeed, some analysts, including renowned terrorism expert Brian Michael Jenkins of the RAND Corporation, have gone so far as to suggest that al Qaeda is already a nuclear terrorist group even without, insofar as we know, possessing a nuclear weapon. His argument is that the group's public propaganda and rather advanced use of international communications, including false images of mushroom clouds in the background of the White House, have allowed the group to achieve one of the goals of classical terrorism—instilling fear in the target population. Although not dismissive of the potential nuclear threat from al Qaeda, Jenkins writes that the group's propaganda is amplified by the 24-7 news cycle and sensational journalism, among other factors. He cites as support a media report that 40 percent of Americans believe it is likely that terrorists will detonate a nuclear bomb in the United States within the next five years.

Numerous analyses of nuclear terrorism tend to focus largely on the supply or demand sides of the problem. In general, physicists tend to focus on the supply side and Russia, while counterterrorism experts tend to focus on the demand side and the Near East and South Asia. In the 1960s and 1970s, questions of nuclear terrorism were generally contemplated by physicists, some of whom had worked on the Manhattan Project. Their motivation was primarily technical: Could someone with basic scientific and engineering skills and no access to classified information build a nuclear weapon? As the study of terrorism developed in the 1970s and beyond, more social scientists started to think about the demand side—the terrorists and what motivated them to attempt to acquire nuclear weapons.

The analysis in this book is not necessarily market-based as that would imply the existence of a normally functioning, competitive, illicit nuclear weapons or materials market with open and transparent buyers and sellers. The illicit nuclear market can best be categorized as imperfect with market distortions, including the overall clandestine nature of the market, national and international export control regimes, national and international government-sponsored sting efforts to take fissile material off the market, elusive customers, numerous middlemen, and questionable suppliers, among other factors.[14] However, in order for nuclear terrorism to happen, the supply of intact nuclear weapons or fissile material must meet the terrorist demand. That condition, as will be illustrated, does not guarantee that a terrorist group will be successful in detonating a nuclear device.

The consequences of a nuclear attack even with an IND would be high and depend on many factors, including yield of the explosion, location of detonation, and prevailing wind patterns. Moreover, economic costs, general fear and panic, and population dislocation are among other consequences. However, as will be discussed more in depth, the detonation of a single IND is not necessarily an existential threat to the United States. Overreaction to such an event—where unintended consequences may come into play—must be vigilantly guarded against as it could lead to an existential threat under certain circumstances. A fair amount of analysis concerning nuclear terrorism focuses almost exclusively on either consequence or probability, which can lead to polarized conclusions when a more balanced approach or set of policy options might be warranted.[15] Policymakers ignore the nuclear terrorism threat at society's peril, but they must also weigh and balance: (1) how a very public focus on the threat in the absence of clear communications to the public on how to respond to the threat might undermine societal resilience; (2) the percentage of resources dedicated to such a problem, given other more likely conventional or even unconventional terrorist attack scenarios; and (3) the potential second- and third-order effects of retaliatory responses postdetonation. In short, it is assessed that terrorist groups must have the intent *and* the logistical, financial, and organizational capacity to develop the requisite capability to construct or otherwise acquire a nuclear weapon and detonate it to constitute a clear and present nuclear terrorism threat.

DEFINING NUCLEAR TERRORISM

When the topic of nuclear terrorism is discussed, it is often assumed that there is one common definition—the detonation of a nuclear weapon, whether that results from the terrorist theft of an intact nuclear weapon or from the building of an IND using illicitly acquired fissile material. That is the focus of this book because the detonation of a nuclear weapon is likely to be the most catastrophic of the numerous nuclear threat scenarios. However, it is not the sole threat, nor is it the most probable threat. As Charles Ferguson and William Potter point out in *The Four Faces of Nuclear Terrorism*, there are four nuclear terrorism threat scenarios under which a terrorist group could

- steal, buy, or otherwise acquire an intact nuclear weapon;
- steal, buy, or otherwise acquire fissile material necessary to construct its own improvised nuclear device;
- acquire radiological isotopes, such as cesium-137 or strontium-90; wrap them in conventional explosives; and detonate the device in a populated area (radiological dispersion device or "dirty bomb"); and
- infiltrate a civilian nuclear power plant and sabotage its operation, resulting in the release of radiation (an intentional Chernobyl).[16]

In 1975 Brian Michael Jenkins defined the nuclear terrorism threat as

a broad spectrum of mischievous to malevolent actions, including the creation of potentially alarming hoaxes, acts of low-level symbolic sabotage, the occupation or seizure of nuclear facilities, acts of serious sabotage aimed at causing widespread casualties and damage, thefts of nuclear material, armed attacks on nuclear weapons storage sites, thefts of nuclear weapons, the dispersal of radioactive contaminants, the manufacture of homemade nuclear weapons, and the detonation or threatened detonation of such devices.[17]

With the benefit of more than thirty years' experience assessing terrorism and nuclear terrorism in particular, Jenkins currently believes:

Nuclear terrorism, upon close examination, turns out to be a work of truly worrisome particles of truth. Yet it is also a world of fantasies, nightmares, urban legends, fakes, hoaxes, scams, stings, mysterious substances, terrorist boasts, sensational claims, descriptions of vast conspiracies, allegations of cover-ups, lurid headlines, layers of misinformation and disinformation. It is hard to separate the truth from the myth. Much is inconclusive or contradictory. Only the terror is real.[18]

The nuclear terrorism threat is relatively diverse. While the focus of this book is on the detonation of a nuclear weapon acquired from a state or constructed by a terrorist group, the successful execution of any of these threats may achieve terrorists' objectives—to instill fear in the minds of a civilian population, to kill as many of them as possible, and to disrupt global commerce. Even actions short of an actual nuclear detonation could help terrorists achieve their objective of instilling fear and anxiety in a population. As Jenkins points out, there is a difference between nuclear terrorism and nuclear terror, the former being the act or events and the latter being about imagination and fear. And "fear is not free. Frightened populations are intolerant. Frightened people worry incessantly about subversion from within."[19] They look for enemies and may be willing to trade some of their civil liberties for security.[20] Fear, in turn, may result in panic and potential overreaction, particularly if accurate information is not shared promptly and effectively with the general public and if policy decisions concerning potential retaliation are made in response to expedient and understandable societal pressures without careful deliberation of potential intended and unintended consequences.

EFFECTS OF NUCLEAR WEAPONS AND ATTENDANT CONSEQUENCES

Nuclear weapons are the most destructive devices ever created by humankind. According to a seminal 1979 study conducted by the Office of Technology Assessment (OTA), the following five physical effects result from the detonation of a nuclear weapon:

- an explosive blast that is qualitatively similar to the blast from ordinary chemical explosives but that has somewhat different effects because it is typically so much larger;

- direct nuclear radiation;
- direct thermal radiation, most of which takes the form of visible light;
- pulses of electrical and magnetic energy, called electromagnetic pulse (EMP); and
- the creation of a variety of radioactive particles, which are thrown up into the air by the force of the blast and are called radioactive fallout when they return to Earth.[21]

The physical effects of the detonation of a nuclear weapon depend on many factors, including (but not limited to) the yield of the explosive device, whether it is detonated in the air above the target or on the ground, the prevailing weather and wind patterns, and the population density of the target area. Various estimates have been given about the effects of a detonation of an IND in any large city. According to Steve Younger, former head of nuclear weapons research and development at Los Alamos National Laboratory, "As a rule of thumb, the death toll from a 10-kiloton weapon, the type that one might expect a lower-level nuclear state to develop, would be about 100,000 people."[22] Professor Allison paints an even starker picture, stating that the effects a ten-kiloton weapon would have on any city would be as follows:

> From the epicenter of the blast to a distance of approximately a third of a mile, every structure and individual would vanish in a vaporous blaze. A second circle of destruction extending three quarters of a mile from ground zero would leave buildings looking like the Murrah building in Oklahoma City. A third circle, reaching out one and one-half miles, would be ravaged by fires and radiation. . . . In Washington [D.C.], a bomb going off at the Smithsonian Institution would destroy everything from the White House to the lawn of the Capitol building; everything from the Supreme Court to the FDR Memorial would be left in rubble; uncontrollable fires would reach all the way out to the Pentagon.[23]

Beyond the immediate effects of a nuclear detonation, there are other extensive and important consequences, such as economic costs and potential civil liberties restrictions. Many of the consequences depend on uncertainties associated with how the threat may be manifested (the modalities of the attack or the number of nuclear weapons a terrorist adversary may possess) and how the U.S. population and government react to a nuclear attack. For example, if a terrorist group delivers an IND by means of a shipping container into a major port, it is likely that commerce would be substantially affected; ports across the country and the world would be shut down for inspection, similar to the grounding of all aircraft in the aftermath of the terrorist attacks of 9/11. In 2004 the RAND Corporation, supported by the Department of Homeland Security's Office of Intelligence Analysis and Infrastructure Protection, conducted an exercise-based research effort that simulated a nuclear terrorist attack on the Port of Long Beach.[24] The research found, inter alia, the following:

- Widespread death, injury, and destruction extends two to three kilometers from the blast center. Initial effects of the attack will include more than five thousand fatalities and tens of thousands of injuries, including several thousand burn victims.
- Due to the relatively low yield of the IND, there is widespread damage and fires in the harbor but relatively little physical damage to the City of Long Beach.
- People within one to two kilometers of the blast area who are not shielded absorb dangerously high doses of radiation. Within ten minutes the mushroom cloud from the detonation reaches twenty thousand feet and begins to spread; the dispersal of fallout will depend on prevailing wind patterns. Heavy local fallout presents the prospect of tens of thousands of deaths.
- As people begin to evacuate the city, initial misinformation or inconsistent information sows confusion and panic. Gridlock occurs on almost all freeways as people attempt to evacuate.
- At the highest levels of government, the focus is on determining if any additional nuclear weapons are present in the country and, if so, where. Action has been taken to close all ports for an indefinite period of time and to order the immediate inspection of all rail and truck traffic carrying containers away from U.S. ports.
- The economic effects of the attack could be far reaching. They would include difficulty in determining when to reopen ports and how to ensure

financial and insurance companies resume operations in the Port of Long Beach and surrounding areas.[25]

The rules and standards of conduct for a post–nuclear terrorist attack environment have yet to be written and represent a substantial element of uncertainty. Some elements of the nonphysical effects of a terrorist nuclear attack are within the government's power to control. For example, will there be an executive or legislatively driven effort to provide the intelligence and law enforcement communities within the United States with enhanced intelligence and surveillance tools, even if temporarily, to discover which individuals within the United States may have been involved in the attack? If so, what will the implications be for civil liberties? With respect to any potential retaliation against a terrorist group or any nation-state that may have facilitated the terrorist attack, what standards of evidence will be applied? Stating that the United States may be willing to act based on imperfect evidence of attribution may strengthen U.S. declaratory policy on actions it may take in the aftermath of a nuclear attack.[26] Will political leadership be able to withstand what would likely be overwhelming societal pressure to retaliate quickly? If nuclear forensic, intelligence, and law enforcement tools are able to identify the origin of the fissile material used in the bomb, and the country of origin is one that is allied with or not hostile toward the United States (for example, Russia or Pakistan), will the United States retaliate against that country for lax nuclear security? To the extent that retaliation for lax security is military in nature (a retaliatory threat against Russia is likely not credible), will the United States risk broad nuclear conflict over the explosion of one nuclear device made with Russian HEU or plutonium? The most important principle here is to guard against overreaction, or against delivering to the terrorist groups that may have detonated a weapon a tactical and strategic victory of a nation living in fear and anxiety. As terrorism expert John Mueller has stated, "The costs of terrorism commonly come much more from . . . overwrought reactions (or overreactions) to it than from anything the terrorists have done."[27]

In short, the physical effects of nuclear weapons are stark and devastating, yet not necessarily existential if the bombs are limited in number. However, the overall consequences of an attack would likely be substantial in magnitude in terms of lives lost and economic costs. The economic consequences are substantial, not only for the country in which the detonation takes place but probably also for the entire global economy. The global financial markets demonstrated amazing resiliency in the aftermath of 9/11, yet if a nuclear attack was conveyed through a shipping container, trade with the United States would likely be halted for some time. Trade would likely slowly resume over time as security at U.S. ports would be increased. As terrorism expert Richard Falkenrath points out, other consequences include:

- *Panic.* "An NBC [nuclear, biological, or chemical] attack against a civilian population would, in all likelihood, trigger panic incommensurate with the real effects of the weapons."[28]
- *Degraded response capabilities.* The government's ability to respond to a nuclear terrorism attack is likely to be constrained as "emergency response personnel such as police officers, firefighters, and paramedics may be the first casualties of an NBC incident."[29] Congressional hearings held in June 2008 also point out the continued lack of preparedness for response to a nuclear attack.[30]
- *Loss of strategic position.* The willingness and/or ability of the United States to defend its interests could be impaired by an actual or threatened nuclear attack. As Falkenrath notes, "The U.S., for example, could be deterred from entering a regional crisis in which its national interests were threatened."[31]

Last, the psychological and social effects of a nuclear attack would be profound and far reaching as any polity subject to such an attack would immediately question one of the fundamental tenets of government—the provision of security to those consenting to being governed. One can foresee the potential for civil liberties to be substantially curtailed for some (one would hope limited) period in the aftermath of a nuclear attack while authorities seek to determine if any additional nuclear weapons may be in the country.

With an understanding of how nuclear terrorism is defined and the effects and potential consequences even crude nuclear weapons could have, it is now possible to provide an overview of the two macro forces that characterize the environment in which terrorists operate as they seek to acquire nuclear weapons or fissile material—supply and demand.

DEMAND AND SUPPLY: THE BASICS

Nuclear terrorism can be characterized as a problem having both demand- and supply-side dimensions. The demand side of the nuclear terrorism issue tends to be more nebulous than the supply side insofar as it involves an assessment of various types of terrorist groups and their diverse motivations, intentions, and capabilities to conduct nuclear terrorism. The good news on the demand side is that according to publicly available current intelligence, there are no indications that any terrorist group has acquired enough fissile material to construct an IND or has stolen, purchased, or otherwise received an intact nuclear weapon. Moreover, despite the reconstitution of elements of al Qaeda Central in the Federally Administered Tribal Areas (FATA) of Pakistan, the U.S.-led global campaign against terrorism has made it relatively more difficult for a decentralized organization to plan and execute the type of complex operation that would be required for a successful nuclear terrorist attack.[32] The bad news on the demand side of the equation is that while many have written al Qaeda's obituary, the group remains a substantial threat.[33] According to the 2007 National Intelligence Estimate (NIE), *The Terrorist Threat to the U.S. Homeland,*

> al-Qa'ida is and will remain the most serious terrorist threat to the Homeland, as its central leadership continues to plan high-impact plots, while pushing others in extremist Sunni communities to mimic its efforts and to supplement its capabilities. We assess the group has protected or regenerated key elements of its Homeland attack capability including: a safe haven in the Pakistani Federally Administered Tribal Areas (FATA), operational lieutenants, and its top leadership.[34]

Al Qaeda has plainly stated it wishes to acquire and use chemical and biological weapons against the United States to kill over 4 million Americans.[35] It is worth noting that Suleiman Abu Ghaith, a Kuwaiti and an al Qaeda spokesman, did not specifically refer to nuclear weapons in his statement justifying the death of millions of Americans. Moreover, al Qaeda may not necessarily be the only terrorist group with the intent, if not necessarily the capability, to attack the United States with WMD. However, intent alone does not constitute a national security threat; while not trivial, intent only becomes clearly and presently dangerous when married to capability. Trends in terrorism also tend to demonstrate that since the 1990s terrorism has become more religiously motivated and, therefore, some argue, less constrained in the potential use of indiscriminate, mass-casualty violence against innocent civilians.[36] In addition, reducing the demand side of the nuclear terrorism threat is a longer-term, international endeavor and lacks a simple solution. For example, demand-side policy remedies include using the full range of power—military, economic, and diplomatic—to ameliorate the underlying causes of terrorism. If the underlying causes of terrorism are addressed over the long term, and terrorist logistical, planning, and operational capabilities continue to be degraded in the short term, the probability of nuclear terrorism will likely decrease.

From a supply-side perspective, if terrorists cannot acquire an intact nuclear weapon from one of nine de facto nuclear weapons states[37] or fissile material from a broader range of states, they will not be able to successfully execute a nuclear detonation. Put another way, if the nine nations possessing nuclear weapons and forty-plus other nations possessing weapons-relevant quantities of HEU or plutonium can protect this material perfectly, to some heretofore nonexistent and exacting international standard, the threat of nuclear terrorism can be eliminated. According to the International Panel on Fissile Materials (IPFM), an independent group of arms control and nonproliferation experts, as of 2007 there were between 1,400 and 2,000 metric tons of HEU and 500 tons of separated plutonium in the global stockpile.[38] The supply-side policy remedy, therefore, is to secure existing nuclear weapons and fissile material such that terrorists are unable to acquire them. "Leakage," or the inadvertent supply of a nuclear weapon or fissile material, is more of a threat than a nation-state intentionally transferring a nuclear weapon or fissile material to a terrorist group for reasons that will be explored later. The good news on the supply side is that since the Cooperative Threat Reduction (CTR) Program was initiated under the congressional sponsorship of Senators Sam Nunn and Richard Lugar in 1991, substantial progress has been made in improving the security of fissile material. The bad news is that there remains a significant amount of fissile material that is not appropriately and effectively protected.[39] Neverthe-less, there are forces in favor of enhanced international protection of fissile material. Nation-states with nuclear weapons are fully aware that, if not pro-tected adequately, those weapons could be used against them if acquired by an international or domestic terrorist or insurgent group. With nuclear weapons comes a built-in incentive to design an effective protection regime. Optimal policies to combat nuclear terrorism proceed concurrently with supply- and demand-side remedies.

A "NUCLEAR AGE" PROBLEM

Notwithstanding a recent increase in public interest in nuclear terrorism, the issue is not new. As Jenkins points out, the fear of nuclear terrorism preceded even contemporary terrorism; it is firmly enmeshed in popular culture through science fiction novels and films going as far back as 1914 and H. G. Wells's *The World Set Free*, which coined the term "atomic weapons" long before the advent of the nuclear age.[40] The nuclear terrorism threat had only potential in the minds of some in the mid-twentieth century, as terrorism at that time was characterized by low-level violence used for limited political purposes. The state-to-state nuclear threat has existed since the dawn of the nuclear age in the mid-twentieth century.[41] While Cold War dangers stemmed from the poten-tially existential threat of global thermonuclear war between nation-states, the threat of nuclear terrorism emanates from a concern that subnational actors, or terrorist groups, might decide to acquire or build and use nuclear weapons. Writing about the potential for a covert nuclear attack between nation-states in March 1945, physicist Leo Szilard stated:

> Clearly, if such [nuclear] bombs are available, it is not necessary to bomb our cities from the air in order to destroy them. All that is necessary is to place a comparatively small number of such bombs in each of our major cities and to detonate them at some later time. . . . The United States has a very long coastline which will make it possible to smuggle in such bombs in peacetime and to carry them by truck to our cities. The long coastline, the structure of our society, and our very heterogeneous popu-lation may make an effective control of such "traffic" virtually impossible.

. . . So far it has not been possible to devise any methods which would enable us to detect hidden bombs buried in the ground or otherwise sufficiently protected against detection.[42]

The CIA recognized the nuclear terrorist threat as early as 1975, when it published *Managing Nuclear Proliferation: The Politics of Limited Choice*. The report concluded:

> If a terrorist group does acquire nuclear explosives, it can rely upon unconventional delivery methods which would be inappropriate for any but the most desperate or irrational state. Any form of transport, airplane, boat, truck, or train could conceivably be employed. Unlike a state, terrorists with a mobile base of operations need not be concerned with the threat of counter-attack, hence they are not subject to the deterrence of defense systems that constrain states.[43]

While the issue of whether terrorists can be deterred will be examined more in depth in chapter 6, the point is that analysts inside and outside the U.S. government have been thinking about and advising policymakers on the threat of nuclear terrorism for decades. Since these early World War II– and Cold War–era assessments made by the intelligence community, several occurrences have taken place: (1) the information revolution has spread the explicit knowledge of how to build a crude nuclear weapon;[44] (2) terrorists have, arguably, become relatively less constrained in the advocacy and potential use of nonconventional weapons as a means of instilling fear in civilian populations; (3) the risks to nuclear material increased in the aftermath of the Soviet Union's dissolution and then decreased as programs such as the Cooperative Threat Reduction Program put nuclear security technologies and practices in place; (4) other countries have developed nuclear weapons yet remain politically unstable, and some (for example, Pakistan) may have active terrorists who have infiltrated military and intelligence organizations; (5) there has been a development of proliferation rings (for example, Abdul Qadeer [A. Q.] Khan's in Pakistan), in which second-tier nuclear countries export nuclear-related technology to other nations wishing to acquire nuclear weapons;[45] and (6) a potential renaissance in nuclear power generation could evolve in response to volatile fossil fuel prices and climate change imperatives and could result in the further spread of nuclear fuel cycle knowledge.

TERRORIST NUCLEAR WEAPONS VERSUS STATE NUCLEAR WEAPONS

Because individuals often equate the failure of nation-states to acquire nuclear weapons with the certain failure of nonstate actors to acquire or build nuclear weapons, it is important to differentiate between a state's nuclear weapons program and an IND that a terrorist group might build. The first difference is that states attempting to develop nuclear weapons will likely want to develop a full-scale nuclear fuel cycle; that is, they may want to have the capability to enrich natural uranium and reprocess spent nuclear fuel for nuclear weapons use. While such an infrastructure-intensive effort is incredibly costly and time consuming (with some states, such as Libya, failing despite substantial investments), if successful the programs may meet the multidimensional motivations that cause states to seek nuclear weapons in the first place.[46] States don't want one, two, or a handful of nuclear weapons; indeed, such small numbers would be destabilizing insofar as they may invite preemptive attacks by regional adversaries. One of Pakistan's primary nuclear weapons concerns, for example, is ensuring that its relatively small nuclear force (estimated to be at least sixty and as many as a hundred nuclear warheads) cannot be eliminated by an Indian first strike.[47] If a nation can enrich natural uranium to be used as fuel for a nuclear power reactor, it can further enrich uranium for nuclear weapons use; such a state is, in the words of former International Atomic Energy Agency director general Mohamed ElBaradei, a "nuclear weapons capable state."[48] The second difference is that states will want to develop nuclear doctrine that governs the command and control over nuclear weapons. It can be especially important in countries in which the military may be prominently involved in politics. Who has operational control over the weapons and decides under which circumstances to use them? The third difference is that states will also want to ensure the security and survivability of nuclear weapons in which they have invested much treasure. Security is important to prevent the "boomerang effect," or having your own weapons used against you. Another difference is that states will want to have some level of certainty that their weapons are reliable and will achieve a certain yield. This final requirement implies some level of nuclear testing or, at a minimum, sophisticated computer modeling.

Yet the nuclear terrorist model is different. Most terrorist groups attempting to acquire or build improvised nuclear weapons are unlikely to:

- have the resources, logistical capability, time, and (if terrorists continue to be kept under a state of constant pressure globally) sustained safe haven to develop a full-scale nuclear fuel cycle;
- develop any formal "doctrine" to govern the use of their nuclear weapon(s), as a single charismatic leader may likely exercise dictatorial control over the weapon should a terrorist group acquire one;
- be concerned with security and survivability as much as they are with hiding the weapon(s) from military, intelligence, and law enforcement services that may be searching for the weapon (if they are aware such a weapon exists); and
- be concerned about the yield of the weapon. Even if it fizzles and achieves a yield of less than one kiloton, a detonation in a U.S. city will still instill massive fear and likely panic—a primary terrorist objective. This is particularly so given that the state of U.S. readiness to respond to a nuclear attack is not highly advanced.[49]

HEU VERSUS PLUTONIUM

Terrorist groups seeking to build an IND would most certainly accept, purchase, or attempt to steal plutonium or HEU. However, given the choice between these two elements, a terrorist with some scientific input would likely target HEU. Plutonium, often referred to as the "most difficult element," has a high degree of toxicity and has to be handled with great care. "Plutonium is a physicist's dream but an engineer's nightmare. With little provocation, the metal changes its density by as much as 25 percent. It can be brittle as glass or as malleable as aluminum; plutonium damages materials on contact and is therefore difficult to handle, store, or transport."[50] By contrast, small quantities of HEU can be readily handled without any significant protection. It is far more malleable than plutonium and can be used in the more basic nuclear weapon design—the gun-type device. Moreover, and important from a terrorist's perspective, HEU is easily shielded from nuclear detection devices, making transportation of the material itself or an IND using HEU less risky. From a nuclear terrorism perspective, then, HEU is the preferred fissile material. An interesting application of game theory to the question of whether governments should prioritize the safeguarding of HEU over plutonium also reaches the conclusion that "a strong emphasis on HEU safeguards is soundly justified. There is some reason to suspect . . . that U.S. efforts to throttle proliferation of plutonium are currently being overfunded and, even more so, that HEU funding should be increased dramatically."[51]

How, then, might a terrorist group with the intent to inflict mass casualties and instill fear in civilian populations acquire a nuclear weapon or fissile material to build an IND? It is to this topic that we turn in chapter 2.

TWO

The Terrorist Pathway to a Nuclear Weapon Detonation

The pathways to a clandestine nuclear attack on the United States have been studied since the 1950s. The critical difference now, of course, is the purveyor of that threat; although Russia continues to target the United States with strategic nuclear weapons today, there is far less concern about a Russian clandestine nuclear attack. Yet examining what was known about a potential clandestine nuclear attack on the United States by the former Soviet Union is pertinent insofar as it provides a context for the means by which any foreign power, nation-state, or terrorist group may convey a nuclear weapon into the United States. In 1951 the CIA drafted an NIE titled *Soviet Capabilities for Clandestine Attack against the U.S. with Weapons of Mass Destruction and the Vulnerability of the U.S. to Such Attack*. The NIE concluded that the Soviet Union, from the least to greatest probability, could:

- "smuggle an atomic bomb through customs as a commercial shipment,"
- conduct a "clandestine attack with civilian aircraft of a type used by U.S. or foreign transoceanic airlines,"
- "[utilize] a merchant ship for delivering an atomic weapon into a key U.S. harbor," and
- "[smuggle] . . . an atomic bomb, especially if disassembled, from a Soviet port into an isolated section of the U.S."[1]

All of these scenarios are very much in play today, but the adversary potentially engaging in them is more likely to be a nonstate actor than a nation-state. Other analysts have built upon this foundation or developed their own terrorist pathways to the bomb. Matthew Bunn, of the Belfer Center for Science and International Affairs at Harvard University's John F. Kennedy School of Government, has developed a unique perspective that illustrates terrorist pathways to the bomb overlaid with the national and international efforts undertaken to block those pathways. There is a fair degree of consensus among experts on the basic steps to a terrorist nuclear weapon. At the most simplistic level, a terrorist acquires (as a direct and willing transfer or through theft or purchase) an intact nuclear weapon from a de facto nuclear weapons state, overcomes any security measures that may be applied to that weapon, transports it to the target destination, and detonates it.[2] Or, in the more likely scenario, a terrorist group acquires (again through direct and willing transfer, theft, or leakage) enough fissile material to construct a nuclear weapon, transports this material to some safe haven where it has brought together a team of experts, assembles the weapon, smuggles it to a country the group wishes to harm, and detonates it. As mentioned above, terrorists may also smuggle fissile material into the target country if they perceived the risks of this method were lower than transporting an intact nuclear weapon across international borders.[3]

There is a basic five-step process once a decision has been made by a radical terrorist group to attempt to acquire and use a nuclear weapon. These steps are:

1. nuclear weapon or fissile material acquisition,
2. nuclear weapon or fissile material transport to a safe haven,[4]
3. "weaponization" of the fissile material,
4. smuggling the weapon to the target country,[5] and
5. detonation.

A further breakdown of these five basic steps by Professor John Mueller of Ohio State University illustrates that terrorists contemplating such an attack have a number of barriers they must overcome. Table 1 provides a set of interrelated but independent tasks a terrorist must successfully complete in order to acquire fissile material, weaponize it, smuggle the weapon to the target country, and detonate it. The factors enumerated support a thesis advanced by Dr. Michael Levi of the Council on Foreign Relations. One shibboleth associated with nuclear terrorism is that the terrorists only need to be right once and they have succeeded. However, according to Dr. Levi, authorities only have to be right once to break the acquisition, weaponization, transportation, and detonation supply chain the terrorist must strive to keep intact. In short, per Dr. Levi, authorities must seek to exploit "Murphy's Law of Nuclear Terrorism . . . what can go wrong might go wrong. . . . A 1995 plot to explode airlines over the Pacific Ocean was thwarted when plotters started a fire while preparing explosives. . . . A defense must be prepared to take advantage of such terrorist error or bad luck, lest a terrorist plot succeed despite such misfortune because the defense fails to exploit it."[6]

While Professor Mueller's scenario raises a number of issues that may not necessarily occur in reality, such as the rapid discovery by authorities of diverted fissile material, the value of the scenario lies in its explanation of the complexities of the nuclear material supply chain. There are numerous opportunities for something to go wrong, either technically, logistically, or operationally, and as Levi points out, if intelligence, law enforcement, and other security professionals are poised to exploit the weakest link in the supply chain, preventing nuclear terrorism becomes more probable.

One central element of assessing various approaches to preventing nuclear terrorism is providing policymakers with a set of myths about it. According to Levi, the following positions should be shared openly with policymakers to undermine existing myths:

- Fissile material and weapons security, while potentially very effective, cannot be perfected. This may "open the door to more realistic discussions of broader defenses."
- There may be "no such thing as a true nuclear black market."
- Making a nuclear weapon is not as simple as surfing the Internet.
- Smuggling fissile material is different from smuggling drugs.[7]

TABLE 1. ATOMIC TERRORIST TASK/BARRIER LIST

Fissile material acquisition	An inadequately secured source of adequate quantities of HEU must be found. The area must be entered while avoiding detection by local police and by locals wary of strangers. Several insiders who seem to know what they are doing must be corrupted. All the insiders must remain loyal throughout the long process of planning and executing the heist, and there must be no consequential leaks. The insiders must successfully seize and transfer the HEU, and the transferred HEU must not be a scam or part of a sting, and it must not be of inadequate quality due to insider incompetence.
Fissile material transport	The HEU must be transported across the country (of acquisition) over unfamiliar turf while its possessors are being pursued.[1] To get the HEU across one or more international borders smugglers must be employed, and they must remain loyal despite the temptations of massive reward money and not generate consequential suspicion in other smugglers using the same routes who may be interested in the same money.
Weaponization	A machine shop must be set up in an obscure area with imported, sophisticated equipment without anyone becoming suspicious.[2] A team of highly skilled scientists and technicians must be assembled, and during production all members of the team must remain absolutely loyal to the cause and develop no misgivings or severe interpersonal or financial conflicts. The complete team must be transported to the machine shop, probably from several counties, without suspicion and without consequential leaks from relatives, friends, and colleagues about the missing. The team must have precise technical blueprints to work from (not general sketches) and must be able to modify these appropriately for the precise purpose at hand over months (or even years) of labor and without being able to test. Nothing significant must go wrong during the long process of manufacture and assembly of the improvised nuclear device. There must be no inadvertent leaks from the team. Local and international police, on high (even desperate) alert, must not be able to detect the project using traditional policing methods as well as the most advanced technical equipment. No locals must sense that something out of the ordinary is going on in the machine shop with the constant coming and going of nonlocal personnel.[3]

Table 1. Continued

Smuggling and transport	The IND, weighing a ton or more, must be smuggled without detection out of the machinery shop to an international border.
	The IND must be transported to the target country either by trusting the commercial process filled with people on the alert for cargo of this sort or by clandestine means, which requires trusting corrupt coconspirators who also know about the reward money.
	A team of completely loyal and technically accomplished coconspirators must be assembled within, or infiltrated into, the target country.
	The IND must successfully enter the target country and be received by the in-country coconspirators.
Detonation	A detonation team must transport the IND to the target place and set it off without anybody noticing and interfering, and the untested and much traveled IND must not prove to be a dud.

Source: Professor John Mueller, "The Atomic Terrorist: Assessing the Likelihood," prepared for presentation at the Program on International Security Policy, University of Chicago, January 1, 2008.

1 In this scenario, the theft is rapidly discovered by authorities. One can reasonably question whether this would happen given less than adequate security at some facilities, particularly nuclear research reactors. Here the question of time becomes essential: How soon after the diversion of HEU is it discovered? The longer the diversion goes undetected, the lower the probability it will be recovered. If small amounts of HEU were pilfered over time by an insider, while the risk may be greater in terms of longer periods of illicit diversion, which may be subject to discovery, it is also possible that poor security may not result in discovery of a more patient acquisition strategy.
2 Some raise doubts about the level of sophistication required in certain machinery. See Peter D. Zimmerman and Jeffrey G. Lewis, "The Bomb in the Backyard," *Foreign Policy*, November–December 2006.
3 It could be argued that if the machine shop were located in isolated areas in the Pakistani FATA, or even within the United States for that matter, that it would be relatively simple to ensure the clandestine nature of the shop and its activities.

Other arguable myths that could be added to Dr. Levi's list include:

- There is a high probability that existing nuclear powers (de jure or de facto) will knowingly transfer intact nuclear weapons to terrorist groups.
- The nuclear terrorist threat is greater today than it was at the height of the Cold War.
- Nuclear terrorism itself represents an existential threat to the United States.
- There are numerous terrorist groups possessing the intent *and the capability* to detonate a nuclear weapon in the United States.

While these points may contravene conventional wisdom, they are compelling and worthy of consideration whenever claims are made that nuclear terrorism is inevitable or unpreventable.

In summary, there are three ways a terrorist can acquire nuclear weapons or fissile material: (1) state sponsorship through a sale or a gift, (2) theft, or (3) a black market purchase made possible by inadvertent leakage of fissile material.[8] For each of these scenarios, if the terrorists acquire fissile material, they must still construct the weapon, and there is considerable debate about whether sophisticated terrorist groups could successfully acquire, build, deliver, and detonate such a weapon. Conventionalists believe it is very possible and even likely. Skeptics think that while it is possible, it is not likely. Terrorism analyst Peter Bergen has stated that with respect to the terrorist paths to a nuclear weapon, "none of those scenarios are remotely realistic outside the world of Hollywood."[9] Let us consider each of these paths briefly.

STATE SPONSORSHIP

Would a nation-state intentionally transfer a nuclear weapon or fissile material to a terrorist group?[10] This concern was one of the numerous justifications for invading Iraq in 2003—the concern that Iraq had WMD or was reconstituting its WMD programs and might share such weapons with al Qaeda or other terrorist groups. It would seem a simple matter of math that "the more states that have nuclear weapons, the greater the probability is that one of those weapons might go astray."[11] Indeed, nuclear proliferation is directly relevant to nuclear terrorism: the more states possessing nuclear weapons and the more fissile material being produced and transported, the greater the target set for terrorist groups seeking to acquire fissile material or intact nuclear weapons. To some, however, such as Peter Bergen, the case of a country voluntarily giving up or selling its nuclear weapons "does not pass the laugh test."[12] How likely is it that a nation-state will sell or give a nuclear weapon or fissile material to a terrorist group?

It has been pointed out that owing to their past and arguably ongoing actions, various states of nuclear proliferation concern might consider exporting an intact nuclear weapon (should they have one), fissile material, or the technical and scientific knowledge that might allow a terrorist group to assemble a nuclear weapon. For example, North Korea is a known exporter of

Scud missile systems, allegedly assisted Syria in the construction of a nuclear reactor, conducted its own second nuclear test in May 2009, continues to launch ballistic missiles in violation of United Nations Security Council resolutions, engages in illegal counterfeiting of U.S. currency, perpetrates global insurance fraud, and has an economic imperative to acquire hard currency given the country's dire financial situation.[13] Iran is a state sponsor of terrorism, has exported substantial amounts of conventional weaponry to other states and nonstate terrorist proxies (including Hezbollah and Hamas), has an active ballistic missile program, and is enriching uranium for what it states are "peaceful nuclear purposes."[14] Pakistan, a nation of 176 million that has been a nominal U.S. ally in fighting terrorism, is a de facto nuclear weapons state and, along with its regional rival, India, tested a nuclear weapon in 1998. Pakistan's current inventory of nuclear weapons is estimated to be between sixty and one hundred.[15] The country has a plethora of Islamist extremists, including the Taliban and al Qaeda, some of whom may have infiltrated the army and Inter-Services Intelligence (ISI). Moreover, Pakistan is plagued by perennial political instability, demonstrated by the assassination of former prime minister Benazir Bhutto in December 2007 and the January 2011 assassination of the governor of Pakistan's Punjab Province Salman Taseer, a secular ally of Pakistan's weakened political leadership. Importantly, Pakistan has engaged in substantial second-tier proliferation, including the provision of nuclear weapons designs, uranium enrichment, and other related technologies to Iran, North Korea, and Libya through the infamous A. Q. Khan network.[16] While concerns remain about the end of A. Q. Khan's house arrest in February 2009, three substantial concerns with respect to Pakistan are the following scenarios: (1) the Taliban or al Qaeda are able to insert one of their members into the nuclear weapons establishment, or leverage sympathetic workers already within the establishment as part of a long-term operation to acquire fissile material; (2) an attempted coup d'état leads to general instability and a movement of nuclear weapons and components, making them more vulnerable; and (3) a coup brings a radical Islamist regime to power. As will be discussed later, Pakistan is indeed the most dangerous country with respect to nuclear proliferation and nuclear terrorism.

State sponsorship of classical, political terrorism, where demands are tactical, limited, and regional, is quite different from providing a weapon of mass destruction capable of annihilating potentially hundreds of thousands of people to an uncontrollable terrorist group. Plausible deniability becomes somewhat more difficult when nuclear weapons are involved; the stakes are simply too high and the list of suspected sources too short. One important element in whether a country decides to intentionally share fissile material or an intact nuclear weapon with a terrorist group is the nuclear attribution abilities of the United States and the international community, and the extent to which a state contemplating such illicit transfers believes the United States and the international community can attribute fissile material pre- or postdetonation back to it. Ostensibly, if the state contemplating such an illicit transfer perceives that the United States and the international community have good nuclear attribution capabilities, it may be less willing to intentionally transfer weapons based on the belief that it would suffer retaliatory consequences.[17] It has been reported that the United States has access to the IAEA's library of nuclear samples from North Korea, obtained before the agency's "inspectors were thrown out of the country, that would likely make it possible to trace an explosion back to North Korea's nuclear arsenal. The North Koreans are fully aware, government experts believe, that the United States has access to that database of nuclear DNA. But when it comes to other countries, many of the library's shelves are empty."[18] Along with numerous other geostrategic factors, the disparities of such nuclear DNA databases may cause the United States to have different policies with respect to how it attempts to deter North Korea, Russia, and Pakistan from transferring fissile material or weapons to a terrorist group.

INTENTIONAL TRANSFERS OF NUCLEAR WEAPONS ARE UNLIKELY

As mentioned above, nation-states acquire nuclear weapons for a variety of complex and interrelated reasons, including (but not limited to) a security imperative, prestige, regional hegemonic desires, various domestic political considerations, and as a sign of global scientific advancement. While an intentional state transfer of an intact nuclear weapon cannot be completely discounted, it seems unlikely a state would be willing to take this risk.[19] First, nation-states invest an inordinate amount of time and resources in the acquisition of nuclear weapons; for those nations that have developed nuclear weapons, the weapons are viewed as the country's "crown jewels." Aside from money, which might be perceived as prolonging national survival, what national interest is served by transferring such highly valued symbols of national power and prestige to a terrorist group whose actions are not only uncontrollable but would almost certainly invite retaliation?

Second, while the status of nuclear attribution and forensics remains imperfect, when these tools are used in combination with other forensic tools, including intelligence and law enforcement, any nation-state willingly transferring nuclear weapons or fissile material to a terrorist group has to be concerned about the potential of massive retaliation from the target country. Whichever state is attacked with nuclear weapons may have a very low evidentiary threshold for culpability and, as a result, may counterattack first and ask questions second. Indeed, it is stated U.S. policy that "the United States will continue to make clear that it reserves the right to respond with overwhelming force—including through resort to all of our options—to the use of WMD against the United States, our forces abroad, and friends and allies."[20]

Third, the relationship between state sponsors of terror and individual terrorist groups is not generally stable over sustained periods of time. That is, what assurances would a nation-state transferring such massive power to a terrorist group have that their own weapons would not be turned against them, in the so-called boomerang effect? Consistent with this argument, terrorism scholar Daniel Byman points out:

> Trust and plausible deniability are inversely related when it comes to state backing of terrorists. Iran trusts Hezbullah and works openly with it, but this close relationship is far from secret. Iran also has ties to a range of Palestinian and Iraqi groups, but while these relationships are more covert, and thus more deniable, they are not built on trust. Thus, Iran lacks deniability for the groups to which it might transfer more advanced systems, but lacks the trust that would make it more likely to transfer advanced systems.[21]

Fourth, another argument posits that seemingly irrational and internationally isolated leaders such as those in North Korea and Iran are more likely than other leaders to sell a nuclear weapon to undermine U.S. national security. While it is true that isolated leaders have historically made many poor choices that were perceived as irrational by the United States, deterrence is based more on fear and emotion than on rationality, as will be discussed in chapter 6. Moreover, as STRATFOR Global Intelligence has found:

> Truly crazed and suicidal leaders have a difficult time becoming leaders of a country even capable of considering trying to develop nuclear weapons. . . . They may have taken risks, but they were generally calculated and they want to enjoy the fruits of their labor. The consequence for miscalculating with nuclear weapons is annihilation—not only for themselves, their family, and the power base that they have toiled to build, but for the entire society.[22]

According to Brian Michael Jenkins, the

> record of state sponsorship of terrorists lends little support to [nation-states selling or giving a nuclear weapon to proxies as a mode of surrogate warfare]. It does not fit the patterns of what we have seen. Apart from bumping off troublesome exiles, or each others' diplomats during war, even state sponsors of terrorism have become more cautious when engaging in larger-scale, higher-risk operations. . . . Providing rockets and tactical missiles is one thing—providing nuclear weapons seems quite another.[23]

Finally, as discussed in chapter 1, nuclear weapons are the ultimate weapon; the combined blast, thermal, radiation, and fallout effects from such weapons are heinous. Both the nation-state that transfers the nuclear weapon and the terrorist group that detonates it run an extremely high risk of delegitimizing their cause by breaking the nuclear taboo. Al Qaeda's tactics, imposition of harsh ideology, and indiscriminate violence in Iraq (specifically in al-Anbar Province) were enough to cause Sunni Muslims to rise up against their Sunni brethren and fight alongside the United States against al Qaeda.[24] The use of nuclear weapons against any Western nation, an action that would likely kill innocent Muslims, may well have a similar effect, only on a more global scale.

Alternatively, although somewhat less persuasively, it could be argued that there may be some circumstances under which a nation-state may knowingly transfer a nuclear weapon or fissile material to a terrorist proxy or to the high-est bidder. If a nation-state was desperate—if it perceived that its survival was at stake—and it believed that a terrorist group had a better chance to success-fully deliver and detonate an existing nuclear weapon against the threatening adversary, it might transfer such a weapon. From a rational thought perspec-tive, given U.S. declaratory policy on retaliation for the use of nuclear weapons against the United States, it does not appear reasonable that any nation would intentionally transfer fissile material to a terrorist group. However, history is replete with examples of what U.S. policymakers perceived to be irrational acts on the part of foreign nations. Indeed, some have posited that North Korea, "which is in desperate economic straits, has already stated its right to sell its nuclear wares."[25] According to the U.S. Intelligence Community, "in April 2005 North Korea told a U.S. academic that it could transfer nuclear weapons to terrorists if driven into a corner."[26] While such statements could be taken at face value, perhaps more accurately they could also be interpreted as part of North Korea's traditional diplomatic modus operandi designed to attract attention and garner assistance. With North Korea's second nuclear test in late May 2009, additional concerns have been raised that even if the country does not use nuclear weapons, it may consider transferring nuclear materials or technology to the highest bidder, which could include a terrorist group.[27] With a low degree of confidence, the infamous and discredited October 2002 Iraq NIE found that "Saddam [Hussein], if sufficiently desperate, might decide that only an organization such as al-Qa'ida, with worldwide reach and ex-tensive terrorist infrastructure and already engaged in a life-or-death struggle against the United States, would perpetrate the type of terrorist attack that he would hope to conduct."[28] The question becomes how best to deter such state sponsorship of nuclear terrorism, a question that will be addressed in chapter 6.

An unwilling transfer could occur if a terrorist group has a close rela-tionship with elements of the nation-state's bureaucracy responsible for con-trolling nuclear weapons.[29] As mentioned previously, for example, civil strife in Pakistan could lead to insiders at Pakistan's nuclear weapons establishment who are sympathetic to the Taliban or al Qaeda taking actions that might make fissile material more vulnerable to terrorist seizure. This would undoubtedly be called a theft by political leadership, or the government would deny any knowledge of the transfer. While this denial may be marginally credible with nuclear-related technology, as in the A. Q. Khan case, target nations may be less willing to subsume counterproliferation under counterterrorism if fissile material or an intact weapon itself was transferred, even "unwillingly," to a terrorist group.

THEFT

A second means by which a terrorist group could acquire a nuclear weapon or fissile material is theft. Nation-states possessing nuclear weapons understand the effects and value of these weapons and secure them accordingly—although not to any unitary and binding international security standard. Moreover, simple "smash and grab" operations against intact nuclear weapons may not, in and of themselves, be successful if the desired end state is a nuclear detonation. While there may be no single standard for how the use of nuclear weapons is controlled, technology exists that allows civilian leadership to prevent the inadvertent or unauthorized use of nuclear weapons. One such technology, known as a permissive action link (PAL), was first developed by the United States during the Cold War and allowed the United States to retain control over tactical nuclear weapons placed on alert posture with non-U.S. delivery units of the North Atlantic Treaty Organization (NATO) in Europe and the Pacific.[30] Permissive action links prevent the unauthorized use of nuclear weapons by causing the weapon to self-destruct (a nonnuclear explosion) if someone tampers with the weapon or attempts to extract its (fissile material) core. While it cannot be assumed that the relatively new de facto nuclear states of India, Pakistan, and North Korea use *advanced* PAL technology, whatever technology they use would require some form of inside information to activate or circumvent the PALs for a detonation once an intact nuclear weapon was stolen. Moreover, older-generation Russian tactical nuclear weapons may not have originally possessed PALs or similar such controls but would likely have been subject to retrofitting with such devices during required maintenance.

It is generally thought that Pakistani nuclear weapons are "de-mated"; that is, the HEU or plutonium is removed and stored separately from the rest of the weapon, and the warhead itself is stored separately from the means of delivery. While some believe this is positive from a security perspective, as the weapons are unlikely to be on hair-trigger alert and an intact nuclear weapon could not be easily stolen, Charles Ferguson of the Council on Foreign Relations points out:

> De-mated warheads may, however, pose a greater security risk than mated warheads. Short of terrorists enlisting insider assistance to teach them how to detonate a fully assembled nuclear weapon, they would have more confidence in exploding bombs they built themselves. Another advantage for terrorists is that presently almost all of Pakistan's nuclear weapons are powered by HEU. By stealing the HEU separated from de-mated warheads, terrorists would have the material they would need to build the simplest improvised nuclear device.[31]

There is no single international standard for how nuclear weapons are secured; nation-states have their own highly classified programs for nuclear weapons security. Most nuclear weapons security regimes involve human, physical, and technical means: Individuals charged with protecting nuclear weapons are screened for reliability and responsibility, generally through personnel reliability programs and training; physical security measures including "guns, guards, and gates" surround facilities housing nuclear weapons; and portal monitors, electronic codes, or PALs protect fissile material and nuclear weapons from diversion or accidental, inadvertent, or unauthorized use. As nuclear weapons states mature, they develop highly secretive nuclear weapons doctrine that specifies the primary purposes of nuclear weapons in a national and regional context, how the weapons are stored, the extent to which they are on alert, and which entity is the final arbiter of nuclear weapons use, among other factors.[32]

Some of the greatest supply-side concerns with respect to theft or leakage of nuclear weapons or fissile material include political instability, corruption, and the security capacity and potential terrorist penetration of entities having control over nuclear weapons.[33] While military elements assigned to protect nuclear weapons tend, in general, to be well organized and disciplined, how these forces will react in the event of a regime change is unknown. As mentioned, the country that raises the most concern from a political stability and nuclear weapon theft or leakage scenario is Pakistan. Pakistan will be discussed more in depth in chapter 5.

BLACK MARKET PURCHASE RESULTING FROM LEAKAGE

The third scenario under which a terrorist could acquire an intact nuclear weapon or fissile material is the purchase of it outright in a black market transaction, which may result from inadvertent leakage due to infiltration, low-level bribery, or a rogue element within a nuclear weapons–possessing government.[34] It is highly unlikely, for reasons stated earlier, that an intact nuclear weapon would be offered for sale on the black market. While there have been reports of Russian "suitcase" nuclear weapons missing and reportedly for sale, none of these weapons have materialized, have been detonated, or have credible threats associated with them; but that does not necessarily mean they don't exist or have not been transferred to nefarious actors.[35] In May 1997 Lt. Gen. Alexander Lebed, national security adviser to Russian President Boris Yeltsin, revealed during a private meeting with U.S. congressmen that some of these Russian weapons were missing. Subsequently, on *60 Minutes* General Lebed stated, "I'm saying that more than 100 out of the supposed 250 are not under the control of the armed forces of Russia. I don't know their location. I don't know whether they have been destroyed or whether they are stored or whether they've been sold or stolen. I don't know."[36] General Lebed's statements were later discounted by Vladimir Denisov, the chair of the commission established by Lebed to the study the issue. Denisov disclosed that the commission's members "were able to match records to actual weapons," or as he put it, they "counted them on fingers."[37] While the United States manufactured small-size, special atomic demolition munitions meant for battlefield use, such as the Davy Crockett, the Soviets developed two versions of a portable nuclear device, the RA-155 for the army and the RA-115-01 for the navy (intended for underwater use).[38] According to nuclear security expert Matthew Bunn, it is plausible that Russian accounting methods may be responsible for any allegedly missing weapons. Bunn stated:

> The way the Russian accounting system works, everything is accounted for on paper. And there's [*sic*] reams of gigantic paper log books. You could easily imagine a situation where Lebed sent somebody to check at a particular facility, and there's a 19-year-old guard there, and he looks in the book and says, "Gee, there's supposed to be 100 here and it turns out there are only 30." And the reason is, there's another log book over

here that the 19-year-old forgot about, that describes how many had been shipped off to such-and-such a place to be dismantled, or something like that.[39]

Stewardship of these suitcase weapons remains one of the many unknowns associated with the nuclear terrorism issue. While a degree of uncertainty remains with respect to the security of these weapons (likely in the minds of both U.S. and Russian officials), the two factors mentioned above—lack of any appearance or use of such weapons (notwithstanding a claim by Chechen terrorists that they had acquired two devices) and the fact that such weapons require continual maintenance by trained technicians—indicate this may not be a clear and present threat. According to Nikolai Sokov, a former Soviet and Russian Ministry of Foreign Affairs official, two main conclusions can be reached about this issue:

> First, the probability that any portable nuclear devices were lost prior to or after the breakup of the Soviet Union appears low. . . . This does not mean that the threat does not exist, but rather that at this moment, it is probably not the most immediate threat to the home security of the United States or to U.S. armed forces abroad. Second, even if any of the devices were lost, their effectiveness would be very low or maybe even non-existent, especially if the loss occurred during the period of greatest risk, in the early 1990s. Without scheduled maintenance, these devices apparently can produce only minimal yield and eventually no yield at all, and can only serve as a source of small amounts of weapons-grade material.[40]

Moreover, a former director of Research Institute No. 4 (the research arm of the Russian Strategic Rocket Forces), Vladimir Dvorkin, confirmed that in addition to "some type of permissive action link device . . . [the weapons] were also protected against attempts to forcibly remove electronic locks. In the event of such an attempt, the weapon automatically switched into a 'non-use' mode and would not explode." [41]

There is, however, no reason for complacency, as both Russia and the United States continue to have tactical nuclear weapons—highly valuable to a terrorist—forward deployed, possibly unprotected by electronic means, and uncontrolled by any verifiable arms control or disarmament treaty. History illustrates that Osama bin Laden and al Qaeda were patient and operationally conservative; that is, the group preferred operations that have a high likelihood of success.[42] Russian officials and the broader global community have great incentives to ensure that small atomic munitions, should they continue to exist, are provided appropriate security. Secretary of Defense Robert Gates, speaking before the Carnegie Endowment for International Peace, stated:

> I have fairly high confidence that no strategic or modern tactical nuclear weapons have leaked. What worries me are the tens of thousands of old nuclear mines, nuclear artillery shells, and so on, because the reality is the Russians themselves probably don't have any idea how many of those they have or, potentially, where they are. And I don't know how much that has changed now. . . . So I think that of the weapons where the Russians know where they are and know what they are, I have pretty high confidence they are under control. What happened maybe during an earlier, more chaotic period or what has happened to some of these older weapons, I think there are some uncertainties.[43]

It is a cause for concern that a Soviet and Russian expert who has had decades of access to the government's most sensitive information with respect to Russian nuclear weapons and fissile material security publicly states "uncertainties" about an "earlier, more chaotic period or what has happened to some of these older weapons." Nevertheless, if such old systems have not been appropriately maintained by trained experts, the danger may be somewhat overstated.

The greater threat with respect to black market purchases is fissile material, which tends to be less adequately secured than nuclear warheads.[44] While nuclear warheads and their delivery mechanisms are under the control of military authorities more accustomed to security, weapons-usable fissile material can be found at foreign civilian facilities that tend not to have as strong a physical security regime or an adequate security culture. According to the Nuclear Threat Initiative (NTI), "Over 130 research reactors continue to operate with HEU in over 40 countries around the world . . . with an estimated 20 tons of HEU in the research reactor fuel cycle worldwide, enough for hundreds of nuclear weapons."[45] While significant progress has been made in securing nuclear weapons and fissile material since the fall of the Soviet Union in 1991, additional work remains to be done, as will be addressed in chapter 5.

While there may be consensus on the terrorist pathways to a nuclear weapon, there is less of a consensus on the threat of any given terrorist group successfully engaging in each step necessary to detonate a nuclear weapon without being discovered along those pathways. Given the catastrophic consequences that would result from detonating a nuclear device in a U.S. or other Western city, few analysts discount the fact that a potential threat exists. Where some analysts differ, however, is on the likelihood that terrorist groups, including al Qaeda, have the capability to successfully execute such an attack without being discovered. The threat may be clear insofar as terrorist intent to acquire unconventional weapons is concerned, but the specific *nuclear* terrorism threat is not present if various terrorist groups are judged not to have the capability to build nuclear weapons.

Before assessing supply and demand, however, an assessment of how fissile material or a nuclear weapon may be compromised and how such compromises may be detected and reported to national and international authorities must be undertaken.

THREE

Fissile Material Compromise— Notification and Detection

As mentioned in chapter 2, the intentional transfer of an intact nuclear weapon from a nation-state to a terrorist group is unlikely, except perhaps in the most extreme circumstances. The greater risk from a nuclear terrorism perspective is that a terrorist group will acquire fissile material and attempt to construct its own IND. How, then, would a compromise of fissile material be detected? Would national and international nuclear security officials be notified in a timely fashion? Is there any global nuclear detection architecture that integrates national and international nuclear security experts? Does a viable black market for fissile material exist? Has enough fissile material been compromised over time to be of concern? What databases track illicit trafficking in nuclear weapons, and how accurate are they?

TRACKING ILLICIT FISSILE MATERIAL TRAFFICKING

There are certain inherent limitations in ascertaining trends in illicit trafficking in fissile material. "First, the number of confirmed cases is relatively small. Second, there is a high probability that the actual number of cases is much larger. . . . Third, the quality and scope of available information is very uneven and often is contradictory."[1] In the aftermath of the collapse of the Soviet Union in 1991, impoverished and opportunistic sellers seem to have been the norm. Of the known illicit trafficking incidents, 68 percent occurred between 1991 and 1999, and many were for relatively small amounts of HEU (of varying enrichment levels) and plutonium. The black market in nuclear and radioactive materials seems to be supplier driven at this point. "Most known thefts of weapons-usable and other nuclear and radioactive material have been committed by impoverished insiders in the hope of improving their desperate financial situation. . . . Because they diverted the material on their own initiative rather than in response to someone's order, the nuclear black market we have seen to date is supply driven."[2]

Another of the unknowns associated with nuclear terrorism is the question of supply-side sophistication. Have the early amateurs who were often caught in sting operations or through their own folly been replaced by more sophisticated suppliers who have adapted to law enforcement, security, and intelligence agency methods to interdict supplies? Are there fewer sophisticated suppliers than some perceive? In March 2010, nuclear security officials from the nation of Georgia arrested two Armenians attempting to sell eighteen grams of HEU, the origins of which remain unclear. There have been at least three cases in which petty criminals and smugglers within the former Soviet Union attempted to sell one hundred to two hundred grams of weapons-grade HEU while claiming to have two kilograms of the material to supply. How and where these unsophisticated suppliers acquired this material remains a mystery, owing in part to the lack of an official Russian explanation to the West that has been covered in open sources. According to *Atlantic*:

> All three [cases] happened in the past five years, well after more-stringent controls on nuclear materials should have been in place. Two involved significant amounts of high-enriched uranium . . . seeming to have come from two separate sources. And all three were carried out by poorly educated amateurs who knew little about the nuclear materials they were trafficking and only wanted to make a quick buck. All three men made foolhardy mistakes—in some cases transporting their atom-bomb materials through functioning border points. . . . What if these three would-be traffickers had been not bumblers but professionals—interested not in money but in ideology, focused on accumulating enough bomb-grade material to assemble a nuclear weapon that could kill millions of people?[3]

These incidents demonstrate one element of the supply-side nature of the black market. The demand side of the market is equally important.

Who are the buyers that compose the demand side of the illicit fissile material market? Al Qaeda has demonstrated through its actions that it is interested in acquiring fissile material. However, given the complex and opaque nature of this market, complete with numerous intermediaries and middlemen, the end users are not always obvious. Successful interdictions often catch individuals or groups in the early to mid-part of the supply chain, thus leaving the end user unknown. By definition, unsuccessful interdictions also leave the end user unknown. In the 1991–2005 period, according to open-source information, buyers were most often undercover police and intelligence officers. "The number of sting operations recorded internationally was 47. Another 315 interceptions in the period resulted from the activities of police and security services, most of which were probably sting operations but could not be positively identified as such."[4] A reasonable conclusion could be that at the peak of danger—the early to late 1990s—suppliers were relatively unsophisticated and trafficked in either "red mercury" or other false fissile material, and buyers were governmental agencies running sting operations.[5] According to public sources, no terrorist group has acquired weapons grade fissile material. However, there is no reason for complacency, as it is clear that various terrorist groups, including Chechen groups, and al Qaeda, have expressed clear and determined interest in acquiring WMD. Given the relative success of U.S. and allied counterterrorism operations against core al Qaeda, including the elimination of senior operational leaders, the extent to which the group has the capability and expertise to plan sophisticated operations, such as nuclear terrorism, remains an open question.

DUELING DATABASES

There are at least two international databases that monitor illicit transactions in nuclear and radioactive materials: one administered by the IAEA, another started by Stanford University and now maintained by the University of Salzburg, Austria.[6] The IAEA, an independent entity related to the United Nations, was established in 1957 as the "Atoms for Peace" organization. The IAEA is charged with seeking "to accelerate and enlarge the contribution of atomic energy to peace, health, and prosperity throughout the world. It shall ensure, so far as it is able, that assistance provided by it or at its request or under its supervision or control is not used in such a way as to further any

military purpose."[7] As part of its charge, the IAEA maintains the Illicit Trafficking Database (ITDB). Established in 1995, the ITDB contains information voluntarily reported and confirmed by participating states (although the
IAEA encourages nonmember states to report as well) on incidents including
"unauthorized acquisition [for example, through theft], provision, possession,
use, transfer, or disposal of nuclear and other radioactive materials, whether
intentionally or unintentionally, with or without crossing international borders, as well as unsuccessful or thwarted acts of the above type. . . . It also
covers the loss of materials and the discovery of uncontrolled materials."[8]

The second database is the Database on Nuclear Smuggling, Theft, and
Orphan Radioactive Sources (DSTO). The difference between the ITDB and
DSTO is that the latter includes incidents that governments may be reluctant
to report and confirm to the IAEA. The DSTO includes incidents reported in
open sources and found credible by the University of Salzburg. Open-source
information may or may not necessarily be as reliable as that which is officially
reported by governments to the IAEA. For comparative purposes, the number
of cases "confirmed to the IAEA by the Russian [Federation] between 1993
and 2005 is less than a third of some 300 cases reported in the press over the
same period."[9] As mentioned above, the inconsistencies between these two
databases limit the analysis of trends in illicit trafficking.

Some who may be sympathetic to the conventionalist school of thought
argue that while these databases are useful, they have relatively limited utility
as "states are loathe to claim missing material when it is seized and much less
ready to accept the possibility that more may be missing and for sale to the
highest bidder. . . . National interests trump the collective security imperative
of closing down the black market."[10] While it may be clear that what is officially reported to the IAEA may indeed be the tip of the iceberg in terms of what
may be available on the black market, and national and multilateral efforts to
further stanch the illicit trade in nuclear materials should be supported, the
complete eradication of the illicit trade, including hoaxes, is unlikely so long as
the forces of supply and demand continue to exist. Yet assumptions that a fully
functional market exists, composed of numerous willing and capable buyers
and sellers, are questionable.

According to the ITDB, for the period 1993–2009 there were 1,773 confirmed incidents reported by member states.[11] During the 1991–2005 period, using the same definition of incident as the IAEA, the DSTO recorded

a total of 1,440 cases, including 1,053 trafficking incidents. According to the International Institute for Strategic Studies, "Over 90 percent of these trafficking cases did not pose a significant threat from the standpoint of either nuclear weapons proliferation or terrorism in that they did not involve weapons-usable nuclear materials or dangerous radiation sources, considered suitable for an effective RDD [radiological dispersion device]."[12] An analysis of IAEA, ITDB, and DSTO data on incidents involving nuclear material illustrates that of all the incidents during the aforementioned time frame, 7 percent involved HEU and 10 percent plutonium. Figures 1 and 2 illustrate the breakdown of nuclear material incidents.

Because terrorists would likely be primarily concerned with HEU or plutonium, the ITDB and the DSTO provide information on the incidents and amounts with respect to this material. According to the IAEA's ITDB, there have been eighteen confirmed incidents involving HEU and plutonium. The

FIGURE 1.
INCIDENTS INVOLVING NUCLEAR
MATERIALS CONFIRMED TO
THE ITDB, IAEA, 1993–2005

FIGURE 2.
INCIDENTS INVOLVING NUCLEAR
MATERIALS, DSTO, 1991–2005

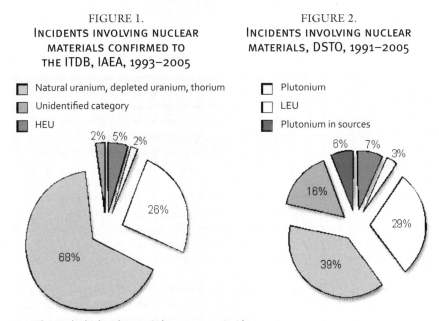

Note: The total is higher than 100% because some incidents involved more than one category of nuclear material.

Source: Data from IAEA, "Trafficking in Nuclear and Radioactive Material in 2005," last updated March 3, 2011, http://www.iaea.org/newscenter /news/2006/traffickingstats2005.html. See also IAEA, "IAEA Illicit Trafficking Database (ITDB)," http://www-ns.iaea.org/downloads/security/itdb -fact-sheet.pdf, for more updated information.

Source: Data from Lyudmila Zaitseva, "Organized Crime, Terrorism, and Nuclear Trafficking: DSTO Case Study 2001–2005" (presentation, Naval Postgraduate School, Monterey, California, July 26, 2006), http://www.nps.edu/academics/sigs/ ccc/conferences/recent/Presentations/ Zaitseva_Monterey_2006.pdf.

DSTO adds seven highly credible incidents involving HEU from 1991 to 2006. Table 2 summarizes these incidents.

A basic summary of fissile material incidents shows that the total of all fissile material stolen (and subsequently recovered), lost, or seized that has been confirmed by national governments to the IAEA is approximately 8.25 kilograms from 1991 to 2006. Of this amount, 5.96 kilograms were weapons-grade HEU (enrichment >85 percent ^{235}U), 1.91 grams were HEU of unde-termined enrichment, and 0.36 grams were plutonium.[13] Even if the lower estimated threshold of HEU required to build an IND is used—twelve to twenty kilograms (implying a sophisticated design and engineering team)— 5.96 kilograms, while of concern, does not reach a clear and present danger threshold.[14] This is particularly true given that there is no information indi-cating that any of these materials were ever meant to be combined; indeed, as they were seized or recovered over a fifteen-year period and include both plutonium and varying enrichment levels of HEU, it seems unlikely they were intended to be combined by any single buyer. However, as mentioned earlier,

TABLE 2. ADDITIONAL HIGHLY CREDIBLE CASES INVOLVING HEU, DSTO, 1991–2006

Incident	Date	Location	Material	Amount (kilograms)
Seizure	October 6, 1992	Podolsk, Russian Federation	HEU (90%)	1.5
Seizure	July 29, 1993	Andreeva Guba, Russian Federation	HEU (36%)	1.8
Seizure	November 28, 1993	Sevmorput, Russian Federation	HEU (20%)	4.5
Loss	1996	Tomsk, Russian Federation	HEU (90%)	.345
Loss	1992–1997	Sukhumi, Abkhazia, Georgia	HEU (90%)	.655
Diversion attempt	1998	Chelyabinsk region, Russian Federation	HEU (unknown %)	18.5
Seizure	2000	Elektrostal, Russian Federation	HEU (21%)	3.7

Source: Lyudmila Zaitseva, "Illicit Trafficking in Radioactive Materials," in *Nuclear Black Markets: Pakistan, A.Q. Khan and the Rise of Proliferation Networks, A Net Assessment* (London: International Institute for Strategic Studies, 2007), 125.

if one assumes this confiscated material represents only the tip of the iceberg, it is indeed a cause for great concern. If, for example, a 1998 case involving 18.5 kilograms of unknown HEU enrichment (never reported to the IAEA by Russia but confirmed by a Russian Ministry of Atomic Energy official) were verified, the total would be 24.5 kilograms, or about half of what it would take to build a gun-type nuclear weapon without a reflector.[15] "As demonstrated by a number of successful diversions . . . the security and control systems at source facilities failed to register the disappearance of significant amounts of weapons-usable material."[16] One of the greatest concerns for the future of securing fissile material, particularly in Russia, is that equipment installed and paid for by the United States continues to be operated and maintained as U.S. funding for the Nunn-Lugar program there begins to phase out.[17]

Some analysts use the narcotics smuggling analogy as an example of how easy it would be to smuggle a nuclear weapon or fissile material into the United States. While this may be understandable insofar as it points out the porous nature of U.S. borders and relatively low estimates of interdiction rates, what it neglects to understand is risk.[18] Drug smugglers are primarily motivated by profit and understand well that there are certain costs of conducting business. These costs certainly include interdiction by governmental authorities. Drug smugglers, like any other business people seeking to maximize profit, will want to decrease their costs by minimizing seizures and, therefore, will adapt their smuggling methods for such purposes. However, losing bales of marijuana or kilos of cocaine or heroin are risks that the drug cartels are willing to accept; they are a simple cost of doing business. Their venture will not fail due to 10–15 percent narcotics interdiction rates.

However, terrorists are not generally motivated by profit but by a complex mix of ideological objectives, sometimes secular, other times religious. If a group has acquired an intact nuclear weapon, or more likely the fissile material to construct its own nuclear weapon, it has dedicated much treasure, time, and energy to the endeavor. The amount of risk, framed as a successful interdiction of the fissile material or intact nuclear weapon, a terrorist is willing to accept is likely to be far lower than that of the drug cartels. This lower risk tolerance may result in more operational conservatism. Failure to get an individual shipment of drugs into the United States is likely viewed by narco traffickers as a learning experience, with the remedy being sending more drugs across the same or another border using different means. While a terrorist may also view failure of shipping fissile material or an IND into the country as an opportunity to learn, it comes with a far higher cost. Failure to the terrorists means not only losing all the effort and to resources put into the effort to acquire the fissile material and to construct a weapon but also failure in the eyes of their global supporters and, perhaps most important, in the eyes of God.[19] This cost may prove too high for terrorists to bear.

Another concern in the nuclear black market is the potential linkages between organized criminal groups and terrorists. It has been documented that some terrorists engage in criminal activities to financially support their activities, enter a country illegally, or engage in document fraud.[20] However, there is a dearth of unclassified, official reporting on documented linkages between organized criminal groups and terrorists with respect to nuclear issues. According to Louise Shelley, a professor at American University, new, organized criminal groups, unlike traditional hierarchical groups such as La Cosa Nostra (Mafia), share one fundamental ideological motivation with terrorists—a desire for an insecure state. Through interaction in prisons and under-governed territories, Shelley argues, terrorists and criminals develop relationships, some of which can be exploited for illicit trafficking in any number of goods, including nuclear materials. Ozersk, a closed city in Russia in which substantial quantities of fissile material were produced throughout the Cold War and in which much HEU is currently stored, has the most drug users per capita in Russia.[21] Unexplained affluence in Ozersk and unofficial parking spaces outside nuclear facility perimeter fences, while not conclusive, could be causes for concern.[22] The primary concern is that an insider or, more than likely, a team of insiders can defeat any technology placed at these facilities through international nuclear security programs, including the U.S. Cooperative Threat Reduction Program. The perennial insider threat, if it succeeds, could provide a terrorist group with a strategic advantage—time to escape the area undetected.[23]

Not all analysts are convinced of the pervasiveness of crime related to the Russian nuclear complex. Although using only a single case study, a team of RAND analysts concluded with respect to the Japanese Aum Shinrikyo group that "Russian officials appear to have been less corrupt, and Russian nuclear materials and expertise more secure, than many analysts in the West have alleged."[24] Moreover, Chechen rebel groups have the intent and likely inside connections to Russian criminal groups and, insofar as it is known, have not acquired a nuclear weapon or fissile material. According to smuggling expert Rensselaer W. Lee, "Most nuclear smuggling networks seemingly lack the principle attributes of organized crime—a continuing criminal conspiracy, a firm organizational structure, and corrupt ties to authorities. Relationships among sellers, brokers, and middlemen are ad hoc, deal-specific, and impermanent. Large Russian or Western mafia syndicates evince little apparent interest in procuring, transporting, or selling nuclear and radioactive assets."[25]

In short, from an economic perspective, it is hard to argue that a fully functioning black market in fissile material is thriving today. Small quantities of fissile material have been offered for sale by unsophisticated opportunists, scam artists, or governments running sting operations. There is evidence that terrorist groups have attempted to procure fissile material, but there is no evidence that they have been successful, to the best of official U.S. knowledge. Yet while the low-hanging fruit in the market—unsophisticated and opportunistic smugglers and criminals—continue to be apprehended, the concern is that dynamic terrorist groups have learned from apprehensions, sting operations, and fraudulent "red mercury" schemes and have adapted their acquisition strategies to avoid detection. There is a dearth of open-source information available on the demand side of the nuclear materials market. As will be discussed below with respect to al Qaeda, there are numerous open-source leadership statements and fatwas indicating the group's self-imposed religious obligation to acquire unconventional weapons. Again, whether al Qaeda has prioritized the acquisition of one type of unconventional weapon over another is an open question. It could, however, be compellingly argued that given a preference for operational conservatism, and that chemical and radiological sources are far more readily available than fissile material, a chemical or radiological attack is far more likely than a true nuclear fission attack by al Qaeda.

If nation-states become aware of fissile material compromise, whether they report such a compromise to international authorities is a political question. However, if a political decision is made to report the compromise, the most appropriate agency to be notified is the IAEA.

THE ROLE OF THE IAEA IN DETECTION AND NOTIFICATION

It is necessary and appropriate to inquire, if there were a compromise of fissile material anywhere in the world, how would the United States know about it? As mentioned earlier, there is a substantial (but decreasing) amount of fissile material stored and in use at over 130 nuclear research reactors in over forty countries. It is the consensus of many experts that the security of this foreign fissile material is not as advanced as it would be in weapons-related facilities.[26] How would the United States and the international community be made aware if HEU used at a research reactor were compromised? Is it possible that even security personnel at the research reactor may not be aware that its material may have been compromised?

Physical protection of fissile material remains the responsibility of the nation-states that own it, thus entangling the fissile material compromise alert and notification function with national sovereignty. As Gary Samore, White House coordinator for arms control and weapons of mass destruction, proliferation, and terrorism, stated, "The structure of nuclear security is fundamentally a sovereign responsibility of nation states . . . it might be nice if there was a world policeman, but there isn't."[27] Former IAEA director general Mohamed ElBaradei, while discussing the emerging nuclear power renaissance, stated in the agency's consultations with countries wanting to start nuclear power initiatives anew that "we stress that the primary responsibility to ensure safety and security [of nuclear activities] lies with the countries concerned."[28] According to Friedrich Steinhausler, professor of physics and biophysics at the University of Salzburg, Austria: "National practices and the resulting levels of security vary considerably between states due to the lack of adequate mandatory standards and large differences in available funds. This results in fortress-like storage facilities with multiple security barriers in nuclear weapons states to facilities housing weapons-usable fissile material protected by unarmed guards, reflecting cultural differences in national threat perception."[29] Arguably, one of the fundamental flaws in the current international fissile material protection regime is that there are few legally binding international nuclear material protection, control, and accounting (MPC&A) standards.[30] ElBaradei, speaking before the United Nations General Assembly, stated that an independent commission tasked with reviewing the IAEA's work concluded, in part: "In order to help address the threat of nuclear terrorism, the Commission urges Member States to negotiate *binding* agreements—not voluntary, as at present—to set effective global nuclear security standards and to give the Agency the resources and authority to help ensure they are implemented."[31] While the

IAEA has certain security standards and provides technical training to nations on these standards, the agency's genesis and mission are based on facilitating national access to civilian nuclear energy. The IAEA does not enter a country to provide fissile material protection and safeguards training unless it is invited to do so by the host government. And, of course, not all nations are members of the Treaty on the Nonproliferation of Nuclear Weapons (NPT), not all NPT members have safeguards agreements, and not all NPT members with safeguards agreements have an Additional Protocol in force.[32] Importantly, India, Pakistan, Israel, and North Korea are not members of the NPT.[33]

If the IAEA is not present, or only intermittently present, and a country is determined to leverage its civilian nuclear infrastructure for military purposes, the probability that the United States will become fully aware of diversions of fissile material from civilian to military programs in a timely fashion is low. This is true with respect to North Korea, with which the United States and four other countries are intermittently negotiating to develop a nuclear disarmament verification regime. Such a regime would allow the six parties to develop some level of confidence in, among other factors, how much plutonium North Korea has reprocessed from spent nuclear fuel. With respect to countries that are members of the IAEA, particularly those that have implemented the Additional Protocol, the IAEA is likely to issue the first warning that fissile material has been compromised or otherwise diverted from civilian application. As Iran is a member of the NPT, IAEA inspectors are monitoring the reported 3,606 kilograms of low-enriched uranium (LEU) and the 25.1 kilograms of uranium enriched to 19.7 percent it has produced at declared nuclear facilities.[34] Undeclared nuclear activities are not, of course, under IAEA watch but may be discovered through aggressive unannounced inspections authorized under the Additional Protocol. As of December 2010, Iran does not currently have an Additional Protocol in force, according to the IAEA.

TECHNOLOGY

Technology plays a role in detecting the compromise of fissile material, clandestine nuclear weapons development or fissile material production, and undeclared nuclear activity in violation of IAEA safeguards agreements.[35] According to the National Research Council, science and technology can contribute to the detection and interdiction of illicit fissile material and crude nuclear devices "in at least two ways: (1) by providing technical means for detecting the movement of special nuclear materials, especially HEU, either in weapons or as contraband, through border transit points and around critical U.S. assets such as ports, cities, and other high-value facilities; and (2) by providing sophisticated data-mining tools for analysis of intelligence on nuclear smuggling and on illicit weapons development programs."[36] For example, an important part of the U.S. Cooperative Threat Reduction Program with Russia has been the installation of certain MPC&A systems, including portal monitoring systems, which would ostensibly activate alarms in the event an insider attempted to smuggle fissile material out of a Russian storage facility. "Ostensibly" is added because one of the greatest threats to fissile material security is insider complicity in shutting down such systems or otherwise defeating them temporarily so that fissile material can be smuggled out. As mentioned previously, the sustainability of such systems remains a core challenge as the United States begins to phase out funding for the Cooperative Threat Reduction Program in Russia.[37] Satellite imagery and environmental sampling are critical detection tools as well. Despite Syrian attempts to camouflage its construction, satellite imagery proved pivotal in identifying the allegedly North Korean–built gas-graphite nuclear reactor at Al Kibar that was bombed by Israel in 2007.[38] From an international perspective, ElBaradei has stated, the IAEA "remains uncomfortably dependent in our verification work on satellite imagery and environmental sampling analysis provided by Member States. We clearly need a minimum independent capability to ensure our credibility."[39] Currently there are no technological silver bullets that will immunize the United States from the threat of nuclear terrorism. Technology is an enabler; it is best integrated into a strategic view of nuclear terrorism and the myriad tools countries can bring to bear to combat the threat.

INTELLIGENCE

As a first line of defense, intelligence has a central role to play in assessing threats, informing export controls, and alerting national authorities to fissile material compromises. As Rolf Mowatt-Larssen, former director of the Office of Intelligence and Counterintelligence of the Department of Energy (DOE) stated, "The task for the Intelligence Community is not easy. We must find something that is tactical in size but strategic in potential impact. We must find a plot with its networks that cut across traditional lines of counterterrorism and counterproliferation. We must stop something from happening that we have never seen before."[40]

The foundation for alerts and notifications to the United States and broader international community that fissile material has been compromised or diverted is intelligence methods and the development of international intelligence, security, and law enforcement liaison relationships. According to John Despres, former staff member of the Senate Select Committee on Intelligence and national intelligence officer for nuclear proliferation in the U.S. intelligence community, "Exchanges of information among Western intelligence and security services can contribute to common assessments and to prompt detection, identification, location, and even interdictions of terrorists and their state supporters before they initiate operations."[41] National law enforcement, security, and intelligence personnel are in the best position to have local relationships built on trust and legitimacy and technologies in place to become aware of compromises of fissile material. While constrained by sovereignty, law enforcement entities nevertheless share a similar culture across national borders and have common crime-fighting missions; therefore, they might be best placed to develop nuclear counterterrorism links. The FBI has developed many of these links through its Legal Attaché program overseas.[42]

National sovereignty and divergent national interests may cause limits to be placed on the types of information and intelligence shared, and the sensitivity of fissile material compromises may cause nation-states that have "lost" the material not to be eager to share that information. Former director of Central Intelligence (DCI) George Tenet seems to have confirmed this when he described how he and an aide were attempting to develop unprecedented intelligence cooperation with Russian KGB officials in the summer of 2003 to resolve questions concerning reported thefts of Russian fissile material or "suitcase nukes." Tenet described a meeting between CIA and KGB officials concerning this matter: "It soon became evident that even high-level pressure had not prepared [the Russian interlocutors] for the intimate forms of concrete cooperation required to deal with the WMD threat. In the final analysis, it was still a game of spy versus spy."[43] This is one reason why the former director of the Department of Energy's intelligence program has recommended that the IAEA develop its own intelligence arm to transcend national borders and cooperated to develop an early warning function for loose nuclear materials or weapons.[44] While such a separate intelligence service would represent a success for collective and international security and is an intriguing concept (driven perhaps by a need to surmount the aforementioned "spy versus spy" mentality), it is also in tension with the national sovereignty imperatives that are an important element of any international body controlled by its constituent member states. Only sustained political leadership at the highest levels, including the possible provision of incentives and disincentives, can overcome such national concerns.

NOTIFICATION FROM FOREIGN POLITICAL LEADERSHIP

Current U.S. declaratory policy is intentionally ambiguous but clearly serious on the consequences any nation-state or nonstate actor would suffer if it assisted a terrorist group in developing a nuclear weapon. It provides: ". . . the United States will hold any state, terrorist group, or other nonstate actor or individual fully accountable for supporting or enabling terrorist efforts to obtain or use weapons of mass destruction—whether by facilitating, financing, or providing expertise or safe haven for such efforts."[45]

The intention of this declaratory policy, an extension of remarks President George W. Bush made in the aftermath of North Korean nuclear tests in 2006, is to deter any nation, particularly North Korea and Iran, from providing any assistance to terrorist groups attempting to develop nuclear weapons. This policy may also provide an incentive for a nation-state to alert the United States that fissile material may have been compromised within its borders in order to avoid retribution in the wake of a nuclear terrorist attack on the United States. However, it could also be argued compellingly that a policy of declared and implied military retaliation against allied states (Russia and Pakistan, for example) for terrorist use of fissile material or a nuclear weapon against the United States constitutes a disincentive for notification cooperation. Physicist Michael Levi of the Council on Foreign Relations writes that a

> U.S. threat will not only affect day-to-day decisions about security—it will also affect decisions in a crisis. The United States and others should want to encourage cooperation from a state's leaders if that state's security sys-

tem fails and nuclear weapons or materials escape its control. In particular, they will want that state's leaders to notify them of any major security failure so that they can mount an intensive effort to prevent an ensuing attack. Deterrent threats would likely undermine that goal. . . . Any possibility that the United States would punish the state for attacks stemming from negligent security practices would sharply discourage leaders of that state from notifying the United States of any actual security failures.[46]

If the United States is notified by Russian authorities that some of its fissile material is missing, the U.S. Intelligence Community, in concert with DOE and the Department of Defense (DOD), Russian authorities, and friendly foreign intelligence services, can work to determine what terrorist group(s) or terrorist group intermediaries may be in Russia, what their most likely escape routes are, and their potential end destinations.

Early detection of fissile material compromises is essential, as there is an inverse relationship between the amount of time a fissile material compromise goes undetected and the ability of authorities to locate it. The more time that elapses between the compromise and the detection of that compromise, the lower the likelihood of timely fissile material recovery. Early detection provides law enforcement, intelligence, and security services with an opportunity to search a smaller geographic area for the compromised material. If the compromised material is rapidly transported away from the source of the compromise through, for example, air transport, the probability of recovery decreases.

Should fissile material overseas be compromised, what capabilities does the United States have to detect the material if a terrorist group attempts to smuggle it (or an intact nuclear weapon) into the country?

U.S. GLOBAL NUCLEAR DETECTION ARCHITECTURE

Assuming that fissile material can be compromised at its source, the United States is in the process of establishing a global nuclear detection architecture to detect the attempted smuggling of radiological and fissile material into the country. The goal is to take advantage of the United States' competitive technological advantage, jettisoning Robert Oppenheimer's infamous 1946 statement that the best tool to detect the smuggling of a nuclear weapon into the United States is a screwdriver to open containers that may be carrying such a device. Dr. Oppenheimer's point was that one had to be close—very close—to a nuclear weapon in order to detect it, particularly if the weapon's fissile material core was shielded.[47] The Department of Homeland Security's Domestic Nuclear Detection Office (DNDO) is the lead federal agency on nuclear detection.[48] The Security and Accountability for Every (SAFE) Port Act (P.L. 109-347), which codified the establishment of the DNDO, did not define the global nuclear detection architecture. The DNDO has defined the architecture as a "multilayered structure of radiological/nuclear detection systems, deployed both domestically and overseas; a well-defined and carefully coordinated network of inter-relationships among them; and a set of systems engineering–based principles and guidelines governing the architecture's design and implementation and evolution over time."[49]

The Government Accountability Office (GAO) has assessed U.S. progress in nuclear detection. It concluded that

> while DNDO has made some progress in strengthening radiation detection capabilities to address critical gaps and vulnerabilities in combating nuclear smuggling (including the land border area between ports of entry, aviation, and small maritime vessels) . . . DNDO is still in the early stages of program development, and has not clearly developed long-term plans, with costs and time frames, for achieving its goals of closing these gaps by expanding radiological and nuclear detection capabilities.[50]

Technologically, the current iteration of deployed nuclear detection architecture uses (handheld) polyvinyl toluene radiation portal monitors (PVT-RPMs) and spectroscopic radiation in the Vehicle and Cargo Inspection Systems (VACIS) located at some U.S. and foreign ports.[51] These systems have inherent limitations, and the DNDO has been exploring the use of Advanced Spectroscopic Portals (ASPs).[52] The GAO "recommended in March 2006 that the DHS analyze the benefits and costs of deploying ASPs to determine whether any additional detection capability provided by ASPs is worth the cost, and would still question the replacement of current-generation equipment with ASPs until DNDO demonstrates that any additional increase in security would be worth the ASPs' much higher cost."[53] In September 2008 the GAO concluded that the DNDO's findings "do not accurately depict the results from the test and could potentially be misleading. . . . The test results provide little information about the actual performance capabilities of the ASPs."[54] In June 2009 the GAO found that the DNDO's recent tests of ASPs "added credibility to the test results," but the GAO continues to question "whether the benefits of ASPs justify the high cost given that DHS criteria for a significant increase in operational effectiveness require only a marginal improvement in the detection of certain weapons-usable materials."[55]

Other groups have found that the relative ease of shielding HEU makes ASPs not worth the increased costs. Based on two field tests and computer modeling, two physicists at the Natural Resources Defense Council (NRDC), Thomas B. Cochran and Matthew G. McKinzie, have found that "existing radiation portal monitors, as well as new Advanced Spectroscopic Portal machines, cannot reliably detect weapons-grade uranium hidden inside shipping containers. They also set off far too many false alarms."[56] Matthew Bunn and Andrew Newman of Harvard University succinctly assess detection technologies, stating, "It is important to understand that neither the detectors now being deployed, nor the Advanced Spectroscopic Portals will have any substantial chance of detecting HEU material with even modest shielding."[57]

The detection systems deployed today are "passive," meaning they detect radioactive materials that "emit a constant stream of gamma rays, neutrons, and alpha and beta particles. Passive detection systems measure these spontaneous emissions without applying any external stimulation such as x-ray, gamma-ray, or particle beams. Two factors severely limit passive detection systems: radioactivity and background radiation. The radioactivity of some sources is low or easily shielded. Background radiation varies dramatically with location, time, and viewing direction."[58]

There is, however, extensive ongoing research and development on "active" detection systems that would provide an external stimulus to radiological and nuclear material, causing the material to emit additional particles and rays that would overcome background noise. Research continues into the efficacy and efficiency of these technologies (including muon radiography, muon beams, and neutron generators) that could serve as the foundation for standoff platforms that could potentially detect the presence of a nuclear weapon or fissile material from the air, prior to its arrival at U.S. borders.[59] As technologies improve, particularly at official ports of entry, it is important to bear in mind that the terrorist threat is dynamic. That is, if terrorists believe there is even a slight chance that their weapon or fissile material may be detected by deployed technology, they are unlikely to attempt to smuggle the material through an official port of entry. The United States appears to be at that point currently, even with detection technology that is not completely effective. If terrorists decide to smuggle a crude nuclear weapon or fissile material across any U.S. border via small aircraft, water-bound pleasure craft, or any other conveyance in between official ports of entry, the importance of having stand-off platforms increases substantially. However, intelligence or law enforcement information would still serve as a force multiplier by forewarning agencies of potential areas of the border across which such materials may be flowing.

The ability to detect fissile material is not an academic matter. While a multilayered defense-in-depth approach will likely continue to be the United States' best method of preventing nuclear terrorism (whether technologies designed to detect fissile material are or are not effective), there is the policy question about the level of resources that should be dedicated to such research and development efforts. As technology improves inexorably, there will always be a compelling argument for continuing basic and applied research and development on nuclear and radiological detection technology, but resource allocation in fiscally austere times can be a zero-sum game. What level of resources should be devoted to nuclear detection research and development versus protection of fissile material and nuclear weapons at their source and to intelligence and law enforcement designed to detect compromises of such material through human and technical means? In a $14 trillion economy, the easy answer might be that the country should dedicate resources to all areas of nuclear terrorism prevention. However, counterterrorism program performance metrics and relative assessments of the effectiveness and efficiency of certain technologies no doubt have a place in making national budgetary decisions.

Finally, there is a temporal dimension to technology research and development as it relates to potential terrorist development of nuclear weapons. At current levels of research and development investment in nuclear and radiological detection technology, it has been estimated that the active detection technologies may not reach effective and efficient milestones for ten to fifteen years.[60] If, as some estimate, terrorists are likely to develop a nuclear weapon in ten years, the terrorists may succeed before the United States has the technology to reliably detect such a weapon. However, skeptics are likely to doubt the ten years to nuclear terrorism estimate, as it blindly accepts that terrorist acquisition of nuclear weapons is only a question of "when, not if." Skeptics might cite President John F. Kennedy's statement in the third presidential debate in 1960 that represented a then widely held view: "There are indications, because of new inventions, that ten, fifteen, or twenty nations will have a nuclear capacity, including Red China, by the end of . . . 1964."[61] It didn't happen. As a skeptic might see it, technical determinism when applied to nonstate actors is sometimes constrained by sound national policy and cohesive international action. Moreover, a skeptic might also cite RAND research indicating that insurgencies don't last forever.[62] The research encourages the United States to adopt a new counterterrorism strategy that deemphasizes heavy U.S. military footprints in Muslim countries and emphasizes the importance of enhanced national and international police and intelligence. The implication is that if the United States can devise and successfully execute a less kinetic and more police- and intelligence-driven counterterrorism strategy, leveraging international law enforcement, security, intelligence, and military forces, it may prove more effective in countering terrorism in general and the threat of nuclear terrorism specifically. Barring any technological breakthrough that may make nuclear weapons far easier to build, if such counterterrorism strategies are successfully executed, al Qaeda's capability to engage in sophisticated international operations such as nuclear terrorism may be substantially degraded over the next decade.

NUCLEAR DETECTION NET ASSESSMENT AND RECOMMENDATIONS

While research and development into active detection systems may prove promising in the ten- to fifteen-year time frame, current detection systems are not effective against a shielded HEU device that a terrorist may attempt to smuggle into the United States. One is left to conclude that the current deficiencies in detection technology make it prudent to (1) place greater urgency on containing and protecting nuclear weapons and fissile material at their source; (2) invest in nonnuclear means of disrupting terrorist networks, plots, and means to support their activities; and (3) continue to invest in research and development for promising detection technologies. Consideration should also be given to mechanisms and practices that would enhance the incentives for nation-states to notify the United States and the international community in the event of a fissile material compromise. On the supply side, fewer fissile material protection sites, with improved protection according to some heretofore nonexistent, binding international security standard, could go a long way to decreasing the risk of nuclear terrorism.

Periodic arrests of opportunistic suppliers of faux fissile material or small amounts of true fissile material should not lead one to conclude that a thriving black market for fissile material exists. Government sting operations have value insofar as they increase uncertainty and risks for potential buyers and suppliers. The knowable unknowns—how much fissile material may be available for sale and which end users may be attempting to purchase it—should be a priority for intelligence, law enforcement, and security services working cooperatively. Yet sting operations and the publicity they create should not be perceived as prima facie evidence that a viable and well-functioning black market exists.

Given this understanding of the methods and measures that may be used to detect and notify the United States and the international community that fissile material or a nuclear weapon may have been compromised, a more in-depth assessment of the demand and supply sides of the nuclear terrorism threat can be undertaken.

FOUR

The Nuclear Terrorism Threat Spectrum—Demand

efore assessing the demand side of nuclear terrorism, a brief examination of the spectrum of views on nuclear terrorism and terrorism threat assessment methodologies will be instructive. Consistent with the conventionalist and skeptic schools outlined previously, there is a broad divergence of nuclear terrorism threat assessments.

The Commission on the Prevention of Weapons of Mass Destruction Proliferation and Terrorism (Graham-Talent Commission) concluded: "Unless the international community acts decisively and with great urgency, it is more likely than not that a weapon of mass destruction will be used in a terrorist attack somewhere in the world by 2013. . . . Terrorists are more likely to be able to obtain and use a biological than a nuclear weapon."[1]

President Barack Obama, speaking in the Czech Republic in April 2009, stated that nuclear terrorism is "the most immediate and extreme threat to global security. One terrorist with a nuclear weapon could unleash massive destruction. Al-Qaida has said that it seeks a bomb. And we know that there is unsecured nuclear material across the globe. To protect our people, we must act with a sense of purpose without delay."[2]

Polling data indicate that the American people are convinced that a terrorist attack upon the United States using nuclear weapons is likely. According to a 2007 Harris Poll, when asked to rate the likelihood of a nuclear bomb exploding in a city in the next five years, 42 percent thought it "likely," 14 percent deemed it "very likely," and 28 percent considered it "somewhat likely."[3] Are the American people correct? How should one assess the nuclear terrorism threat?

When considering the threat of nuclear terrorism, it is worthwhile to understand how terrorism threat assessment affects allocation of counterterrorism resources. As numerous experts have posited, including national security personnel at the GAO:

> Much of the federal efforts to combat terrorism have been based on vulnerabilities rather than an analysis of credible threats. . . . What is important about intelligence agency [terrorism] threat assessments is the critical distinction between what is conceivable or possible and what is likely in terms of the threat of a terrorist attack. Some of the public statements made by intelligence community officials about the terrorist [chemical, biological, radiological, or nuclear (CBRN)] threat do not include important qualifications to the information they present. Based upon our reading of the classified threat documents, such as national intelligence estimates, such qualifications include the fidelity and amount of credible intelligence, the terrorists' intentions versus their capabilities, whether the target is military or civilian, whether the target is international or domestic, and whether the enemy is a government or terrorists without foreign government sponsorship.[4]

Similarly, terrorism expert Brian Michael Jenkins points out that there is a clear distinction between pre- and post-9/11 terrorism threat assessment practices. He states that the National Commission on Terrorist Attacks Upon the United States (hereafter the 9/11 Commission) "described the government's lack of foresight and preparedness as a 'failure of imagination.' That made it imperative not just to outgun the terrorists but also to out-imagine them. Instead of starting at the front end with terrorism intentions, the analysis now started at the back end by identifying a vulnerability, postulating a hypothetical terrorist foe, and building a scenario—invariably a worst-case scenario with terrible consequences."[5] Open societies have infinite vulnerabilities that invariably lead to competitive debate about which vulnerability and attendant set of consequences is more important. This is not to say that vulnerability analysis has no utility; clearly it does with respect to assessing consequences. However, vulnerability assessment should not supplant sound threat assessment practices.

RISK CALCULATIONS AND NUCLEAR TERRORISM

The overall level of risk of a nuclear attack by terrorists can be defined as the product of the consequence of a nuclear detonation and the threat of the same, expressed as the probability that a terrorist group will be able to acquire or build and detonate a nuclear weapon successfully ($R = C \acute{} P_t$, where $t =$ intent + capability, and $C =$ consequence). Since probability can be difficult to assess with any validity and reliability, we are often left with consequence. As Jenkins points out, "Since it is difficult to estimate the probabilities of an attack, threat advocates make it a contest of consequences. Indeed, most current assessments of terrorist threat are consequence-driven . . . the possibility of tens of thousands or hundreds of thousands of casualties trumps the probability of occurrence. Even a 1 percent chance becomes an unacceptable risk requiring preventative or preemptive action."[6] It would seem NBC News military analyst William Arkin concurs, as he has written:

> To many though, the [9/11 attacks] merely confirmed a decades-old presumption that if they could, terrorists would acquire weapons of mass destruction, and they would also use them. This threat is . . . amorphous, in that it cannot be measured in warheads or forces and cannot be "deterred" in the traditional sense. It is also based on faith and completely divorced from intent, political realities, and technological possibilities. But because the consequences of failure are so high, it is a threat that never really goes away. Could terrorists really obtain sufficient material and put together all of what would be needed to manufacture a nuclear weapon? I'll go out on a limb and say, not after 9/11.[7]

In order to constitute a threat, a terrorist group must have the intent *and* the capability to successfully execute such an attack. Capability is difficult to assess with a high degree of confidence, but from a policymaker's perspective it may be the best practice to assume some level of capability and seek to disprove it. As terrorism expert Daniel Byman suggests, "Intent is not the same as capability. For more than five years now, al-Qa'ida has tried to repeat its murderous feats of 9/11—and it has failed. The ten-foot-tall jihadist monster that menaced us on 9/11 is weaker than we supposed, and much of this weakness stems from successful U.S. counterterrorism."[8] Intent in the absence of capability does not translate into an immediate threat. However, intent in and of itself is very dangerous, particularly if it is manifested by terrorist groups that have empirically demonstrated logistical, financial, and operational capabilities to undertake substantial terrorist attacks. The national objective, then, is to use all the tools of national power—diplomatic, intelligence, military, economic, and financial—to ensure such groups do not develop the capability to acquire, build, and detonate even an IND. Capability is dynamic and must be closely and continuously monitored; innovative intelligence methods designed to monitor and blunt terrorist nuclear capability are essential. While intent can be relatively simple to assess—public statements of terrorist group leaders can be quite revealing—assessing capability takes analysts and policymakers into the murky world of intelligence and many unknowable unknowns, many of which have been mentioned earlier.[9] According to Charles Allen, former DHS undersecretary of intelligence, "Although we have an understanding of terrorist intent to acquire nuclear weapons, we are less certain about the terrorists' capability to acquire or develop a nuclear device. . . . I do not believe that any terrorist organization currently has developed a nuclear device."[10]

Moreover, intent and capability might not necessarily be independent variables. That is, if terrorists determine that the risks of failure are too high or that more conventional (and reliable) weapons will help them achieve their goals with a lower level of risk and cost, this may affect their intent to use nuclear weapons.[11] Given the horrific consequences of a nuclear detonation in a U.S. city, many analysts argue that the likelihood of nuclear terrorism is nearly irrelevant; if there is even a relatively small probability of terrorist success, or if the probability is trending upward, the country must take immediate measures to prevent such an attack. Former vice president Richard Cheney infamously stated, "If there's a 1 percent chance that Pakistani scientists are helping al-Qa'ida build or develop a nuclear weapon, we have to treat it as a certainty in terms of our response. It's not about our analysis, or finding a preponderance of evidence. . . . It's about our response."[12] Such a position (some would refer to it as worst-case scenario planning), while comprehensible, has far-reaching ramifications for national security policy, resource allocation decisions, and assessments of real and opportunity costs.[13] Preventive war, while having a place in a spectrum of available options in a national security crisis, tends to place a premium on nearly infallible intelligence—a characteristic that is not necessarily inherent to the intelligence discipline, where ambiguity and incompleteness are the rule, not the exception. The central interpretation of the "precautionary principle" built into a 1 percent doctrine is that it is better to be safe than sorry. However, one of the essential dilemmas for policymakers, according to analysts Robert Hahn and Cass Sunstein, is that "it is not clear what to do if one wants to be 'safe.' How safe is safe enough?"[14] Michael Krepon, a nuclear weapons expert at the Henry L. Stimson Center, stated, "When worst-case scenarios do not materialize, those who issued dire warnings can take credit. And if attacks do occur, the alarmists can always say, 'I told you so.'"[15] Worst-case scenarios set the evidentiary bar for action—up to and including preemptive military actions—very low, which can have enormous long-term effects on the United States' standing in the world, as well as cause the United States to incur substantial human and financial costs.

Worst-case scenario–based planning can also yield substantial opportunity costs. As Daniel Byman suggests:

> While such worst-case scenarios can highlight U.S. weaknesses and lead to more robust plans, they are too often more sensational than real, and too frequently disconnected from the goals and capabilities of actual terrorist groups. The result is what scholar Leif Wenar has called a "false sense of insecurity." At the moment the threat to the United States is real, but not existential. Al-Qa'ida will not destroy the United States. Unfortunately, too many analyses emphasize the worst possible case, and too few consider the very real limits of our adversaries and their objectives.[16]

As mentioned earlier, however, while the direct effects of a detonation of an IND may not in and of themselves be existential, should the United States overreact, then the effects of those overreactions might put the country on an unforeseen and dire path. For example, in the aftermath of a nuclear terrorist detonation in the United States, should leadership substantially curtail civil liberties for an indefinite period of time, suspend the Constitution, execute martial law, or engage in an ill-conceived (conventional or nuclear) retaliatory military attack on a country with strategic nuclear forces capable of targeting U.S. leadership, population centers, and critical infrastructure targets concurrently, then the country might be moving in the direction of either an existential threat or one that so changes the character of our society, political institutions, and norms that the threat could possibly be considered existential. Yet this threat lies within the realm of reaction, a variable that can be controlled internally through leadership, communication, and societal resilience.

THE DEMAND SIDE

The demand side of the nuclear terrorism issue concerns the terrorists who are attempting to acquire either intact nuclear weapons or sufficient fissile material to construct such a destructive device. The demand-side analog to the nuclear terrorism supply-side argument—"no loose nuclear weapons, no loose fissile material, no nuclear terrorism"—is "no sophisticated nuclear-capable terrorists, no nuclear terrorism." Each argument stretches credulity but makes the point that decreasing both supply and demand is essential in reducing the overall risk of nuclear terrorism. While the supply-side problem and set of reasonable policy solutions to prevent nuclear terrorism are fairly clear (even if not necessarily easy to execute in a timely and effective manner), the demand side is relatively more complex. Here we are attempting to get inside the head of the terrorist to understand myriad motivations, intentions, potential self-restraints, and diverse and uncertain capabilities to successfully execute a catastrophic attack.

In the Cold War, adversarial military forces were arranged in such a manner as to be susceptible to intelligence collection. Soviet military capabilities were relatively transparent, yet their intentions remained opaque. Today, arguably, the situation is exactly the opposite as we believe we understand the intentions of al Qaeda and other terrorists groups but are less well informed on their nuclear capabilities. An assessment of global terrorism trends and their relationship to nuclear terrorism is a good starting point for analysis.

GLOBAL TERRORIST TRENDS AND NUCLEAR TERRORISM

In April 2008 administration officials and other experts testified before the Senate Homeland Security and Government Affairs Committee on the threat of nuclear terrorism. The former director of Department of Energy (DOE) intelligence and counterintelligence as well as DHS's former undersecretary of intelligence, two of the country's foremost experts on this matter, provided their assessments of the threat in both open and closed (classified) congressional sessions.[17] These officials, in general, would likely find their views closer to those of the conventionalists than to those of the skeptics, as no one wants a nuclear attack to occur, particularly during his or her tenure. It could be argued that policymakers' perceived penalty for threat overestimation is far smaller than that associated with threat underestimation. One demonstration of the conventionalist school of thought was made by the director of DOE intelligence and counterintelligence when he stated, "It would be a mistake, however, to view nuclear terrorism strictly through the prism of the threat posed by al-Qa'ida today. . . . Increasing numbers of disaffected groups are turning to violence. . . . We must guard against conventional thinking that places limits on the art of the possible for terrorist action."[18] While there may be little disagreement with each of these discrete thoughts, when taken together and viewed through the prism of nuclear terrorism threats to the U.S. homeland, this line of reasoning would likely have little credible value in skeptics' eyes. One such skeptic, former deputy national intelligence officer for transnational threats Glenn Carle, stated:

> We do not face a global jihadist "movement," but a series of disparate ethnic and religious conflicts involving Muslim populations, each of which remains fundamentally regional in nature and almost all of which predate the existence of al-Qa'ida. . . . Al-Qa'ida is the only global jihadist organization and is the only Islamic terrorist organization that targets the U.S. homeland. Al-Qa'ida threatens to use chemical, biological, or nuclear weapons, but its capabilities are far inferior to its desires.[19]

With respect to the limited destructiveness of terrorism, another skeptic, Professor John Mueller of Ohio State University, stated: "Even with the September 11 attacks included in the count . . . the number of Americans killed by international terrorism since the late 1960s . . . is about the same as the number killed over the same period of time by lightning, or by accident-causing deer, or by severe allergic reaction to peanuts."[20]

Newsweek correspondent Fareed Zakaria summarized terrorist trends by stating, "If you set aside the war in Iraq, terrorism has in fact gone way down over the past five years."[21] This differs substantially with official assessments of terrorist trends, which generally have shown significant increases in global fatalities from terrorism over the 1998–2006 period. Zakaria cites *Human Security Brief 2007*, a study published by Simon Fraser University in Canada, which finds:

> The expert consensus in the West is that the threat of global terrorism is growing. . . . The consensus view of the various Western intelligence agencies is in turn supported by statistics from three databases. . . . The National Counterterrorism Center [NCTC] . . . has data that show that the number of terrorist attacks—and fatalities they cause—have increased steeply worldwide from 2005 to 2006. . . . Similarly, U.S.-based Memorial Institute for the Prevention of Terrorism (MIPT) . . . shows fatalities from terrorism worldwide increasing sharply from 2003—as does the relatively new National Consortium for the Study of Terrorism and Responses to Terrorism (START) dataset from the University of Maryland. The reason . . . that the NCTC, MIPT, and START global fatality tolls rise so dramatically after 2003 is because all three datasets are counting a large percentage of *all* civilian deaths in Iraq's civil war as deaths from "terrorism."
>
> Since the concept of terrorism remains contested, the counting rules used by the NCTC, MIPT, and START are as legitimate as any others. But they are unusual because counting the intentional killing of civilians in civil wars as "terrorism," as all three datasets do, is a sharp departure from customary practice.[22]

Similarly, a Congressional Research Service report found that "some would argue that NCTC data attributable to Iraqi casualties, which are largely the product of sectarian violence, rampant criminal activity, and homegrown insurgency, grossly distort the terrorism picture and perhaps should not be attributed to terrorist activity."[23]

The terrorist threat has evolved since the events of September 11, 2001. Testifying before the House Committee on Homeland Security in February 2011, Secretary of Homeland Security Janet Napolitano summarized the evolving terrorist threat to the U.S. homeland as one in which there has been a "rise in the number of terrorist groups inspired by al-Qaeda ideology—including (but not limited to) al-Qaeda in the Arabian Peninsula (AQAP) from Yemen, al-Shabaab from Somalia, and Tehrik-e-Taliban Pakistani (TTP)." Not only have these groups sponsored or been linked to terrorist attacks against the U.S. homeland (AQAP with Nidal Hassan, Fort Hood 2009, and with Umar Abdulmutallab, failed aircraft bomb December 2009 and printer toner cartridge bomb attempt October 2010; and TTP with Faisal Shahzad, Times Square, New York City, bomb attempt June 2010), they are also, according to Napolitano, "trying to inspire individuals in the West to launch their own, smaller-scale attacks, which require less . . . sophisticated planning."[24]

Regardless of numeric trends in global fatalities resulting from terrorism, analysts of nuclear terrorism are left to ponder the question of what exactly is the "art of the possible" and how it differs from the art of the impossible. A skeptic might ask which terrorist groups specifically have the intent *and* capability to construct a nuclear weapon, deliver it to the United States, and successfully detonate it. Are the intelligence and law enforcement communities aware of millennial and apocalyptic groups that are more advanced, well connected, well financed, and technically capable in their quest for nuclear weapons than were Aum Shinrikyo or Chechen terrorist groups, for example? If so, what are the identities and capabilities of those groups? If Aum Shinrikyo (which was very well financed and recruited some of Japan's best scientists) and the Chechen terrorist groups (which had proximity to large quantities of fissile material and had alleged contacts with Russian organized crime) could not go nuclear, how successful might less well-financed and less technically capable terrorist groups be?

While there is near-universal agreement that if terrorists could acquire nuclear weapons, it would represent a clear and present danger to U.S. national security, consensus does not exist among policymakers, scholars, and other interested observers on the complex question of whether terrorist groups have the intent, motivation, and capability to acquire, build, weaponize, deliver, and detonate a nuclear weapon. Moreover, analysts also differ on the probability of such an attack, which has a clear temporal dimension.

An assessment of some of the various underlying assumptions and basic arguments associated with the skeptic and the conventionalist schools of thought is instructive. Table 3 reflects several relatively simplified core assumptions and arguments that are explored in greater depth in the supply and demand sections of this book. One of the greatest divergences between the two schools of thought lies in whether analysts believe that terrorist groups have the technical, engineering, and logistical skills to build a nuclear weapon. Some analysts, including physicists who have experience in nuclear weapons design, are diametrically opposed on this question.

TABLE 3. COMPETING NUCLEAR TERRORISM THREAT
ASSUMPTIONS AND ARGUMENTS

Issue	Conventionalists	Skeptics
Are terrorist groups rational?	Assume all groups have potential for nuclear terrorism and may be irrational/unpredictable.	Assume all terrorists have malevolent intent but all may not be interested in nuclear terrorism. All groups not necessarily irrational or unpredictable; some act strategically.
Which terrorist groups credibly threaten the United States with nuclear terrorism?	Not simply al Qaeda; numerous, and perhaps unknown, groups might attack the United States with a nuclear weapon. Core al Qaeda remains a threat.	Largely concerned with al Qaeda as the only group that has specifically threatened the U.S. homeland. Core al Qaeda operations capability degraded but not defeated.
If a terrorist group acquires a nuclear weapon or builds an IND, will it detonate it?	Yes. If not in the United States, then in other Western countries that represent "softer" targets.	Not necessarily. Terrorists may act in a parastatal manner. May use to deter attacks against safe haven(s).
Are terrorist groups operationally conservative?	No. Should not allow historic precedents to rule out "breakout" and increasingly violent techniques, like nuclear terrorism.	Yes. Tend to stick with what works—operationally and technically.
Can terrorist groups be deterred from nuclear terrorism?	Unlikely. "Expanded" deterrence for enabling states might work.	Possible by increasing the terrorists' perceived risk of failure—operationally, politically, and theologically.
Would a state provide a nuclear weapon to a terrorist group?	Yes. Mercantilist states have sold nuclear technology and advanced conventional weapons. Why not a nuclear weapon?	Unlikely. States realize attribution capabilities may lead to massive retaliation even without irrefutable evidence. Little plausible deniability.

Table 3. Continued

Issue	Conventionalists	Skeptics
Could terrorist groups acquire an intact nuclear weapon on the black market?	Possibly. Russian "suitcase" nukes or special atomic demolitions question not fully resolved.	Unlikely. Even if acquired, unlikely to have ability to override potential detonation codes or successfully deconstruct.
Could terrorists acquire enough fissile material on the black market to build an IND?	Yes. There is no way of reliably knowing how much material may have been lost, especially in the early to mid-1990s. In one unofficial instance, 18.5 kg of HEU were nearly stolen from Russia.	Possible, but unlikely given imperfect state of market, increasing security for fissile material, government stings, international collaboration. Only 5.96 kg of HEU in illicit trafficking according to official IAEA data.
Do any terrorist groups have the capability to construct an IND (gun-type) device?	Yes. Once fissile material is acquired, it is quite possible a terrorist group could recruit necessary skill sets to construct an IND. No need to test. Machine tools are low tech and available.	Possible. While challenge is not insurmountable, it is exceedingly difficult to do, even once fissile material is acquired. "Explicit" knowledge does not constitute "tacit," experience-based knowledge.
Can terrorist groups transport and detonate an IND in the United States?	Possible given porous borders, ineffective detection technology, and technical assistance on detonation.	Possible, yet many steps involved, absolute loyalty required, and numerous transportation risks exist.
What is the probability of terrorist nuclear detonation within the United States in the next decade?	Conceivable. Medium- to high-range probability.	Vanishingly small probability.
What is the status of al Qaeda's nuclear knowledge?	Dynamic; assume recruitment for technicians, chemists, metallurgists, and engineers continues.	Elemental based on "safe house" documents seized. Counterterrorism, nuclear security efforts constraining recruitment.
What happens if the Iranians make nuclear weapons?	Will result in cascading proliferation; stimulus for regional, civilian nuclear programs; increased nuclear terrorism risks; and regional destabilization.	May not necessarily lead to cascading proliferation. Extended deterrence and U.S. security guarantees might preclude proliferation. If not, regional deterrence dyads may develop as in India/Pakistan.

Table by author.

THE "ACQUISITION-USE" THESIS

Many analysts and senior governmental leaders unquestionably believe that if al Qaeda acquired a nuclear weapon it would use it almost immediately at a location with the lowest risk of discovery. It is also the consensus judgment of the U.S. Intelligence Community, which concluded, "We assess that al-Qa'ida will continue to try to acquire and employ chemical, biological, radiological, or nuclear materials in attacks and would not hesitate to use them if it develops what it deems is sufficient capability."[25] According to former director of Central Intelligence George Tenet, "We established beyond any reasonable doubt that al-Qa'ida had a clear intent to acquire chemical, biological, and radiological/nuclear weapons, to possess not as a deterrent but to cause mass casualties. The assessment prior to 9/11 that terrorists were not working to develop strategic weapons of mass destruction was simply wrong. They were determined to have, and to use, these weapons."[26] This judgment may be valid and is based largely on all-source intelligence analysis. Policymakers responsible for protecting U.S. national security have prudent and clear incentives to assume al Qaeda would use nuclear weapons against the United States if it acquired them; any other position makes them vulnerable to dereliction of duty charges. However, as nonproliferation expert Lewis Dunn has concluded, it is appropriate to consider the assumption that "acquisition equals use" because if the null hypothesis is true—that is, acquisition does not equal use—there may be important policy implications. According to Dunn, if acquisition does not equal use, "actions to enhance deterrence would take on greater importance—and feasibility—as a complement to more active measures against Usama bin Laden and al-Qa'ida."[27]

Policymakers' prudent assumption that al Qaeda's acquisition of nuclear weapons equals use of nuclear weapons is based on a number of factors, including but not limited to (1) al Qaeda's public statements and positions justifying the use of WMD to kill 4 million–10 million Americans; (2) the belief by al Qaeda or any other terrorist group that once it acquires a nuclear weapon, it has already incurred certain "sunk costs"—substantial time, effort, and money spent in acquisition—that provide an internal pressure for the group to use the weapon (if the weapon is not used, all was for naught); (3) if a potential target state discovers that a terrorist group has acquired a nuclear weapon, the target state's preemptive actions may be no different than if the terrorist group had actually used the weapon; in essence, from the terrorist group's perspective, once discovered it may be in a use-it-or-lose-it position; (4) the perception that al Qaeda may be irrational or has an apocalyptic view of destroying the world in order to save it; and (5) al Qaeda's demonstrated activities involving other unconventional weaponry, such as chemical weapons.

There are some, however, who might argue that certainty about terrorist intentions and motivations concerning nuclear weapons may be unwarranted. The automatic "if acquisition, then use" thesis may not necessarily be true as a terrorist group (such as al Qaeda) may make a strategic calculation that (1) if a nuclear weapon is acquired, it has more options than immediate detonation; (2) using weapons indiscriminately may cause the Ummah (Muslim community) to rise up in revolt in a global version of the Anbar Awakening in Iraq; and (3) using nuclear weapons may hasten the demise of the group given that a nuclear attack anywhere in the Western world is likely to unleash unprecedented and direct attacks against core al Qaeda in Pakistan and against al Qaeda affiliates globally. Terrorist analysts Chris McIntosh and Ian Storey argue:

> The arguments made in favor of the probability of nuclear terrorism rely on a series of false equivalencies and a fundamental misreading of the way recent events implicate our broad understanding of terrorist strategy. . . . Since the 1980s the [nuclear terrorism] debate has largely centered around the probability of acquisition; if a terrorist organization successfully acquires a nuclear capacity, proponents of the nuclear terrorism scare believe it is only a matter of time before that weapon will be used against the United States. This conventional formulation assumes that a terrorist organization has only two choices once acquisition occurs—either to use it or not. Presumably, an organization wouldn't desire such a capacity unless they wished to use it, so there is an implicit equation between acquisition and use.[28]

McIntosh and Storey's arguments about the expanded set of choices terrorists have post–nuclear weapons acquisition are predicated on the belief that terrorist organizations are strategic actors whose actions can be modeled. According to these analysts, "In spite of conventional wisdom, there is every reason to believe that . . . attempting to understand terrorist strategy through the lens of basic strategic rationality is a methodologically legitimate and scientifically worthy enterprise."[29] McIntosh and Storey expand the two perceived options that terrorists have post acquisition of nuclear weapons to five options, as outlined in figure 3.

According to McIntosh and Storey, blackmail implies that the organization declares that it has a nuclear weapon and identifies the conditions that will induce an attack. Besides the need to establish the credibility of a nuclear capability claim (by perhaps providing documentation of the design or even a nuclear detonation), nuclear blackmail is problematic because the target state has no way of being ensured that terrorists will surrender their nuclear weapons if it complies with their demands. Opacity implies that an organization admits a nuclear capacity but does not identify the conditions that would stimulate an attack. Latency implies a situation in which a terrorist group does not confirm it possesses a nuclear capacity but does publicly state the conditions under which it would detonate a nuclear weapon in pursuit of its goals. Dormancy implies that after weapon acquisition the terrorist group neither chooses to publicly identify the conditions that would trigger a nuclear attack nor publicizes the acquisition of the weapon itself; the organization would keep the "bomb in the basement."[30] McIntosh and Storey highlight that there are certain opportunity costs associated with a terrorist group's choices regarding nuclear use. "Most obviously, an organization that moves from a policy of dormancy to blackmail cannot easily return to dormancy or latency—those options have been foreclosed."[31]

From a terrorist's motivational and intent perspective, McIntosh and Storey conclude that "nuclear terrorism is improbable in the extreme. Although the names and actors have changed and terrorism has come to dominate strategic thought across the globe, America's metropolitan centers have no more to fear than they ever have from the possibility of nuclear terrorism."[32] They base this conclusion on three premises. First, there are relatively high opportunity costs of detonating a nuclear weapon when and if terrorists acquire one. The Cold War's "stability-instability" paradox holds "empirical weight—nuclear acquisition does not make nuclear policy the only means of aggression. . . . Nuclear acquisition does not necessarily foreclose the panoply of other directions the [terrorist] campaign could conceivably take."[33] Second, as mentioned above, a nuclear terrorist attack against a Western, industrialized nation

FIGURE 3.
Terrorist Options: Post–Nuclear Weapons Acquisition

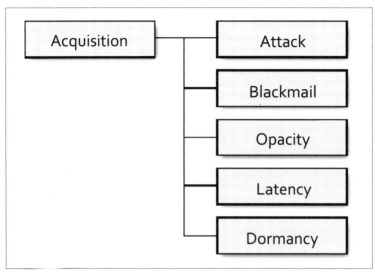

Source: Chris McIntosh and Ian Storey, "Between Acquisition and Use: Examining the Improbability of Nuclear Terrorism," January 29, 2008.

would call into question the very survivability of the terrorist group. While it may be difficult to deter terrorist groups by punishment for many reasons (a subject that will be explored more in depth later), a terrorist nuclear attack "does carry with it a considerable potential threat to the continued survival of the organization. . . . This potential manifests itself in two ways: internal threats of disintegration and external threats to continued operations and survival of the terrorist organization."[34] Third, the conflation of capitulation and surrender works against nuclear terrorism:

> For a terrorist organization, even complete capitulation [of the target state] does not end the threat to their organization. . . . It is conceivable that a nuclear attack on Manhattan combined with a request to remove all U.S. troops from Iraq might result in U.S. withdrawal, but there is virtually no scenario under which that would cause the U.S. to give up and cease hostilities against the organization responsible. In other words, capitulation would occur, while the potential costs to the organization *in-*

crease. In an interstate war, the opposite is true—capitulation or surrender almost always results in the threat decreasing.[35]

Similarly, nonproliferation analyst Dunn raises the issue that if al Qaeda acquired nuclear weapons, it might surprise the world by not using them. According to Dunn, "Bin Laden's statements about nuclear weapons (and defensive jihad), a look at his goals, and 'state-like' action by al-Qa'ida all provide starting points for that speculation" that bin Laden himself will be highly influential in the debate over whether to use nuclear weapons.[36] "From all three [aforementioned] perspectives, bin Laden and his immediate lieutenants might, under some conditions, regard nuclear weapons as 'too valuable to detonate.'" In one of the only post-9/11 interviews of bin Laden, he was asked by Pakistani journalist Hamid Mir: "Some Western media claim that you are trying to acquire chemical and nuclear weapons. How much truth is there in such reports?"[37] Bin Laden allegedly responded, "I heard the speech of American President Bush yesterday [October 7, 2001]. He was scaring the European countries that Usama wanted to attack with weapons of mass destruction. I wish to declare that if America used chemical or nuclear weapons against us, then we may retort with chemical and nuclear weapons. We have the weapons as deterrent."[38] Mir, however, may not be an entirely reliable source; since the October 2001 interview he has provided numerous accounts of the conversation with varying messages, some of which have bin Laden and Ayman al-Zawahiri claiming to have nuclear weapons, others seeming to have de-emphasized nuclear weapons.[39] As was soon discovered as a result of Operation Enduring Freedom, documents seized in al Qaeda safe houses in Afghanistan showed that the status of al Qaeda's nuclear weapons capability at that time was nascent.

With respect to al Qaeda's goal of establishing an Islamic Caliphate, nuclear weapons use, according to Dunn, could be a double-edged sword. On the one hand, such a devastating blow against the United States would demonstrate al Qaeda's power and might be "perceived as a method of diverting U.S. energies, thereby disrupting counterterrorist actions." On the other hand, the use of a nuclear weapon could substantially undermine the goal of establishing an Islamic Caliphate by (1) "awakening a giant," causing the United States and numerous allies to significantly increase global counterterrorism activities in ways that are unforeseen but may be ruthless, and (2) foreclosing the option of al Qaeda's seizing power in one state and using any nuclear weapon it may possess to deter the United States or any other power from invading (an invasion that would undermine the nascent theocratic regime that al Qaeda would likely envision as the foundation of the Caliphate).[40]

Options short of nuclear detonation are explicitly raised here to allow the reader to understand some of the underlying assumptions about nuclear terrorism. The nuanced meaning of the term "use" is illustrative as it forces the analyst and policymaker to think anew about some scenarios that may have been anticipated in the context of nation-to-nation nuclear exchanges but have not necessarily been fully considered with respect to nonstate actors such as terrorist groups.

Empirically speaking, because there have been zero incidents of nuclear terrorism as defined herein, there are no exact-match case studies from which to learn. However, there have been at least four cases in which terrorists have used chemical, biological, or radiological weapons against adversaries or noncombatants.[41] In one case, Chechen terrorists placed a dirty bomb in a Moscow park but did not detonate it. The most prominent of the chemical weapon cases is Aum Shinrikyo's use of sarin nerve gas in the Tokyo subway in 1995.

TERRORIST USE OF WMD: THE CASE OF AUM SHINRIKYO

While the scope of this book is limited to nuclear terrorism, if one views biological and chemical weapons as potential "gateway" terrorist WMD (an assertion that is arguable), it may prove useful to briefly consider one of the more prominent cases of WMD use by a terrorist group. According to terrorism expert Bruce Hoffman, Aum's use of sarin gas in the Tokyo subway in 1995 "marked a significant historical watershed in terrorist tactics and weaponry. Previously, most terrorists had shown an aversion to the esoteric and exotic weapons of mass destruction popularized in fictional thrillers. . . . Radical in their politics, the majority of terrorists were equally conservative in their methods of operation."[42] Aum crossed this threshold, yet the results were less than catastrophic.

Designated as a foreign terrorist organization by the U.S. Department of State (DOS), Aum is a Japanese group formerly led by the charismatic Shoko Asahara, a partially blind owner of a chain of yoga schools in Japan. Asahara was apocalyptic in his views; he was obsessed with the idea of nuclear war, particularly between the United States and Japan. Prior to their nuclear weapons acquisition efforts, Asahara and Aum attempted to gain power through Japanese electoral politics. It was not until the electoral effort failed that Asahara turned the group toward "viewing Japanese and Western society as the enemy and advocated pursuing violent means to bring about Armageddon."[43] Asahara apparently believed that a U.S.-Japanese war would trigger Armageddon. Aum recruited over three hundred scientists in fields such as medicine, biochemistry, biology, and genetic engineering from some of Japan's top universities. The group was well financed; Aum's ventures reportedly yielded annual revenue approaching $1 billion. Aum first attempted to acquire nuclear weapons from contacts made at a relatively high level in Russia. According to a RAND study, senior Aum leader Hayakawa Kiyohide spent much time and money exploring Russia's advanced weapons market. "He made eight trips to Russia in 1994. He kept a personal notebook—eventually confiscated by authorities—which included the phrase 'Nuclear warhead. How much?'"[44] What was meant by this passage is unclear. Was it simply a note or perhaps related to an actual negotiation? Notwithstanding some contacts with Russian nuclear scientists and senior-level officials, including former vice president Alexander Rutskoy and the head of Russia's Security Council Oleg Lobov, and payments from Aum to certain Russian officials for pet projects, Aum was unable to purchase a nuclear warhead.[45] Undeterred, Aum was also pursuing a parallel acquisition strategy focused on fissile material. Believing that Australia would not be harmed at Armageddon, Aum "bought a sheep farm at Banjawarn in 1993 to test chemical weapons and mine uranium. . . . However the cult found little uranium."[46]

Despite its prodigious financial resources and scientific support—at the height of instability in the former Soviet Union—Aum did not succeed in acquiring a nuclear weapon or fissile material. The group failed for numerous reasons.[47]

- While Aum may have had access to numerous scientists, it did not apparently have access to the right type of scientists, those having the appropriate nuclear, physics, engineering, electronics, explosives, and metallurgy skills to build a nuclear weapon. Corrupting a Russian official to sell a nuclear warhead would have negated the necessity of having these scientists available (although detonation may still have required technical knowledge to overcome any potential permissive action links or other safety devices on the weapon). Depending on the path terrorists take to nuclear weapons, there are certain skill sets that they must have lest their efforts fail. Aum did not succeed in recruiting the appropriate personnel; intelligence, military, and other elements of U.S. national power must ensure that al Qaeda similarly fails.

- Russian nuclear weapons security was better than many in the West believed. In the early aftermath of the collapse of the Soviet Union, the early to mid-1990s, a period arguably thought to be the most dangerous, the security of Soviet fissile material was relatively poor. While it is not clear if Aum specifically targeted fissile material, the bottom line is that Russian security officials may have had more integrity than was previously thought. Aum may simply not have known which officials were most susceptible to bribery, yet Aum's well-financed effort was ultimately rebuffed.
- Aum apparently had certain ideological constraints, including a deadline of Armageddon in 1995. If Asahara could not use nuclear weapons as a catalyst to induce a U.S.-Japanese war and Armageddon, Aum would try chemical agents, which they perceived to be easier to weaponize and detonate. While al Qaeda may have a longer time frame than Aum had, it may make similar cost-benefit assessments of the effort to build nuclear weapons, particularly if the group perceives that its international influence is decreasing and it needs a successful mass-casualty attack (using any type of weapon) to remain a viable international threat.

After failing at nuclear weapons acquisition, Aum turned to chemical weapons, and thus the 1995 sarin attack in Tokyo.[48] Yet Aum did not give up entirely on nuclear acquisition. In 2000 Japanese police searches of Aum facilities "revealed classified information about nuclear facilities in Russia, Ukraine, PRC, South Korea, and Taiwan."[49] Moreover, it was also determined that Aum members hacked into classified computer networks to acquire the data.

If Aum's nuclear weapons acquisition efforts failed, why and how might other, perhaps less well-funded and less scientifically oriented, groups attempt the same clandestine goal and expect different results?

WHY, HOW, AND WHO?

The primary questions to be asked about the demand side of nuclear terrorism are why, how, and who. Why are certain terrorist groups interested in nuclear terrorism? What is their motivation? Once there is an understanding of the motivation, one can marry this motivation to the ever-important "how" question of nuclear weapons capability. While intent and motivation to acquire nuclear weapons are dangerous enough by themselves, when married to capability, they become a clear and present danger to national and international security. Finally, motivation and capability can be related to an understanding of the third question, "who"—which groups may represent the greatest nuclear terrorism threat?

As mentioned earlier, there is a relationship between intent and capability; in some instances intent can drive capability and in others capability can drive intent. While a terrorist group may continue to state in its propaganda that it is interested in acquiring a nuclear device, it may not, in reality, dedicate its relatively scarce resources to such an attempt, choosing instead to focus on more reliable conventional weapons–based attacks while pursuing a nuclear weapons propaganda campaign. As nonproliferation expert William Potter and terrorism expert Gary Ackerman point out, some terrorist groups might also have their intent to use nuclear weapons influenced by happenstance; that is, should one of the nations in which a group has a presence experience extreme political instability and that nation has nuclear weapons, it may be possible for the group to acquire nuclear weapons. Even if that terrorist group had not considered the use of nuclear weapons previously, it might opportunistically develop the intent as a result of governmental collapse.[50]

The concept of risk and how different terrorist groups assess risk is also central to the relationship between intent and capability. If a terrorist group is operationally conservative, by definition preferring to rely on tried and effective conventional explosives to achieve limited political objectives, it is unlikely it will dedicate substantial, if any, resources to acquiring nuclear weapons. While nuclear weapons can be used to achieve limited political objectives, many terrorist groups may perceive the attendant time, effort, resources, and level of failure risk as disproportionate to those objectives. Some groups may fear a backlash against their cause should they use nuclear weapons, which almost by definition kill indiscriminately.

WHY: MOTIVATION

Drawing upon prior research, Potter and Ackerman have distilled a series of motivations terrorist groups may have for engaging in nuclear terrorism. While a comprehensive assessment of terrorist motivation is beyond the scope of this book, the following is a list of compelling reasons why a terrorist group might dedicate substantial time, energy, and treasure to acquiring nuclear weapons:

Mass casualties. Some terrorists wish to acquire and use a nuclear device to cause mass casualties. Al Qaeda leadership, based on religious decrees, fatwas, videos, and other public pronouncements, would like to kill 4 million–10 million Americans, a number analogous to the number of Muslims they believe the United States and its Middle Eastern allies have killed in the world. It is recognized that nuclear weapons could be used to inflict mass casualties, and as mentioned earlier, even a "fizzle" nuclear detonation could lead to the deaths of tens of thousands. Numerous terrorism experts, including Brian Michael Jenkins, have reviewed the historical arc of terrorism and concluded that the trend toward mass-casualty infliction clearly exists. However, it does not necessarily flow from this trend that nuclear terrorism is inevitable. According to Jenkins:

> The constraints that limited terrorism violence in the past have clearly eroded. This does not mean that all terrorists are devoted to carnage—those with political agendas still must calibrate their violence to their cause. Nonetheless, al-Qa'ida's continuing quest for 9/11-scale events, evident in various terrorist plots uncovered since 9/11, sustains fears that terrorists will eventually acquire and use true weapons of mass destruction. Thus far, our worst fears have not been realized: The "what ifs" remain "what ifs." There is no inexorable march to Armageddon, but it cannot be ruled out.[51]

The intersection of mass-casualty terrorism with unconventional weapons is one that has been studied extensively by terrorism scholars. In a March 2001 study concerning the motives and outcomes of mass-casualty terrorism, terrorism expert John V. Parachini calls into question the conventional wisdom that terrorists will inexorably move to use unconventional weapons to maximize casualties and garner a premium on their investment. In six mass-casualty case studies, three of which used unconventional weapons (Rajneeshee, 1984; Liberation Tamil Tigers Eelam [LTTE], 1990; and Aum Shinrikyo, 1995) and three of which used conventional weapons (World Trade Center, 1993; Oklahoma City bombing, 1995; and Africa embassy bombings, 1998), Parachini concludes that "the attacks with conventional high explosives, in contrast [to the attacks with unconventional weapons], were spectacularly successful."[52] As a result, Parachini finds:

> The mixing of incidents involving [conventional and unconventional weapons] has created an inchoate sense of fear and policy maelstrom. As a result, American counterterrorism policy may mistakenly focus too much attention on unconventional weapons attacks rather than mass-casualty attacks regardless of weapons material. Extrapolating from the consequences of incidents involving high explosives to potential incidents involving unconventional weapons leads to an exaggerated sense of the likelihood and consequences of a perceived newly emerging terrorist threat. . . . While government has a responsibility to protect its citizens from even low-probability events that may present catastrophic consequences, a critical part of the task for policymakers is to find the right balance of effort between low- and high-probability attacks.[53]

Similarly, terrorism expert Gavin Cameron of the Center for Nonproliferation Studies at the Monterey Institute of International Studies finds that "the problem with the heightened focus [on WMD terrorism] is that it involves a conflation of two largely separate concepts: that of mass-destruction terrorism and that of terrorism using nonconventional weapons. Preparations for the former are being justified on the basis of an increased incidence of the latter. However, there is a very considerable difference between the two concepts, and it is far from clear how they relate to one another."[54]

The outcome of such a debate leads to the conclusion that counterterrorism resources may be best directed against mass-casualty attacks regardless of the type of weapons used in the attacks. Given what Richard Falkenrath has stated is the "unknowability" of a WMD terrorist attack, the central counterterrorism policy conundrum is what is the optimal allocation of counterterrorism resources and how can those resource levels be simultaneously directed at

(1) the highest probability attack scenarios likely using conventional weapons (or even a radiological dispersion device or biological weapon) to inflict mass casualties and (2) low-probability scenarios that have high consequences such as a nuclear weapon attack. Moreover, what types of performance measurements are being used to ascertain the rate of return on various counterterrorism investments, and what actions are taken based on those performance assessments?[55] While this question is beyond the scope of this book, it is one policymakers must face every day, for none want to be caught with a resource allocation strategy that underestimates the next attack scenario.

Inordinate psychological impact. Terrorism is a tactic used to evoke terror. As Brian Michael Jenkins stated as early as 1975, "The primary attraction to terrorists in going nuclear is not necessarily the fact that nuclear weapons would enable terrorists to cause mass casualties, but rather the fact that almost any terrorist action associated with the words 'atomic' or 'nuclear' automatically generates fear in the minds of the public."[56] Precisely because nuclear weapons are such heinous weapons, with mushroom clouds and images of devastated Hiroshima and Nagasaki indelibly etched in the minds of so many, nuclear terrorism's allure to terrorist groups is powerful. As part of its propaganda strategy al Qaeda has disseminated images of the White House with a mushroom cloud behind it and the U.S. Capitol in the aftermath of a nuclear attack. Through such propaganda, al Qaeda may have become what Jenkins refers to as "the world's first terrorist nuclear power without, insofar as we know, possessing a single nuclear weapon. . . . Al-Qa'ida is certainly the first terrorist group to have a nuclear policy."[57] The key, according to Jenkins, is that nuclear terror (driven by imagination and fear) is separate and distinct from nuclear terrorism (the act of a nuclear detonation conducted for terrorist purposes). With one nuclear detonation, or even with a successful radiological attack, anywhere in the world, a terrorist group may potentially be able to achieve not only quasi-statehood but also inflict upon civilians a sense of powerlessness, fear, and vulnerability. It is for this reason that the resiliency of the American people, according to Stephen Flynn of the Council on Foreign Relations, sustains "the United States' global leadership and economic competitiveness. . . . Periodically, things will go badly wrong. The United States must be prepared to minimize the consequences of those eventualities and bounce back quickly. Resilience has historically been one of the United States' greatest national strengths."[58] Social and economic resilience is part of "deterrence by denial," or an attempt to deter terrorists by denying their goals to eviscerate an economy or bring a nation to its knees politically. For example, if the United States can convince terrorist groups that even if they are able to detonate one or a handful of nuclear weapons within the country they will not forever cripple the U.S. economy or cause the U.S. political system to fall, it will have influenced the deterrence equation. This is the core of deterrence by denial. The concept of terrorist deterrence will be explored more in depth in chapter 6.

Prestige. Nation-states attempt to acquire nuclear weapons for myriad reasons beyond a security imperative. One of these reasons is to achieve prestige, to demonstrate that they have joined the exclusive de facto set of nine nuclear weapons states. For a nonstate actor such as a terrorist group, to acquire or construct a nuclear device demonstrates that the group—against all odds, the international community, and international nuclear nonproliferation norms—has acquired the power of a nation-state. The prestige that such an achievement, however disastrous from the West's perspective, would bring to any terrorist group would be profound. As former DCI George Tenet, someone who would most likely identify with the conventionalist school of thought as outlined herein, stated: "If they manage to set off a mushroom cloud, they will make history. Such an event would place al-Qa'ida on par with the superpowers and make good bin Laden's threat to destroy our economy and bring death into every American household."[59]

Incentives for innovation and escalation. According to Potter and Ackerman, "In a milieu in which terrorist groups may have to compete with rival groups for 'market share' of media attention and constituency support, terrorist decision makers may feel compelled to outdo the destruction wrought by previous attacks."[60] If a terrorist group were able to detonate an IND anywhere in the world, it would gain unrivaled attention. However, it is also possible that such attention may bring with it condemnation not only from the immediate target of the attack but also, depending on the nature of the attack, from the perceived terrorist group's constituency itself. Notwithstanding numerous al Qaeda–inspired justifications for the use of WMD against nonbelievers, there appears to be a debate within the international Muslim community, or Ummah, about the legitimacy of killing Muslims and innocent civilians. For example, the terrorist bombings of civilian hotels in Jordan in

2005 led to street protests against al Qaeda. Al Qaeda's number-two leader, Ayman al-Zawahiri, warned Musab al-Zarqawi, al Qaeda's nominal leader in Iraq (now deceased), that beheading and killing other Muslims might alienate the al Qaeda constituency.[61] Several former intellectual leaders of terrorist groups, including al Qaeda, have written (sometimes while in prison) what have been referred to as recantation books, or works that criticize the religious underpinnings and justifications for terrorist violence as a perversion of true Islam. Perhaps the most infamous is a treatise that was written by Sayyid Iman al-Sharif (otherwise known as Dr. Fadl), a former leader of the Egyptian terrorist group al Jihad, the original core of al Qaeda.[62] Ayman al-Zawahiri has attempted to refute the recantations in his own writings.[63] These debates within al Qaeda and the international jihadist movement about the appropriateness of certain actions, including indiscriminate killing, may have an effect (some would argue only a marginal one) on al Qaeda's WMD acquisition efforts.

Mass destruction and area denial. Nuclear weapons achieve the twin terrorist goals of attacking the target country's infrastructure and denying the country use of a certain area through contamination. Depending upon the geographic area hit (for example, Manhattan or an important sea port), there can be far-reaching economic consequences.

Atomic fetishism. Some terrorist groups, such as Aum Shinrikyo, are led by charismatic individuals who seem to have a fixation with nuclear weapons. Perhaps driven by the fact that Japan is the only nation against which a nuclear weapon has ever been used, or a fascination with science fiction, Aum's leader Shoko Asahara seemed to be obsessed with unconventional weapons.

Revenge and other "expressive" motives. It is also possible that groups that believe they have been victims of extraordinary crimes against humanity, such as genocide, may be capable of "unrestrained levels of violence in the pursuit of revenge against their perceived prosecutors."[64] Given the two bloody wars that the Chechens have fought with Russia, this motivation may apply to them. Yet the Chechens chose not to detonate a radiological dispersion device they placed in a Moscow park in 1996. The self-restraint the Chechens exercised in not detonating the RDD could be attributable to many factors. One may be that they simply calculated that in the context of their contemporaneous goals and the desire to restart negotiations with the Russians, escalating the conflict to another level might not have met their political objectives. An alternative explanation might be that the Chechens did not want to cross the threshold into the use of unconventional weapons, positing that such an action might unleash another ferocious Russian counterattack against them.

Ideology. The worldview or body of doctrine that a terrorist group holds could arguably be one of the most important factors influencing whether it attempts to acquire and use nuclear weapons. One idea that approaches consensus among terrorism scholars is that "groups motivated by religion, which are focused on cosmic as opposed to mortal concerns, are far more prone to engage in attacks involving mass casualties and hence are more prone to use nuclear weapons or other means of mass destruction."[65] As terrorism expert Jessica Stern points out, "People join religious terrorist groups partly to transform themselves and to simplify life. . . . Because they believe their cause is just, and because the population they hope to protect is purportedly so deprived, abused, and helpless, they persuade themselves that any action—even a heinous crime—is justified. They know they are right, not just politically, but morally. They believe that God is on their side."[66]

According to terrorism expert Bruce Hoffman:

> The most salient motive—as the al-Qa'ida and Aum cases demonstrate—remains one involving some religious or theological imperative, whereby a group animated by a desire to decisively attack an enemy state and its population (perhaps in order to deliver a stunning knockout blow) . . . deliberately embarks on such a course of action. But it would be a mistake to see such motivations involving CBRN terrorism as exclusively within the purview of religious terrorists.[67]

Supporting Hoffman, Ackerman and Potter point out that not all religious groups are equally likely to pursue mass destruction, stating that "possessing an ideology with a religious character may at most be a contributing factor to any desire to engage in nuclear terrorism."[68]

Although no taxonomy of Islamist terrorist groups and their attendant worldviews may be entirely satisfactory, terrorism adviser Rohan Gunaratna has stated that the spectrum of Islamist groups includes four main categories, with areas of overlap between them: (1) the revolutionary, (2) the ideological, (3) the utopian, and (4) the apocalyptic.

Revolutionary Islamist groups seek to "legitimize violence by advocating and practicing collective decision-making—and do not kill members of their own community with whom they differ."[69] Groups that fit into this category, according to Gunaratna, include Egyptian Islamic Jihad and Palestinian Hamas.

Ideological Islamist groups "have a coherent discourse of political violence. . . . They offer a systematic set of ideas that justify violence, the use of which is highly regulated and controlled from above and carefully tailored to suit political and social contexts. . . . They have a widespread constituency mutually reinforced by a social services machinery which . . . serves to limit the scale and scope of violence."[70] Islamist groups fitting into this category include Hezbollah and the Islamic Group of Egypt. Some might argue that Hamas, with its extensive social services network within the West Bank and Gaza Strip, might also fit into this group.

Utopian Islamist groups seek "to destroy the existing order. . . . They have no rational political approach or strategy, and endorse no traditional social structure; they are reinventing tradition."[71] There are two stages of a development. In the first stage, according to Gunaratna, groups seek to destroy the established political order yet only kill employees of the state to do so. In the second stage, utopian groups target the existing social, economic, and cultural order; innocent civilians are targeted; and the group moves from utopian to apocalyptic. Examples of terrorist groups in the first-stage category include the Taliban, which operates primarily in Afghanistan and Pakistan; the Salafist Group for Call and Combat of Algeria (GSPC); and (until the 9/11 attacks) al Qaeda, according to Gunaratna.

Apocalyptic Islamic groups "use collective violence but are indiscriminate. They firmly believe that they have been divinely ordained to commit violent acts and are the most likely to engage in mass-casualty, catastrophic terrorism. Many specialists believe that they lack the patient, systematic approach needed to develop the elaborate organization, trained personnel, and equipment by which potent chemical, biological, radiological, or nuclear agents can be produced."[72] Terrorist groups fitting into this category, according to Gunaratna, include al Qaeda and the Armed Islamic Group of Algeria. Gunaratna observes, "Al-Qaeda's suicidal crashing of a hijacked passenger aircraft into the World Trade Centre—a non-political, non-military, and non-governmental target—was a deliberate attack on human beings and their private economy, also on what had become a potent cultural symbol. Its motives were unambiguous. By its decision to conduct a mass-casualty attack, al-Qaeda moved from being a utopian Islamist group to an apocalyptic one."[73]

However, opinion among terrorism experts differs over whether al Qaeda should be categorized as apocalyptic. In general, apocalyptic groups advocate and have had as their focus an end of time prophecy. "Contrary to popular belief, al-Qaeda has never sought an apocalyptic goal. Closer examination suggests that it is a very practical group, with clear aims and objectives, but one that is capable of chameleon-like maneuvering."[74] This view is supported by the Department of Energy's former director of intelligence and counterintelligence Rolf Mowatt-Larssen, who believes that al Qaeda acts very strategically. According to Larssen, also a former CIA employee, a decision by al Qaeda leaders to carry out a nuclear attack would not be made lightly. "They would come to a conclusion . . . where they would justify the use of a nuclear or some other weapon of mass destruction in what they would consider rational terms. In other words, how it would help them fulfill specific goals they have."[75] The question concerning the extent to which al Qaeda might restrain itself from detonating a nuclear weapon remains an open one that will be addressed further.

In short, then, at the highest level of abstraction, terrorist motivations to conduct nuclear attacks can be categorized as being either secular or divine. On the one hand, secularists "see nuclear weapons in much the same way national governments do: possession is useful; use is to be avoided." Divinists, on the other hand, "see nuclear weapons as instruments of ultimate destructive power, of divine revenge and retribution, a trigger for Armageddon. . . . For 'divinists' acquisition means use, not possession."[76] However, whether even pure divinists have the capability to steal or construct an IND remains the question nation-states continue to dedicate substantial resources to answering. Reading the statements of Osama bin Laden and other al Qaeda leaders, replete with references to Allah, the Prophet Mohammed, the restoration of the Caliphate, and entreaties to Muslims to undertake jihad (part of their religious obligation) and assist in the goal of acquiring nuclear weapons, it is clear that al Qaeda uses the divine to motivate and recruit. Effective as such imploring statements may be at recruitment, this approach may also have some limitations, as will be discussed later.

How: Capability

As has been mentioned earlier in this book, the fact that certain groups, including al Qaeda, have the intent to acquire and use nuclear weapons is enough to warrant those groups a high priority for intelligence, diplomatic, and military measures to learn more about and prevent their nuclear capability. But there is a more fundamental debate underlying discussions about any particular terrorist group. This debate concerns whether it is possible for groups having no access to classified information, yet potential access to requisite quantities of fissile material, to construct a crude nuclear device. As mentioned in table 3, this is one of the core disagreements between conventionalists and skeptics. Conventionalists are more likely to believe that, if provided fissile material, it is possible that a small group having the appropriate skill sets could construct and detonate a device. Skeptics, including some who have designed nuclear weapons, concede it is plausible, but they are more likely to believe that it would be very difficult for terrorists to construct a nuclear weapon undetected.

The conventionalists would be far more compelled to believe that there are numerous terrorist groups beyond al Qaeda that either have or have within their reach the logistical, technical, and financial capability to construct a nuclear weapon. Conventionalists would likely cite the following resources as evidence:

- In 1964 scientists at the Lawrence Radiation Laboratory (subsequently renamed the Lawrence Livermore National Laboratory) wanted to test the proposition that well-trained individuals without access to classified information could design a workable nuclear weapon. Labeled the "Nth Country Experiment," the project had the purpose of discovering if "a credible nuclear explosive can be designed, with a modest effort, by a few well-trained people without contact with classified information. The goal . . . should be to design a nuclear explosive which, if built in small numbers, would give a small nation a significant effect on their foreign relations."[77] The laboratory recruited two postdoctoral physicists to run this experiment. While they did not have access to classified information, they did have access to the laboratory's extensive unclassified library, which housed information on such topics as critical-mass numbers, compiled through "tedious, dangerous research."[78] The physicists also had access to an anonymous team of expert bomb designers if they wanted to test certain experiments, for instance, those that may have involved high explosives.[79] The physicists assumed their nameless country had "more resources than Ghana, but less than an industrialized nation."[80] Over the 1964–1967 period, the physicists were able to develop a viable "implosion-type" nuclear weapon design. They did not choose the gun-type design, believing that would have been too easy.[81] Skeptics would argue, however, that having a viable design does not necessarily mean the group could have actually built the weapon.

- In the late 1960s and early 1970s theoretical physicist Theodore B. Taylor became concerned with nuclear terrorism. While in his twenties and thirties, Taylor worked in the Theoretical Division at Los Alamos Scientific Laboratory, "where he was a conceptual designer of nuclear bombs. He designed the Davy Crockett, which in its time was the lightest and smallest fission bomb ever made."[82] When asked how easy it would be for terrorists to build an atom bomb, he responded, "Very easy. Double underline. Very easy."[83]

- In 1977 the congressionally chartered Office of Technology Assessment (OTA) was asked the question, "Could a nonstate adversary design and construct its own nuclear explosive?" The response was:

Given the weapons material and a fraction of a million dollars, a small group of people, none of whom have ever had access to the classified literature, could possibly design and build a crude nuclear explosive device. The group would have to include, at a minimum, a person capable of searching and understanding the technical literature in several fields, and a jack-of-all-trades technician. They would probably not be able to develop an accurate prediction of the yield of their device, and it could be a total failure because of either faulty design or faulty construction. If a member of the group is careless or incompetent, he might suffer serious or fatal injury. However, there is a clear possibility that a clever and competent group could design and construct a device which would produce a significant nuclear yield.[84]

- A 2006 article in the journal *Foreign Policy* updated and operationalized OTA's conclusion by providing one path through which Osama bin Laden and al Qaeda could build a nuclear weapon *within the United States*. With a notional budget of about $5.5 million, a team of nineteen people (using the 9/11 personnel figures) or less, machine tools that the authors state are readily available on the open market, an out-of-the-way U.S. location at which to construct the weapon, and a requisite amount of fissile material purchased on the black market for approximately $4 million, the authors conclude, "Although building a nuclear device remains an expensive, complex undertaking out of reach for most organizations, a well-financed group that seeks to kill very large numbers of people may well find it an irresistible option."[85] While compelling and possible, their argument is based on economics, calculating that spending $5 million is the most efficient means for terrorists to kill up to one hundred thousand people. Although this may be true, skeptics might argue that the terrorists contemplating such an attack may have more complex motivations and strategic considerations, such as organizational survival and questions about whether such an indiscriminate and unprecedented attack would cause support within the Ummah to substantially weaken, that might dissuade them from executing a nuclear attack even if they were capable of doing so.

- Noted Nobel laureate physicist Luis W. Alvarez, one of the few individuals who accompanied the *Enola Gay* on its historic mission, has taken a similar position. According to Alvarez, who was responsible for monitoring the energy from the Hiroshima explosion while aboard the *Enola Gay*,

With modern, weapons-grade uranium, the background neutron rate is so low that terrorists, if they had such material, would have a good chance of setting off a high-yield explosion simply by dropping one half of the material onto the other half. Most people seem unaware that if separated ^{235}U is at hand, it's a trivial job to set off a nuclear explosion, whereas if only plutonium is available, making it explode is the most difficult technical job I know. . . . Given a supply of ^{235}U, however, even a high school kid could make a bomb in short order.[86]

- The *Final Report of the National Commission on Terrorist Attacks upon the United States* concluded, "A nuclear bomb can be built with a relatively small amount of nuclear material. A trained engineer with an amount of highly enriched uranium or plutonium about the size of a grapefruit or an orange, together with commercially available material, could fashion a nuclear device that would fit in a van like the one Ramzi Yousef parked in the garage of the World Trade Center in 1993. Such a bomb would level lower Manhattan."[87]
- John Coster-Mullen, a truck driver from Wisconsin without a college degree, through painstaking research over a decade constructed the first accurate replica of Little Boy, the gun-type nuclear weapon dropped on Hiroshima, Japan, in August 1945. While Mr. Coster-Mullen did not acquire fissile material, his book, *Atomic Weapons: The Top Secret Inside Story of Little Boy and Fat Man*, outlines nearly precise specifications of the bomb's components.[88]

Skeptics, meanwhile, provide supporting evidence that, while not impossible, it would be particularly difficult for a nonstate actor to construct a nuclear weapon. Some skeptics may concede that it is possible for a sophisticated terrorist group to acquire the requisite technical skill sets necessary to construct a nuclear weapon. However, skeptics are more likely to focus on the entire supply chain of terrorist activities that must be executed flawlessly in order for a terrorist to acquire the fissile material necessary,[89] construct the device, and deliver it to a target area all while maintaining complete operational security and group cohesion. From a technical perspective, skeptics might cite the following sources as being authoritative.

Stephen M. Younger, a former Los Alamos National Laboratory official in charge of nuclear weapons research and development and subsequently head of the U.S. Defense Threat Reduction Agency, is skeptical of those who believe constructing nuclear weapons could be done by a high school kid, as Alvarez asserted. According to Younger,

> It would be wrong to assume that nuclear weapons are now easy to make, that once the secret was out anyone could read the instruction book and make one with materials found around the house. I am constantly amazed

when self-declared "nuclear weapons experts," many of whom have never seen a real nuclear weapon, hold forth on how easy it is to make a functioning nuclear explosive. In fact, and thank goodness, there are some significant challenges. . . . While it is true that one can obtain the general idea behind a rudimentary nuclear explosive from articles on the Internet, none of these sources has enough detail to enable the confident assembly of a real nuclear explosive. . . . There are tricks of the trade that even the most complete set of instructions won't contain. . . . You need a working knowledge of how parts fit together, what tolerances are permitted or required, the compatibility of material.[90] To be specific uranium is a material so hard that it is used in armor-piercing tank ammunition. It is exceptionally difficult to machine. . . . Another challenge to the would-be nuclear power is how to choose the right tolerances. . . . "Just put a slug of uranium into a gun barrel and shoot it into another slug of uranium" is one description of how easy it is to make a nuclear explosive. However, if the gap between the barrel and the slug is too tight, then the slug may stick as it is accelerated down the barrel. If the gap is too big, then other, more complex issues may arise. . . . Even advanced industrial nations had a remarkably difficult time solving problems that seem "obvious" to experienced weapons designers.

Is the danger of terrorists getting a nuclear weapon overblown, something that we can ignore? Unfortunately not, since there is still the possibility that terrorists could buy, steal, or be given a device from an established nuclear power. The good news is that even the best-financed and best-organized terrorist group would be hard-pressed to take a stolen or purchased piece of special nuclear material and convert it into a nuclear weapon. In addition to the design and materials, they would require machine shops, explosives testing ranges, sophisticated diagnostic equipment, and more. The bad news is that . . . more and more small countries are crossing the technological threshold that would permit them to make a weapon on their own. . . . The more countries that have nuclear weapons, the greater the probability is that one of these weapons might go astray.[91]

Nobel Prize–winning economist Thomas Schelling stated in a seminal article published in 1982 that the terrorist construction of a nuclear weapon from illicitly acquired fissile material "makes strong demands on an organization. Highly qualified scientists and engineers are required. . . . It appears to require a group of significant size, high professional quality, and excellent organization and discipline to convert unauthorized or illicitly obtained materials into a useable weapon."[92]

Friedrich Steinhausler, professor of physics and biophysics at the University of Salzburg, has written that while terrorists could steal an advanced nuclear weapon from a nuclear weapons state, if the terrorists chose to build a crude nuclear device, they would face a numbers of hurdles that, while high, are not insurmountable. According to Steinhausler,

> The construction of a crude nuclear device requires teamwork, better still, tacit governmental support. Even if the terrorists should have gained possession of sufficient amounts of weapons-grade nuclear fissile material, it is still a major technical challenge to actually build such a device. . . . Should terrorists intend to use a crude nuclear device . . . they would need to have the following:
>
> - Basic knowledge in physical and chemical properties of fissile materials; radiation physics; physical principles of explosive devices, particularly about shaped charges; and electronics;
> - Access to a workshop with advanced equipment . . . ;[93]
> - A sufficient amount of nuclear weapons–grade material needed for building a crude nuclear device (about 25 kg of HEU [using a reflector], 8 kg of plutonium), at least 50 kg of high explosives, and a supply of krypton switches;
> - Machining capabilities for the production of complex shapes (tolerance: about 10E-10m); and
> - Ceramic (cerium sulfide) crucibles, electric furnace, argon-filled enclosure, freon gas, and vacuum pumps.
>
> Despite the multiple technical and logistical hurdles discussed, many of them are not insurmountable for a determined terror organization, especially if operating with tacit support of a sympathetic state and willing to deploy suicide commandos.[94]

Karl-Heinz Kamp, former security policy coordinator of the Konrad Ade-nauer Foundation in Berlin, Germany, and currently affiliated with the NATO Defense College in Rome, Italy, was an early skeptic of a terrorist group's ability to construct a crude nuclear device. Writing in 1996 Kamp stated,

> The idea that terrorists can readily build a bomb is naïve. After all, a number of countries with vast resources and a wide range of scientific and technical personnel have struggled unsuccessfully to produce nuclear weapons. Iraq's nuclear weapons program, which was exposed after the [1991] Persian Gulf War, is an example of a costly, time-consuming, and ultimately unsuccessful quest for a nuclear device. . . . Although the probability is low, the cost of nuclear terrorism is grave enough to deserve continuing attention.[95]

With respect to the comparison of Iraq's program to develop nuclear weapons with that of a terrorist group, conventionalists would conclude with compelling evidence that a nation-state's efforts to develop nuclear weapons are far different from those of a terrorist group. As mentioned earlier, nation-states desire to build more than a handful of tested and accurate weapons to be used for various purposes, including regional deterrence. A terrorist group, however, could be satisfied with one or two crude and untested nuclear devices. Nation-states tend to want to develop their own fissile material, while a terrorist group wants only to acquire the material in any manner possible. While this is true, one has to wonder whether nation-states determined to acquire nuclear weapons have not pursued parallel nuclear weapons development paths—an expedited program to develop a crude nuclear device using acquisition methods similar to those of a terrorist group and an indigenous nuclear weapons program centered on the nuclear fuel cycle. If, for example, Iran tested a nuclear weapon and Saudi Arabia decided it wanted nuclear weapons as a hedge against Iran, it might pursue parallel paths. First, it might attempt to purchase a few nuclear weapons from its ally Pakistan. Second, it might concurrently pursue the long-term development of its own civilian nuclear power program. How the extension of a U.S. nuclear umbrella to Saudi Arabia might influence regional governments' actions is unclear.

Christoph Wirz and Emmanuel Egger, senior physicists in charge of nuclear issues at the Spiez Laboratory, the Swiss nuclear, biological, and chemical defense establishment, illustrate a number of practical obstacles to the manufacture of a gun-type, crude nuclear device:

- Uranium ignites spontaneously in the air at 150–175 degrees Celsius (C).
- Uranium is chemically toxic and radioactive. Highly enriched uranium exhibits more than one hundred times as many disintegrations per time unit as natural uranium.
- When cooling down from its melting point (at 1,132.2 degrees C) to room temperature, uranium undergoes two phase transitions. The density thereby increases by more than 8.5 percent. A change of 8.5 percent in density results in a change of approximately 18 percent critical mass.
- It is not possible to check whether or not the two subcritical masses fit together.

As Wirz and Egger state, "The hurdles for terrorists to get a nuclear weapon are extremely high. The probability of terrorist use of such a weapon is, therefore, extremely low. To build a nuclear weapon is a difficult task, even for countries. Iraq tried it fifteen years ago with a project on the scale of US$10 billion and seven thousand employees, and did not succeed."[96]

Brian Michael Jenkins, while suggesting that the debate over whether a terrorist group could acquire the necessary know-how and equipment to fabricate a nuclear device has yet to be resolved, states, "There is no evidence that they [terrorist groups] have this knowledge now, and what little we know about their capabilities suggests that they do not." He states further that there is a need to "underscore the complexity of [the debate's] key assumption: Terrorists must have the requisite fissile material, which means a sufficient quantity of highly enriched uranium or plutonium, plus some other nonfissile strategic materials. Theoretically, there are several ways for terrorists to obtain these items. Theoretically, just about anything is possible."[97]

Perhaps one of the most balanced analyses concerning the question of whether a terrorist group can construct a nuclear device was written by J. Carson Mark, a former division leader of Los Alamos National Laboratory's Theoretical Division, and several colleagues.[98] Mark and his coauthors reached the following conclusions regarding a crude device based on early design principles:

- Such a device could be constructed by a group not previously engaged in designing or building weapons, provided a number of requirements were adequately met.
- Successful execution would require the efforts of a team having knowledge and skills in addition to those usually associated with a group engaged in hijacking a transport or conducting a raid on a plant.
- To achieve rapid turnaround (that is, the device would be ready within a day or so after obtaining the material), careful preparations extending over a considerable period would have to have been carried out, and the material acquired would have to be in the form prepared for.
- The amounts of fissile material necessary would tend to be large—certainly several and possibly ten times the so-called formula quantities.
- The weight of the complete device would tend to be large, probably more than a ton.
- The conceivable option of using oxide powder (whether uranium or plutonium) directly, with no post-acquisition processing or fabrication, would seem to be the simplest and most rapid way to make a bomb. However, the amount of material required would be considerably greater than if metal were used. To approach crystal density would require a large and special press, and the attempt to acquire such an apparatus would constitute the sort of public event that might blow the cover of a clandestine operation.
- Devices employing metal in a crude design could certainly be constructed as to have nominal yields in the ten-kiloton range; witness the devices used in 1945.
- There are a number of obvious potential hazards in nuclear weapon construction, among them those arising in the handling of high explosives, the possibility of inadvertently inducing a critical configuration of the fissile material at some stage in the procedures, and the chemical toxicity or radiological hazards inherent in the materials used. Failure to foresee *all* the needs on these points could bring the operation to a close; however, all the problems posed can be dealt with successfully provided appropriate provisions have been made.

Net Assessment: Can Terrorists Build a Nuclear Weapon?

Naturally, one would prefer to have a definitive answer to this question. Given the fallibility of intelligence, however, definitive answers provided with a high degree of confidence are rare. Blind faith in technical determinism is unwarranted. It is likely neither impossible nor exceedingly easy for a terrorist group to construct a nuclear weapon even if it had the requisite amount of fissile material. Assessments of terrorist capability are largely based on analysis of classified and open-source information and intelligence, informed speculation, and assumptions that may or may not be valid. Under certain sets of circumstances and making certain assumptions, anything is possible and can be accepted on faith. As mentioned throughout, stochastic assessments of a successful nuclear detonation range from near zero to near one over varying time frames. It seems that the answer to the "build" question is a function of at least three fundamental issues. Table 4 summarizes some conditions that, if met, substantially increase the probability that a terrorist group may develop the capability to build an improvised nuclear device.

First, do the terrorists have a safe haven from which to operate in the long term and either tacit or explicit state assistance? Such a safe haven or state assistance can substantially enhance the chances for terrorist success. The concept of extended deterrence that is directed at preventing nuclear or nuclear-capable nation-states from assisting terrorist groups in becoming nuclear states will be discussed more in depth in chapter 6. Safe havens, however, do not necessarily need to be in nuclear- or nearly nuclear-armed nations; such nations or semiautonomous ungoverned areas within nations can provide a safe base of operations for a terrorist group's clandestine procurement networks, terrorist training, and covert test and construction facilities. For example, although Afghanistan is a member of the NPT, it did not have a civilian nuclear power generation program. According to nonproliferation expert David Albright, despite open-source reporting on al Qaeda's possible nuclear acquisition efforts based out of the country, "the IAEA showed little inclination to investigate these reports. The IAEA was also unmotivated to inspect Afghanistan because Kabul has no declared nuclear activities, and the IAEA traditionally has minimized its activities in such nations."[99] After reviewing documents that had been located in al Qaeda safe houses in Afghanistan, Albright concluded, "If

TABLE 4. CONDITIONS AFFECTING WHETHER TERRORISTS
CAN BUILD NUCLEAR WEAPONS

Condition	Implication
Have terrorists been able to acquire sufficient fissile material to build a weapon?	The acquisition of high-grade fissile material can facilitate, yet not guarantee, terrorist success. If materials of varying enrichment, density, and form are acquired, the process of weaponization becomes more difficult, although not necessarily insurmountable if appropriate metallurgists and chemists are part of the team.
Have terrorists been able to recruit the required scientific, engineering, and technical personnel, including those with "tacit" knowledge of nuclear weapons construction?	Tacit knowledge is, arguably, a critical path to success in a nuclear terrorism plot. In the absence of tacit knowledge, trial and error efforts could increase the risk discovery.
Do terrorists have a safe haven from which to operate and/or tacit or explicit state sponsorship?	Safe havens allow terrorists to operate in an unimpeded fashion, thus facilitating the aggregation of personnel, equipment, and knowledge to plan a sophisticated attack. Even tacit state support can substantially advance a terrorist nuclear plot without guaranteeing its success.

Table by author.

al-Qa'ida had remained in Afghanistan, it would have likely acquired nuclear weapons eventually."[100]

Second, have the terrorists been able to recruit the required scientific, engineering, and technical personnel, including those who have tacit knowledge of nuclear weapons construction? How much do the United States and other nations participating in the Global Threat Reduction Initiative (GTRI) know about the global universe of individuals who possess these skill sets? What are their identities, travel patterns, levels of job security, and potential associations with jihadists? How vulnerable to terrorist recruitment are these individuals? What mechanisms and foreign intelligence liaison relationships and practices are in place to trigger notification of the United States or a friendly foreign intelligence service that such an individual is or may be facilitating any terrorist group's construction of a nuclear weapon or acquisition of fissile material? What incentives are in place to encourage foreign intelligence services to share sensitive nuclear intelligence with the United States?

Third, have terrorists been able to acquire a sufficient amount of fissile material to build a weapon? While acquisition of this material may be the greatest hurdle, acquisition in and of itself, particularly if the material's loss is detected soon after diversion, does not necessarily guarantee success as indicated above. Moreover, if the fissile material acquired by the terrorists is of varying enrichment, density, and form, the process of weaponization—the actual construction of the weapon—will be more difficult, although perhaps not prohibitively so if the appropriate chemical and metallurgical specialists are part of the terrorist team.

If these three conditions are met, it would seem that the odds likely favor the terrorist in terms of narrow conditions for constructing a nuclear weapon. However, depending on where such a weapon may have been constructed, successful detonation in the United States does not automatically flow from a successful construction effort.

Just about every study, blue-ribbon commission, or panel addressing the question of the United States' ability to prevent a terrorist group's use of WMD has featured prominently the importance of intelligence and law enforcement tools to learn more about, among other areas of interest, the capability of terrorist groups to construct or otherwise acquire and detonate a nuclear device.[101] The penetration of terrorist cells, enhanced human intelligence collection, adoption of rigorous and interdisciplinary approaches to WMD intelligence assessments, and targeting of signals intelligence to intercept communications facilitating clandestine WMD procurement networks are all elements of an integrated intelligence strategy to prevent terrorists from acquiring the necessary know-how and material to construct, buy, or be gifted a crude nuclear device.

With an understanding of potential terrorist motivations to conduct an attack and of the possible capability of terrorist groups to construct an IND, we can now look to the "who" question. Which existing terrorist groups have the motivation and, importantly, have demonstrated through their actions the logistical, financial, and operational skills to successfully build and detonate such a device?

WHO: TERRORIST GROUPS
One of the most important questions to be addressed on the demand side of nuclear terrorism is which groups may constitute a clear and present nuclear

terrorism threat, as defined by those that have the motivation, the intent, *and* the capability to inflict a nuclear attack on the United States. There are, of course, different perspectives on this issue, and there is a temporal dimension to the question. Terrorism expert David Rapoport's research has demonstrated that, historically, terrorism tends to develop and wane along certain waves, "a cycle of activity—which can last up to 40 years—characterized by expansion and contraction phases: rise, floodtide of violence, and ebb."[102] The question becomes not only how long the terrorism threat from al Qaeda lasts but which groups might replace it and how long the broader threat of Islamic extremism might last. As the National Intelligence Council has stated, "Terrorist groups who form the crest of each wave usually dissolve before the entire wave does, and their decay contributes to the breaking of the wave. Al-Qa'ida's weaknesses—unachievable strategic objectives, inability to attract broad-based support, and self-destructive actions—might cause it to decay sooner than many people think."[103]

The nuclear weapons learning curve for terrorists, while steep, is not stagnant. Over time, and particularly if not constantly pressured by kinetic and nonkinetic means, terrorists have the opportunity to learn more about nuclear weapons, attempt to acquire fissile material, and recruit trained technical personnel who can build and detonate a nuclear device.

A skeptic might argue that if a notional nuclear terrorism attack is confined to one successfully directed against the United States itself and not necessarily U.S. interests, allies, or troops overseas, there are few groups that may constitute a clear and present threat. They might argue further that global support for al Qaeda is waning, even among Muslim populations, and groups that might succeed al Qaeda may not necessarily have the same sophisticated operational and logistical capabilities to execute a nuclear attack.[104] Given the same constraints, the conventionalists might argue that limiting the threat set to al Qaeda is an approach that lacks imagination; it is too backward looking, limiting, and linear. Conventionalists might point to the emergence of Aum Shinrikyo in Japan, a group that was not necessarily on the radar screen of Japanese security and law enforcement agencies, as proof that "black swans" can and do emerge. Are there Aums within the United States? Conventionalists might also argue that given the diffusion of nuclear-related technology, if it is not al Qaeda that threatens the United States with nuclear terrorism, it will be another terrorist group—perhaps one even more sophisticated than al Qaeda. Of course, such a scenario is possible, but simply because it is possible does not mean it is probable.

Writing in 1975, Jenkins posited, with prescient caveats, that there was an inverse correlation between a terrorist group's intentions to cause mass casualties and its capability to carry out complex and sophisticated operations. Under such a framework, Jenkins thought—consistent with former CIA director Michael Hayden's assessment in chapter 1—that smaller terrorist groups (sometimes led by mentally unstable individuals), while having perhaps the highest levels of intent and willingness to use nuclear weapons, had the lowest level of capability to construct or otherwise acquire a nuclear weapon. Larger terrorist groups, while having more human, logistical, and operations resources at their disposal, had substantial constituencies that would cause them to be more cautious. His prescient caveats warned that the motivation and capability curves are not stationary. He pondered that a technical breakthrough (perhaps decreasing the amount of fissile material necessary for nuclear weapons) could make nuclear weapons more accessible. While thankfully this has not occurred yet, it remains a possibility. Jenkins posited that a worldwide resurgence of ethnic conflict or the emergence of large groups claiming divine inspiration could increase motivation and decrease terrorist self-restraint. Such actions would shift the intention line. "More actors, including large organizations, might be willing to commit nuclear terrorism. This is exactly what happened."[105]

Given that intentions and capabilities are not static and clearly have changed with time and international developments, which groups today may present an imminent nuclear terrorism threat? With respect to potential attacks against the U.S. homeland, while al Qaeda may not be the only group, it is certainly the highest priority and worthy of a brief summary.

Al Qaeda and Nuclear Weapons

In the U.S. Intelligence Community's 2010 Annual Threat Assessment provided to Congress, former director of National Intelligence (DNI) Dennis C. Blair stated:

> We judge that if al-Qa'ida develops chemical, biological, radiological, or nuclear (CBRN) capabilities and has operatives trained to use them, it

will do so. Counterterrorism actions have dealt a significant blow to al-Qa'ida's near-term efforts to develop a sophisticated CBRN attack capability, although we judge the group is still intent on its acquisition.[106]

There are few analysts who would doubt this statement of al Qaeda's intent to acquire WMD. Yet al Qaeda's nuclear capability remains unknown, and past attempts by al Qaeda to use other WMD have not been effective in achieving its goals, as will be outlined later.

Others have chronicled extensively the nuclear-related activities of al Qaeda.[107] Separating the facts of al Qaeda's capability for nuclear terrorism from sensationalized fiction remains a challenge as the reliability and validity of sources are oftentimes unknown. Moreover, as Jenkins points out, there tends to be a circular feedback mechanism concerning al Qaeda's activities or alleged nuclear activities. As al Qaeda's nuclear propaganda is picked up and amplified by media sources, al Qaeda affiliates light up chatter in Internet jihadist chat rooms. It is picked up by intelligence agencies and reflected in governmental leader statements, which sow additional fear. The al Qaeda terrorist threat is real and tangible; the nuclear threat from al Qaeda, however, remains unclear. While evidence exists that the group is interested in all WMD, the relative level of effort al Qaeda has dedicated to various WMD types is unknown, as are the group's nuclear capabilities.

This section will attempt to separate al Qaeda intentions and capabilities into what is known and unknown. First, it is worthwhile to provide a brief overview of expert assessment on the current strength of al Qaeda. Al Qaeda is now over twenty years old and has been under attack for over nine years. Under those circumstances, how is the group holding out? The stronger the core al Qaeda, the greater the likelihood that sophisticated terrorist operations might be successful.[108] Second, a brief assessment of what al Qaeda has said about nuclear weapons is in order. As Jenkins points out, al Qaeda's communications and propaganda tempo seems to vary inversely with its operational tempo. Bin Laden once stated that he viewed 90 percent of the global jihadist struggle as a media war that sows constant fear and anxiety in target populations. Notwithstanding this observation, al Qaeda propaganda and leadership statements with respect to their desired acquisition and potential use of nuclear weapons cannot be ignored. Third, a summary of some of the more salient developments in al Qaeda's quest for nuclear weapons will be discussed. Finally, some factors that have an impact on al Qaeda's quest for nuclear weapons will be offered.

Al Qaeda at Twenty

Edward M. Gistaro, former national intelligence officer for transnational threats, assessed in 2008 the status of al Qaeda in the following manner:

> In spite of successful U.S. and allied operations against al-Qa'ida, especially the death of important al-Qa'ida figures since December 2007, the group has maintained or strengthened key elements of its capability to attack the United States in the last year.

- First, al-Qa'ida has strengthened its safe haven in Pakistan's FATA by deepening its alliances with Pakistani militants and pushing many elements of the Pakistani government authority from the area.
- Second, despite some significant losses, al-Qa'ida has replenished its bench of skilled mid-level lieutenants capable of directing global operations. . . . While it sometimes can take several months to replace these individuals, al-Qa'ida has developed succession plans, can reshuffle leadership responsibilities, and promote younger commanders with years of battlefield experience to senior positions.
- Third, bin Laden and his deputy, Ayman al-Zawahiri, continue to maintain al-Qa'ida's unity and its focus on their strategic vision and operational priorities, although security concerns preclude them from running the organization day-to-day.[109]

At least two other respected terrorism analysts Peter Bergen and Bruce Hoffman have also cautioned against the premature claim of the death of al Qaeda. According to Bergen, "It's conventional wisdom that al-Qa'ida the organization has been largely destroyed and an ideological movement inspired by al-Qa'ida has replaced it, spawning a new generation of 'homegrown' or 'self-starting' terrorists . . . but it would be wrong to conclude that . . . the central al-Qa'ida organization is no longer a threat. Such a view underestimates the resiliency of al-Qa'ida. . . . In fact more than at any time since

September 11, Usama bin Laden's deadly organization is back in business."[110] Bergen cites as evidence core al Qaeda's role in the London bombings of July 2005; al Qaeda demonstrated it "was able to conduct simultaneous bombings in a major European capital thousands of miles from its base on the Afghan-Pakistan border."[111] Other points of core al Qaeda resiliency, according to Bergen, include:

- the continuing vitality of al Qaeda's propaganda division, al Sahab;
- the broad ideological and strategic influence bin Laden and Zawahiri continue to exercise over the organization;
- al Qaeda's ability to still attract other militant groups, such as the Algerian GSPC, to its standard; and
- its new training ground in Pakistan, indicating that the organization will continue to be a significant threat. "Terrorist plots have a much higher degree of success if some of the cell's members have received training in bomb making and operational doctrine in person. For example, two of the London July 7, 2005, suicide bombers received al Qaeda training in Pakistan."[112]

Lest it be thought that Bergen believes al Qaeda is ten feet tall or has ultimate staying power in its global war, he clarifies that the group has made substantial blunders and will ultimately lose.[113] Bergen points out that al Qaeda has four strategic weaknesses:

- *Al Qaeda keeps killing Muslim civilians.* "This is a double whammy for al-Qa'ida as the Koran forbids killing civilians and fellow Muslims."[114] Attacks on Muslim civilians in Saudi Arabia, Indonesia, Jordan, and Iraq have substantially undermined popular support for al Qaeda.[115] According to the National Intelligence Council, "Although determining precisely the number of Muslims worldwide who have died in al-Qa'ida attacks is difficult, examination of available evidence suggests that at least 40 percent of the victims have been Muslims."[116]
- *Al Qaeda has not created a mass political movement.* Unlike Hamas, for example, al Qaeda does not run social welfare services, schools, hospitals,

or clinics for its "constituents." According to the National Intelligence Council, "Despite sympathy for some of its ideas and the rise of affiliated groups in places like the Mahgreb, al-Qa'ida has not achieved broad support in the Islamic world. Its harsh pan-Islamist ideology and policies appeal only to a tiny minority of Muslims."[117]

- *Al Qaeda has expanded its list of enemies.* "It's very hard to think of a category of person, institution, or government that al-Qa'ida does not oppose. Making a world of enemies is never a winning strategy."[118]
- *Al Qaeda has no positive vision.* What al Qaeda actually wants is restoration of the Caliphate. "In practice that means Taliban-style theocracies stretching from Indonesia to Morocco. A silent majority of Muslims don't want that."[119] According to the National Intelligence Council, in one study of public attitudes toward extremist violence "there is little support for al-Qa'ida in any of the countries surveyed—Algeria, Egypt, Jordan, Kuwait, Lebanon, Morocco, Qatar, Saudi Arabia, United Arab Emirates, and Yemen. The report also found that majorities in all Arab countries oppose jihadi violence, by any group, on their own soil."[120]

In concurrence with Gistaro and Bergen, Bruce Hoffman has stated:

Ongoing investigations increasingly suggest that recent terrorist threats and attacks—the August 2006 plot to blow up ten planes in-flight from Britain and crash them into American cities, the July 2005 suicide bus and subway bombings in London, and the two separate operations foiled in Britain during 2004 . . . were all in fact coordinated in some way by al-Qa'ida and not (as commonly assumed) cooked up by homegrown terror groups.

Rather than al-Qa'ida R.I.P. then, we face an al-Qa'ida that has risen from the grave. Its dispersion following Operation Enduring Freedom has not meant that al-Qa'ida has become decentralized. The movement in fact is just as hierarchical as before; its chain of command, however, admittedly is less effective and more cumbersome. But this is a reflection of how al-Qa'ida has been able to adapt and adjust to changes imposed on its operations by the U.S.-led war on terrorism.[121]

There are, however, dissenting opinions of the continuing strength of core al Qaeda. Few would deny that al Qaeda's senior leadership continues to plot, recruit, and train individuals within Pakistan's Federally Administered Tribal Areas to attack the United States. Yet, while not discounting the threat from al Qaeda or declaring victory over the group, NCTC director Michael Leiter stated, "Because of a series of ... successful endeavors, core al-Qa'ida and its ability to project threats to Western Europe and the United States is much lower than it was last year, and I think in many ways lower than it has been for quite some time. . . . Their ability to train and deploy recruits has been seriously diminished over the past year."[122]

Another dissenting opinion is provided by Mark Sageman, a forensic psychiatrist and terrorism consultant. Sageman states, "I am skeptical of a resurgent al-Qa'ida Central. The evidence mustered in support is anecdotal and without any explanation of the dynamics underlying the fluctuations in al-Qa'ida operations."[123] One of the disagreements between Sageman and Hoffman centers upon the extent to which al Qaeda Central has provided more than simple inspirational leadership to bands of local terrorist "wannabes." Hoffman believes, based on supporting evidence from a number of terrorist attacks since 2001, that al Qaeda Central has provided substantially more than inspiration to local terrorist groups, including major assistance in operational training in Pakistan. Sageman disagrees, believing that the trend is moving in the direction of a "leaderless jihad." He states, "Al-Qa'ida Central is of course not dead, but it is still contained operationally. It puts out its guidance on the Internet, but does not have the means to exert command and control over the al-Qa'ida social movement." Others have concluded that if one accepts the position that al Qaeda is increasingly becoming a networked and decentralized organization, the conventional wisdom that this type of organization may be stronger than a hierarchical-based organization may be flawed. Two international policy (but admitted nonterrorism) experts have analyzed the structural arguments underpinning the consensus that "it takes a network to fight a network" and argue:

International relations scholars have been too quick to draw parallels to the world of the firm where a networked organization has proven well adapted to the fast-moving global marketplace. They have consequently overlooked issues of community and trust, as well as problems of distance, coordination, and security, which may pose serious organizational difficulties for illicit networks. Although there is much we do not know about this network, the evidence in the public domain suggests al-Qa'ida is subject to many of the same weaknesses that have beset clandestine networks in the past.[124]

Known al Qaeda Statements and Positions vis-à-vis WMD: Intent

Al Qaeda has a prolific propaganda machine that churns out videos of al Qaeda leaders and operations; jihadist messages and statements; altered pictures depicting mushroom clouds in Washington, D.C.; and numerous other propaganda items. Authentic al Qaeda statements concerning nuclear weapons, particularly from the leadership, should not be ignored. According to Peter Bergen, "The most reliable guide to what al-Qa'ida and like-minded groups will do has long been what bin Laden says."[125] Al Qaeda and its leadership have made a handful of statements about nuclear weapons that are worth considering. Some of the more salient comments include:

- Approximately five years after al Qaeda commenced its CBRN weapon acquisition efforts, in a 1998 interview with Pakistani journalist Rahimullah Yusufzai, bin Laden stated,

  To seek to possess the weapons that could counter those of the infidels is a religious duty. If I have indeed acquired these weapons, then this is an obligation I carried out and I thank God for enabling us to do that. And if I seek to acquire these weapons, I am carrying out a duty. It would be a sin for Muslims not to try to possess the weapons that would prevent the infidels from inflicting harm on Muslims. But how we would use these weapons if we possess them is up to us.[126]

- In June 2002 Suleiman Abu Ghaith, a Kuwaiti cleric and al Qaeda spokesman, posted a statement on the Internet saying that "al-Qa'ida has the right to kill four million Americans, including one million children, displace double that figure, and injure and cripple hundreds of thousands."[127]

According to Ghaith, as many Muslims had died at the hands of the United States or the apostate regimes it supports in the Middle East.

- Because a religious justification for terrorism activities must be developed prior to any operational activity, al Qaeda sought and received such a justification in May 2003. The justification came in the form of *A Treatise on the Legal Status of Using Weapons of Mass Destruction against Infidels*, authored by Nasir bin Hamid al-Fahd, a respected Saudi cleric. While jailed in Saudi Arabia, al-Fahd allegedly recanted some religious fatwas and pronouncements, but it is unclear if the aforementioned WMD treatise is among them. The treatise makes two main arguments:

  - *On killing women and children.* "It has been established that the Prophet forbade the killing of women and children. However, if you put these hadiths [oral traditions relating to the words and deeds of Mohammed] together, it will become apparent that the prohibition is against killing them intentionally. If they are killed collaterally, as in the case of a night attack or invasion when one cannot distinguish them, there is nothing wrong with it. Jihad is not to be halted because of the presence of infidel women and children."[128]
  - *On killing innocent Muslims.* Any detonation of a nuclear device in a populated area of the United States would likely kill innocent Muslims. After tracing numerous scholars whose writings say the killing of innocent Muslims is prohibited, al-Fahd reinterprets these writings: "If we accept the argument [that it is impermissible to kill innocent Muslims], we should entirely suspend jihad for no infidel land is devoid of Muslims. As long as jihad has been commanded . . . and Muslims have continuously acted on that basis, and it can be carried out only in this way, it [killing of innocent Muslims] is permitted."[129]

Al Qaeda's Nuclear Quests: Capability

The different types of information available on al Qaeda's quest for nuclear weapons are summarized in table 5. So as not to reproduce the work others have already performed well, this section will provide only brief highlights of the more salient developments. There is a plethora of information about al Qaeda's WMD acquisition efforts in open sources. Some of the information

TABLE 5. AL QAEDA AND NUCLEAR WEAPONS

Type/status	Nuclear weapons
Reports and allegations	Attempted or successful purchase of Soviet origin suitcase bombs (1998, 2001, 2002) Attempted purchase of fissile materials (1998, 2000, 2001)
Hard evidence	Contacts with Pakistani nuclear scientists (2001) Afghanistan-seized documents (2001, 2002) Arrests, interrogations, and detainee testimony (1998, 2001, 2002, 2003, 2004)

Source: Lewis A. Dunn, *Can al-Qaeda Be Deterred from Using Nuclear Weapons?* (Washington, DC: National Defense University, July 2005).

has been corroborated by official sources in public, while much of it remains uncorroborated. However, at least in the public domain, there appears to be a substantial lack of information on al Qaeda's specific nuclear capabilities other than the documents that were found in al Qaeda safe houses in Afghanistan by U.S. forces and journalists as a result of the U.S. invasion of Afghanistan in late 2001. It is highly probable that interrogations of captured al Qaeda operatives, including Khalid Sheik Mohammed, have yielded raw information that may have proven valuable for assessing al Qaeda's nuclear capabilities, but this information remains classified. There is little public information about al Qaeda's nuclear activities since the events of 9/11. Nevertheless, official U.S. government sources have gone on record as stating that they do not believe that al Qaeda, or any other terrorist group, has been successful in its efforts to acquire either an intact nuclear weapon or enough fissile material to construct its own crude nuclear device.[130] David Albright's conclusion about al Qaeda's projected nuclear capability in the absence of the U.S. invasion of Afghanistan bears repeating: "If al-Qa'ida had remained in Afghanistan, it would have likely acquired nuclear weapons eventually."[131] While Pakistan's FATA today is a far less hospitable environment for sophisticated terrorist attack planning than pre-2001 Afghanistan, the extent to which al Qaeda's nuclear knowledge has advanced remains an open question, insofar as open-source information can determine.[132]

SUDAN: 1992–96

Al Qaeda's activities to acquire nuclear weapons started in the early 1990s

when Osama bin Laden, having left Afghanistan after the Soviet Union's re-
treat in 1989, was living in Sudan. Using his financial resources and personal
wealth, bin Laden established a relationship with the National Islamic Front
(NIF), which was in control of Sudan at the time. According to terrorism
analyst Michael Scheuer, bin Laden's financial support to the NIF gave him
access to the state-owned Military Industrial Corporation, which was likely
used as a front to acquire necessary technologies for CBRN weapons. During
this time al Qaeda was tricked by numerous scams in which alleged HEU,
sometimes referred to as "red mercury," was offered for sale.[133] In February
2001, when Osama bin Laden was on trial in absentia for the 1998 bombings
of U.S. embassies in Kenya and Tanzania, an al Qaeda prosecution witness, Jamal Ahmad al-Fadl, testified that al Qaeda was willing to spend $1.5 million to
acquire uranium. According to terrorism expert Rohan Gunaratna: "Although
the intelligence community reported in the late 1990s that al-Qa'ida had acquired uranium in Khartoum and hired Egyptian and Pakistani physicists to
research the development of nuclear weapons, it seems the group may have
been duped. Intelligence sources now believe that criminals sold al-Qa'ida
irradiated canisters purported to contain uranium stolen from Russian army
bases, whereas in fact the content would have had no military value whatsoever had it been passed on to rogue nuclear scientists."[134]

AFGHANISTAN: 1996–2001
Osama bin Laden, expelled from Sudan after relations with the NIF turned
sour, returned to Afghanistan shortly after the Taliban took control of the
country and quickly established a close relationship with the regime and its
leader, Mullah Omar. Bin Laden's "Arab Afghan" fighters, who fought to
eject the Soviet Union from Afghanistan from 1979 to 1989, now fought
alongside the Taliban against its adversaries, including, among others, the
Northern Alliance. With respect to the extent to which the Taliban assisted al
Qaeda in its nuclear weapons activities, David Albright concludes, "Considering the Taliban's close cooperation with bin Laden, nuclear transfers may have
taken place under the cover of the Afghani government's civil activities."[135]

It was also during this period that a friendly (foreign) intelligence service shared information with the United States that, according to former DCI
George Tenet, a Pakistani nongovernmental organization called Ummah Tameer-

e-Nau (UTN–Islamic Reconstruction) was lending its "expertise and access to the [Afghani] scientific establishment in order to help build chemical, biological, and nuclear programs for al-Qa'ida."[136] UTN's founder, Sultan Bashirrudan Mahmood, was a former director of the Pakistan Atomic Energy Commission (PAEC) and an individual who was reportedly forced out of his job in 1999 due to official concerns about his "vocal advocacy of producing extensive amounts of weapons-grade plutonium and enriched uranium to help equip other Islamic nations with nuclear arsenals."[137] According to Pakistani officials, Mahmood "had experience in uranium enrichment and plutonium production, but was not involved in bomb-building."[138] Another UTN board member, Chaudhiry Andul Majeed, was a prominent nuclear scientist who retired from the Pakistani Institute of Nuclear Science and Technology.

According to George Tenet, the CIA passed the information about UTN–al Qaeda contacts to Pakistan, which called the UTN officials in for questioning. "Pakistani intelligence interrogators treated the UTN officials deferentially . . . they were seen as men of science, men who had made significant contributions to Pakistan."[139] Subsequently, in the fall of 2001, a Western intelligence service informed the CIA that Mahmood and Majeed, in August 2001, had met with Osama bin Laden and Ayman al-Zawahiri in Afghanistan. "There, around a campfire, they discussed how al-Qa'ida should go about building a nuclear device."[140] Reportedly, bin Laden indicated to Mahmood and Majeed that "he had obtained, or had access to, some type of radiological material that he said had been acquired for him by the radical Islamic Movement of Uzbekistan. . . . Pakistani officials said they have been unable to verify those claims."[141]

After the 9/11 attacks, understandably the interest and concern in these UTN–al Qaeda contacts increased intensely. Tenet was dispatched by President George W. Bush to Islamabad to meet with Pakistani President Pervez Musharraf. There he and an aide (Rolf Mowatt-Larssen) attempted to persuade a skeptical Musharraf that al Qaeda was a nuclear threat to the United States and perhaps to Pakistan. Tenet encouraged Musharraf to investigate UTN aggressively, look at elements of the Pakistan Army and ISI that might be penetrated by al Qaeda, and inventory Pakistani fissile material. According to Tenet, Musharraf complied at least with respect to UTN by allowing a U.S. polygraph team to assist in the UTN investigation. With the assistance of the

U.S. polygraph team, Pakistan "eventually obtained confessions that added important new details to the story. Mahmood . . . even provided a hand-drawn rough bomb design that he had shared with al-Qa'ida leaders. . . . It appears we had disrupted the organization in the early stages of its efforts to ply trade with al-Qa'ida."[142]

According to U.S. officials, both Mahmood and Majeed did not have the appropriate skills to build a nuclear weapon, leading one official to conclude that the meeting between Mahmood, Majeed, bin Laden, and al-Zawahiri was akin to the "the blind leading the blind." Subsequent interrogations provided evidence that al Qaeda, at that time, lacked technical expertise. One official reportedly stated, "If [al Qaeda] had been handed the plans for a nuclear bomb, the worst they could have done is used them as kindling to start a fire."[143] While this may be true, it represents a snapshot in time and, conventionalists may argue, discounts the resiliency and resourcefulness of al Qaeda. Perhaps of greater concern is that while Mahmood and Majeed may not necessarily have had the appropriate skills to construct a nuclear weapon, they were in a position to know individuals who did have these skills and were ideologically inclined to support al Qaeda. Whether such individuals have been directed to al Qaeda remains an open question, at least insofar as open sources may be concerned.

More pieces of evidence on al Qaeda's nuclear capabilities were documents seized by U.S. and allied intelligence and military personnel, as well as journalists, in al Qaeda's Afghanistan safe houses during Operation Enduring Freedom. It is unclear if the documents were truly left behind by al Qaeda and Taliban forces retreating under siege or if they were intentionally left behind as disinformation. In January 2002 former DCI George Tenet informed Congress that rudimentary diagrams of nuclear weapons were found in a suspected al Qaeda safe house in Kabul. The U.S. Intelligence Community assessed that "these diagrams, while crude, describe essential components—uranium and high explosives—common to nuclear weapons."[144] In November 2001 Cable News Network (CNN) representatives in Afghanistan found a document titled (in Arabic) "Superbomb." According to David Albright, who reviewed the document with CNN, it "has some sections that are relatively sophisticated and others that are remarkably inaccurate or naïve. . . . Nor is it a cookbook for making nuclear weapons, as many critical steps to make a nuclear weapon are missing from the document. The [nuclear weapons] designs are not credible. If someone obtained separated plutonium and built this design, it would not function as an atomic bomb. Rather, it would be a radiological dispersion device."[145] Just as important as what was found in Afghanistan was what was not found. According to Albright, "No evidence . . . has emerged that al-Qaeda obtained any nuclear weapons, despite bin Laden's statement to a Pakistani journalist . . . in which he claimed to have both nuclear and chemical weapons." Moreover, U.S. experts took environmental samples at about one hundred sites in Afghanistan, which "did not reveal the presence of plutonium or enriched uranium at any of these sites."[146]

Net Assessment: Al Qaeda's Nuclear Weapons Capability

While official sources are not always valid and reliable (as was the case all too tragically with respect to WMD in Iraq), available open-source evidence, including official government testimony, seems credible with respect to al Qaeda not currently possessing nuclear weapons. According to the Commission on Intelligence Capabilities of the United States Regarding Weapons of Mass Destruction (Robb-Silberman Commission), "The community appears to have been correct in its assessment of the low probability that al-Qa'ida had built a nuclear device or obtained sufficient material for a nuclear weapon."[147] However, given al Qaeda's stated intentions and demonstrated activities to acquire nuclear weapons, it would not be a surprise to discover that al Qaeda, despite the international community's best efforts to prevent it, had acquired some amount of fissile material. Sun Tzu, in *The Art of War*, cautions, "He who exercises no forethought but makes light of his opponents is sure to be captured by them." The dangers of underestimating al Qaeda, or any other terrorist group that may have the sophistication to successfully execute a catastrophic terrorist attack, are portentous. However, overestimation also has its costs, including the creation of an enduring climate of fear and the opportunity costs and attendant vulnerabilities that are associated with preparing for the wrong type of attack. Classified intelligence sources and methods may contradict open-source estimates of al Qaeda's nuclear knowledge and capability. Because there may be no definitive answers for al Qaeda's nuclear capability (owing to myriad factors, not the least of which is incomplete and fallible intelligence), a series of questions might shed some light on this topic:

Intelligence—validity, reliability, and confidence. In the aftermath of the erroneous conclusions reached by the intelligence community with respect to WMD in Iraq, the community continues to rebuild its credibility with policy-makers and the public. What does the U.S. Intelligence Community conclude with a high degree of confidence about al Qaeda's nuclear capabilities? How confident is the intelligence community about al Qaeda's nuclear activities within its current safe haven, the Federally Administered Tribal Areas within Pakistan? With what level of confidence does the intelligence community judge that the illicit proliferation activities of the A. Q. Khan network have ceased? Are there any residual linkages between the vestiges of the Khan network and al Qaeda–affiliated or sympathetic groups? How confident is the intelligence community that it understands the identities of scientists and technologists globally, particularly within Pakistan, and the extent to which these individuals may not only be sympathetic to the Pakistan Taliban, Afghani Taliban, or al Qaeda but also be willing to take action based on these sympathies? How confident is the intelligence community that al Qaeda has not established other safe havens around the world, perhaps in nonnuclear nations, that could act as clandestine proliferation network hubs designed to acquire fissile material? How confident is the intelligence community that al Qaeda's nuclear know-how has not progressed since the seizure of the "Superbomb" article and other material in the immediate aftermath of Operation Enduring Freedom? How confident is the intelligence community that if al Qaeda affiliates or in-termediate brokers approached Russia, North Korea, or Pakistan to acquire either an intact nuclear weapon or fissile material, the United States would become aware of that approach in a timely fashion? Given the recent assassina-tion of a Salman Taseer, the governor of Pakistan's Punjab Province, by one of his own bodyguards, if these guards are screened through the same Personnel Reliability Program as Pakistan's nuclear security guards, does this decrease the U.S. government's confidence in Pakistan's nuclear weapons and material security?[148] To what extent have extremist forces infiltrated those responsible for protecting Pakistan's nuclear weapons and material?

Current nuclear weapons possession and their possible use. If al Qaeda pos-sesses nuclear weapons already, as some allege, it has had ample time to use them to undermine U.S. national security, which has as one of its components a vibrant U.S. economy. Why has al Qaeda not already used such weapons?

The absence of evidence is not evidence of absence. However, al Qaeda is not omnipotent. The United States has been engaged in two wars in largely Muslim countries (an abhorrence to al Qaeda) that have consumed substantial amounts of U.S. resources since 2001. Given that (1) U.S. troops continue to invade and "occupy" Muslim countries; (2) the United States continues to support Israel, a government that is an undeclared nuclear power, and took no action against it for bombing Syria's Al Kibar reactor in 2007; (3) the United States continues to support the apostate regime in Saudi Arabia; and (4) Islamic jurisprudence has provided justification for the use of nuclear weapons against innocent women and children, including Muslims in infidel lands, the additional impetus that is necessary for al Qaeda to execute an "American Hiroshima" is unclear.[149] It could be argued that given al Qaeda's operational history of attacking early in new American presidential administrations and its concurrent goal to undermine the U.S. national economy, the period of late 2008 or early 2009 would have been auspicious for a devastating nuclear attack. During times of presidential transition, numerous national security personnel are not in place,[150] and since 2008 the U.S. economy has experienced a deep recession. Any potential al Qaeda attack could also happen outside U.S. borders but still be directed against U.S. national interests and thus be successful in "bleeding" the U.S. economy. Even if an al Qaeda attack were to occur within U.S. borders, a mass-casualty conventional attack (such as that in Mumbai, India) or an RDD or biological attack may not be out of the question. Some would argue that, although perhaps not as spectacular as 9/11, these scenarios are far more likely than a nuclear attack. Skeptics would argue that, given al Qaeda's modus operandi, there have been ample opportunities for the group to attack the United States with nuclear weapons. For a variety of reasons, it has not happened.

Potential al Qaeda self-restraint. Al Qaeda's messages and leadership statements arguing that it is permissible to indiscriminately kill Muslims and women and children who may be living in infidel nations indicate that the leadership is aware of the potential negative effects a nuclear attack could have on the support for the organization in the Ummah. As mentioned earlier, al Qaeda's second in command, Ayman al-Zawahiri, has directly and vehemently refuted a number of recantation books that condemn al Qaeda's killing of Muslims. To what extent, if at all, will al Qaeda consider such recantation

books and general concerns within the Ummah about the indiscriminate killing of Muslims as it makes strategic decisions about whether to use nuclear
weapons should it acquire them? Will actions that have the potential to enhance self-restraint (including reinforcing an ambiguous declaratory policy
that "all means necessary" will be used to exact retribution from any nation-
state or nonstate actors that use nuclear weapons against the United States,
its interests, or its allies) have any effect on al Qaeda decision making? What
actions can the United States take in cyberspace, where many of al Qaeda's
recruitment and inspirational activities take place, to demonstrate to al Qaeda
that a nuclear attack will be perceived by the Ummah as a substantial violation
of widely accepted Islamic jurisprudence and norms? How can the United
States reinforce the belief that a failed al Qaeda attempt to detonate a nuclear
weapon will be interpreted as a massive failure in the eyes of the Prophet?

Al Qaeda's perception of its continued viability and international relevance.
To what extent does al Qaeda's perception of its continued viability and global
relevance influence whether the group would execute a nuclear attack if it possessed nuclear weapons? Some might argue that if al Qaeda perceived its global influence was waning and it was becoming more of a nuisance and less of a
serious threat, the group might be more willing to undertake a nuclear attack
designed to illustrate to the world that the group is still relevant, remains the
predominant international threat, and has achieved nation-state status with its
demonstrated nuclear capacity.

Gaining legitimacy and the question of whether to use weapons. If al Qaeda
does have or should later acquire or build a nuclear weapon, it has more than
the simple two options of use or not use. While there are numerous paths to
a nuclear weapon, one oftentimes not discussed is that "rather than begging
nuclear weapons from a sympathetic government, al-Qa'ida or its spinoffs may
soon become the government in any of perhaps a dozen countries."[151] Citing
historical examples of how terrorist groups entered the mainstream of political discourse, including the Bolsheviks in Russia, Hamas in Palestine, and the
Stern Gang in Israel, Forecasting International (FI) states, "Bin Laden and
his senior advisers can be expected to attempt to enter mainstream politics in
much the same manner. FI believes they could be successful."[152] If al Qaeda
morphs into a political party that aspires to rule a nation, not only does the deterrence equation change, as the movement would have targets that could be

held at risk, but also even if it did eventually possess nuclear weapons, it may use them more to deter invasion than as a mass-casualty terrorist device. It may be plausible that if al Qaeda were able to take over Iran, Somalia, Sudan, Yemen, Libya, Syria, Pakistan, Afghanistan, or any other state as a base for its grandiose idea of a Caliphate expanding from Morocco to Indonesia, nuclear weapons then might be viewed more for their deterrent value than as a tool to compel the West to take certain actions.

Al Qaeda's strategic decision making. Al Qaeda is a strategic operation that calculates violence based on its perception of whether those actions can achieve the group's desired objectives. It may not be traditionally deterred by punishment, but is it possible that it could be deterred by denial of achieving its objectives? If al Qaeda makes strategic calculations, one has to consider the extent to which it may reflect on its miscalculation that the United States was a paper tiger, in that the United States has not retreated in its pursuit of al Qaeda (notwithstanding the arguably diversionary war in Iraq). How does al Qaeda think that the United States and the rest of the international community would react to al Qaeda's detonating a nuclear weapon in New York, London, or Moscow? Does al Qaeda believe it can continue to exist even as a decentralized movement in the aftermath of such a potentially devastating attack that would likely be nearly universally condemned? If al Qaeda has doubts about the Ummah's support for nuclear weapons use, it might impact its strategic decision-making process. Efforts by prominent Muslim clerics, particularly those who may have had leadership roles in al Qaeda, to amplify denunciations of violence should be strongly encouraged and supported.

The true strength of core al Qaeda. Given that al Qaeda has remained under pressure since the attacks of 9/11, has core al Qaeda and its central leadership retained the ability to plan and direct the execution of such a sophisticated attack? As mentioned earlier, there are stark differences of opinion among terrorism experts on this matter. It may be one thing for core al Qaeda to plan and train locally inspired al Qaeda affiliates to conduct, for example, simultaneous transportation-based attacks with low-technology weapons, yet it may be entirely another for the group to acquire fissile material, construct a weapon, smuggle it into the United States (assuming it was not constructed in the United States or was detonated overseas), transport it to a point of detonation, and then successfully detonate it.

Security of al Qaeda's terrestrial and cyber safe havens. Al Qaeda's safe haven in Pakistan's Federally Administrated Tribal Areas could be central to its ability to plan and coordinate other sophisticated attacks on the United States, up to and including a nuclear attack. As Michael Leiter has stated, "The FATA has provided [al Qaeda (AQ)] with a safe haven from which they can recruit, train, and send operatives to the West. They also use the relative sanctity of the region in order to produce media statements and maintain the pace of AQ propaganda to the Muslim and, increasingly, the Western world."[153] Yet Pakistan has become increasingly aggressive in attacking the Taliban in the Swat Valley as well as in South (but not yet North) Waziristan, putting safe havens under new domestic pressure. The United States also continues to ratchet up pressure in ungoverned areas of Pakistan, including through the aggressive (and controversial) use of unmanned aerial drones.[154] Skeptics would argue that it may be extremely difficult to prepare and direct the successful execution of a sophisticated terrorist attack such as nuclear terrorism while Hellfire missiles continue to fall on the very land from which such an attack may be planned.

"While the world has witnessed al-Qa'ida's ability to form common cause with extremists across the globe, metastasizing outside of its traditional safe havens, its most sophisticated plotting against the West is still guided by a smaller cadre of extremists working out of these frontier areas in Pakistan."[155] Although the cyber safe haven may not necessarily be of direct use to any al Qaeda nuclear operation, it can provide financial and other material support that could assist in a nuclear operation's supply chain. What mechanisms are in place to assess the performance of U.S. cyber operations against al Qaeda? How have these performance assessments served to improve the targeting of U.S. cyber operations against al Qaeda?

In a world where terrorism will not be completely eradicated, many societies remain open, nuclear security is imperfect, and nuclear weapons continue to exist, there may always be a risk of nuclear terrorism. National leaders must act globally not only to undermine the root structural causes of international terrorism but also to continue to put pressure on terrorist groups that may have the capability to engage in all forms of mass-casualty terrorism, including nuclear terrorism. All means of national and international power—hard and soft power alike—must be harnessed to continue to degrade any terrorist group's capability to acquire or build nuclear weapons. For if there are no terrorist groups capable of acquiring or building a nuclear weapon, the risk of nuclear terrorism becomes infinitesimal. A number of demand-side variables affecting nuclear terrorism are included in table 6. Yet, a defense-in-depth approach to reducing the risk of nuclear terrorism has another integral component that can further reduce nuclear terrorism risk: supply-side measures to ensure that fissile material is adequately protected. It is to these supply-side strategies we now turn.

TABLE 6. DEMAND-SIDE VARIABLES AFFECTING NUCLEAR TERRORISM

Variable	Impact and questions
Global counterterrorism effectiveness. Some have stated that poverty and lack of economic opportunity are the primary causes of international jihadism. While these factors may be one element among a complex mix of root causes of terrorism, so too are broader attitudes toward specific U.S. policies, particularly in the Middle East. The United States' vital national interests, however one may define them, are inviolate and should not be held hostage to extremist demands. However, to the extent that U.S. vital national security interests can be defended and advocated in a manner that does not engender hatred and perceptions of imbalance, the better the United States will be able to advance its interests.	What are the root causes of terrorism, and what tools does the international community have at its disposal to address these concerns? How effective is the United States and the international community in ameliorating the root causes of international terrorism? What level of political will are countries willing to exert to address some of these underlying causes? How effective is the United States at winning the ideological battle with Islamic radicalism? How effective are the United States and the global community at stanching the lifeblood of international terrorism— the ability of terrorist groups to continue to recruit, fund, and support new terrorists to implement their extremist agenda?
Convincing terrorist groups through strategic communications and other means of messaging that the risks of failure in any nuclear plot are substantial and increasing.	What specific measures have been taken to reinforce the message to terrorist groups that the risks of undertaking such an operation outweigh the potential benefits? How effective are U.S. public diplomacy efforts to reinforce this message, among many other, to terrorist groups and those on whose behalf terrorists claim to be operating? Are U.S. homeland security efforts, particularly those aimed at detecting fissile material in transport, perceived by a terrorist group as marginally increasing the risk of detection given the current status of technological development in this area?
Communicating to terrorists that the United States has advanced consequence management capabilities and a resilient society.	Are the roles and responsibilities of federal, state, and local homeland security, defense, and first responders clear? It appears clear, as some studies have documented,[1] that state and local resources would be quickly overwhelmed in responding to a nuclear attack. It would seem prudent, then, as some have advocated,[2] for the federal government to act quickly to assume a leadership role in response to a nuclear attack; no other level of government can marshal the resources and logistics of federal response.

Table by author.

1 See the *Preventative Defense Project*, a research collaboration of Stanford and Harvard Universities, co-directed by former defense secretary William J. Perry and Ashton B. Carter, former assistant secretary of defense for international security policy.
2 See Ashton B. Carter, Michael May, and William J. Perry, "The Day After: Action Following a Nuclear Blast in a U.S. City," *Washington Quarterly*, Autumn 2007.

FIVE

The Nuclear Terrorism Threat Spectrum—Supply

This chapter assesses the various supply-side variables that may enable a terrorist group. If unmatched by supply, demand for nuclear weapons or fissile material by terrorists does not constitute a clear and present national security threat. There remains in the world, however, a substantial number of nuclear weapons and stockpiles of fissile material. Perfect supply-side security, while a reasonable goal, thus may not necessarily be achievable.

From a global nuclear terrorism supply-side perspective, according to former director general of the IAEA Mohamed ElBaradei,

> In recent years . . . sophisticated extremist groups have shown keen interest in acquiring nuclear weapons. In parallel, nuclear material and nuclear material production have become more difficult to control. Energy security and climate change are driving many countries to revisit the nuclear power option. But with that, there is also an increasing interest in mastering the nuclear fuel cycle to ensure supply of the necessary nuclear fuel. The concern is that by mastering the fuel cycle, countries move dangerously close to nuclear weapons capability. . . . Roughly 27,000 nuclear warheads remain in the arsenals of nine countries. Strategic reliance on these weapons by countries and their allies undoubtedly motivates others to emulate them.[1]

The increasing demand for a nuclear power option to which Dr. ElBaradei refers is a nuclear power renaissance that will be discussed later. While the long-term energy trend illustrates increasing prices for fossil fuels, nuclear power requires substantial capital outlays that if not readily provided by the private sector in the absence of governmental loan guarantees could limit any nascent nuclear power renaissance. Moreover, as the events of March 2011 at the Fukushimi Daiichi nuclear power plant in Japan demonstrate, the concern about the safety of nuclear power has not been eradicated.

The possible convergence of political instability in some regions of the world and nuclear weapons has been a cause for concern on the supply side of nuclear terrorism for over a decade. The 2006 *Quadrennial Defense Review* Report noted:

> Several other WMD-armed states, although not necessarily hostile to the United States, could face the possibility of internal instability and loss of control over their weapons. The lack of effective governance in many parts of the world contributes to the WMD danger, providing opportunities for terrorist organizations to acquire or harbor WMD. The prospect that a nuclear-capable state may lose control of some of its weapons to terrorists is one of the greatest dangers the United States and its allies face.[2]

SUPPLY SIDE: THE ENABLERS OF NUCLEAR TERRORISM

Given that terrorist groups are highly unlikely to master the nuclear fuel cycle on their own, they are dependent upon others who have done so to acquire or construct a nuclear weapon. While state sponsorship would significantly assist a terrorist group in its attempt to develop nuclear weapons, it is not a necessary precursor, as outlined in chapter 4. It should be made explicit that with regard to any state sponsorship of nuclear terrorism, the United States' interest is to develop an appropriate mixture of incentives and disincentives for countries to (1) secure fissile material and nuclear weapons, (2) notify the United States when fissile material or nuclear weapon security has been compromised, (3) cooperate with the United States and the international community in locating missing material or weapons, and (4) assist the United States and the international community in preventing additional attacks should a terrorist succeed in detonating a single nuclear weapon anywhere in the world.[3]

On the supply side of the nuclear terrorism balance sheet, there are at least six factors that must be taken into consideration:

1. Massive amounts of HEU and plutonium in global civilian and military stockpiles (mostly in Russia and the United States) and the potential for leakage (inadvertent or otherwise) of these materials and other nuclear-related technologies to terrorist groups[4]
2. U.S. and Russian tactical nuclear warheads in forward deployed positions
3. The potential for political instability or a successful political coup to lead to a de facto nuclear weapons state losing control over any of its existing nuclear weapons or fissile material
4. HEU used in commercial applications—largely as fuel for foreign civilian research reactors—and perhaps not as secure as HEU in military applications[5]
5. A potential renaissance in nuclear power, perhaps leading to additional countries mastering the nuclear fuel cycle
6. Threshold nuclear weapons states, such as Iran, crossing into the nuclear club. If Iran develops and tests a nuclear weapon, some argue that the nuclear domino theory would apply; that is, it is likely that Saudi Arabia and possibly Egypt might follow.[6] Whether Saudi Arabia in particular decides to develop or purchase its own nuclear weapons likely depends on the extent to which the Saudi leadership believes the United States has the political will and capability to protect it from a nuclear-armed Iran. Would the United States place Saudi Arabia, like South Korea and Japan, under its nuclear umbrella in order to prevent it from making a decision to build or buy nuclear weapons? While a fascinating national security question, it exceeds the bounds of this book.

As national security scholars Daniel Byman and Robert Litwak point out with respect to the supply side of nuclear terrorism, unintentional leakage of fissile material is likely to be the most important problem. If leakage is the primary supply-side problem, one would think it would be reasonable for the U.S. Intelligence Community to develop a risk-based assessment of which countries and, more directly, which facilities across the world represent the highest nuclear security risk. The former director of the DOE's intelligence and counterintelligence program revealed in congressional testimony that on August 28, 2006, the

Nuclear Materials Information Program (NMIP) was established via National and Homeland Security Presidential Directive (NSPD-48/

HSPD/17). [The] NMIP is an interagency effort managed by the Department of Energy. . . . While the specifics of the NMIP are classified, the goal of NMIP is to consolidate information from all sources pertaining to worldwide nuclear materials holdings and their security status into an integrated and continuously updated management system.[7]

The NMIP informs other U.S. government programs including, but not limited to, the Global Threat Reduction Initiative. As referenced earlier, in April 2009, President Obama committed to securing all vulnerable nuclear materials worldwide in four years. Since that time, six nations have eliminated or transferred to secure storage all HEU in their territory.[8] Nuclear security expert Matthew Bunn points out that the NMIP serves as an important baseline by which to judge the progress of President Obama's initiative to secure all vulnerable nuclear material worldwide by 2013. As will be addressed in chapter 7, one of the central challenges to this goal is the national political sensitivities surrounding information related to nuclear weapons and nuclear materials. Unless nation-states determine that the international security threat of nuclear terrorism is greater than the myriad reasons for which they developed nuclear weapons, they are generally unwilling to share this most sensitive information.

GLOBAL HEU AND PLUTONIUM STOCK

How much fissile material has been produced and is currently in global stockpiles? According to the IPFM, as of December 2010 the fissile material stockpile was between 1,400 and 1,600 metric tons of HEU and approximately 500 tons of separated plutonium.[9] In addition to the approximately 9,400 existing (deployed, in reserve, and awaiting dismantlement) nuclear warheads the United States possesses and the 14,000 warheads Russia has, this material could be used to generate thousands more nuclear weapons or, if not appropriately secured, be illicitly transferred to unauthorized parties.[10] As mentioned earlier, relatively small quantities are necessary to build a crude IND, yet only 5.96 kilograms of HEU has been involved in official, reported illicit transactions. Securing fissile material is also relatively more difficult than is generally understood. According to Siegfried Hecker, a metallurgist and emeritus director of the Los Alamos National Laboratory, there are five characteristics of fissile material that must be understood in order to establish a comprehensive safeguards system for such material:

1. Existing inventories of fissile material are far larger than the amount required for a nuclear bomb. According to a 1994 DOE study on U.S. plutonium production, the United States had produced or acquired 111,400 kilograms of plutonium since 1943.[11] In 1994 the total inventory was 99,500 kilograms. "Although there are explanations for the 'missing' 11,900 kilograms, the uncertainties between physical inventories and accounting are many times the amount required for a bomb."[12] Indeed, the amount of "missing" material is enough for hundreds of nuclear weapons.[13] The uncertainties about Russia's production and current stockpiles of fissile material are beyond those in the United States, as Russia's accounting system was based more on production quotas than control and accounting. As Joseph Cirincione, vice president for national security at the Center for American Progress, stated, "The amount of weapons-usable nuclear material in Russia may not even be known by the Russian government."[14]

2. Fissile material exists in every imaginable form. HEU and plutonium "are not like gold bricks at Fort Knox. . . . [They] are highly reactive metals that oxidize rapidly. . . . Furthermore, plutonium is constantly created and destroyed during reactor operation and transmutes into other elements over time."[15]

3. Fissile material exists in many locations, not just in a few storage vaults. The issue of applying a Fort Knox gold standard has been raised by numerous advocates of enhanced security, but there are numerous ways in which fissile material is unlike the gold at Fort Knox, not the least of which is that the amount of gold in Fort Knox is known for certain. There are no such certainties with fissile material. Moreover, both gold and HEU are used in many places where security does not approach that which is afforded the gold at Fort Knox.

4. Fissile material, particularly plutonium, is difficult to measure and handle owing to its high radiotoxicity.

5. Military secrecy hampers safeguards and transparency. "Although secrecy is necessary to protect a state's nuclear weapons program, excessive secrecy . . . impede[s] implementation of a rigorous safeguards system."[16]

Given this understanding of the inherent difficulties in implementing rigorous national MPC&A systems (part of overall security capacity), it is possible to combine this information with other factors to assess an individual country's nuclear terrorism risks. Table 7 outlines a modified view of how Daniel Byman assesses three leakage indicators for countries possessing nuclear weapons: (1) security capacity, (2) corruption perception levels, and (3) terrorist penetration risk. To these indicators, a political stability index score has been added to capture the extent to which political instability may affect leakage or the inability of a nation to continue to secure its nuclear weapons or fissile material. The most dangerous combination would be a country possessing nuclear weapons that has low political stability, weak security capacity, high corruption perception levels, and high terrorist penetration risks. It is recognized that there are distinct interactions among these criteria. For example, while any of the nuclear countries might have high security capacities, if the same country has a high corruption perception level it could mean that nuclear industry insiders may constitute a considerable threat.

The countries of greatest concern are, arguably, Pakistan, Russia, North Korea, and Iran. As Iran is currently not a de facto nuclear nation, we will consider the other three nations separately. However, transcending the country-based approach is necessary in any assessment of nuclear terrorism risk, as HEU-fueled nuclear reactors also constitute a risk on the supply side.

PAKISTAN

Two of the primary nuclear risks in South Asia are, first, a miscalculation leading to a preemptive strike and perhaps a nuclear war between India and Pakistan and, second, terrorist acquisition of Pakistani-origin nuclear weapons or fissile material. The Pakistani nuclear weapons program began in earnest in 1972 and came to fruition with a nuclear test in 1998. According to the Natural Resources Defense Council, Pakistan, which is not a state party to the NPT, has approximately "sixty nuclear weapons and is busily enhancing its nuclear weapons capabilities."[17] According to David Albright and Paul Brannan of the Institute for Science and International Security, imagery analysis from early 2009 indicated Pakistan is making significant progress on the second and third reactors at the Khushab plutonium production facilities.[18]

TABLE 7. LEAKAGE CHARACTERISTICS OF NUCLEAR WEAPONS STATES

Country	Security capacity	Political stability index [a]	Corruption levels [b]	Terrorist penetration risk	Overall risk
China	High	High	High	Low	Low
France	High	High	Low	Low	Low
India	Medium	Medium	High	Low	Low
Iran [c]	Medium	Medium	High	Medium	Medium
Israel	High	Low	Medium	Low	Low
North Korea [d]	High	High	High [c]	Low	Medium
Pakistan	Medium	Low	High	High	High
Russia	Medium [e]	Medium	High	Low	Medium
United Kingdom	High	High	Low	Low	Low
United States	High	High	Low	Low	Low

Source: Data from Daniel Byman, "Do Counterproliferation and Counterterrorism Go Together?" *Political Science Quarterly* 122, no. 1 (2007): 33.

(a) Based on D. Kaufman, A. Kraay, and M. Mastruzzi, *Governance Matters III: Governance Indicators for 1996–2002* (Washington, DC: World Bank, 2003), World Bank Policy Research Working Paper 3106. Available at http:///worldbanks.org/wbi/governance/ pubs/govmatters2001.htm, accessed July 17, 2008.
(b) Corruption levels are based on Transparency International's "Corruption Perception Index 2007." Available at http://www.transparency.org/policy_research/surveys_indices/cpi/2007, accessed July 17, 2008.
(c) Iran is not a nuclear weapons state but is included given its nuclear program and the country's alleged attempt to move beyond the peaceful application of the nuclear fuel cycle.
(d) North Korea is not included in Transparency International's assessment; its corruption score is based on the nation's participation in narcotics trafficking, counterfeiting of U.S. currency, and alleged illicit transfers of nuclear knowledge.
(e) Russian security capacity is assessed as medium due to the massive amounts of HEU and plutonium stockpiles Russia possesses and the wide number of disparate facilities at which its nuclear complex is housed.

Pakistan is of greatest concern to the United States due to many factors. One of these factors is the infamous nuclear proliferation activities of A. Q. Khan, the ringleader of a group of associates responsible for transferring nuclear equipment (mostly uranium enrichment centrifuge technology) and, allegedly, advanced nuclear weapons design information to Libya, North Korea, and Iran.[19] According to *Oxford Analytica*, "There are grounds for doubt that Khan was a 'rogue element' operating on his own [as asserted by former president Pervez Musharraf in his memoir]. . . . It is hard to imagine that

Khan could have functioned without some level of cooperation by Pakistani military personnel and intelligence services."[20] Indeed, the Associated Press has reported that Khan disavowed his earlier statements that the Pakistani government was not a party to the nuclear transfers, saying, "The [Pakistani] army had 'complete knowledge' of the shipment of P-1 [centrifuges used for uranium enrichment] to North Korea and that . . . it must have gone with [Musharraf's] consent."[21] Pakistani leadership has not allowed American representatives or those of the IAEA to interview Khan, released from house arrest in February 2009; as the father of the Pakistani nuclear weapon he is considered by many Pakistanis as a national hero. Some astute observers have raised concerns that the A. Q. Khan network, considered completely dismantled by Pakistani authorities, may still be in operation. Mark Hibbs, a journalist with *Nucleonics Week* who has been following the Khan network and proliferation in general for years, stated in June 2007:

> I must admit that my concern about the issue of A. Q. Khan and illicit networks and smuggling is far greater today than it's ever been. These networks . . . morph over time. . . . Arresting A. Q. Khan, arresting half a dozen other people who were involved in it, isn't enough. There were many, many, many people in this business and all of them have not been identified. . . . People that were working in the network and at a fairly early stage jettisoned themselves away from organizations that were working with it are in a position—because they've got the blueprints, because they have the knowledge, because they have the order books and laundry lists—they can become dormant for as long as they feel necessary for them to safely reemerge at some future point.[22]

Pakistan has a large and growing presence of Taliban and al Qaeda terrorists, particularly in the undergoverned (at least by official authorities) FATA. Graham Allison of Harvard University has pointed out that "extremists are everywhere: in the madrassas [Islamic schools], in the intelligence services, in the military, and among the general public."[23] Pakistan formally recognized the Taliban government in Afghanistan shortly after it seized power in 1996. It was reported that senior CIA officials secretly visited Pakistan and strongly encouraged its military and civilian leadership to take more action to ensure that links between radical militants in Pakistan and the country's ISI were severed.[24] While the ISI does not have a direct role in protecting Pakistan's nuclear arsenal or fissile material, similar allegations of terrorist penetration have been made about the Pakistan Army. Numerous cease-fire arrangements between the Pakistani Taliban and the central government have backfired; the Taliban implemented a perverted and radical form of sharia that has alienated the populace in the Swat Valley, thus causing mass exodus. The Taliban has not laid down its arms as promised in the agreement with the government and has attempted to expand its influence in the North-West Frontier Province and surrounding regions.[25] According to Bruce Riedel, former CIA officer and current Brooking Institution scholar, Pakistan "has more terrorists per square mile than any place on earth, and it has a nuclear weapons program that is growing faster than any place else on earth."[26]

Another great concern with respect to Pakistan and nuclear terrorism is political instability. Many observers of South Asian national security point out there were numerous attempts to assassinate President Musharraf, and the assassination of Benazir Bhutto in December 2007 only raised concerns about nuclear security during and in the aftermath of political transitions. In January 2011 Salman Taseer, the governor of Pakistan's Punjab region, was assassinated by his own bodyguard, reportedly for speaking out against Pakistan's anti-blasphemy laws. From 1999 to November 2007 Pervez Musharraf was both the Pakistani president and army chief. Although Musharraf retained his title of president after stepping down from his military post under domestic and international pressure, his position was weakened as a result of losing control over the army, a central force within Pakistan.

Political instability in Pakistan does not bode well for nuclear security. Moreover, according to the Congressional Research Service, the loss of human life related to Islamist militancy was greater in 2007 than in the previous six years combined.[27] According to Thomas Donnelly of the American Enterprise Institute, "It is hard to escape the conclusion that Pakistan began as and remains a profoundly unsettled and unsettling political phenomenon, both internally and internationally."[28] Adding to this political instability, President Musharraf resigned his post as president of Pakistan in August 2008, a development that supports the argument that Pakistan may continue to be the most dangerous country in the world with respect to the potential for nuclear terrorism. In February 2008 parliamentary elections were held, resulting in the seating of a coalition led by Benazir Bhutto's husband, Asif Zardari. Zardari was subsequently elected president. Political warfare between President Zardari and opposition leader and former prime minister Nawaz Sharif has been intense; one issue is the reseating of Iftikhar Chaudhry, the Pakistani Supreme Court's chief justice (previously dismissed by President Musharraf).[29] While Pakistan became more aggressive against the Taliban in the Swat Valley in the spring and summer of 2009, continued internecine political warfare and assassinations will surely sap the country's ability to unite in the purpose of economic development and combating terrorism and insurgency over the long term.[30]

Given this instability and internal unrest, the security of the country's nuclear weapons is of grave concern.[31] Prior to her assassination, Benazir Bhutto expressed unease about the security of Pakistan's nuclear weapons, stating, "We need to maintain Pakistan's stability. If there is no stability, then I'm afraid the controls could weaken."[32] Even more recently, Mohamed ElBaradei reportedly stated, "The effects of any new war in the Middle East and the Islamic world could have repercussions, not only in Iran but . . . in Pakistan, a nation with many internal problems. . . . I fear a system of chaos or extremist regime in this state, which has thirty or forty nuclear weapons."[33] The U.S. Intelligence Community, however, appeared to retain confidence in Pakistani nuclear weapons security as recently as February 2008, when Director of National Intelligence Michael McConnell testified: "We judge the ongoing political uncertainty in Pakistan has not seriously threatened the military's control of the nuclear arsenal, but vulnerabilities exist. The Pakistani army oversees the nuclear program, including security responsibilities, and we judge that the army's management of nuclear policy issues—to include physical security—has not been degraded by Pakistan's political crisis."[34]

The essential questions with respect to Pakistan and nuclear terrorism are as follows: (1) How secure are Pakistan's nuclear weapons? What doctrine and command and control methods are in place to ensure that nuclear weapons and technology do not leak into terrorist hands? (2) In the event of a political coup or assassination by Islamic jihadists, how would a new regime, possibly hostile to the United States and other regional powers, view and control nuclear weapons? (3) To what extent are nuclear weapons insiders, those charged with building and protecting nuclear weapons, sympathetic to Islamic jihadists; that is, what is the "insider threat?" (4) If the Taliban seizes territory close to nuclear weapons storage sites and the army decides to move the weapons components, how vulnerable are these components during transfer? (5) Is another A. Q. Khan network possible or a situation in which nuclear-trained scientists share their knowledge with terrorist groups such as al Qaeda?[35] (6) How effective has U.S. nuclear security assistance to Pakistan been? An indirect but related proliferation concern is that "Pakistan may decide, as a matter of state policy, to extend a nuclear umbrella (or engage in nuclear sharing) with one or more Middle East states, especially if Iran acquires a nuclear device."[36] Given national sovereignty and secrecy surrounding these issues, each of these questions is difficult to answer with any high degree of certainty. There are, however, a number of open sources that can shed light on at least some of these questions.

PAKISTANI NUCLEAR DOCTRINE

Perhaps the most dangerous time in a country's nuclear maturity is that immediately preceding and after a nuclear weapons test—the point at which a country successfully and verifiably crosses the nuclear threshold. This is so because during this period the country is likely to be in the relatively early stages of developing its nuclear doctrine: who exactly will control the nuclear weapons and how, under what circumstances their use will be contemplated, and who has the ultimate decision-making authority on use.

The central question becomes how the newly nuclear-armed nation resolves the "always/never" dilemma of how to control its nuclear forces.[37] Emerging nuclear powers "always" want their nuclear weapons to be survivable and capable of a retaliatory strike to deter an adversary's first strike, but they "never" want their weapons to be used in an unauthorized manner. This has implications for how weapons are stored and under which circumstances the weapons might be deployed. The "always" side of the dilemma calls for nuclear weapons to be mobile, stored in a decentralized manner, and on hair-trigger alert, with control over these weapons possibly devolved to field commanders to ensure the weapons could be used should national leaders become incapacitated in a first strike. The "never" side of the dilemma calls for weapons components and delivery mechanisms to be stored separately, yet in a centralized location; not to be on hair-trigger alert; and to have only a few select leaders with the authority to authorize the weapons' use. Pakistan's primary adversary in the region is India, a country larger in geography, conventional military forces, and unconventional weapons. Pakistan and India have fought three full-scale wars (1947, 1965, and 1971) and continue to engage one another through proxies over the disputed territory of Kashmir.[38] On at least three occasions, Pakistan has placed its nuclear weapons on alert status, and in two of these instances Pakistan removed its nuclear weapons from storage facilities.[39] The problem becomes one of relative threat perceptions. If Pakistani leaders view India as their prime threat, they will err on the side of "always"; U.S. leaders might view unauthorized use or terrorist acquisition of a nuclear weapon or fissile material as the greatest threat and thus urge Pakistani leaders to err on the side of "never." Pakistan has only recently begun to view the Taliban and al Qaeda as the central threat to national security. According to Mahmood Shah, a retired security official in northwest Pakistan who reportedly often reflects military thinking, "Finally the mind-set has changed. . . . There is a realization that the threat to Pakistan is not Indian divisions and tanks, it is a teenage boy wearing a jacket [full of explosives]."[40] How pervasive this position is within the ruling elite remains an open question.

Pakistan has no formally declared nuclear doctrine; the terms "minimum credible deterrent" and "minimum defensive deterrence" have been used to characterize its nuclear doctrine.[41] While the exact meaning of these terms remains somewhat nebulous, the essence is that Pakistan's nuclear doctrine is "aimed solely at deterring any conventional or nuclear threat from India."[42] According to three senior Pakistani officials, "Deterrence was the sole aim and a small nuclear arsenal was considered adequate. Of course, minimum cannot be defined in static numbers."[43] According to some analysts, given regional conventional force asymmetries, "it is generally assumed that a nuclear first strike is a principal part of Pakistan's nuclear doctrine."[44] A purposely vague nuclear doctrine is likely to remain unclear with respect to "redlines," or threshold actions taken by India that might trigger Pakistan's first use. Political instability or civil war in Pakistan could, however, serve as a catalyst for either India or Pakistan to seriously contemplate a preemptive nuclear strike.[45]

PAKISTANI COMMAND AND CONTROL

Pakistan's command and control comprises three components: (1) the National Command Authority (NCA), (2) the Strategic Plans Division (SPD), and (3) the Strategic Forces Commands (SFC, Army, Air Force, Naval) (see figure 4).[46] The NCA, established in 2000, consists of ten members: the president; the prime minister; the chairman of the Joint Chiefs of Staff; the ministers of defense, interior, and finance; the director-general of the Strategic Plans Division; and the commanders of the army, air force, and navy. The NCA chairman, the president of Pakistan, casts the final vote.[47] The NCA was put on a legally binding basis when President Musharraf formalized its authorities under the National Command Authority Ordinance of 2007. While a legal basis for nuclear command and control may be symbolically important, the extent to which such legal authorities are recognized and implemented during a period of extreme political instability or revolution is uncertain. The SPD serves as the secretariat to the NCA and is in charge of "developing and managing Pakistan's nuclear capability in all dimensions. . . . The SFC is responsible for planning and control as well as operational directive for nuclear weapons deployment and use."[48]

Pakistan stores its nuclear warheads in a de-mated fashion, meaning that the warheads are stored separately from the delivery mechanisms and that the warhead components themselves are also stored separately. While this may make a preemptive attack against these weapons more difficult and possibly prevent an intact weapon from being stolen, from a vulnerability to terrorism

FIGURE 4.
PAKISTAN'S NUCLEAR COMMAND AND CONTROL HIERARCHY

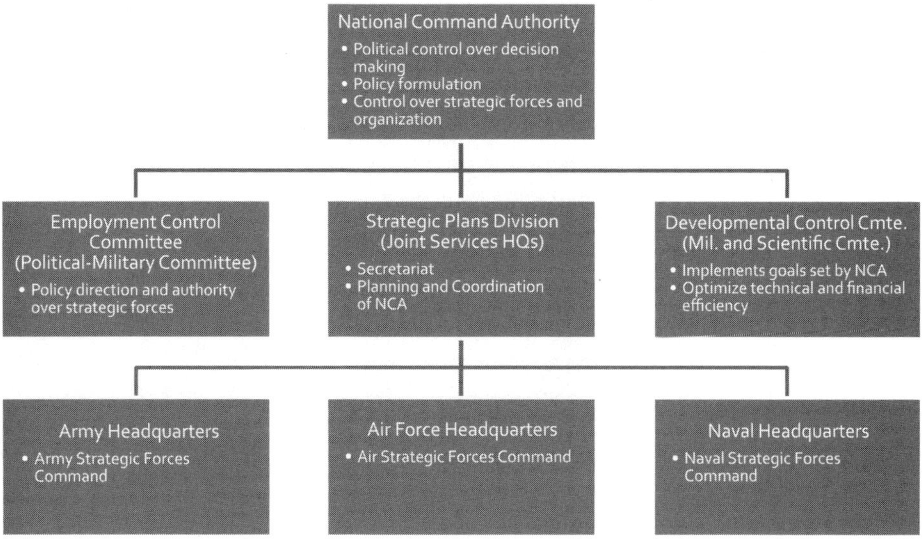

Source: Mahmud Ali Durrani, "Pakistan's Strategic Thinking and the Role of Nuclear Weapons," Occasional Paper 37 (Albuquerque, NM: Cooperative Monitoring Center, July 2004), 50, http://www.cmc.sandia.gov/cmc-papers/sand2004-3375p.pdf.

perspective it is not necessarily positive. More storage facilities means more people involved in securing the weapons components (including fissile material), more targets, more transportation, and, as a result, potentially more vulnerabilities to terrorist attacks. The potential insider threat within Pakistan's nuclear weapons establishment may continue to raise doubts in the minds of Pakistani leaders. It has been reported that President Musharraf "attempted to purge the military and intelligence services of officers he considers overly sympathetic to the Taliban and other extremist religious groups. He fired the country's top intelligence chief and reassigned other key officials two hours before the U.S. started bombing Afghanistan."[49] According to Pakistan security expert Dr. Stephen Cohen, however, "Pakistan has a homegrown personnel reliability program, but even this could be circumvented by a determined conspiracy."[50] This thought is echoed by Pervez Hoodbhoy, the chairman of the Department of Physics at Quaid-e-Azam University in Islamabad, who stated, "Safety procedures and their associated technologies are only as safe as the men who use them. . . . The deliberate nurturing of jihadism by the state has, over thirty years, produced extremism inside parts of the military and intelligence. Today, some parts are at war with the others. . . . We Pakistanis live in a state of denial."[51]

Former president Musharraf himself seems to have exhibited some of this denial when he reportedly stated to former U.S. director of Central Intelligence George Tenet that he did not believe terrorists could build nuclear weapons. Tenet recounts in his memoir that when he was briefing Musharraf shortly after the United States learned that Pakistani scientists had met with Osama bin Laden and Ayman al-Zawahiri in 2001 to discuss nuclear weapons, President Musharraf stated, "But Mr. Tenet, we are talking about men hiding in caves. Perhaps they have dreams of owning such weapons, but my experts assure me that obtaining one is well beyond their reach."[52]

U.S. NUCLEAR SECURITY ASSISTANCE TO PAKISTAN

The U.S.-Pakistani relationship has ebbed and flowed, not unlike many other relationships between nation-states.[53] Stephen Cohen stated, "Pakistan used to be an important state because of its assets, but it is important now because of its problems. . . . It has become virulently anti-American, it was the worst proliferator of advanced nuclear and missile technology, and it continues to harbor—partially involuntarily—extremists and terrorists whose dedicated mission is to attack the United States."[54] In the aftermath of the Soviet invasion of Afghanistan in 1979, Pakistan and its military and intelligence services became conduits and proxies through which the United States fought the Cold War. This period is sometimes referred to as the "Reagan jihad" against Communism, as U.S. resources flowed to various official and unofficial sources within Pakistan and Afghanistan (including mujahideen fighters), with the end goal being ejecting the Soviet Union from Afghanistan. After the Soviet Union withdrew from Afghanistan in 1989 and subsequently dissolved in 1991, U.S. interest in Afghanistan and Pakistan waned. In 1998, after the Indian and Pakistani nuclear weapons tests, the United States sharply curtailed any aid it was providing to Pakistan. The terrorist attacks of 9/11 transformed the U.S.-Pakistani relationship as Pakistan became an ally in the global war on terrorism. Pakistan has received more than $10.4 billion in overt assistance by the end of fiscal year (FY) 2010 and more then $8 billion in reimbursements for its support of U.S.-led counterterrorism efforts.[55] According to the Congressional Research Service, "Pakistan has conducted unprecedented and largely ineffectual counterterrorism operations in the country's western tribal areas, where al-Qa'ida operatives and their allies are believed to enjoy 'safe havens.'"[56] Given the resurgence of the Pakistani Taliban in the spring of 2009 and the displacement of civilians as the Pakistan Army battles insurgents in the Swat Valley, the United States has provided an additional $100 million in humanitarian assistance and another $10 million in other, unspecified defense-related assistance.[57] Some members of Congress, however, have expressed substantial concern that U.S. military assistance provided for counterinsurgency purposes could free up additional resources for Pakistan to continue to increase the size of its nuclear arsenal.[58] The United States has also provided direct aid to Pakistan for nuclear weapons and fissile material security.

There is an age-old conundrum in nuclear weapons security, borne out of the 1968 NPT as well as U.S. law (the Atomic Energy Act of 1946, as amended), that must be addressed when considering nuclear security assistance to nonnuclear weapons states. Under the terms of the NPT, Article I, each nuclear weapons member state "undertakes not in any way to assist, encourage, or induce any non-nuclear weapons state to manufacture or otherwise acquire nuclear weapons or other nuclear explosives, *or control over such weapons or explosive devices* [emphasis added]."[59] Similarly, U.S. law has numerous provisions that prevent assistance to aspiring nuclear weapons states. As David

Albright has stated, whether such assistance is permissible may depend on the technology involved: "Assisting Pakistan to improve the security of its nuclear weapons storage facilities may be permissible. However, assistance that improves the safety and security of a nuclear warhead itself may also significantly improve Pakistan's ability to deploy a warhead on a ballistic missile and may be prohibited under the NPT."[60] One must weigh the costs and benefits of rigid adherence to such reasonable and legally defensible restrictions. The NPT provides a norm against nuclear proliferation, and norms are important. Violating norms should not be taken lightly; violating laws should not be tolerated. However, if violating a norm means that de facto nuclear weapons states with potential nuclear security vulnerabilities, substantial political unrest, and significant internal terrorist presence are provided with services and training to close those security gaps, the norm should be revisited.[61] If domestic laws cease to adequately reflect U.S. interests, the legislative process may amend them, as has happened numerous times with the Atomic Energy Act of 1946.

In the immediate aftermath of the terrorist attacks of 9/11, President Musharraf moved Pakistan's nuclear weapons to six undisclosed sites.[62] The reported and ostensible reasons for the move were that the country was "fearful of possible strikes against the country's nuclear facilities" and "to remove them from air bases and corridors that might be used by the United States in an attack on Afghanistan."[63] In the wake of Pakistan's nuclear tests in 1998, the provision of nuclear security assistance was reportedly considered and rejected by the United States. However, since 2001, according to a *New York Times* report, the United States has spent over $100 million on a highly classified program to help secure Pakistan's nuclear weapons.[64] Little public information is available on the exact types of assistance that have been provided. However, reportedly, what has been provided is assistance with physical security measures; border control technologies; personnel reliability programs, including training for Pakistani personnel in the United States; as well as the construction of a nuclear security training center in Pakistan.[65] It has also been reported that "much of that [$100 million effort] has petered out, and American officials have never been permitted to see how much of the money was spent, the facilities where the weapons are kept, or even a tally of how many Pakistan produced."[66] Reportedly, in light of heightened concern over an increasingly aggressive Taliban, U.S. and Pakistani officials have initiated behind-the-scenes consultations to enhance the United States' role in securing Pakistan's nuclear weapons up to and including "a proposal to ship some highly enriched uranium to the United States for disposal."[67] Pakistan uses both HEU and plutonium for nuclear weapons purposes; HEU is also used as a fuel for some Pakistani nuclear reactors.

While there has been conflicting information about whether permissive action link technology was offered to Pakistan, it appears that a functionally similar, equivalent code-lock device exists today.[68] Some sources offer that PAL assistance was offered by the United States but rejected by Pakistan because it perceived that the provision of such technology was simply a ruse for U.S. intelligence gathering or that the technology would allow the United States to essentially have a "kill switch" on Pakistani nuclear weapons.[69] According to Bruce Riedel, a former CIA officer, "It's worth remembering that on their list of potential threats to their nuclear assets, the United States is number 1, and terrorists and fundamentalists are further down the line."[70] Other sources state that the United States did not offer PAL technology for two essential reasons: legally it violates U.S. and international law (and is classified), and sharing it would allow Pakistan to learn too much about U.S. nuclear weapons systems.[71] While the United States has provided significant counterterrorism, economic, humanitarian, and nuclear security assistance to Pakistan, given the sensitivity surrounding nuclear weapons and Pakistan's suspicions about U.S. intentions vis-à-vis its nuclear weapons (among other factors), there are limits to how much the United States and the international community can help Pakistan enhance the security of its nuclear weapons, fissile material, and nuclear scientists and technicians.

It should be made clear that what has not been part of the dialogue between the United States and Pakistan are any potential U.S. contingency plans that would involve the United States entering Pakistan to seize its nuclear weapons in the event a jihadist regime assumed power in a coup. However, former secretary of state Condoleezza Rice tacitly acknowledged such planning in her confirmation hearing. In response to a question about what would happen to Pakistan's nuclear weapons if there were a radical Islamist coup, Secretary Rice answered, "We have noted this problem, and we are prepared to try to deal with it."[72] However, numerous analysts have noted the extreme difficulty in successfully executing such a complex mission, particularly if the United States is not invited in by the government of Pakistan—however that may be defined in a political crisis.[73] According to one report, military and nuclear experts believe that "the bottom line is that if a real-life crisis broke out, it is unlikely that anyone would be able to assure the American president, with confidence, that he knew where all of Pakistan's weapons were—or that none were in the hands of Islamic extremists."[74]

As concerns about Pakistan's political stability and security over its nuclear weapons increased in late 2007 and early 2008, the country dispatched Lt. Gen. Khalid Kidwai, head of the aforementioned Strategic Plans Division, to assure the West that Pakistani nuclear weapons security is "fool-proof."[75] According to various media accounts and Kidwai's presentation summaries, it appears that Pakistani nuclear weapons security includes (1) a force of ten thousand troops assigned to guard the country's nuclear facilities overseen by the SPD; (2) enhanced physical security perimeters at nuclear facilities; (3) a personnel reliability program that has subjected two thousand nuclear scientists to extensive background checks;[76] (4) some "functional equivalent" to permissive action links; (5) implementation of the "two-man rule," which requires that two men be present to authenticate the codes that call for the release of nuclear weapons; and (6) enhanced nuclear technology export controls designed to prevent recurrences of A. Q. Khan–type secondary proliferation.[77] Some have questioned the personnel reliability program, pointing out two primary concerns: first, that all such systems are imperfect (witness Aldrich Ames's espionage in the U.S. Intelligence Community) and, second, that the ISI is conducting the vetting for individuals assigned to sensitive nuclear facilities and that certain factions within the ISI may continue to be sympathetic to the Taliban.[78] Moreover, in terms of the effectiveness of U.S. nuclear security assistance, according to one report, "After more than four years, no one in Washington has a clear sense of whether the small, covert American program to help Pakistan secure its weapons and laboratories is actually working. Kidwai has been happy to take the cash and send in progress reports, but auditors from Washington have been rebuffed whenever they have asked to see how, exactly, the money was being spent."[79]

NET ASSESSMENT: PAKISTAN

The bottom line with respect to Pakistan and nuclear terrorism is that while the country has substantially improved its nuclear security since 2001 and exhibited no systemic failures, there are limits to U.S. knowledge and intelligence.[80] Pakistan represents a potentially toxic mixture of relative political instability, proximity to terrorist groups with international reach, and possible terrorist penetration of institutions responsible for security of the country's nuclear weapons and related technologies. There is an argument for differentiating between the security of nuclear weapons themselves, on the one hand, and the concern about secondary proliferation of nuclear technology and know-how, on the other hand. According to former deputy secretary of state Richard Armitage, "I think most observers would say that they [nuclear weapons] are fairly secure. They have pretty sophisticated mechanisms to guard the security of those." Yet as mentioned above, other experts continue to express concern that the vast tentacles of the A. Q. Khan network are in danger of reappearing, particularly given Khan's release from house arrest in February 2009. Separately, concerns continue regarding the extent to which Pakistani nuclear scientists may be susceptible to jihadist recruitment. The 2001 meetings between Pakistan Atomic Energy Commission scientists (Majeed and Mahmood) and Osama bin Laden mentioned earlier still give many experts cause for concern. How many other scientists, perhaps with more direct knowledge of nuclear weapons construction, are willing to or have already met with al Qaeda? How much does the U.S. Intelligence Community know about the identities, travels, and activities of Pakistani nuclear weapons scientists?

Finally, from a U.S. policy perspective, as terrorist expert Daniel Byman points out, the United States must realize and consciously weigh and balance the fact that its counterterrorism and counterproliferation policies with respect to Pakistan exist in tension. According to Byman, "For now, the United States has emphasized counterterrorism, accepting Pakistan's rather pathetic excuse with regard to A. Q. Kahn's network in order to preserve cooperation on counterterrorism and maintain decent relations in general."[81] Moreover, Pakistan's nuclear security and counterterrorism activities, while core issues for U.S. national security, are not best addressed in a vacuum. As Pakistan expert Stephen Cohen stated recently, "Short-term strategies regarding terrorism and nuclear technology should not get in the way of long-term strategies to stabilize Pakistan. We should devote as much attention to shoring up Pakistan's broken institutions and helping Pakistanis resolve their permanent political crisis as we devote to terrorism and nuclear issues. For, if we fail to do the former, the latter will certainly become more acute."[82] Given continued political instability within Pakistan, U.S. efforts to support groups within the nation that are trying to build enduring democratic institutions able to meet the needs and demands of Pakistan's growing population (including for security, economic development, and education) may yield the greatest long-term security benefits.

Some have advocated a "nuclear deal" for Pakistan similar to the civilian nuclear cooperation deal the United States concluded with India through which "Pakistan would receive support in its civilian nuclear program in exchange for greater assurances regarding the security of its nuclear assets and technology, and transparency regarding past leakages."[83] Indeed, it is reported that Pakistan's foreign minister, Shah Mehmood Qureshi, citing Pakistan's energy needs, recently stated that "Pakistan should be eligible for the same facility."[84] However, Pakistan's historical record of proliferation warrants extreme caution. If any such civilian nuclear cooperation deal is considered with Pakistan, it must be tightly tied to nonproliferation and nuclear security goals, with explicit milestones, transparency, and verification mechanisms put into place. Moreover, given the U.S.-India nuclear cooperation deal and the November 2008 terrorist attacks in Mumbai, India, it would appear reasonable to increase diplomatic efforts to work with Pakistan and India to continue to pursue a dialogue over the disputed territory and potential nuclear flash point of Kashmir. Enhanced nuclear safeguards and transparency should be encouraged, and careful cost-benefit studies of providing certain nuclear security technologies to Pakistan should be explored to bolster Pakistani nuclear weapons security.

RUSSIA

The Soviet Union ceased to exist in December 1991. It left in its wake a sprawling nuclear establishment, thousands of nuclear warheads, a relatively impoverished Russia, and an extremely damaged Russian national psyche and morale.[85] Seeing the potential threat to which these conditions could lead, Senators Richard Lugar and Sam Nunn were instrumental in passing the Soviet Nuclear Threat Reduction Act in 1991 (Public Law 102-228). The goal of the act was to reduce the threat emanating from the dissolution of the Soviet Union that, by default, made Kazakhstan, Ukraine, and Belarus nuclear weapons states as Soviet nuclear weapons were stationed on their newly sovereign soil. The program called for assisting Russia and the states of the former Soviet Union in the dismantling and destruction of nuclear weapons, providing security for nuclear weapons transportation and storage, as well as securing of fissile material. This assistance was renamed the Cooperative Threat Reduction Program in 1993, and among other achievements, it led to Kazakhstan (April 1995), Ukraine (June 1996), and Belarus (November 1996) becoming nonnuclear weapons states as each nation shipped former Soviet nuclear weapons stationed on its soil to Russia.[86] Russia, as the legal successor to the formerly Soviet Union, became responsible for securing over 25,000 nuclear weapons and hundreds of metric tons of fissile material; at the time it did not necessarily have the financial resources to accomplish this task. One Russian nuclear weapons plant manager informed journalist William Langewiesche that during the Soviet era "anyone stealing nuclear material in the Soviet Union was committing a state crime. He became a state criminal! So, there was fear. Real fear. If something got lost somewhere—maybe a piece of paper or materials, or there was a mismatch in balance of plutonium—a person understood that he would be exiled forever."[87] The plant manager continued, "But when this . . . change took place, of course, people felt more . . . *freedom* I would say." The change to which the nuclear plant manager was referring was the implosion of the Soviet Union.

Russia represents a classic case of the Willie Sutton argument—he robbed banks because that was where the money was—as applied to nuclear terrorism. While it is not necessarily the case that a nuclear terrorist would head to Russia to acquire a nuclear weapon or fissile material simply because there is a lot of it there (a terrorist may well head anywhere he determined a weapon or fissile material is most vulnerable and easily accessible), the vast repositories of nuclear weapons and fissile material in Russia represent what might be considered by a terrorist a target-rich environment. According to *The Global Fissile Material Report, 2010*, Russian stockpiles of HEU and plutonium total approximately 1,380 (1,250 HEU, 130 Plutonium for weapons) metric tons.[88] The Natural Resources Defense Council has estimated that Russia has approximately 10,000 nuclear warheads, including those categorized as active, in reserve, or awaiting dismantlement under various arms control agreements with the United States.[89] Of these 10,000 warheads, approximately 2,050 are tactical nuclear weapons, a portion of which are dedicated to missile defense.[90]

Tactical or nonstrategic nuclear weapons are of particular concern from a nuclear terrorism perspective for a number of reasons. First, the weapons are generally intended for battlefield use and are, therefore, forward deployed at numerous sites, thus increasing the nuclear weapons target set for terrorists. Second, some of the older tactical nuclear weapons, if they have not been updated through periodic maintenance, may not necessarily be equipped with permissive action links, possibly decreasing one hurdle terrorists must surmount to detonate a nuclear device if they were to acquire one. Third, the weapons tend to be small and thus easily transported. Fourth, while the trend in both the United States and Russia since 1991 has been to decrease the numbers of these weapons unilaterally and significantly, there are still a substantial number of deployed tactical nuclear weapons, and as a class of weapons they are not governed by any formal and verifiable arms control agreements.[91]

In addition to tactical nuclear weapons, another supply-side concern is the size of the Russian nuclear weapons complex; it is vast, composed of over three hundred buildings at over forty facilities across the country.[92] The sheer size of the complex and relatively large number of personnel represent another opportunity for terrorists to make inroads to opportunistic insiders looking to profit from their insider status. According to journalist William Langewiesche, "Possibilities abound for an insider job, and though the deal would be fraught with the chance of betrayal, the potential advantages are huge: insiders could neutralize any practical defenses, pass through the gates with a load of un-shielded HEU undetected, and provide a getaway team with a head start that could be measured in weeks or months."[93] The potential solutions, or at least the means that may increase the probability that illicit insider transactions are caught early on, are a complex mix of personnel reliability programs, two-man rules whenever material is touched or moved, bar code scanners to move away from paper inventories, and instilling, or perhaps reinvigorating, a culture of security. The security culture question is interesting insofar as

> in the Soviet days [working in one of the ten closed cities], you were a trusted person, an elite person, if you were working in these facilities. And we come along, and we say, "Okay, you're not allowed to go into the vault by yourself anymore. You need one or two other people with you every time you unlock that door." [Fissile material security] is a very

complicated thing. Bricking up windows is part of the solution, but it's not everything.[94]

THE U.S. INTELLIGENCE COMMUNITY'S VIEW

At the direction of Congress, since the late 1990s the U.S. Intelligence Community has conducted an annual review of Russian nuclear weapons and fissile material security. The most recent years for which versions of these reports are openly available are 2002, 2004, and 2006. The U.S. Intelligence Community has consistently stated that it is concerned with undetected smuggling of weapons-usable nuclear material. The language has changed only slightly over the years.

- 2002—"Weapons-grade and weapons-usable nuclear materials have been stolen from some Russian institutes. We assess that undetected smuggling has occurred, although we do not know the extent or magnitude of such thefts. Nevertheless, we are concerned about the total amount of material that could have been diverted over the last ten years."[95]
- 2004—"We find it highly unlikely that Russian authorities would have been able to recover all the material reportedly stolen. We assess that undetected smuggling has occurred, and we are concerned about the total amount of material that could have been diverted or stolen over the past thirteen years."[96]

The language in 2006 was similar. The CIA raised other concerns about Russian nuclear weapons and fissile material security, including:

- *The insider threat.* "Russia's nuclear security has been slowly increasing over the last several years, but we remain concerned about vulnerabilities to an insider who attempts unauthorized actions as well as to potential terrorist attacks."[97]
- *Terrorist targeting of Russian nuclear facilities.* "Since the September 2001 terrorist attacks in the United States, President Putin and other Russian officials have conducted a public campaign to provide assurances that terrorists have not acquired nuclear weapons. Russian officials have reported, however, that terrorists have targeted Russian nuclear weapon stor-

age sites. Russian authorities reportedly thwarted two terrorist attempts in 2002 and 2003 to gain access to Russian nuclear weapons storage facilities in the European part of Russia."[98] In addition to these instances, "two Chechen sabotage and reconnaissance groups reportedly showed a suspicious amount of interest in the transport of nuclear munitions."[99]

Moreover, Russia has also been the target of numerous terrorist attacks, demonstrating the relative power of terrorist groups within Russia and particularly groups located in the Caucasus region, including Chechen terrorist groups. These attacks include:

- *Moscow theater—2002.* In October 2002 about 50 Chechen rebels seized the Theatrical Center in Dubrovka in Moscow during a showing of the Russian musical *NORD-OST.* The *NORD-OST* terrorist attack, as it became known, led to the death of at least 129 hostages and 39 terrorists after Russian special forces pumped an unknown chemical into the theater's ventilation system and subsequently raided the theater.
- *Beslan—2004.* In 2004 a Chechen-affiliated terrorist group seized a school in Beslan, Northern Ossetia, Russia. Over 1,000 people were taken hostage. Two days after the seizure there was an explosion in a gymnasium where the hostages were being held that led to intense gunfire between terrorist and government forces. According to a report, 186 children, 124 civilians, 11 teachers, 10 Russian soldiers, and 2 government employees were killed.[100]
- *Moscow—2011.* On January 24, 2011, a terrorist attack against Moscow's busy Domodedov airport killed at least 35 people. While no group officially claimed responsibility for the attack, Russian official have numerous suspects within the Caucasus region.[101]

While not a realized attack with real-world casualties, in 1996 Chechen separatists threatened to turn Moscow into a desert by using radioactive waste. The group reportedly tipped off Moscow law enforcement to a radioactive package containing cesium-137 it had placed in Moscow's popular Izmailovsky Park. The device was located by police prior to detonation.[102] The incident illustrated that a terrorist group within Russia had access to radioactive material. Why the Chechen terrorist group did not detonate the weapon remains uncertain. According to terrorism expert Brian Michael Jenkins,

> Chechen rebels would appear to be the terrorist group best positioned to obtain a Russian nuclear warhead or fissile material. . . . They see their rebellion as an existential struggle. They have been brutalized by two bloody wars. They are willing to kill in quantity, as they have demonstrated in a number of large-scale attacks. They would also seem to have the capability. They live in Russia. They speak the language. The leaders have money. Reportedly, they have connections with organized crime. Some have served in Soviet and Russian armed forces. . . . And yet, despite this, insofar as we know, the Chechens have not succeeded in acquiring a nuclear weapon or fissile materials. They have made no overt assaults on Russian nuclear weapons storage sites that we know of. . . . And they did not detonate the one dispersal device they had. Either the Chechens have decided that in the context of their conflict, going nuclear makes no sense, or getting nuclear bombs in Russia is not as easy as it looks.[103]

Despite ongoing concerns about Russian fissile material security, substantial progress has been made since 1991 through the Cooperative Threat Reduction Program.

COOPERATIVE THREAT REDUCTION PROGRESS

According to the GAO, considerable progress has been made in upgrading Russian security throughout the weapons complex since the early 1990s. The GAO found that from FY 1993 through FY 2006 the Department of Energy (largely through its MPC&A program launched in 1995) and the Department of Defense (largely though the Cooperative Threat Reduction Program) have spent approximately $2.2 billion to "provide security upgrades and other assistance at sites in Russia and other countries that house weapons-usable nuclear materials and warheads."[104] This is only part of the broader U.S. assistance program focusing on reducing the threat posed by potentially vulnerable nuclear warheads, material, and expertise. According to Anthony Wier and Matthew Bunn of the Belfer Center for Science and International Affairs at Harvard University, from FY 1992 to FY 2006, approximately $8.2 billion (in 2005 dollars) have been allocated to this cause.[105]

How Much Nuclear Security Has the United States Purchased?

What were the results of these expenditures? The Nunn-Lugar "Scorecard" (figure 5) illustrates progress to date. While the results of this program go beyond issues that may directly pertain to detecting, dissuading, and preventing nuclear terrorism, they are nevertheless relevant insofar as they demonstrate U.S. and Russian commitments to fulfilling their NPT obligations and may assist allied powers in cooperating on nuclear nonproliferation and other matters relating more directly to nuclear terrorism.

Another official attempt at assessing Cooperative Threat Reduction Program performance and making recommendations for the future was undertaken in 2001. In 2001 then secretary of energy Bill Richardson requested that former Senate majority leader Howard Baker and former White House counsel Lloyd Cutler cochair a group to review and assess the DOE's nonproliferation programs in Russia and make recommendations for their improvement. The Baker-Cutler report concluded, in part: "Current nonproliferation programs in the Department of Energy, Department of Defense, and related agencies have achieved impressive results thus far, but their limited mandate and funding fall short of what is required to address adequately the threat."[106]

One of the attendant recommendations in the report was an "enhanced national security program . . . that could be carried out for less than 1 percent of the U.S. defense budget, or up to a total of $40 billion over the next eight to ten years."[107] The goal was to develop a strategic plan to "secure and/or neutralize in the next eight to ten years all nuclear weapons–usable material located in Russia and to prevent the outflow from Russia of scientific expertise that could be used for nuclear or other weapons of mass destruction."[108]

The progress of various U.S. nuclear security and nuclear nonproliferation programs will be addressed more specifically in chapter 7. However, a brief mention here—relative to Russia—is necessary. In December 2010 the GAO assessed the progress that the DOE and DOD have made through these programs and summarized it as follows:

- *Nuclear material (DOE).* The DOE has completed a combination of rapid and comprehensive upgrades at 195 of 214 (91 percent) buildings (at 37 sites) with nuclear material in Russia.

FIGURE 5. THE NUNN-LUGAR "SCORECARD"

The Nunn-Lugar Scorecard
Destroying Weapons & Materials of Mass Destruction through Cooperation

CTR

Soviet Declared Amounts		Reductions to date	Percent of 2012 Targets	2012 Targets
13300	Warheads Deactivated	7599	82%	9222
1473	Intercontinental Ballistic Missiles (ICBM) Destroyed	791	73%	1078
831	ICBM Silos Eliminated	498	77%	645
442	ICBM Mobile Launchers Destroyed	180	67%	267
48	Nuclear Weapons Carrying Submarines Destroyed	32	91%	35
936	Submarine Launched Ballistic Missiles (SLBM) Eliminated	659	95%	691
728	SLBM Launchers Eliminated	492	87%	564
906	Nuclear Air-to-Surface Missiles Destroyed	906	100%	906
233	Bombers Eliminated	155	100%	155
194	Nuclear Test Tunnels/Holes Sealed	194	100%	194
	Nuclear Weapons Transport Train Shipments	503	81%	620
	Nuclear Weapons Storage Site Security Upgrades	24	100%	24
	Biological Monitoring Stations Built & Equipped	20	36%	55

Ukraine, Kazakhstan and Belarus are Nuclear Weapons Free

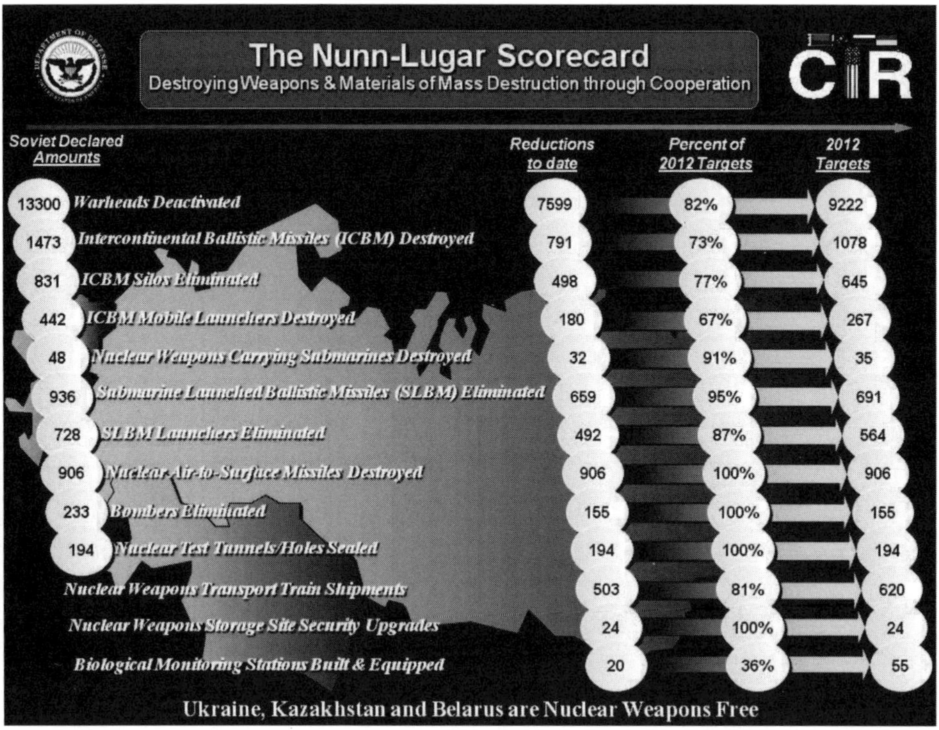

Source: Senator Richard G. Lugar's website, "The Nunn-Lugar Scoredcard," http://lugar.senate.gov/nunnlugar/scorecard.html, updated March 2011.

- *Nuclear warheads (DOD and DOE).* The DOE and DOD have completed a combination of rapid and comprehensive MPC&A upgrades at 73 of the 97 (75 percent) planned warhead sites.[109]

NET ASSESSMENT: RUSSIA

It is an undeniable fact that the security of Russian nuclear weapons and fissile material has improved markedly in the last nineteen years as a result of numerous factors, not the least of which are the U.S. MPC&A and Cooperative Threat Reduction Programs. Numerous reviews have reached relatively similar conclusions, with differences in assessments based on their definitions of what is being counted in which countries and whether it is according to planned governmental work, or what should be completed based on views independent of government plans. Beyond the GAO, nuclear security expert Matthew Bunn has reviewed the progress and concluded that through FY 2010, it can be summarized as:

- *Comprehensive upgrades on buildings with weapons-usable nuclear material in the former Soviet Union:* 84 percent (210 out of 250) complete. As political sensitivities outlined previously illustrate, a number of buildings in Russia still contain weapons-usable material, and the United States and Russia have not reached an agreement to include them in nuclear security plans.
- *Security upgrades on Russian nuclear warhead sites:* completion of 97 warhead storage sites of the estimated 110–130 nuclear warhead sites in Russia.[110]

"Most importantly, Russia's economy has stabilized and has been growing steadily for years; nuclear workers are getting paid an above-average wage, on time, largely ending the desperation that motivated some nuclear thefts or theft attempts in the 1990s; and the central government has established much firmer control over key sectors and facilities."[111]

However, substantial challenges lie ahead for security of Russian fissile material, one of which may be a relatively complacent, yet arguably accurate, attitude about the threat of nuclear terrorism. In June 2006, under the auspices of the Military-Industrial Commission and the Ministry of Defense, Russia released a white paper on nonproliferation.[112] According to the white paper, while Russia categorizes nuclear terrorism as "the greatest threat," at the same time it "estimates that the risk of terrorists acquiring or building a nuclear weapon is extremely low. Instead, it concludes that the greatest risk is the possibility that terrorists might acquire radioactive materials to build a radiological device."[113]

Moreover, as will be addressed in chapter 7, at the April 2010 nuclear security summit in Washington, D.C., the following Russian government statement was made: "There are no vulnerable nuclear materials or facilities in its territory, which would raise concerns due to their security level."[114] This attitude may be a result of Russian conflation of nuclear weapons associated with nation-state programs and those associated with nonstate actors. However, as outlined earlier, the skeptic school of thought would likely agree with the Russian assessment that a dirty bomb attack is far more likely than an IND attack. Notwithstanding the progress that has been made in Russian nuclear weapons and fissile material security, sustaining this security as funding for the U.S. Cooperative Threat Reduction Program phases out and Russia assumes greater fiscal stewardship is perhaps the greatest challenge.

Sustainability of the nuclear security systems and mechanisms that the United States has assisted Russia in installing and implementing is a major future challenge. In 2002 Congress mandated that the DOE work with Russia to develop a sustainable MPC&A system to be solely supported by Russia by 2013.[115] Journalist William Langewiesche relays one story that demonstrates the importance of sustainability from an interview he conducted with an American technician with a decade of experience in the secret cities of the Urals. The U.S. official was discussing with a Russian plant worker the efficacy of a radiation portal monitor to track whether radioactive materials were leaving certain areas of the city. In response to the American's question about how the portal monitoring system was working, the Russian responded, "Oh, we shut it off most of the time because it is always going off." Why? asked the American. The Russian responded, "Well . . . it's the people on the buses. People go fishing in the lake, and when they catch fish and bring them out on the bus, they set off the radiation monitor. And then we've got to respond." The American remarked to Langewiesche, "Just when you think you've nabbed a terrorist, what you've really nabbed is a radioactive fish."[116] According to the GAO, while the DOE has developed sustainability guidelines and is working with officials at the Federal Agency for Atomic Energy of the Russian Federation (Rosatom) to develop joint sustainability plans, several challenges could impact the DOE's "ability to prepare Russia to sustain security upgrades at its own sites that house weapons-usable nuclear material, including: (1) access difficulties at some sites, (2) the limited financial ability of some Russian sites to maintain DOE-funded MPC&A equipment, (3) lack of certification of some DOE-funded MPC&A equipment, and (4) delays in installing the MPC&A Operations Monitoring system at Rosatom facilities."[117]

Importantly, notwithstanding the "reset" of U.S.-Russian relations, a revanchist Russia could jeopardize the U.S.-Russian partnership on nuclear security. The August 2008 Russian military invasion of its sovereign and Western-aligned neighbor Georgia caused a pause in U.S.-Russian cooperation. Georgia has been one of the preferred routes of nuclear materials smuggling. The United States has been working with Georgian officials to install radiation detection devices at various locations throughout the country. While such technologies installed at official border crossing points may do little to prevent smuggling of materials across age-old smuggling routes (in March 2010 two Armenians reportedly smuggled eighteen grams of HEU [89.4 percent enriched] into Georgia by train, allegedly circumventing detection by concealing the material in a lead-lined cigarette package[118]), at a minimum they may provide a disincentive to trafficking nuclear material through the country. However, the Russian invasion has not only caused U.S. DOE officials to leave the country but also opens the more fundamental question of the status of Russia's post–Cold War relations with the rest of the world.

In any complex, multifaceted international relationship, such as the U.S.-Russian relationship, one or more issues may have the potential to derail the broader relationship over the short term. Yet today's international dilemmas and common threats to international security, such as nuclear proliferation and nuclear terrorism, require cooperation and coordination among major world powers. Consistency of purpose and action among Russia, China, the United States, the United Kingdom, France, and Germany with respect to Iran's alleged nuclear weapons program, for example, would provide a diplomatic united front to undermine any efforts by Iran to weaponize its civilian nuclear program. A central tenet of the Obama administration's "reset" of U.S.-Russian relations, is further reductions in strategic nuclear arms through the New Strategic Arms Reduction Treaty (START).[119] In the Obama administration's first summit with Russia, President Obama and President Medvedev announced a number of common interests and initiatives designed to enhance nuclear security and strengthen the nuclear nonproliferation regime. In a speech at Moscow's New Economic School on July 7, 2009, President Obama named a number of other common interests, including "a strong, peaceful, and prosperous Russia"; "reversing the spread of nuclear weapons and preventing their use"; and "isolating and defeating violent extremists."[120] The most tangible outcome of the July 2009 summit was the Joint Understanding for a follow-on treaty to replace START, which was due to expire in December 2009.[121] In December 2010, the U.S. Senate provided its advice and consent to ratification of New START, which, inter alia, limits the numbers of deployed strategic nuclear warheads to no more than 1,550 each. While the reduction of U.S. and Russian strategic nuclear arms may not cause countries of nuclear proliferation concern to jettison their nuclear programs, it demonstrates firm steps in implementing U.S. and Russian obligations as outlined in Article VI of the NPT. Other nuclear security commitments supported by President Obama and President Medvedev at the July 2009 summit included:

- a renewed commitment to the nuclear security initiatives outlined in Bratislava in 2005, including the repatriation of spent HEU fuel from research reactors;
- continued progress in meeting the terms of the U.S.-Russia Plutonium Disposition Agreement;
- development of new types of LEU fuels for possible conversion of research reactor cores;
- the continued importance of minimizing the use of HEU in civilian applications;
- continued improvement in physical security systems at nuclear facilities;
- assistance provided to other nations to carry out their WMD nonproliferation obligations under United Nations Security Council Resolution 1540; efforts to increase the overall effectiveness of international safeguards in promoting the peaceful use of nuclear energy;
- continued research into methods and mechanisms for the provision of reliable nuclear fuel cycle services (for example, nuclear fuel banks); and
- expanding the Global Initiative to Combat Nuclear Terrorism (GI).

As will be further addressed in chapter 7, if sustainable progress can be made in all of these initiatives, as well as President Obama's commitment to securing all vulnerable fissile material around the world by 2013, the risk of nuclear terrorism will certainly decrease substantially. Yet effective implementation of such initiatives in many instances pits national interests against collective international security interests, a situation that demands sustained, high-level political commitment and leadership to surmount.

NORTH KOREA AND IRAN

Two countries labeled as part of the "axis of evil" by President George W. Bush in January 2002, North Korea and Iran also present a nuclear terrorism risk. At the most elemental level of analysis, the more nations that possess nuclear weapons, the wider the nuclear weapons and fissile material target set for terrorists and the greater the risk of nuclear terrorism. It should be mentioned, however, that despite the risk factors, historical precedent indicates that no state possessing nuclear weapons has ever transferred an intact nuclear weapon to a nonstate actor. Of course, there has been extensive secondary proliferation among nations attempting to acquire nuclear weapons, whereby substantial nuclear-related technologies have been shared. The extent of North Korea's and Iran's (alleged) nuclear weapons programs and the means to prevent them from advancing are beyond the scope of this book. However, a brief summary of their programs is useful in understanding the potential nexus to nuclear terrorism.

NORTH KOREA

North Korea has been considered a de facto nuclear power since its nuclear tests in October 2006 that, according to the U.S. Intelligence Community, "produced an estimated yield of less than one kiloton, well below the yield of other states' first nuclear test."[122] The North Korean nuclear program appears to have improved since 2006, at least insofar as the yield of the nuclear blast. In May 2009 North Korea conducted a second nuclear test; this time the nuclear yield, as assessed by the Office of the Director of National Intelligence, was "a few kilotons."[123]

The earliest international agreement on nuclear matters on the Korean Peninsula was the 1991 Joint Declaration on the Denuclearization of the Korean Peninsula, signed after U.S. President George H. W. Bush announced (in September 1991) that the United States would unilaterally withdraw its nuclear weapons from South Korea. Under the terms of the 1991 Joint Declaration, North and South Korea agreed "not to test, manufacture, produce, receive, possess, store, deploy, or use nuclear weapons."[124] The agreement also bound the two sides to forgo the possession of "nuclear reprocessing and uranium enrichment facilities." North Korea clearly violated this agreement. The second major agreement on nuclear matters was the 1994 Agreed Framework. Bilateral talks between the United States and North Korea resulted in the U.S.–North Korea Agreed Framework of 1994, which called for a freeze of the North Korean nuclear program in exchange for the provision of light-water nuclear reactors and fuel oil. Ultimately, North Korea reneged on its commitments under the bilateral accord by clandestinely developing a uranium enrichment program and, as U.S. intelligence discovered, by participating in a deal in which North Korea traded ballistic missiles to Pakistan in exchange for HEU technology and materials through the infamous A. Q. Khan network.[125] The Agreed Framework broke down in 2003. In the third major initiative on nuclear matters on the peninsula, the United States and the world community (in the form of six-party talks with Russia, South Korea, North Korea, Japan, China, and the United States) have been engaged with North Korea, albeit intermittently, in negotiations to disarm the country's nuclear program since 2003.[126]

The most recent substantive progress made in six-party agreement negotiations, concluded in February 2007, moved toward the implementation of the September 2005 Six-Party Joint Statement. Under the 2005 Joint Statement of the Fourth Round of the Six-Party Talks, North Korea committed to "abandoning all nuclear weapons and existing nuclear weapons programs and returning, at an early date, to the Treaty of the Non-Proliferation of Nuclear Weapons, and to IAEA safeguards."[127] Under the 2007 agreement North Korea committed to (1) freeze its nuclear installations at the Yongbyon site, (2) subsequently disable all North Korean nuclear facilities, and (3) provide a declaration of "all nuclear programs."[128] In exchange, based on verified progress (the "action for action" principle) in meeting agreed-upon denuclearization goals, the North Koreans were offered normalization of relations, including removal of the country from the United States' list of state sponsors of terrorism.[129]

According to Christopher Hill, former assistant secretary of state for East Asian and Pacific affairs, North Korea made progress in, among other areas, disablement of three core nuclear facilities at Yongbyon and the provision of nineteen thousand pages of documents concerning its plutonium production program. North Korea must undertake additional initiatives in other areas, including providing verifiable responses to questions about its uranium enrichment activities, the extent to which it supplied Syria with nuclear-related technologies to build a nuclear reactor, and human rights, including information about Japanese abductees.[130] While its motivations remain unclear, North Korea asked the IAEA to remove seals and all surveillance mechanisms from the nuclear reprocessing plant at Yongbyon.[131] This seems consistent with prior North Korean behavior in this "one step forward, two steps backward" series of negotiations. The main point of contention continues to be the establishment of a robust verification regime, including environmental sampling, by which outside inspectors would be able to verify what North Korea has declared. Moreover, North Korea has been less than forthcoming about its uranium enrichment programs. John Bolton, former U.S. representative to the United Nations, was highly critical of the Bush administration for removing North Korea from the state sponsors of terrorism list, believing it was "the final crash and burn of a once aspiring global effort to confront and reverse nuclear proliferation."[132]

As mentioned above, the U.S. Intelligence Community reported in 2006 that North Korea (in 2005) stated to a U.S. academic that it could transfer nuclear weapons to terrorists if driven into a corner. Given this statement and North Korea's prior aberrant international behavior in trafficking ballistic missiles and other military material, a threat was issued to North Korea in 2006 by President George W. Bush. Kim Jong-Il was warned that the "transfer of nuclear weapons or material" to other countries or terrorist groups "would be considered a grave threat to the United States" and that North Korea would be held "fully accountable."[133] In this instance, the warning to North Korea was left vague, perhaps intentionally. How "fully accountable" was to be defined remains wide open. Would the United States go to the United Nations Security Council and demand tougher sanctions, revisit its policy of providing food aid unconditionally, or attack North Korea militarily? While there may be some circumstances under which a declaratory policy is left deliberately vague, threats can be perceived as being more credible if they are more direct.[134] It should be clear that this warning was enabled, at least in part, by the nuclear attribution abilities of the United States. The North Korean nuclear threat is unique in that the international community, through the IAEA, has access to a library of nuclear samples from the country that would facilitate the ability to trace a terrorist nuclear explosion back to North Korea. North Korea continues to exhibit behavior of great concern regarding proliferation and regional stability, including testing missiles (unsuccessfully) that could be long-range, allegedly sinking a South Korean naval vessel—the *Cheonan*—and killing nearly fifty sailors, launching artillery attacks against disputed islands, and revealing new uranium enrichment facilities.[135]

IRAN

Unlike North Korea, Iran is not currently a de facto nuclear power. However, Iran continues to enrich uranium in violation of United Nations Security Council resolutions. According to the IAEA, through its extensive enrichment operations Iran has produced up to 3,606 kilograms of LEU.[136] While this may or may not be a sufficient amount of LEU to make the estimated 25–50 kilograms of HEU necessary for a nuclear weapon,[137] Iran would have to (1) make the political decision to develop a nuclear weapon (if such a decision has not already been made), (2) continue to enrich the LEU from 5 percent ^{235}U to a minimum of 20 percent needed for weapons-usable HEU (but more likely to 85 percent for weapons-grade HEU—and it seems to have the technology and ability to do so having already produced 25.1 kilograms of UF_6 enriched to 19.7 percent),[138] and (3) design a viable nuclear weapon using HEU, a capability about which there is uncertain judgment. Iran has spent vast treasure and time to develop this LEU.[139] Iran's uranium enrichment facilities, and its centrifuges in particular, in late 2009–2010 were damaged by computer malware known as Stuxnet.[140] The "worm" caused certain industrial safety and control systems to fail by covertly changing the frequency of certain types of frequency converters that control the speed of the centrifuge motors. The full extent of the damage is unknown with a high degree of certainty, yet according to the Institute for Science and International Security, approximately a thousand centrifuges at Iran's Natanz fuel enrichment plant were destroyed.[141]

If Iran is working to develop its own nuclear weapon, a claim it vehemently denies, it is unlikely to sell this material to any terrorist group, except perhaps under the most extreme circumstances under which the survival of the regime is at stake. According to the most recent publicly available U.S. Intelligence Community NIE, "We judge with high confidence that in the fall of 2003, Tehran halted its nuclear weapons program; we also assess with moderate-to-high confidence that Tehran at a minimum is keeping open the option to develop nuclear weapons."[142] The NIE clearly defines a "nuclear weapons program" as "Iran's nuclear weapons design and weaponization work and covert uranium conversion–related and uranium enrichment–related work; we do not mean Iran's declared civil work related to uranium conversion and enrichment."[143] However, as has been demonstrated numerous times throughout history, intelligence is a fallible human endeavor. According to former IAEA director general Mohamed ElBaradei, Iran, an NPT member state, continues to undermine complete transparency with respect to its nuclear activities.[144] While some progress has been made with Iran, ElBaradei has stated, "I regret that we are still not in a position to achieve full clarity regarding the absence of *undeclared* nuclear material and activities in Iran. This is because the Agency has not been able to make substantive progress on the so-called alleged studies and associated questions relevant to possible military dimensions to Iran's nuclear programme."[145]

The central conundrum with respect to uranium enrichment is that the same technology and processes used to enrich the concentration of ^{235}U from 0.7 percent in natural uranium to 3–5 percent for use in nuclear reactors and is legal under the NPT can also be used to further enrich uranium to 85 percent ^{235}U, or weapons-grade uranium, which is illegal under the NPT.[146] Iran maintains that its enrichment activities are solely in pursuit of civilian nuclear purposes. The international community believes Iran may be pursuing a nuclear weapons program and has passed numerous United Nations Security Council resolutions (for example, 1696 [2006], 1737 [2006], 1747 [2007], 1803 and 1835 [2008], and 1929 [2010] demanding that Iran comply with the IAEA requirements for nuclear program transparency and cease all uranium enrichment activities. The resolutions also detail sanctions for Iranian noncompliance. Iran continues to expand and enhance centrifuge designs and operations, as demonstrated by the public access Iranian president Mahmoud Ahmadinejad provided to his tour of the enrichment facility at Natanz in April 2008. Boasting about the addition of six thousand new, second-generation (IR-2) centrifuges to the existing three thousand centrifuges, President Ahmadinejad stated, "The nuclear victory of Iran is the start of the ever-increasing destruction of the imperialistic state."[147] International Atomic Energy Agency officials have reportedly estimated that Iran has enough components and material to make ten thousand centrifuges.[148] Among other arguments, Iran has never accepted the legal basis for sanctions, and international talks designed to bring Iran into compliance, or get it to disgorge its LEU in exchange for nuclear fuel, continue to make minimal progress.[149]

As the world's preeminent state supporter of terrorism, Iran has an established history of working with terrorist groups, which it often uses as proxies to advance its interests in the Middle East. Yet empirical evidence demonstrates Iran may at least be aware that the use of nuclear weapons by one of Iran's proxies against the United States would almost certainly result in immediate and devastating retaliation. As counterterrorism expert Daniel Byman notes, "Perhaps not surprisingly, Iran has not transferred chemical or biological weapons or agents to its proxies, despite its capability to do so."[150] Byman also notes that Iran's proxies, primarily Lebanese Hezbollah, "appear to recognize the 'red line' drawn by the United States and other powers with respect to terrorist use of [WMD]. . . . Moreover, their current tactics and systems enable them to inflict considerable casualties."[151] This is not to say that there are no circumstances under which Iran would transfer fissile material or an intact nuclear weapon, should it develop one, to a terrorist group. However, Iran would likely have to perceive its very existence as being threatened—perhaps by an imminent invasion or even an invasion that successfully routed its elite Revolutionary Guard Forces—before it might turn to such a risky course of action.

Israel, a nation profoundly threatened by a potential Iranian nuclear weapon, has made no secret of its readiness to preemptively strike the Iranian nuclear establishment.[152] Some have speculated that Israel, perhaps as supported by other nations, may have been the originator of the Stuxnet malware.[153] Given the schisms in the Iranian polity and power structure in the aftermath of the contested June 2009 presidential election, the regional and international repercussions of such an Israeli preemptive attack are uncertain.[154] However, if such a kinetic attack were to take place, it is not unreasonable to expect enhanced Iranian nationalism, perhaps manifested through a more resolute commitment to build nuclear weapons; regional and perhaps international increases in terrorism; and potential oil supply disruptions out of the Persian Gulf.

NET ASSESSMENT: IRAN AND NORTH KOREA

The aberrant international behavior of both Iran and North Korea is cause for an abundance of caution when negotiating with them in a bilateral or multinational setting and for the adoption of a "trust but verify" approach to all interactions. North Korea exports ballistic missiles to numerous foreign nations, has supported terrorism in the past, counterfeits U.S. currency, and engages in illicit narcotics trafficking.[155] Iran is the most active state sponsor of terrorism today, it actively works to undermine U.S. national security activities in Iraq and Afghanistan, and its current president has stated publicly a desire to see Israel eventually eliminated.[156]

However, it is not necessarily axiomatic that such aberrant behavior extends to the provision of intact nuclear weapons, fissile material, or nuclear-related technologies to terrorist groups. First and foremost these regimes, like all others, value survival. As mentioned previously, one must consider that even active state supporters of terrorism understand that terrorist groups can be uncontrollable and could take actions that boomerang against their sponsors. Certain nations also have no plausible deniability when it comes to their support of certain terrorist groups—Iran and Hezbollah, for example. It could also be argued that through years of negotiation with the United States over nuclear matters, North Korea may have become familiar with U.S. nuclear attribution capabilities.

North Korean and Iranian leadership may or may not perceive U.S. retaliatory policy to be credible. While there may be some limited and extreme circumstances under which North Korea and Iran might provide a nuclear weapon or fissile material to a terrorist group (outlined earlier), the leaders would have to calculate that their regimes could survive a potential retaliatory U.S. attack with "all our [U.S.] options." As will be discussed in chapter 6, deterrence does not require a leader be "rational"; fear is enough. As the notable Swiss philosopher Jean-Jacques Rousseau wrote in *The Social Contract*, "Man's first law is to watch over his preservation; his first care he owes to himself; and as soon as he reaches the age of reason, he becomes the only judge of the best means to preserve himself; he becomes his own master."[157] The U.S. and international response to 9/11 was strong and resolute; if they wish to remain in power, foreign state leaders who provide terrorist groups with nuclear weapons or fissile material would have to have a high degree of confidence that even their clandestine support of terrorist nuclear activities could remain hidden. Given the combination of intelligence, law enforcement, and nuclear forensic and attribution tools, it is likely that, over time, the genesis of a nuclear attack against the United States or its allies could be determined, and the evidentiary threshold may by very low.

The supply-side focus of nuclear terrorism should not be fixated on national de jure or de facto nuclear weapons states. As mentioned earlier, any terrorist attempting to construct an IND is likely to use the less sophisticated of the two basic nuclear weapons designs, the gun-type device. While plutonium can be used in a gun-type device, because of its high spontaneous fission activity it does not work as well as HEU for this purpose.[158] To obtain HEU, terrorists may not necessarily gravitate to those locations having the most fissile material; it is far more likely they will search out the most vulnerable sources. As a result, another area of international vulnerability with regard to nuclear terrorism is the civilian use of HEU.

HEU IN CIVILIAN COMMERCE

HEU is used in both military and civilian applications, and experts generally agree that HEU used in civilian applications (research reactors, critical and subcritical assemblies, and medical isotope production) is less secure than HEU dedicated to military purposes.[159] As part of the competing U.S. and Soviet "Atoms for Peace" programs launched in the 1950s, hundreds of HEU-fueled nuclear power reactors were built domestically and for export to over forty countries.[160] According to members of Princeton University's Program on Science and Global Security, "Atoms for Peace and similar programs created problems for the countries that supplied nuclear know-how and technology as well as those who were being encouraged to pursue it, fueled regional rivalries, and became the bane of the international community."[161] Lightly irradiated spent fuel at research reactors around the world "would require some chemical processing before [it] could be used in a bomb, [but] most groups with skills needed to make a nuclear bomb from HEU metal would be able to put together the skills needed to get HEU from HEU research reactor fuel."[162] One case that demonstrates some of the hazards of nuclear research reactors is the Pelindaba Nuclear Research Center in South Africa.

THE CASE OF PELINDABA NUCLEAR RESEARCH CENTER

In November 2007 the Pelindaba Nuclear Research Center in South Africa was penetrated.[163] The facility targeted within the complex housed one hundred kilograms of weapons-grade HEU, possibly enough for two to four nuclear weapons. According to reports, two groups of four armed criminals attacked the facility from different directions in what appears to have been a coordinated attack. According to the South African Nuclear Energy Corporation, one group of technically sophisticated criminals deactivated several layers of security, including a ten-thousand-volt electric fence. While images of the men breaching the fence were captured on closed-caption television, no guards were watching the monitors. The breach of the fence and reported lack of security personnel monitoring the closed-caption cameras imply that there could have been insider collusion. Another element that indicates possible insider collusion is that there is a dispute over the amount of time it took guards to get to the control room. The off-duty guard who was in the control center and was shot by the intruders when they entered it claims it should have taken no more than three minutes, and it was reportedly twenty-four minutes before they arrived.[164] One group of intruders was able to break into an emergency control center, breach an electronically sealed control room, and spend nearly forty-five minutes "inside one of South Africa's most heavily guarded 'national key points'—defined by the government as any place or area that is so important that its loss, damage, disruption, or immobilization may prejudice the Republic."[165] A second group of four attackers failed in their attempt to break in. An off-duty security guard was shot when he discovered the break-in but was able to trigger an alarm. The four armed intruders nevertheless were able to escape through the same fence breach through which they entered.

The government of South Africa fired the two guards who should have been monitoring the security cameras. However, the South African government maintains it does not know the motivation for the attack and does not believe it was a coordinated terrorist attack having the aim of acquiring HEU stored at Pelindaba. In the course of the investigation following the incident, the South African government did not interview the guard who was shot in the intrusion until a team from CBS News's *60 Minutes* arrived and started to ask questions about the incident. The U.S. government has offered to convert Pelindaba's reactor to operate on LEU from HEU but has been rebuffed by the South African government.

The resolution of the event remains somewhat mysterious. Local police arrested three suspects a week after the attack and subsequently released them. The South African Nuclear Energy Corporation suspended six employees. No group, terrorist or otherwise criminal, claimed responsibility for the attack, and public details about the event remain elusive. The IAEA, at the request of the South African government, visited Pelindaba in January 2008 to exchange views of the lessons learned. The IAEA team of experts concluded that "there was no evidence that sensitive nuclear areas were under any threat at any time during the incident. It recommended specific proposals for security training and equipment to the South African authorities." Finally, the group stated that the security upgrade plan at Pelindaba, started in 2006, "provides an 'appropriate basis' for ensuring physical protection of nuclear material and nuclear facilities at the site."[166]

This case is important insofar as it demonstrates the global nature of the HEU and nuclear terrorism problem. Too often the focus is on Russia or Pakistan as sources of fissile material, but as table 8 illustrates, there may be more vulnerable material located across a broad range of non-weapons states. Moreover, questions could be asked about the extent to which the U.S. Intelligence Community was aware that the Pelindaba plant had been successfully penetrated just two years earlier. Was the Intelligence Community aware that "a senior facility official was assassinated in June 2007?"[167] Was the Intelligence Community providing information to requisite State Department, DOE, and DOD personnel about the potential vulnerabilities and threats to the HEU at Pelindaba? Today the Intelligence Community and other security-related agencies are working to refine a prioritized list of vulnerable nuclear facilities and nuclear materials, known as the (classified) Nuclear Materials Information Program. As will be discussed more in chapter 7, the value of such a list is to prioritize facilities with the most vulnerable nuclear materials and work with national officials bilaterally or multilaterally either to remove the vulnerable material or to secure it in place.

As outlined in chapter 1, the global stockpile of military and civilian HEU is estimated to range between approximately 1,400 and 2,000 metric tons.[168] The IPFM estimates that "very roughly, one hundred tons of HEU are in the fuel cycles of civilian research reactors worldwide and in Russia's nuclear-powered civilian vessels. Most civilian HEU is in the NPT nuclear weapons states. About ten tons are in nonnuclear weapon states."[169] These 100 tons of civilian application HEU would be sufficient for over one thousand gun-type nuclear weapons and more than twice as many implosion-type weapons. According to the IPFM, "International efforts to convert HEU-fueled research reactors to LEU have reduced the annual demand of the material by about

TABLE 8. NUMBER OF NON-WEAPONS STATES THAT HAVE POSSESSED MORE THAN ONE KG OF HEU

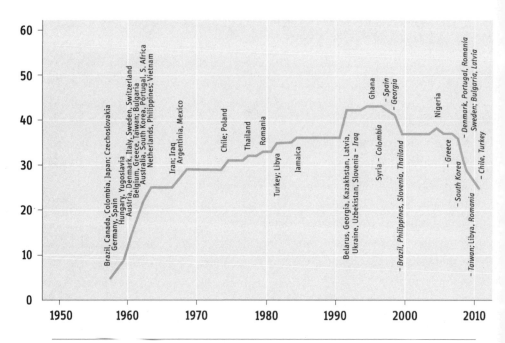

Source: International Panel on Fissile Material, *Global Fissile Materials Report 2010: Balancing the Books—Production and Stocks,* http://www.fissilematerials.org/ipfm/site_down/gfmr10.pdf.

250 kilograms [of HEU] per year. Yet, there are still about 100 sites in 40 countries where the material can be found in significant quantities, at operational or shut down, but not yet decommissioned HEU-fueled reactors."[170]

Numerous sources, including the IPFM, the Institute for Science and International Security, and the Center for Nonproliferation Studies, have catalogued and tracked this material. Table 8 illustrates where HEU in the civilian sector resides. As the table demonstrates, terrorists searching for approximately fifty kilograms of HEU have no shortage of states to target. Fissile material security is only as good as the weakest link in the chain.

SECURITY STANDARDS AND CIVILIAN HEU USE

Despite the significant amount of fissile material in global stockpiles and in civilian research reactors, with widely varying levels of security, today there is no single global set of standards for fissile material security. United Nations Security Council Resolution 1540, passed April 28, 2004, calls for "all States, in accordance with their national procedures, [to] adopt and enforce *appropriate effective* [emphasis added] laws which prohibit any non-State actor to manufacture, acquire, possess, develop, transport, transfer, or use nuclear, chemical, or biological weapons and their means of delivery, in particular for terrorist purposes."[171] The resolution discusses, at a very generic level, export control laws, physical protection measures, border control, and measures to account for and secure nuclear, chemical, and biological materials and technologies; it never defines "appropriate effective." The IAEA provides training to nations on physical security measures at a nation's request, but ultimately, the states themselves are responsible for passing their own laws and developing their own security standards.

The United States has played a leading role in building international norms against the use of HEU in civilian commerce, with occasional setbacks. China's nuclear test in 1974 led to the creation in 1978 of the U.S.-led Reduced Enrichment for Research and Test Reactors (RERTR) program, an effort to reduce the role of HEU in civilian commerce globally. Though the subject of various bureaucratic battles over the years, the RERTR program continues to exist today as part of the broader Global Threat Reduction Initiative.[172] The GTRI has three goals: (1) convert research reactors from the use of HEU to LEU, (2) remove or dispose of excess WMD-usable nuclear and radiological materials, and (3) protect at-risk WMD-usable nuclear and radiological materials from theft and sabotage. According to the DOE–National Nuclear Security Administration (NNSA), the GTRI has made substantial progress, including:

- Converting or verifying the shutdown of a cumulative 62 HEU research reactors.[173] By 2018 the program's goal is to convert 129 HEU reactors to LEU fuel. If additional reactors are not added to the 129, the program is 43 percent complete. While some reactors can convert using existing LEU, new fuels are in the process of being developed for other reactors that cannot use standard LEU.
- Removing 589 kilograms of Russian-origin HEU and 1,290 kilograms of Russian-origin plutonium, enough to make more than seventy-five nuclear bombs. By 2015 the program's goal is to remove or dispose of

about 2,200 kilograms of Russian-origin HEU from civilian sites. If no more HEU is targeted for removal or disposal, the program is currently 27 percent complete.

- Removing 1,146 kilograms of U.S.-origin HEU. The program's goal is to remove or dispose of about 1,250 kilograms of HEU from civilian sites, enough for fifty crude nuclear weapons. If no additional U.S.-origin HEU is added, the program is 92 percent complete.[174]

Other assessments of the progress made with respect to research reactors have been provided by Matthew Bunn of Harvard University's Belfer Center for Science and International Affairs. According to Bunn, through FY 2010, nearly all of the global HEU-fueled research reactors have been upgraded to meet IAEA security recommendations, but some upgrades would not be enough to defend against terrorist or criminal capabilities.[175]

While these results are impressive and have decreased the threat of nuclear terrorism by decreasing the amount of fissile material most vulnerable to terrorist targeting, substantial progress remains to be made. For example, according to Bunn, two-thirds of U.S. HEU abroad is not covered by a U.S. take-back offer.[176] According to physicists Frank von Hippel and Alexander Glaser, the Department of Energy's list of HEU reactors is incomplete. They state, "Current efforts largely exclude reactor types that make up half of the world's HEU-fueled reactors: critical assemblies and pulsed reactors. Worldwide, there are at least 38 HEU-fueled critical assemblies and 19 HEU-fueled pulsed reactors."[177] Citing the 1995 RERTR Program Execution Plan, these reactors are, according to Glaser and von Hippel, categorized as "research reactors using HEU fuels that are not part of the RERTR Program." The pulsed-power and critical assembly reactors, the two physicists say, could be decommissioned and replaced with highly accurate computer simulations. Moreover, Russia, which accounts for 33 percent of the world's HEU reactors and more than 50 percent of the world's civilian HEU, "has yet to make a commitment to convert or decommission any of its own HEU-fueled research reactors."[178]

It has been thirty years since the inception of the RERTR program, and today there remain one hundred sites across forty countries that possess HEU in civilian commerce. As the DOE states, some material may not be targeted for disposal or removal if it is stored in a secure location or has an "acceptable" disposition path. It could be argued that because of many factors—not the least of which are sovereignty, differences in national assessment of the nuclear terrorism threat, economic and financial concerns stemming from the elimination of HEU from civilian commerce, and national pride and prestige—some nation-states may never acquiesce to a total elimination of HEU from civilian commerce. According to some experts, technical hurdles to the elimination of HEU from civilian commerce are being overcome, yet the political hurdles to complete elimination appear to be more intransigent. Nonproliferation expert William Potter provided the following comprehensive list of reasons for such intransigence:

> The most significant obstacles to delegitimizing the commercial use of HEU are political and strategic in nature. They pertain to questions about the relative importance of combating nuclear terrorism vis-à-vis other international challenges, including nuclear weapons disarmament; an allergic reaction by some states to any efforts to limit anything in the civilian nuclear sector, even if it has no technical or commercial justification; considerations of status and prestige, as well as fear of losing out on the benefits of research on what was once "cutting-edge" technology; the potential perception of a HEU phase-out initiative as one mainly of interest to the developed/Northern world; and the possibility that ostensibly civilian HEU stocks are seen by some capitals as a strategic asset and/or hedge to preserve future nuclear weapons options.[179]

While the United States has been at the forefront of efforts to delegitimize HEU in civilian commerce, Anya Loukianova and Cristina Hansell of the James Martin Center for Nonproliferation Studies assert that the United States might consider the following actions to provide greater incentives for other nations to eliminate the use of HEU in civilian commerce:

* lead by example—consider declaring additional HEU to be in excess of military needs in exchange for other countries' deeper engagement in HEU reduction efforts;
* rescind the Burr Amendment (to the 2005 Energy Policy Act), which loosened restrictions on the export of HEU; and

- engage in international evaluations of the threats posed by HEU and develop new recommendations for securing and managing HEU.[180]

While the delegitimization of HEU in civilian commerce is attempting to put the "nuclear genie back in the bottle" (to some extent), the nuclear power industry may be (or maybe not given Japan's nuclear crisis at the Fukushima Daiichi nuclear power plant) headed for a renaissance, another potential concern for nuclear terrorism.

A GLOBAL NUCLEAR POWER RENAISSANCE . . . IN PERIL?

The civilian nuclear power industry is experiencing substantially renewed interest globally. According to the Congressional Research Service, "New permit applications for 30 reactors have been filed in the United States, with another 150 planned or proposed globally, with about a dozen already under construction."[181] According to Mohamed ElBaradei, as recently as ten years ago nuclear power had stopped growing. "Now, it is seen as offering part of the solution to surging global demand for energy, uncertainty about energy supply, and concern about climate change. In the last two years, 50 Member States have expressed interest in considering the possible introduction of nuclear power and asked for Agency support."[182] Whether this renewed interest materializes into operating plants remains an open question and a function of many factors, including but not limited to (1) safe operations of nuclear power plants, as the Three Mile Island (United States, 1979) and Chernobyl (Ukraine, 1986) accidents substantially undermined global support for nuclear power (whether the Fukushima Daiichi [Japan 2011] nuclear crisis has the same effect remains to be seen); (2) cost and available financing (nuclear power plants require multibillion-dollar capital investments and perceptions of unsafe operation will increase risk and, therefore, likely undermine private sector financing for such projects); (3) price of fossil fuels (if the long-term trend continues upward, nuclear power generation may become increasingly attractive); (4) investment in renewable energy such as wind and solar power; (5) effective and efficient technologies to handle the disposition of spent nuclear waste; and (6) the extent to which the international community takes decisive and binding action on measures to ameliorate climate change by decreasing carbon emissions.

There are currently 443 nuclear power plants operating globally, generating 368 gigawatts or approximately 15 percent of the world's electricity. The United States uses nuclear power to generate about 20 percent of its total electrical needs. The comparative figures for others nations include France, 78.1 percent; South Korea, 38.6 percent; Germany, 31.4 percent; Japan, 30 percent; Russia, 16 percent; South Africa, 4.4 percent; Pakistan, 2.7 percent; India, 2.7 percent; and China, 1.8 percent.[183] The nuclear power generation business was essentially moribund after the aforementioned accidents at Three Mile Island and Chernobyl. The March 2011 earthquake, tsunami, and subsequent nuclear crisis in Japan may have a similarly chilling effect on any nuclear power renaissance. Demand for electric power, nevertheless, will increase (or decrease) with global economic growth (or contraction), so it is likely that nuclear power will continue to be an element in industrial nations' portfolio of power generation sources.

There are two main reasons for the renewed interest in nuclear power generation today: the likely long-term trend in fossil fuel price increases and a desire to provide electricity without continuing to produce a large amount of greenhouse gases, primarily carbon. However, some Middle Eastern nations that have expressed an interest in enhanced nuclear power may have done so for reasons that transcend these two ostensible purposes.[184] Official rationales offered by these countries include powering water desalinization plants, diversifying their energy industries in the face of increasing energy demand, and furthering economic and scientific development.[185] Two large regional powers in the Middle East (and rivals with neighboring Iran), Turkey and Egypt, are exploring the option of building seven nuclear power plants—four in Egypt and three in Turkey, respectively—over the next decade.[186] According to nonproliferation expert Joseph Cirincione, "This is not primarily about nuclear energy. It's a hedge against Iran. They're starting their engines. It takes decades to build a nuclear infrastructure, and they're beginning to do it now. They're saying 'If there's going to be an arms race, we're going to be in it.'"[187] Mohammed ElBaradei has reportedly stated, "You don't really even need to have a nuclear weapon. . . . It's enough to buy yourself an insurance policy by developing [nuclear power generation] capability, and then sit on it. Let's not kid ourselves: Ninety percent of it is an insurance policy, deterrence."[188]

From a nuclear terrorism perspective, the primary concern with a potential renaissance in commercial nuclear power generation is the mastery of the nuclear fuel cycle and an increased demand for nuclear fuel, which would mean more fissile material in commerce and transportation. If more nations determine that they must master uranium enrichment and spent fuel reprocessing in order to indigenously produce their own nuclear fuels, the terrorist target set will broaden substantially.

In order for commercial nuclear power to expand internationally without an attendant increase in enrichment and reprocessing, nations developing new nuclear power generation plants must forgo their "inalienable right," preserved under Article IV of the Nonproliferation Treaty, for the "development, research, production, and use of nuclear energy for peaceful purposes without discrimination and in conformity with Articles I and II of the Treaty. . . . All parties to the Treaty undertake to facilitate, and have the right to participate in, the fullest possible exchange of equipment, materials, and scientific and technological information for peaceful uses of nuclear energy."[189]

Whether a country is willing to forgo this "inalienable right" is a complex question determined by myriad factors, including but not limited to national pride and sovereignty, economic and financing issues, political and strategic issues, and the extent to which the country wants to maintain the option at some later date to develop nuclear weapons.

According to the State Department, the United States has been working both unilaterally and multilaterally with the IAEA "to ensure that countries with peaceful nuclear programs will have reliable access to nuclear fuel at a reasonable cost, thereby eliminating any rational economic incentive for acquiring enrichment or reprocessing capabilities."[190] Some countries, including the United Arab Emirates, Jordan, Saudi Arabia, and Bahrain, have signed memorandums of understanding with the United States to "rely on the market for fuel rather than create indigenous enrichment and reprocessing capabilities."[191] Since the entry into force of the NPT in 1970, the IAEA has been working on various efforts to multilateralize the nuclear fuel cycle. According to the IAEA, in the late 1970s and early 1980s many international fuel bank options were advanced yet "eventually surrendered under pressure from competing interests driven by the dynamics of the Cold War: nationalism, economics, and mistrusts and limits of technology."[192] However, the idea of an international nuclear fuel bank, in some form or fashion, may be coming to fruition. In September 2006 the Nuclear Threat Initiative, with direct support from billionaire investor Warren Buffett, pledged $50 million to the IAEA to "help create a low-enriched uranium stockpile to support nations that make the sovereign choice not to build indigenous fuel cycle capabilities."[193] The offer was conditional upon the following two factors: (1) the IAEA approves the establishment of this reserve, and (2) one or more member states contribute an additional $100 million in funding or an equivalent value in LEU to jump-start the reserve.[194] The multilateral fuel bank initiative was further supported recently with a $32 million pledge by the European Union.[195] In December 2010, after years of trying, the IAEA Board of Governors created such a multilateral fuel bank. While this development is very positive from a nuclear terrorism perspective, it does not address other multifaceted reasons that motivate nation-states to want their own uranium enrichment plants.[196]

In the longer term, the United States has proposed, through the Global Nuclear Energy Partnership (GNEP), a program to work with other nations to "help provide reliable, emission-free energy with less of the waste burden than old technologies and without making available separated plutonium that could be used by rogue states or terrorists for nuclear weapons."[197] Under the GNEP, the DOE is "developing advanced reprocessing (or recycling) technologies to extract plutonium and uranium from spent nuclear fuel, as well as an advanced reactor that could fully destroy long-lived radioactive isotopes. . . . Although long a goal of nuclear power proponents, the reprocessing of spent fuel is also seen as a weapons proliferation risk, because the plutonium extracted for new reactor fuel can also be used for nuclear weapons."[198] As a result, one of the primary goals of the GNEP is to develop fuel recycling technologies that will not result in the production of pure plutonium that could be used in nuclear weapons. Arms control and nonproliferation experts, including Frank von Hippel of Princeton University, Edwin Lyman of the Union of Concerned Scientists, and others, are vehemently opposed to the GNEP for four essential reasons:

- While the DOE is promoting the GNEP program on the basis of nonproliferation, according to these experts it has had the exact opposite effect. Since the GNEP's inception, eight countries "have notified the IAEA that they reserve the right to pursue enrichment and reprocessing technologies, including South Africa and Argentina, which are considering reviving their enrichment programs."[199] The GNEP has also, according to this group, violated the DOE's own goal of "no more separated plutonium."

- The cost of the GNEP, according to this group, is likely to be prohibitive. Citing data from a study done by the DOE's Idaho National Laboratory, the group stated that the GNEP reprocessing program would cost over $1 billion per year *more* than the current once-through system using light-water reactors.[200]

- Reprocessing would result in huge additional volumes of liquid, high-level waste. "As a result, contaminated sites at Hanford, WA, Savannah River Site, SC, and West Valley, NY, have required massive clean-up efforts that have and continue to cost billions of dollars. It is astonishing how DOE could propose a vast new reprocessing program when it has failed to effectively deal with the legacy wastes from prior reprocessing facilities."[201]

- Finally, according to this group, many in the civilian nuclear industry do not consider the GNEP a viable solution. In the report *Nuclear Power Joint Fact-Finding*, the group cites a coalition of nuclear utilities—including Exelon, Entergy, Southern Nuclear, GE Energy-Nuclear, Duke Energy, and others—as concluding that the "GNEP is not a strategy for resolving either the radioactive waste problem or the weapons proliferation problem" and that "critical elements of the GNEP are unlikely to succeed."[202]

NET ASSESSMENT: NUCLEAR POWER RENAISSANCE

The bottom line on enhanced nuclear power generation globally is that it remains only a potential; a similar massive increase in nuclear power was projected in the 1970s and never materialized. Today, if nation-states find it economical (very much an open question when full-cycle costs from construction to the disposition of spent fuel are considered), it is possible that such an endeavor may "inevitably lead to a further increase in the stock and flows of uranium and plutonium, materials that are fundamental parts of the nuclear fuel cycle and could be used to make nuclear weapons."[203] There are, however, many reasons why nation-states might make a decision to pursue nuclear power—perhaps as a security hedge—even if it is not economical. For increased nuclear power generation to be implemented in a nuclear terrorism risk-neutral manner, the front and back ends of the nuclear fuel cycle must be tailored to reduce (elimination may be impossible) proliferation risk. On the front end, all future reactors should be powered by LEU, and the multilateral nuclear fuel bank created in December 2010 could provide the fuel to discourage any additional indigenous uranium enrichment. On the back end of the fuel cycle, reprocessing of spent fuel resulting in more plutonium production should be actively discouraged. While further research and development on reactor technologies may help with the back end of the fuel cycle, disposition of spent fuel today remains a contentious issue. As mentioned previously, terrorists are far more likely to use HEU in a gun-type device than they are to use plutonium. However, any grade of plutonium can be used to fashion a nuclear device, and far less of it is needed for this purpose. Nuclear power and fossil fuels are not the only means of generating electricity; renewable energy should find some place in the international energy mix.

SUPPLY-SIDE FORCES: A SUMMARY

Since the dissolution of the Soviet Union in 1991, substantial progress has been made in protecting nuclear weapons and fissile material. The sustainability of the Cooperative Threat Reduction and MPC&A Programs will continue to be a challenge as U.S. funding for programs in Russia is phased out by 2013. As mentioned in chapter 4, in an April 2009 speech in Prague, President Obama stated, "Today, I am announcing a new international effort to secure all vulnerable nuclear material around the world within four years. We will set new standards, expand our cooperation with Russia, and pursue new partnerships to lock down sensitive materials."[204]

Numerous sources, however, have found that while the administration is in the process of developing a plan to achieve these goals, in its FY 2010 budget Congress did not reflect the urgency outlined in the Czech Republic speech. According to Andrew Newman and Matthew Bunn of Harvard University, the $1.3 billion FY 2010 budget to improve controls over nuclear weapons, security of fissile material, as well as nuclear expertise overseas was ". . . essentially the same as the FY 2009 appropriation and $30 million less than that FY 2008 appropriation."[205] This view is also held by Kenneth Luongo, president of the Partnership for Global Security. Referring to the FY 2010 budget, Mr. Luongo stated,

> This budget provides an adequate stream of funding for the important
> mission of preventing nuclear and biological terrorism, but it is not suf-

ficient to meet the Obama administration's commitment to secure "all nuclear weapons and material at vulnerable sites within four years" as well as its other ambitious WMD security objectives. The budget . . . needs to be significantly increased across the board if there is any hope of meeting the President's high-priority WMD proliferation prevention goals. A stagnant or modestly increased funding profile will be inadequate and amount to business as usual.[206]

The FY 2011 budget request asks for an increase of $320 million for key NNSA and DOD programs that support the president's effort to secure all vulnerable nuclear material in four years. According to Luongo, the Defense Authorization Act for FY 2011 approved the full request, but the Continuing Resolution (under which the government is operating in February 2011) did not appropriate the funds.[207]

While the United States and Russia have made substantial progress in securing Russian nuclear weapons and fissile material, a revanchist Russia could undermine the future cooperation necessary for these countries to implement their pledges on nuclear security made at the July 2009 summit. Russia's level of political commitment and self assessment of vulnerable nuclear materials in its territory may also be waning. Moreover, while the Russian economy has prospered and the country, as a result, has the financial capacity to pay its nuclear managers a respectable wage regularly, much of Russia's wealth relies on highly priced commodities, a market that is notoriously volatile.

With respect to Pakistan, the resurgence of al Qaeda and the increasingly assertive Taliban, combined with political instability and possible penetration of the army and ISI by individuals sympathetic to extremist ideology, perhaps makes this country the most dangerous from a nuclear terrorism perspective. While much about Pakistan's nuclear weapons security and the extent to which the United States has provided assistance to enhance that security remains classified, it appears that a reasonable amount of assistance has been provided, and U.S. officials in a position to know appear confident that Pakistan's nuclear weapons are secure. The January 2011 assassination of the governor of Pakistan's Punjab region by his own bodyguard—and the country's reaction to that event—is cause for continuing concern on numerous levels, not the least of which is the reaffirmation that radical ideologues can and have penetrated positions of trust. Any country's nuclear security is only as good as its weakest link, and continued political instability and rising radicalism in Pakistan present increasing nuclear terrorism risks.

While North Korea and Iran represent substantial threats to the nuclear nonproliferation regime, given their aberrant international behavior, this risk may not necessarily extend to the provision by either country of an intact nuclear weapon or fissile material to a terrorist group. Analysts must always be cautious about projecting a rational standard of decision making onto other nations. However, it is an ironclad law of politics and international relations that regimes value their survival dearly. The U.S. declaratory policy on the actions it would take if nuclear weapons were used against it or against its friends and allies will likely provide even irrational actors a cause for hesitation before they sell nuclear weapons or fissile material to uncontrollable terrorist groups. As David Kay, a former United Nations weapons inspector, stated with respect to nuclear unknowns vis-à-vis Iran, "What are the command-and-control arrangements for Iran's nuclear program? Where is President Mahmoud Ahmadinejad in this mix?"[208] President Ahmadinejad may have a tendency to make incendiary statements, but to what extent is he actually in control of policy, particularly on military and nuclear matters? If not the U.S. declaratory policy on retribution for a nuclear terrorist attack, the simple fact that nuclear weapons and fissile material are the "crown jewels" of a nation, demonstrating its scientific progression and possibly serving as a regional deterrent, will likely give pause to a nation considering nuclear weapons or fissile material transfer to any nonstate actor. There may be situations under which, for example, North Korea or Iran (should it develop nuclear weapons) might sell or otherwise transfer nuclear weapons or fissile material to a terrorist group, but these situations appear very limited.

The use of HEU in civilian applications continues to constitute a nuclear terrorism risk. While momentum seems to be moving in the direction of banning such use, a number of nations remain holdouts, including those producing radiological sources for medical use such as South Africa. Russia continues to power civilian icebreaker ships with HEU and has not committed explicitly to converting or decommissioning its HEU-fueled research reactors. Politically and strategically, some nonnuclear weapons states refuse to cede their "inalienable right" to any technologies or processes that are useful for both civilian nuclear power and nuclear weapons. International norms against the use of HEU in civilian commerce are essential. Incentives designed to encourage states to convert or decommission HEU-fueled nuclear facilities or relinquish their HEU for LEU or specialty fuels are a movement in the right direction.

Secondary proliferation networks, particularly those networks that may have had success in the past and went underground in the aftermath of Pakistan's house arrest of A. Q. Khan, also remain a concern. Combating clandestine procurement networks that could be leveraged just as easily by nonstate actors as by nation-states will remain a cause for which the international community must remain ever vigilant. Integrated and cooperative intelligence, law enforcement, and border security efforts are likely to be the most successful tools in the fight against these networks.

Finally, it should not go without mention that the United States has had its own share of problems with respect to nuclear weapons and nuclear weapons component security. In the last few years, there have been two instances in which U.S. custodianship over its own nuclear weapons, or critical components for them, has been deemed inadequate. The first incident occurred in August 2006 but was not discovered until March 2008. It involved the shipment to Taiwan, a nonnuclear nation that China (a nuclear weapons state) continues to believe is one of its provinces, of four nuclear weapon nose-cone fuse assemblies. Reportedly, the Defense Logistics Agency shipped the fuse assemblies to Taiwan instead of four replacement battery packs for use in Taiwan's fleet of UH-1 Huey helicopters.[209] The fuse is meant to detonate the nuclear warhead on a Minuteman III intercontinental ballistic missile (ICBM) as it nears the ground. In the second instance, in August 2007 advanced cruise missiles carrying the W80-1 nuclear warhead were mistakenly loaded onto a B-52 bomber for a flight from Minot Air Force Base, North Dakota, to Barksdale Air Force Base, Louisiana. While the weapons remained in air force custody and control at all times, the mistake was not recognized until the aircraft landed at Barksdale, which meant that the nuclear weapons were "unaccounted for during the approximately 3 ½ hour flight between bases."[210]

These two incidents led Secretary of Defense Robert Gates to commission a study of nuclear weapons security. Ostensibly, as a result of these incidents and subsequent investigative findings, the secretary of defense fired the air force's top civilian and military leaders.[211] A task force led by former secretary of defense James Schlesinger and established by the secretary of defense to examine nuclear command and control concluded that the air force should "convert its existing Air Force Space Command—which now has responsibility for the service's land-based nuclear missiles but not other nuclear weapons—into an organization called Air Force Strategic Command. The new organization would 'be held accountable for the efficacy of the nuclear mission.'"[212] The air force is in the process of standing up the Global Strike Command, which, according to former air force secretary Michael Donley, "restores the necessary focus on the nuclear missions [and] provides a clear chain of command for all Air Force nuclear forces."[213] Notwithstanding these two nuclear security incidents, given the generally sound security that the United States affords its nuclear weapons and fissile material it is unlikely that terrorists would acquire a nuclear weapon or fissile material for a nuclear weapon from within the United States. More troubling, however, may be the state of security of the approximately 150–240 tactical nuclear weapons the United States has deployed in Europe.[214] According to the air force's own blue-ribbon study, which conducted numerous European field visits, "A consistently noted theme throughout these visits was that most sites require significant additional resources to meet DOD security requirements."[215] Beyond the resource question is the issue of nuclear weapons becoming relatively less important to the air force as mutually assured destruction becomes less relevant to U.S. national security.[216]

While this treatment of the supply side of the nuclear terrorism issue is not necessarily comprehensive, it provides the reader with an understanding of the major issues facing global powers today as they attempt to prevent terrorist groups from acquiring nuclear weapons.

We turn next to the relationship between nuclear terrorism and nuclear deterrence. Are terrorist groups that are contemplating nuclear terrorism deterrable? If not, how effective is extended deterrence? What is the status of U.S. and international nuclear forensics?

SUPPLY-SIDE VARIABLES AND TRENDS AFFECTING NUCLEAR TERRORISM

Numerous variables and trends affect the probability of a nuclear terrorist attack. Some of these variables and questions pertaining to them are outlined in table 9.

TABLE 9. SUPPLY-SIDE VARIABLES AFFECTING NUCLEAR TERRORISM

Variable	Impact and questions
Protection (or removal) of fissile material at the source—status and effectiveness. As is documented throughout this book, as a result of the Cooperative Threat Reduction and other programs, the protection of fissile material, particularly within the former Soviet Union, is much improved. However, additional vulnerable materials need to be secured or removed.	To what extent is Russia going to provide the necessary resources and attention to sustain the programs, technologies, and practices that it was provided through the Cooperative Threat Reduction Program? Has the creation of the Nuclear Materials Information Program been translated into a concrete action plan to secure fissile material that is determined to be most vulnerable? Can President Obama's commitment to secure all vulnerable fissile material in four years be implemented?
Protection of tacit nuclear weapons know-how—status and effectiveness. The more nuclear-trained scientists and technicians willing to assist terrorists, for ideological or monetary reasons, the greater the danger on the supply side.	Does the international community, or at least national nuclear authorities in de facto or de jure nuclear states, know the identities and sympathies of its nuclear scientists? What measures are in place to guard against nuclear scientists who may be motivated to provide their expertise to al-Qaeda or other terrorist groups not by financial gain but by jihadist or other radical ideology?
Amount of fissile material in commerce—increasing or decreasing. A nuclear power renaissance could lead to substantially more HEU and plutonium entering commerce, and that would result in more transportation of these dangerous materials and greater opportunities for terrorists to target them when they may be most vulnerable.	To what extent are appropriate incentives in place to cause countries to take actions that may be in the international community's security interest yet might not be in the sovereign nation's commercial or strategic interests? How are the demands of long-term energy security balanced with long-term international nuclear security?
Continued production of fissile material for weapons purposes—increasing or decreasing. According to the International Panel on Fissile Materials, India (a non-NPT member and country with which the United States has a civil nuclear cooperation agreement), Israel (a major U.S., non-NATO ally), Pakistan (a U.S. ally in the global war on terrorism), and North Korea continue to produce fissile material for nuclear weapons. The greater the amount of weapons-grade fissile material produced, the greater the target base for terrorist groups.	What is the level of political will countries are willing to exert to encourage the cessation of weapons-grade fissile material production? How does the United States weigh and balance its counterterrorism versus counterproliferation goals with respect to India, Israel, North Korea, and Pakistan?
Amount of strategic nuclear weapons in U.S. and Russian possession. The United States and Russia possess 95 percent of global fissile material and nuclear weapons, which, some argue, make it incumbent upon them to lead by example by decreasing the importance of nuclear weapons in their defense postures.	Some have suggested that the United States and Russia could achieve the same level of strategic deterrence as today at strategic nuclear warhead levels in the range of 850 warheads each.[1] New START limits of 1,550 strategic warheads each could, arguably, go lower. Will a revanchist Russia interested in regaining its superpower status derail strategic arms control? Will U.S.-Russian differences over issues such as ballistic missile

The United States continues to have tactical nuclear weapons deployed in Europe, and Russia continues to possess nonstrategic nuclear weapons, in part, because of the presence of U.S. tactical warheads in Europe. Decisions about U.S. tactical nuclear weapons are based on these weapons being viewed by some as critical for the NATO alliance and by others as an attractive terrorist target.	weapons on European soil?[2] In the context of the ongoing Nuclear Posture Review, perhaps it is appropriate to reconsider the benefits the forward deployment of such systems provide to U.S. and allied security against the potential international security vulnerabilities such systems may create.
Successful international community efforts in detecting undeclared nuclear activity in NPT countries. A substantial number of countries that have safeguards agreements with the IAEA have not signed the Additional Protocol that provides for, among other measures, enhanced inspection procedures designed to detect undeclared nuclear activities. Without such authorities, arguably, undeclared nuclear activities or diversions of fissile material in civilian applications could increase illicit trafficking in fissile materials.	Does the IAEA have the appropriate legal authorities and level of resources to effectively execute its expanded mission, particularly with respect to the implementation of U.N. Security Council Resolution 1540 and the IAEA's Additional Protocol? What incentives and disincentives can be put in place to encourage the increased adoption of Additional Protocols?
Extent to which nuclear threshold countries, like Iran, continue to enrich uranium or reprocess spent nuclear fuel in order to develop HEU or plutonium. The U.S. Intelligence Community concluded that in 2003 Iran ceased its nuclear weapons program (defined rather parochially). Yet Iran continues to violate the terms of numerous U.N. Security Council resolutions and to deny requests for information from the IAEA on potential programs to develop nuclear weapons.	How willing is the international community to continue to confront Iran should it decide to jettison the NPT and overtly pursue a nuclear weapons program? If it is indeed "unacceptable" for Iran to become a nuclear power, how effective would a preemptive attack against Iran's nuclear weapons infrastructure be? Is delaying the Iranian nuclear weapons program for an undetermined period of time considered a success? Would an attack on Iranian facilities " . . . do more to spur than to delay the country's acquisition of nuclear weapons?"[3]
Extent to which, if at all, the international community implements the multinational nuclear fuel bank, which could provide nuclear reactor fuels in exchange for commitments from countries desiring civilian nuclear power not to pursue uranium enrichment and spent fuel reprocessing.	How are the NPT's "inalienable rights" to pursue technology for peaceful use of nuclear power balanced against fuel bank participation, which may require commitments not to pursue uranium enrichment?

Table by author.

1 See Testimony of Robert L. Gallucci, dean of the Edmund A. Walsh School of Foreign Service, Georgetown University, before the Subcommittee on Strategic Forces of the Senate Armed Services Committee, March 21, 2007.

2 See Steve Andreasen, former director for defense policy and arms control on the National Security Council from 1993 to 2001, "With Nuclear Weapons, a Lot Can Go Wrong," in StarTribune.com, Minneapolis–St. Paul, Minnesota, June 26, 2008. For arguments in favor of retaining U.S. nuclear weapons in Europe, see Report of the Secretary of Defense Task Force on DoD Nuclear Weapons Management, Phase II: Review of the DoD Nuclear Mission, December 2008.

3 See Mark Fitzpatrick, The Iranian Nuclear Crisis: Avoiding Worst-Case Outcomes, International Institute for Strategic Studies, Adelphi Paper 398, November 2008. According to Fitzpatrick, "In the aftermath of an unprovoked attack, Iran could be expected to withdraw from the NPT and engage the full resources of a unified nation in a determined nuclear-weapons-development programme."

SIX

Nuclear Terrorism, Deterrence, and Attribution

One of the central questions on nuclear terrorism is, can sophisticated terrorist groups be dissuaded from acquiring nuclear weapons? Should any such group acquire a nuclear weapon, can it be deterred from using it? The United States has extensive experience with deterrence, the vast majority of which was developed in the context of the Cold War competition between the United States and the Soviet Union. Yet the doctrine of mutually assured destruction tends not to fit neatly into a nonstate actor context. Unlike nation-state weapons, terrorist weapons do not come with a "return address." Can traditional and nontraditional sources of nuclear deterrence theory and practice play a role in deterring nuclear terrorism?

A question more fundamental than deterring nuclear terrorism is, can terrorism itself be deterred? Classical deterrence transcends theory, policy, and doctrine; it is a dynamic process that relies not necessarily on the rationality of national leaders but on emotion and fear.[1] Even actors perceived as "irrational" experience emotion and fear. "To be most effective, deterrence must create fear in the mind of the adversary—fear that he will not achieve his objectives, fear that his losses and pain will far outweigh any potential gains, fear that he will be punished."[2] Clarity and ambiguity are important in deterrence, the former insofar as the specific actions a country wants to deter and the latter regarding a target country's response should the aggressor party not be dissuaded from taking action. Similarly, the perception of a target state's decision-making process as overly coolheaded and rational may actually work against effective deterrence. "It hurts to betray ourselves as too fully rational and cool-headed. The fact that some elements may appear to be potentially 'out of control' can be beneficial to creating and reinforcing fears and doubts within the minds of an adversary's decision-makers."[3]

In order for deterrence to work, it is essential to understand what the United States' vital national interests are and to articulate the specific act or acts the country wants to prevent. What value does the country place on certain assets? It must be clear that "what we seek to deter has such a direct and strong relationship to our most important national interests, with few if any options but to carry through on our deterrent threat, that we can, and will, act. Thus, deterrence statements tied to direct defense of the homeland carry an inherently stronger credibility than deterrent threats extended on behalf of others."[4] Statements and declaratory policies of the United States with respect to the actions it may take in the aftermath of a nuclear terror attack on the homeland may be perceived by state and nonstate adversaries as being more credible than extended deterrence.

Classical deterrence has two main elements. The first is deterrence by punishment—dissuading an adversary from taking particular and specific actions (without saying what is permitted) by making that adversary aware that if it does act, the target state has the military resiliency and redundancy to counterattack massively against highly valued targets, whether they are represented by leadership, population centers, military installations, communication nodes, or economic targets. It was deterrence by punishment, or variations on mutually assured destruction, that operated between the United States and the Soviet Union during the Cold War. The second, arguably more subtle, element of deterrence is deterrence by denial, a process through which potential target countries attempt to dissuade aggressor states or nonstate actors from taking particular actions by denying them the achievement of their political, military, or economic goals. This is accomplished by demonstrating to the potential aggressor state or nonstate actor that any actions it takes against the target state would *not* have the desired effect. For example, if a terrorist wants to devastate an economy, economic and financial resiliency must demonstrate that no matter what the attack pattern or how high the immediate consequences, any terrorist action will fail to substantially undermine the ability of the country both to recover and to continue to employ its factors of production to grow the economy over time.

Two other elements of deterrence are worthy of mention and differentiation: extended deterrence and expanded deterrence. For this book's purposes, *extended deterrence* refers to positive security guarantees, which are represented by the extension of the U.S. nuclear security umbrella to other nations. The United States has extended its nuclear umbrella to NATO, South Korea, and Japan in a successful effort to prevent these nations from developing their own nuclear weapons (many of which are capable of doing so) in response to regional threats. *Expanded deterrence* applies to the case of terrorism, as it implies that while the terrorists themselves may not be deterrable, those who may enable them with financial, material, and other support may be.

EVOLUTION OF DETERRENCE AS APPLIED TO TERRORISM

A brief sketch of how post-9/11 thought on deterring terrorism and thus nuclear terrorism has evolved may prove helpful. The first *National Security Strategy* following the attacks of 9/11 said: "Traditional concepts of deterrence will not work against a terrorist enemy whose avowed tactics are wanton destruction and the target of innocents; whose so-called soldiers seek martyrdom in death and whose most potent protection is statelessness."[5]

This is a fairly static conceptual application of the deterrence process. Coming as it did in the few months following the attacks of 9/11, it represents a relatively inchoate level of understanding. However, thought continued to evolve as the United States gained more experience with and insight into the extremist mind and motivation. The 2006 *National Strategy to Combat Terrorism* further developed a concept of tailored deterrence:

A new deterrence calculus combines the need to deter terrorists and supporters from contemplating a WMD attack and, failing that, to dissuade them from actually conducting an attack. Traditional threats may not work because terrorists show a wanton disregard for the lives of innocents and in some cases for their own lives. We require a range of deterrence strategies that are tailored to the situation and the adversary. We will make clear that terrorists and those who aid or sponsor a WMD attack would face the prospect of an overwhelming response to any use of such weapons. We will seek to dissuade attacks by improving our ability to mitigate the effects of a terrorist attack involving WMD—to limit or prevent large-scale casualties, economic disruption, or panic. Finally, we will ensure that our capacity to determine the source of any attack is well known, and that our determination to respond overwhelmingly to any attack is never in doubt.[6]

This conceptualization of deterrence, as applied to nonstate actors, recognized that (1) the deterrence process could be tailored for use against nonstate actors, (2) the declaratory policy of an overwhelming response against a nation-state that assists a terrorist group in the acquisition of nuclear weapons and against nonstate actors themselves contemplating the use of nuclear weapons against the United States was a central element of expanded deterrence, (3) deterrence by denial would be an element of tailored deterrence and would be implemented by supporting societal resiliency and responding rapidly to the possible use of nuclear weapons against the United States, and (4) enhancing unilateral and multilateral nuclear attribution efforts and technologies that would allow the United States to determine, in the aftermath of any nuclear attack, where the fissile material in the bomb originated would be important. Nuclear attribution as a potential deterrence tool will be discussed more in depth later.

In October 2006 North Korea conducted its first nuclear weapons tests. Given that the U.S. Intelligence Community had reported that in 2005 North Korea had informed a U.S. academic that it could transfer nuclear weapons to terrorists if driven into a corner, this was cause for grave concern. President George W. Bush stated in a speech to the National University of Singapore shortly after the North Korean tests:

In this region, the most immediate threat of proliferation comes from North Korea. America's position is clear: The transfer of nuclear weapons or materiel by North Korea to states or non-state entities would be considered a grave threat to the United States, and we would hold North Korea fully accountable for the consequences of such action. For the sake of peace, it is vital that the nations of this region send a message to North Korea that the proliferation of nuclear technology to hostile regimes or terrorist networks will not be tolerated.[7]

This language was subsequently expanded by former national security adviser Stephen Hadley as he addressed the Fifth Anniversary of the Proliferation Security Initiative, a multilateral initiative designed to interdict shipments of WMD, their delivery mechanisms, and related materials using existing national legal authorities. Hadley broadened the commitment beyond just North Korea to all nations and added nonstate actors:

> Deterrence policy targeted at those states, organizations, and individuals who might assist terrorists in obtaining or using WMD can help the terrorists—help prevent the terrorists from ever gaining these weapons in the first place. The terrorists may not be deterrable themselves, but those they depend on for assistance may well be. The United States has made clear for many years that it reserves the right to respond with overwhelming force to the use of weapons of mass destruction against the United States, our people, our forces, and our friends and allies. Today we also make clear that the United States will hold any state, terrorist group, or other non-state actor or individual fully accountable for supporting or enabling terrorist efforts to obtain or use weapons of mass destruction—whether by facilitating, financing, or providing expertise or safe haven for such efforts.[8]

This statement would seem to cover leakage scenarios or situations under which, for reasons of lax security, fissile material leaks out of a supplier nation unintentionally. This scenario leads to a necessary discussion (see "Expanded Deterrence" section that follows). Moreover, does the reference to an "overwhelming response" in the context of nuclear terrorism connote that the United States will use nuclear weapons in response to a nuclear terrorist attack? What the United States may do if an adversary is ultimately not deterred is left intentionally ambiguous.

DETERRING TERRORISTS

Today, it remains the case that there is no comprehensive national strategy on how to deter terrorism. According to terrorism expert Brian Michael Jenkins, "We have islands of understanding of how to deter terrorists. But there is no champion for it within the government. We don't have an organization within the government to do it."[9] Air force Gen. Kevin P. Chilton, the four-star chief of the United States Strategic Command, reported, "We continue to work on the deterrence problem . . . to flesh out the concept."[10] Referring to traditional deterrence in the Cold War, General Chilton reportedly stated, "I am a little concerned we have maybe taken our eye off that ball [deterrence below the strategic level] over the past 15 years."[11] Much work remains ongoing with respect to development of a national approach to deterring terrorism. However, the 2008 *National Defense Strategy*, while stating that nuclear weapons and the ability to retaliate militarily will remain central to U.S. deterrent posture as long as nuclear weapons remain in the world, recognizes that "deterrence may be impossible in cases where the value is not in the destruction of a target, but the attack and the very means of attack, as in terrorism."[12] Similarly, some analysts, such as Jenkins, do not believe deterrence of nuclear terrorism is reliable. In the case of al Qaeda and its potential use of nuclear weapons, Jenkins believes the best path forward to prevent nuclear terrorism is to "wipe them [al Qaeda] out now."[13]

The efforts to apply deterrence to terrorism amount to disruption, and government sources reportedly have stated that the "preferred way to combat terrorism remains to capture or kill terrorists, and the new emphasis on deterrence in some way amounts to attaching a new label to old tools."[14] According to the Council on Foreign Relation's Michael Levi, "There is one question that no one can answer: How much disruption does it take to give you the effect of deterrence?"[15] Yet there is a keen awareness among U.S. counterterrorism policymakers and practitioners that, as Michael Leiter, director of the NCTC, stated, "showing the barbarism of groups like al-Qa'ida is, ultimately, our strongest weapon in this 'long struggle.' . . . And we must win this struggle . . . by using all elements of national power—diplomacy, foreign aid, non-governmental organizations, and the like—to show that it is al-Qa'ida, not the West, that is truly at war with Islam."[16] When all elements of national power are being leveraged effectively (and how to assess counterterrorism performance and adjust programs based on that assessment remains a challenge), then, as Levi states, the sum total of disruption will be deterrence.

Applying deterrence to terrorism requires an understanding of the potential limitations of deterrence. According to Brad Roberts, national security analyst at the Institute for Defense Analysis, "Deterrence is not irrelevant to the effort to combat terrorism and to reduce the risks of WMD terrorism. But nor is it foundational to strategy in the way that it was during the Cold War. Deterrence is but one of many tools of influence and not always the most promising one."[17] Others have concluded that deterrence may be too narrowly defined to be relevant to countering terrorism. Paul K. Davis and Brian Michael Jenkins of RAND concluded, "The concept of deterrence is both too limiting and too naïve to be applicable to the war on terrorism. It is important to conceive an *influence* component of strategy that has both a broader range of coercive elements and a range of plausible positives, some of which we know from history are essential for long-term success."[18] If, for example, the United States is dealing with an apocalyptic terrorist group that takes its direction from God, deterrence may prove ultimately unsuccessful, as secular disincentives to refrain from executing a nuclear attack may be ignored.

With these limitations in mind, one of the core components of deterrence and dissuasion is the need to understand the culture and mind-set of the adversary one is attempting to influence. What does that adversary hold dear? How does a country attempting to deter an adversary from taking certain actions, with the full range of elements of national power, hold at risk what that adversary values most? While some terrorist groups may have safe havens, generally nonstate actors do not hold any territory dear, thus making it difficult to implement a traditional retaliatory military strike against such territory. Deterrence, then, has to delve deeper into the mind and culture of individual terrorist groups and terrorist leaders.

What does al Qaeda in particular value, and how can what it values be held at risk? Various governmental and academic assessments have illustrated that al Qaeda holds its reputation within the Islamic community (reinforced through al Qaeda's advanced communications capabilities) to be of paramount importance.[19] While they may not have "return addresses," according to Ambassador Dell Dailey, the former State Department coordinator for counterterrorism, "al Qaeda's and other terrorists' center of gravity lies in the information domain, and it is there that we must engage it."[20] As was mentioned in chapter 4, bin Laden recognized that 90 percent of the terrorism battle is waged in the media. An aggressive and creative strategy of denying al Qaeda an effective use of the media may prove useful. While the United States has had some successes in the cyber realm, progress has been uneven, and it continues to build its information warfare capabilities.[21]

Another method of deterring terrorists is to discredit their activities in the eyes of the Ummah. Al Qaeda's perversion of Islam and killing of innocent Muslims have been condemned by numerous influential clerics and individuals formerly affiliated with al Qaeda. If the United States and its allies can amplify this message, they will demonstrate to al Qaeda that they can damage its reputation among the Ummah, which may, arguably, enhance any self-restraint the group might exercise in its decision-making process. This may need to be done with the hand of the United States hidden so the message is perceived not as U.S. propaganda. Moreover, additional study needs to be dedicated to why certain terrorists abandon terrorism; once the underlying factors are understood, the United States and its allies can exploit those issues and work against another element terrorists hold dear—their ability to continue to recruit new members with impunity.[22] Terrorist group leaders also hold dear their authority over their groups, yet there are often vehement disagreements among leaders. Group cohesion could be undermined by sowing dissent with disinformation campaigns. Continuing to attack the creative manner in which terrorists finance their operations can weaken another area terrorists hold dear—their ability to raise funds across the globe, oftentimes on a local scale through criminal activity.[23]

Another method of deterring terrorists is by practicing deterrence by denial. Building on the theme that the resiliency of the United States is essential to deterrence, Davis and Jenkins conclude, "Deterrence depends significantly on convincing organizations such as al-Qa'ida and those who support it that any notion of defeating the United States—much less 'bringing the United States down'—is ridiculous."[24] Clearly al Qaeda is attempting to apply a lesson it learned fighting against the Soviet Union in Afghanistan to its global battle with the United States and its allies, conjecturing that the United States is a paper tiger that has no staying power or appetite for a long-term struggle. As domestic support for the Afghanistan war decreases with distance away from September 11, 2001, defeating al Qaeda in the region by waging a successful (and long-term) counterinsurgency there becomes increasingly problematic. Focusing inward, deterrence by denial involves hardening of certain national assets most likely to be targeted by al Qaeda; perhaps more important is preparing society, without perpetuating debilitating fear, to respond to attacks with the resolve to pick up the pieces and forge ahead in the aftermath.

Effective and efficient consequence management is an important element of deterrence by denial. There is an important strategic communications element to consequence management. That is, in order for deterrence by denial to be effective, terrorists must be convinced that the United States is so well prepared for a nuclear attack that while any such attack will be viewed as a catastrophe, it will certainly not cause the nation to quiver in fear and succumb to terrorist demands. Societal resilience, or the ability of the United States to absorb a nuclear terrorist attack and continue as a viable and strong nation-state, is essential to deterrence by denial.

As outlined previously, it is highly unlikely that any terrorist group will have success creating its own fissile material. Therefore some argue that it may be more effective to deter those nation-states that possess fissile material and nuclear weapons from transferring these goods to terrorist groups. Doing so expands deterrence to those potential nation-state enablers that do have a "return address."

EXPANDED DETERRENCE

As already mentioned, terrorist groups are unlikely to be able to develop an indigenous nuclear fuel cycle infrastructure and are, therefore, reliant upon states to provide them directly or indirectly, intentionally or unintentionally, with a nuclear weapon or the fissile material with which to build a crude nuclear device. If the international community can protect nuclear weapons and materials at their source and prevent states from either intentionally or, perhaps more likely, unintentionally transferring such materials to terrorists or to black market intermediaries, the risks of nuclear terrorism can be substantially decreased. One method for doing this is to deter all nations possessing such material from providing it to terrorists. For reasons outlined earlier, the intentional transfer of an intact nuclear weapon to a terrorist group is unlikely except, perhaps, in the most extreme circumstances. The more probable scenario is the unintentional leakage of fissile material from a state that possesses it either directly to a group affiliated with terrorism or to an intermediate broker who may peddle it to the highest bidder. According to Robert Gallucci, former dean of the Edmund A. Walsh School of Foreign Service and former State Department nonproliferation official:

Because the United States confronts terrorists who cannot be deterred by the threat of retaliation, it should look for a way to deter governments from deliberately transferring or inadvertently leaking fissile material to terrorists. During the Cold War, the United States threatened retaliation to prevent ballistic missile attack precisely because it could not defend against one. Now, we need to prevent the transfer of nuclear weapons or materials to terrorists. Intentionally done or not, we cannot block these transfers, so we should again consider promising retaliation if we are attacked.[25]

Part of the underpinning logic of this expanded deterrence is a doctrine of negligence. Under this doctrine, the carrot of U.S. and international financial assistance to secure fissile material is balanced with the stick of military retaliation that "commits the United States to retaliation with conventional or nuclear forces, depending on the situation, if insecure fissile material storage leads to nuclear terror. Where the proximate cause [the terrorist] is unavailable for deterrent retaliation, and the mediate cause [the noncompliant state] does not fully respond to positive incentives, deterrence of the mediate cause through commitments of retaliation is an effective alternative."[26] While current policy on deterring nuclear terrorism does not specifically mention inadvertent leakage of fissile material, it does state that "the United States will hold . . . any state . . . fully accountable for . . . enabling terrorist efforts to obtain or use weapons of mass destruction." This could clearly be interpreted as targeting inadvertent leakage from Russia, Pakistan, North Korea, Iran, or any state that possesses fissile material.

Graham Allison of Harvard University posits that answering the question of whether states can be deterred from providing fissile material or nuclear weapons depends on the answers to two other fundamental questions. First, can the United States or the international community attribute the weapon to its source? Second, and perhaps of greater political complexity, "how will accountability [for the state transferring the material or weapon] be defined politically, and how can it be enforced?"[27] Whether the United States and the international community can unambiguously attribute a nuclear weapon to a particular country remains an open question with U.S. attribution abilities differing across countries. What the United States would do if it was attacked with a terrorist IND and it discovered the nation from which the material leaked would depend on a complex set of variables, including the political and security calculations of the U.S. president, the circumstances surrounding the detonation, and which country was found culpable. If that country was North Korea, the United States has already issued a fairly clear statement, albeit with intentionally ambiguous means, that any transfer from North Korea to a terrorist group is unacceptable. Allison advocates that the international community more clearly define accountability as part of an enhanced global alliance against nuclear terrorism, a new initiative that would provide countries that joined it with benefits and requirements. Such an initiative, as outlined later, seems promising if sufficient political will can be mustered internationally to move from voluntary to mandatory methods designed to prevent nuclear terrorism. While many nations may view the threat of nuclear terrorism seriously, some remain complacent. Moreover, those nations that view the threat seriously may not necessarily advocate international accords that bind them to specific and concrete prevention measures, with potential political and financial consequences should they not comply.

RUSSIA, PAKISTAN, AND EXPANDED DETERRENCE

There are numerous problems with expanded deterrence and the doctrine of negligence, some of which are recognized by proponents of these concepts but are nevertheless accepted as "least worst" options. First and foremost among these is the problem of allies and friendly foreign states, mainly Russia and Pakistan. In order for any threat to be credible, the adversary must perceive that the threatening country is locked into taking (ambiguous but serious) action if the adversary takes certain explicit actions. While the United States has had its differences with Russia recently over, inter alia, the placement of limited ballistic missile defenses in Poland and the Czech Republic to protect against potential Iranian ballistic missiles and the Russian invasion of the Republic of Georgia, the Cold War is over. Nevertheless, Russia currently has thousands of nuclear warheads on alert and continues to hold U.S. targets at risk. The United States has spent billions assisting Russia as it secures its vast amounts of fissile material. Moreover, Russia has its own internal problems with terrorism, as manifested by, among others, the Chechen terrorists (one group suspected by Russian officials as having some linkages to the January 21, 2011, bombing of Moscow's Domodedov Airport that killed at least thirty-five people), a violent group against which Russia remains engaged in sporadic yet protracted battle.

Pakistan remains a nascent and fragile democracy and an ally in the war on terror. The United States has assisted Pakistan, albeit to a lesser extent than Russia, with nuclear weapons and fissile material security. Pakistan is home to numerous radical Islamist groups, including the Taliban and al Qaeda. As outlined in chapter 5, the United States has provided Pakistan with approximately $10 billion in military assistance since 2001, and the country is currently facing an economic crisis that could further undermine its stability. One of the greatest worries with respect to Pakistan is the fear that a radical Islamist group may take over the country or infiltrate its nuclear weapons establishment and facilitate terrorists' seizure of fissile material or nuclear warheads in transit.[28]

Given these factors in the U.S.-Russian and U.S.-Pakistani bilateral relationships, any threat that the United States would attack these countries militarily if fissile material inadvertently leaked from them to a terrorist group seems incredible. Even a flexible response under which the United States might threaten a limited conventional retaliation against Russian military force stretches credulity, as such a threat would be difficult to implement given unintended consequences and the fact that any attack on Russia could potentially lead to thermonuclear war.[29] Similarly with Pakistan, even limited military strikes against the government (as opposed to al Qaeda forces in the FATA) would directly undermine stability in the country and region and likely lead to an inadvertent regime change, which would endanger U.S. interests in the country and region as a radical Islamist regime may replace the current government and would risk a broader India-Pakistan war.

Both Russia and Pakistan have been relatively complacent about the threat of nuclear terrorism, believing construction of a nuclear weapon may be beyond the abilities of terrorists. This complacency notwithstanding, the threat of retaliation against Russia and Pakistan for the inadvertent transfer of fissile material, some argue, is an anachronism. As Michael Levi of the Council on Foreign Relations stated, "A threat to retaliate following an attack on the United States would . . . do little, if anything, to shift the Russian or Pakistani calculus: the possibility that terrorists might use nuclear weapons against Moscow or Islamabad is already far more motivation to pursue strong security than the possibility of U.S. action following a terrorist attack on the United States might be, particularly because a terrorist nuclear strike would inflict a far higher toll than any U.S. retaliatory action could."[30]

Robert Gallucci argues that "the threat [of retaliation] should not be made lightly against either Russia or Pakistan." However, writing in 2006 Gallucci stated:

Neither Moscow nor Islamabad has been made to understand the priority and urgency of [nuclear security] cooperation to the United States. . . . In the first instance, a mix of economic and political inducements, including sanctions, might be tried to persuade these nations to work as hard as possible, unilaterally and bilaterally, to control or eliminate their fissile material stockpiles and adequately secure nuclear weapons. If this conventional approach fails, the United States should consider expanding the deterrent threat to convey our intent to treat a nuclear attack on the United States as an attack by the perpetrator and the country from which the material was obtained. Such a threat would remain even if the transfer were *not* authorized, but *only* if that government had failed to be fully cooperative in controlling its fissile material and weapons.[31]

As manifested by the Russian government's statement at the April 2010 nuclear security conference, some Russian officials believe that there are no vulnerable materials in Russia. In Pakistan, following the assassination of a Pakistani government official by his own bodyguard (a radical Islamist) in January 2011, the government must take caution to ensure no similar infiltration of those individuals guarding nuclear weapons or fissile materials has taken place. How best does the United States judge, then, if these two allied nations are failing to be fully cooperative in the effort to secure nuclear weapons and fissile material? In the absence of effective international security enforcement mechanisms for nuclear security that would likely be view by many nations as an infringement on national sovereignty, the action lies at the nation-state level and the primary tools of influence are seemingly the traditional carrot and stick. But the reality is that the carrot can and has been used far more often than the stick, and when and if the stick is used, it may not necessarily be in the form of a military retaliation but in the form of reduced carrots.

Whether the stick is used against any nation will depend on numerous factors, not the least of which is the identity of the country from which the nuclear material leaked, and the worldview of the president serving at the time of the potential nuclear detonation in the United States. As will be addressed, given that the first question that will be asked in the aftermath of any terrorist nuclear detonation will be are there any more, confrontation may quickly turn to cooperation.

Skeptics of a policy of retaliation against Pakistan and Russia believe that retaliation not only undermines essential cooperation that is necessary to secure fissile material but also discourages cooperation between parties if material is compromised.[32] Such cooperative efforts include (1) timely notification to the United States of a compromise, (2) assistance in locating the fissile material or weapons if they are compromised, and (3) in the event of a detonation, assistance in preventing any additional nuclear attacks. Eschewing retaliation against Russia and Pakistan does not mean, however, that they are not held responsible for nuclear security. To the contrary, the United States should communicate very openly and clearly that it will continue to hold these nations accountable for day-to-day security of their nuclear weapons and fissile material. Michael Levi offers the following possibilities for holding Russia and Pakistan accountable: "The United States might tie its willingness to sell sensitive nuclear technologies to Russia to adherence to high security standards, might condition military sales to Pakistan on nuclear security efforts, or might more generally make clear that poor nuclear security practices will damage bilateral relations more broadly. What is essential, though, is that in the aftermath of any loss of nuclear material—or even worse, following a nuclear attack—international focus is squarely on cooperation rather than confrontation."[33] According to Ashton Carter, while the first instinct of government officials after an explosion would be to figure out retaliation, "that would probably give way to an effort to seek cooperation of Pakistan or Russia to figure out where the stuff came from, what else was lost, and to hunt down the remaining bombs rather than punish the government that lost them."[34]

NORTH KOREA

In contrast to Russia and Pakistan, another country of great proliferation concern, North Korea, may be a candidate for a more traditional expanded deterrence threat of retaliation. Why is North Korea different? First, as a closed society, North Korea has no internal terrorist threat to speak of and, therefore, has little domestic incentive to ensure that its nuclear weapons and fissile material stocks are adequately secured. Second, experts, including former secretary of defense William J. Perry, have argued that North Korea is a potential security disaster with "the overriding reason [being] the possibility that a North Korean nuclear bomb will end up in one of our cities, not delivered by a missile, but by a truck or freighter."[35] Similarly, Levi believes the North Korean case is "fundamentally different [from the case of Russia and Pakistan] because there is a genuine possibility that North Korean leaders might intentionally transfer nuclear weapons or material to a terrorist group if they did not fear retaliation."[36] North Korea has been boastful of its nuclear weapons as a deterrent, and U.S. regional allies, including South Korea and Japan (countries that would bear the brunt of any counterattack), usually caution against provocative U.S. acts that may result in North Korean military adventurism.[37] While Pakistan's nuclear proliferation activities (with or without the knowledge of Pakistani political leadership) have arguably done more damage to international security than North Korea's, Pakistan is central to the war on terrorism. However, should the Pakistani government fall and a radical Islamist regime come to power, traditional extended deterrence arguments might, conceivably, also be applied to Pakistan.

Central to any discussion of expanded deterrence as applied to terrorism is the United States' ability to attribute a nuclear weapon or nuclear material to a particular country after the weapon has been detonated. It is to this topic we now turn.

NUCLEAR ATTRIBUTION—RETALIATION OR COOPERATION?

Nuclear forensics is one element of a broader field known as nuclear attribution. Nuclear attribution attempts to ascertain the provenance of fissile material seized predetonation or postdetonation. Nuclear forensics

> is the technical means by which nuclear materials [fissile material and its products, precursors, and associated materials], whether intercepted intact or retrieved from post-explosion debris, are characterized [as to composition, physical condition, age, provenance, history] and interpreted [as to provenance, history, and implications for nuclear device design].

Nuclear forensics works best in conjunction with other law enforcement, radiological protection dosimetry, traditional forensics, and intelligence work to provide the basis for attributing the materials and/or nuclear device to its originators. Nuclear forensics is a piece of the overall attribution process, not a stand-alone activity.[38]

Figure 6 shows the various elements of the nuclear attribution process.

As outlined above, nuclear attribution can be a source of deterrence. If countries or nuclear weapons scientists working for those counties are aware that their fissile material can be traced back to them, it may deter them from transferring that material to terrorists.[39] If nuclear attribution is to serve as a deterrent, it is essential that an adversarial country believe that the international community has the ability to trace the material or weapon back to it. According to the American Academy for the Advancement of Science (AAAS):

A believable attribution capability may help to discourage behavior that could lead to a nuclear event. The chain of participants in a nuclear terrorist event most likely includes a national government or its agents, since nearly all nuclear weapons–usable material is at least notionally the responsibility of governments. A forensics capability that can trace material to the originating reactor or enrichment facility could discourage state cooperation with terrorist elements and encourage better security for nuclear weapons–usable material. In addition, most terrorist organizations will not have members skilled in all aspects of handling nuclear weapons or building an improvised nuclear device. That expertise is found in a small pool of people and credible attribution capability may deter some who are principally motivated by financial, rather than ideological, concerns.[40]

Nuclear forensics for attribution can be used both pre- and postdetonation. That is, if fissile material is uncovered in the black market by law enforcement or intelligence officials, nuclear forensics can attempt to identify where that material came from. Similarly, in the event of a nuclear detonation, samples and debris (sometimes microscopic quantities of radioactive materials) can be compared to samples from identified sources to contribute to the determination of bomb provenance. Nuclear attribution, then, relies to a great

FIGURE 6. ELEMENTS OF NUCLEAR ATTRIBUTION

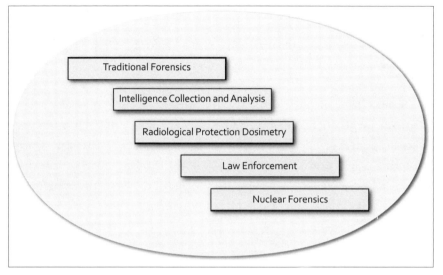

Source: Data from American Physical Society and AAAS, *Nuclear Forensics: Role, State of the Art, Program Needs, 2008,* accessed November 1, 2010, http://iis-db.stanford.edu/pubs/22126/APS_AAAS_2008.pdf.

extent on information and samples of foreign fissile material. Some national governments and the IAEA have nuclear samples databases that, through various chemical, physical, and isotopic processes, yield "signatures" for fissile material.[41] These databases are essential because they serve as a baseline for comparing of fissile material interdicted predetonation or in debris postdetonation. According to the United Kingdom's Royal Society, "These databases contain technical information about characteristic features of civilian and military nuclear material and fuel cycles from around the world."[42]

As one would expect given the extreme sensitivity of nuclear weapons, nations that have overt or covert nuclear weapons programs are not eager to share samples of their fissile material with international bodies. What the United States and IAEA do have for international fissile material samples is highly classified. It has been reported that the

IAEA has a library of nuclear samples from North Korea, obtained before the agency's inspectors were thrown out of the country, that would likely make it possible to trace an explosion back to North Korea's nuclear arsenal. The North Koreans are fully aware, government experts believe, that the United States has access to that database of nuclear DNA. But when it comes to other countries, many of that library's shelves are empty. . . . Senior American nuclear experts have said that the huge gap is one reason that the Bush administration is so far unable to make a convincing threat to terrorists or their suppliers that they will be found out.[43]

If this is true, then the United States' attribution abilities with respect to Pakistan (not an NPT signatory) and Russia (a country that has made great efforts to protect its nuclear weapons secrets) may not be as advanced as with respect to North Korea. According to William Dunlop and H. P. Smith of Lawrence Livermore National Laboratories, one of the Department of Energy laboratories having an expertise in nuclear forensics:

> Foreign access to the debris [postdetonation] is one thing; access to [fissile material] stockpile data for purposes of comparison is quite another. Even if Russia or another country were attacked, current diplomatic realities make it unlikely that a government would grant foreign experts access to relevant stockpile data. In the Russian case, one suspects that the Kremlin would choose to treat the problem as a Russian problem at least until the source [of the fissile material leak] were known to them, a period of time ranging from a week to several weeks to an indefinite future.[44]

What does this mean for the incentives or disincentives that may be in place for notification of the United States if fissile material is compromised? If the United States has more advanced attribution abilities with respect to North Korea, and North Korean leadership believes the United States has this ability, then North Korea has a stronger incentive to notify the United States if its fissile material goes missing. Conversely, with respect to Russia and Pakistan, if the leadership of these countries believe they can mask fissile material compromises or that the United States and the international community have weak attribution abilities, they may perceive they have little incentive to notify the United States if any of their fissile material is compromised.

CURRENT NUCLEAR ATTRIBUTION CAPABILITIES

What is the current status of global nuclear attribution capabilities? According to the AAAS, "The problems of a declining pool of technically competent scientists, the need for new technology, and the utility of international cooperation all point to the need for a new set of initiatives in order to maximize the potential impact in nuclear forensics."[45] There are a number of ways to improve attribution in the interest of enhancing early reporting of fissile material compromise.[46]

- *International cooperation.* One way to improve nuclear forensics and attribution, as has been suggested by both the American Academy for the Advancement of Science and the United Kingdom's Royal Society, is to enhance international technical cooperation. According to the AAAS, "Such cooperation should include enlarging and properly gaining access to existing international and other [nuclear sample] databases and linking them so as to enable prompt data access." In June 2007 former senator (and current vice president) Joseph Biden advocated that the United States should take the lead in creating an international nuclear forensics library that "could house actual samples of nuclear material contributed by participating countries, validated data about their material, or binding agreements to provide predetermined data in the immediate aftermath of an attack or smuggling incident."[47] He recognized that such a library "cannot guarantee that in the wake of an attack the world could assign blame to a country, but it could be a critical tool in narrowing an investigation and debunking wild rumors or allegations."[48]

- *Bilateral agreements.* If multilateral cooperation on nuclear forensics is a "bridge too far," others have suggested starting with bilateral agreements, perhaps between the United States and Russia, to form a credible forensics team in which "each partner, individually, and then jointly, examines what data could be provided to a carefully chosen and controlled bilateral team."[49] Livermore scientists have stated that one of the positive spin-offs of the Cooperative Threat Reduction Program has been "the close working relationship between a long-standing and unchanging team of experts from the Department of Energy laboratories and the Russian Navy. As with most human relationships, a bond of trust was formed over the years based on professionalism and a sense of purpose. The same could be true of the suggested bilateral forensics team."[50]

- *Additional trained personnel.* According to the AAAS, the field of nuclear forensics is shrinking, with many experts in this field prepared to retire soon. The AAAS suggested funding of nuclear forensics programs at universities designed to "produce at least three to four new Ph.D.s per year in relevant disciplines."[51] The Nuclear Forensics and Attribution Act (Public Law 111-140) took initiative in this area.

- *Development of advanced field equipment.* Development of such equipment, not currently available, would "allow the necessary [postdetonation] measures to be made rapidly and accurately at a number of sites."[52]

- *Public pronouncements of general capabilities.* While there is an obvious balance to be struck with respect to how much information a country wants to reveal about its nuclear forensic and attribution capabilities, to have any deterrent effect an adversary must believe that the country attacked has a well-developed nuclear attribution capability.

- *Evidentiary standards.* While nuclear forensics and attribution may not be perfect, if it is stated publicly that the United States might not assume the full burden of proof and would possibly take retaliatory action based on incomplete information and analysis, it could cause states to reconsider the provision of fissile material to a terrorist group.

With this understanding of (1) the nuclear terrorism threat, (2) terrorist pathways to nuclear weapons, (3) supply and demand factors affecting the probability of nuclear terrorism, and (4) the extent to which nuclear terrorism may or may not be deterrable, a consideration of U.S. and international strategies and initiatives in response to the nuclear terrorism threat can be undertaken.

SEVEN

U.S. and International Strategies and Initiatives to Prevent Nuclear Terrorism

Nuclear terrorism is not a new threat, yet in the wake of the attacks of September 11, 2001, it took on a renewed urgency. New programs at both the national and international levels were initiated and some existing programs gained enhanced levels of support. Notwithstanding this renewed support, the threat of nuclear terrorism, whatever its probability, remains with us today as a function of fissile material still at risk, the continuing diffusion of nuclear-related technology through clandestine networks and possibly through a nuclear power renaissance, and a continuing WMD threat from al Qaeda. Positive developments concerning nuclear terrorism—including U.S. and Russian efforts to deemphasize nuclear weapons by decreasing their number of strategic nuclear warheads, continued Cooperative Threat Reduction Program progress, successful efforts to repatriate or remove vulnerable fissile material, a nuclear nonproliferation regime that still stands despite challenges, counterterrorism progress in undermining the capability of terrorist groups to undertake sophisticated operations, and high-level political support for securing remaining vulnerable fissile material—temper some of the pessimism that surrounds this issue.

The purpose of this chapter is to provide a brief overview of some of the main U.S. and international programs intended to prevent nuclear terrorism. As many of these supply-side nuclear terrorism risk reduction measures have been mentioned previously, the discussion will be relatively brief, adding new details where necessary. Supply-side measures are tangible and, arguably (at least at the conceptual level), more easy to understand if not implement. As nuclear security expert Matthew Bunn has argued, "The easy things have been done already. There are deep secrecy, national sovereignty, complacency, political, and bureaucratic impediments to getting this job done."[1]

As the primary purpose of counterterrorism initiatives is to prevent all forms of terrorism, up to and including nuclear terrorism, they will not be discussed in depth here. However, it should be clearly recognized that just as consolidating and locking up fissile material are sound methods to prevent nuclear terrorism, continuing to undermine al Qaeda using all elements of national power—counterterrorism and homeland security related—and addressing the underlying causes of terrorism can be as valuable in reducing nuclear terrorism risks. Just as the West may never see complete nuclear security, it may never completely eradicate terrorism, but it can be marginalized and managed. Broader counterterrorism and homeland security efforts—including such nonnuclear endeavors as increased border patrols, undermining terrorist group efforts to raise and transfer funds and to recruit new members, targeted nuclear intelligence collection and analysis, and law enforcement—are essential elements of countering nuclear terrorism and will be addressed further.

Internationally, numerous efforts to combat nuclear terrorism have been taken at the initiative of the United Nations' IAEA.[2] The international treaties and conventions most relevant to nuclear terrorism include but are not limited to the Nuclear Nonproliferation Treaty, the IAEA Convention on the Physical Protection of Fissile Materials, the International Convention on the Suppression of Acts of Nuclear Terrorism, and United Nations Security Council Resolutions 1373 and 1540. Moreover, the Nuclear Suppliers Group and the Zangger Committee work to ensure that technologies relating to nuclear weapons are not sold or otherwise transferred to states and nonstate actors wishing to acquire nuclear weapons.

U.S. STRATEGY FOR COMBATING WMD

The U.S. strategy for combating WMD, while broader than nuclear terrorism, has as one of its primary goals the prevention of nuclear terrorism. The strategy has three primary pillars: nonproliferation, counterproliferation, and response. Figure 7 depicts these three basic lines of defense. These lines of defense can be treated as a series of independent layers or, perhaps more appropriately, as an interdependent system. Layered defense structures are attractive for many reasons, not the least of which is that as a system they can be effective, even though each individual layer represents imperfect security. According to a 2004 Defense Science Board report:

> With multiple layers, each layer need not be highly effective in order for the overall effectiveness to be high. If the layers require different tactics or technologies to penetrate, the attacker's job is considerably more difficult. This indicates a fundamental synergy between a layered defense and the capability to detect the threat by intelligence indicators, including from law-enforcement activities. A more capable and varied defense means that the attacker must mount a larger operation to penetrate it. A larger operation has more (and more observable) signatures. More people with more skills must be recruited and trained; more money must be obtained and laundered; the operation takes longer; and the attacker must surveil the defense more intensively. By increasing the signature of attack planning, the likelihood of discovery increases commensurately. This, in turn, could allow the defenses to be surged, further increasing effectiveness.[3]

FIGURE 7. MULTILAYERED DEFENSE-IN-DEPTH NUCLEAR COUNTERTERRORISM APPROACH

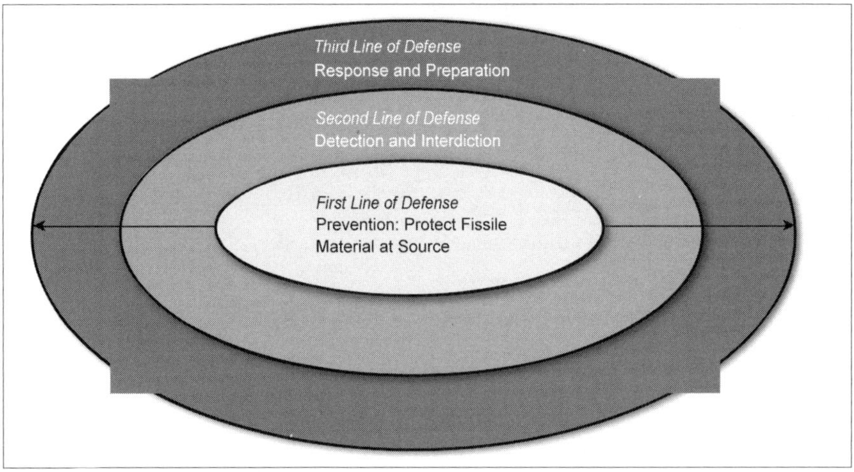

Third Line of Defense
Response and Preparation

Second Line of Defense
Detection and Interdiction

First Line of Defense
Prevention: Protect Fissile
Material at Source

Sources: Data from Chairman of the Joint Chiefs of Staff, *National Military Strategy to Combat Weapons of Mass Destruction*, February 13, 2006, http://www.defense.gov/pdf/NMS-CWMD2006.pdf; and "National Strategy to Combat Weapons of Mass Destruction," National Security, Presidential Directive-17, December 2002, http://www.fas.org/irp/offdocs/nspd/nspd-17.html.

Appropriately located at the core of the strategy are initiatives designed to consolidate and secure nuclear weapons and fissile material. Yet, as Michael Levi of the Council on Foreign Relations posits, given that no defense is perfect (massive stockpiles of fissile material and the potential for insider corruption are not short-term phenomena), it is unrealistic to expect perfect security. If one assumes, then, that fissile material security is imperfect, other elements of the system must be prepared to support the primary layer. Nonnuclear tools should be emphasized. Levi states:

> When policymakers discuss defenses against nuclear terrorism, they tend to focus on nuclear-specific tools, such as nuclear materials security, radiation detection, and nuclear forensics. But we have seen that beyond the core of material and weapons security, defense against nuclear terrorism is as much about bread and butter counterterrorism and homeland security as it is about nuclear-specific measures. Interdicting nuclear smuggling, for example, is as much about detecting terrorists as it is about detecting plutonium; disrupting any nuclear black market may be as much about constraining terrorist financing as it is about nuclear stings; stopping terrorist groups from converting nuclear materials to a nuclear weapon may be as much about denying sanctuary as it is about controlling specialized machine tools or potential bomb components.[4]

Nonproliferation generally concerns bilateral or multilateral means of preventing nonnuclear states and nonstate actors from acquiring nuclear weapons, usually through "diplomacy, arms control, multilateral agreements, threat reduction assistance, and export controls. . . . We must ensure compliance with relevant international agreements, including the Nuclear Nonproliferation Treaty. . . . We will . . . pursue new methods of prevention, such as national criminalization of proliferation activities and expanded safety and security measures."[5] Moreover, nonproliferation measures, according to U.S. strategy, also include (1) strengthening the NPT and the IAEA, including the "ratification of an IAEA Additional Protocol by all NPT States . . . ; (2) negotiating a Fissile Material Cutoff Treaty that advances U.S. interests, and (3) strengthening the Nuclear Suppliers Group and the Zangger Committee."[6] U.S. government programs that fall under the first line of defense include, among others, the Cooperative Threat Reduction Program and various MPC&A programs, located within the Departments of State, Energy, and Defense (see appendix C for a summary of core U.S. government programs to prevent nuclear terrorism).

Counterproliferation measures tend to be more involved in detection and interdiction, both of which are implemented internationally and domestically through various U.S. programs. The Proliferation Security Initiative (PSI) is a prime example of counterproliferation. A voluntary multilateral arrangement (over ninety countries currently participate), the PSI program stresses international cooperation and development and sharing of best practices in the use of existing national enforcement tools to interdict illicit transfers of WMD technologies and their means of delivery.[7] Counterproliferation also requires that "the U.S. military and appropriate civilian agencies be prepared to deter and defend against a full range of possible WMD deployment scenarios."[8] Deterrence involves, among other measures, threats of ensured retaliation for acts by any power, intentionally or otherwise, to aid a terrorist group in its nuclear activities. The U.S. strategy of combating WMD also envisions counterproliferation encompassing "defending against WMD-armed adversaries, including in appropriate cases through preemptive measures."[9]

U.S. government programs that fall under the second line of defense, some of which are designed to "extend U.S. borders out" and detect any illicit fissile material or weapons before they reach U.S. shores, include the Proliferation Security Initiative (interdiction); the Second Line of Defense: Core program (DOE-NNSA, works to equip foreign partners, largely though not exclusively within the former Soviet Union, with radiation detection equipment at border crossings, airports, and seaports); the Second Line of Defense: Megaports Initiative (DOE-NNSA, provides radiation detection equipment to key international seaports); the Container Security Initiative (DHS, provides screening of high-risk containerized cargo at fifty-eight foreign ports before it is loaded onto ships bound for the United States); the Secure Freight Initiative (DHS and DOE, sends radiological detection equipment to overseas ports to scan containers for risk); and export control and border-related security assistance (U.S. Department of State, draws on knowledge from other agencies to support foreign nations in the development of effective export controls). Two other important programs that reside both here and in the third layer of defense are the Nuclear Emergency Search Team (NEST) and the DOE–NNSA–Joint Technical Operations Team (JTOT). In existence since 1975, NEST is composed of U.S. Department of Energy personnel and is called upon to find and defuse a nuclear device should one go missing.[10] Radiation maps of high-risk geographic areas within the United States assist in allowing NEST to spot anomalously high levels of radiation emissions that may represent nuclear devices in U.S. cities. The JTOT program "provides specialized technical capabilities in support of the Federal Bureau of Investigation and the Department of Defense to render safe a nuclear or radiological weapon or device before it does any damage. In addition, they determine if the weapon or device is safe to move for further analysis and safe to ship to a site for disposition."[11]

Finally, the response function involves managing the consequences of the use of WMD against the United States or its allies. As outlined above, it would appear that for numerous reasons this is a relatively weak pillar of the overall approach to preventing WMD terrorism. The consequences of a nuclear attack, even a "fizzle" yield, in a U.S. city will be physically, psychologically, and economically substantial. First responders, including public health agencies and hospitals, in the immediate area will rapidly be overwhelmed. As numerous officials have testified, given the scale of the damage from a nuclear explosion and the potential national ramifications, including possible mass exodus from large metropolitan areas, the federal government is the only entity with the response and rescue resources substantial enough to respond. Given the experience responding to Hurricane Katrina, when state and local resources were quickly overwhelmed, some have argued that a decision should be made that as soon as federal assets can be put in place, federal authorities will be in the lead, as directly supported by state and local personnel.[12] Currently that is not the case, as the federal "response force is a scalable, dedicated force that is prepared to reinforce state and local responders when they request federal assistance."[13] Nevertheless, the Department of Defense seems to be taking the lead in developing WMD response capabilities. By 2011 the Department of Defense plans to have twenty thousand troops inside the United States trained "to help state and local officials respond to a nuclear terrorist attack."[14] The Pentagon is in the process of establishing three rapid-response CBRN Consequence Management Response Forces (C-CMRF), which will join approximately eighty National Guard units trained in CBRN response.[15]

In order to integrate these three pillars of combating WMD, there are four enabling functions: (1) intelligence collection and analysis of WMD, (2) research and development to improve the United States' ability to respond to threats, (3) bilateral and multilateral cooperation, and (4) targeted strategies against hostile states and terrorists.

ENABLING FUNCTIONS

As mentioned, intelligence has an important role to play across all layers of defense. Among other measures, intelligence assists in:

- assessing nuclear terrorism threats (terrorist intentions and capabilities with respect to nuclear weapons);
- detecting, exploiting, and, if appropriate, shutting down clandestine nuclear procurement networks after all valuable intelligence about the extent of the networks' activities have been discovered and utilized;[16]
- informing export controls;
- locating illicit material in transit for interdiction; and
- alerting national authorities to fissile material compromises.

According to the 2002 *National Strategy to Combat Weapons of Mass Destruction*, "Improving our ability to obtain timely and accurate knowledge of adversaries' offensive and defensive capabilities, plans, and intentions is key to developing effective counter and nonproliferation policies and capabilities."[17] As mentioned earlier, "the Intelligence Community must find something that is tactical in size but strategic in potential impact. We must find a plot with its networks that cut across traditional lines of counterterrorism and counter-proliferation. We must stop something from happening that we have never seen before."[18] Yet, as has been demonstrated with intelligence failures relating to WMD in Iraq, intelligence is and will remain fallible.[19] While beyond the scope of this book, some of the more prevalent maladies affecting intelligence analytical tradecraft include a lack of effective interdisciplinary approaches, mirror-imaging (projecting rationality onto foreign decision makers), and the "layering effect" (failing to question underlying and long-standing assumptions), among others.[20] Moreover, these problems can be compounded when nuclear specialists studying the supply side of nuclear terrorism are not integrated with terrorism analysts studying the demand side of nuclear terrorism. According to physicist Michael Levi of the Council on Foreign Relations, "Nuclear experts often hold intuitive assumptions about terrorism that are not borne out in the actual study of terrorist groups."[21] Levi also points out that strategic intelligence assessments of nuclear terrorism must go beyond worst-case assessments and should "interweave expertise on nuclear weapons with expertise on terrorism [interdisciplinary analysis], . . . identify a wide range of possible and credible [nuclear plot] options, . . . [and] go beyond passive collection and reasoning by analogy to active operations designed to understand terrorist approaches to nuclear plots."[22] The development of the Nuclear Materials Information Program, outlined in chapter 5, is an example of the U.S. Intelligence Community taking the initiative to support U.S. policy by prioritizing which fissile material sources overseas are at the greatest risk.

With respect to research and development, it is essential to be able to detect, tag, track, trace, and interdict nuclear material. According to the 2002 WMD strategy, "The United States has a critical need for cutting-edge technology that can quickly and effectively detect, analyze, facilitate interdiction of, defend against, defeat, and mitigate the consequences of WMD."[23] Enhanced international cooperation and targeted strategies against nations engaged in proliferation, such as North Korea and possibly Iran, complete the enabling functions.

NATIONAL STRATEGY IMPLEMENTATION PERFORMANCE

A number of studies have considered the U.S. government's performance in implementing its national strategy to combat WMD. In 2008 an independent review panel cochaired by Robert Joseph, former staff member of the National Security Council in the administration of President George W. Bush, and Ashton Carter, current undersecretary of defense for acquisition, technology, and logistics, concluded: "DOD and the U.S. Government as a whole have not fully implemented [the national strategies articulated in presidential guidance]. Performance has fallen short in all three pillars of the *National Strategy to Combat WMD*: prevention, protection, and response."[24] In another study, the 9/11 Public Discourse Project assessed a grade of D to the U.S. government's effort to prevent terrorists from acquiring WMD. While reviewing the substantial progress that has been made in the Cooperative Threat Reduction Program, among others, the 2005 progress report on the 9/11 Commission's WMD recommendation found "the size of the problem still dwarfs the policy response. Approximately half of former Soviet nuclear materials still lack adequate security protection."[25] More recently, the Partnership for a Secure America (PSA) issued a study assigning an overall grade of C to the U.S. government's efforts to implement the pillars of nuclear terrorism prevention, as outlined in the 2002 WMD strategy. Specifically, the PSA found:

- *Prevention* (cooperative nonproliferation and counterproliferation, grade C+). Nonproliferation programs limited primarily by lack of interagency coordination and long-term strategy, a mismatch of U.S. and foreign expectations, and new multilateral counterproliferation initiatives lacking U.S. follow-through.
- *Detection/interdiction of weapons and materials* (grade B). A tenfold increase in port security funding, 90 percent of U.S.-bound cargo pre-screened, and public and private sector collaboration still inadequate.
- *Integration of U.S. government programs* (grade D). Authority and budgets stove-piped across multiple agencies, and poor coordination between traditional security and development agencies.[26]
- *Long-term sustainment of programs* (grade D). Lack of host country buy-in to ongoing program goals, policies too short term in focus, and human engagement programs underfunded.[27]

Given some of the proposed and ongoing Obama administration initiatives related to combating nuclear terrorism and improving global security of fissile material, these assessments will need to be updated, yet it may be premature to do so.

Building on the momentum of the April 2010 nuclear security summit, the Obama administration submitted to Congress in April 2011 legislation required to ratify an amendment to the convention on the physical protection of nuclear material and the international convention for the suppression of acts of nuclear terrorism. The goal is to update U.S. criminal code to strengthen the ability to investigate and prosecute acts of nuclear terrorism.

U.S. NUCLEAR TERRORISM MACHINERY: WHO IS IN CHARGE?

Part of the challenge of analyzing nuclear terrorism is understanding the broad range of entities within the U.S. government that have some role to play in preventing or responding to nuclear terrorism. Numerous assessments of the U.S. government's attempts to prevent nuclear terrorism have raised the issue of inadequate intragovernmental coordination.[28] According to *World at Risk*, the report of the Commission on the Prevention of Weapons of Mass Destruction Proliferation and Terrorism, "Information provided to the Commission by various agencies revealed nearly 200 interagency committees and working groups that address WMD, counterproliferation, and counterterrorism issues."[29] A dramatized illustration of the lack of any central coordinator came in the Nuclear Threat Institute–produced film titled *Last Best Chance*. At one point, the notional president (played by former senator Fred Thompson), surrounded by his national security advisers in the situation room to discuss missing nuclear material, asks, "Who in this group is responsible for nuclear terrorism?" All hands in the room are raised. He then asks, "And who is in charge?" All hands are lowered. The notional president then mutters, "I guess Harry Truman was right," alluding to Truman's statement that "the buck stops here." Should the nuclear terrorism threat be handled by someone at the National Security Council who also has responsibility for a number of other major national security programs? Who coordinates the various U.S. government programs designed to secure foreign sources of fissile material? Who has the responsibility to integrate U.S. nuclear security programs with U.S. counterterrorism programs for maximum effectiveness and efficiency in combating nuclear terrorism? A recent study by the PSA found that despite impressive accomplishments made in the U.S. nuclear security programs,

> the nonproliferation programs, as currently configured, are neither providing the maximum return on government investment, nor accomplishing their goals at a pace commensurate with the urgency of the threat. Much of the blame for these inefficiencies can be laid on the doorsteps of host governments. . . . A lack of a sense of urgency over the nature of the threat [and] enduring Cold War hostilities have all conspired to frustrate . . . their ultimate objective. Like these foreign partners, the United States Government has also erected its own barriers to success . . . in three broad areas: lack of interagency coordination, unrealistic expectations, and inefficient oversight of program implementation. . . . It is common for multiple agencies to simultaneously plan and pursue similar opportunities on

the ground in the former Soviet Union . . . only to then learn of each other's efforts through their host partners.[30]

Pursuant to Public Law 110-53, Implementing the Recommendations of the 9/11 Commission Act of 2007, the Office of the United States Coordinator for the Prevention of Weapons of Mass Destruction Proliferation and Terrorism was established. Under the law, the coordinator and the deputy coordinator of the office "shall be appointed by the President, by and with the advice and consent of the Senate."[31] Under current law, the coordinator is to have the following responsibilities:

1. Serving as the principal advisor to the President on all matters relating to the prevention of weapons of mass destruction (WMD) proliferation and terrorism.

2. Formulating a comprehensive and well-coordinated United States strategy and policies for preventing WMD proliferation and terrorism, including—

    (a) measurable milestones and targets to which departments and agencies can be held accountable;

    (b) identification of gaps, duplication, and other inefficiencies in existing activities, initiatives, and programs and the steps necessary to overcome these obstacles;

    (c) plans for preserving the nuclear security investment the United States has made in Russia, the former Soviet Union, and other countries;

    (d) prioritized plans to accelerate, strengthen, and expand the scope of existing initiatives and programs, which include identification of vulnerable sites and material and the corresponding actions necessary to eliminate such vulnerabilities;

    (e) new and innovative initiatives and programs to address emerging challenges and strengthen United States capabilities, including programs to attract and retain top scientists and engineers and strengthen the capabilities of United States national laboratories;

    (f) plans to coordinate United States activities, initiatives, and programs relating to the prevention of WMD proliferation and terrorism, including those of the Department of Energy, the Department of Defense, the Department of State, and the Department of Homeland Security, and including the Proliferation Security Initiative, the G-8 Global Partnership Against the Spread of Weapons and Materials of Mass Destruction, United Nations Security Council Resolution 1540, and the Global Initiative to Combat Nuclear Terrorism;

(g) plans to strengthen United States commitments to international regimes and significantly improve cooperation with other countries relating to the prevention of WMD proliferation and terrorism, with particular emphasis on work with the international community to develop laws and an international legal regime with universal jurisdiction to enable any state in the world to interdict and prosecute smugglers of WMD material, as recommended by the 9/11 Commission; and

(h) identification of actions necessary to implement the recommendations of the Commission on the Prevention of Weapons of Mass Destruction Proliferation and Terrorism. . . .

3. Leading inter-agency coordination of United States efforts to implement the strategy and policies described in this section.

4. Conducting oversight and evaluation of accelerated and strengthened implementation of initiatives and programs to prevent WMD proliferation and terrorism by relevant government departments and agencies.

5. Overseeing the development of a comprehensive and coordinated budget for programs and initiatives to prevent WMD proliferation and terrorism, ensuring that such budget adequately reflects the priority of the challenges and is effectively executed, and carrying out other appropriate budgetary authorities.[32]

In a statement of administration policy, the George W. Bush administration wrote that it "opposes the creation of the new position of the U.S. Coordinator for the Prevention of WMD Proliferation and Terrorism. The position is unnecessary given the extensive coordination and synchronization mechanisms that now exist within the executive branch, including the September 2006 National Strategy for Combating Terrorism, which sets forth a comprehensive multi-layered strategy to combat the threat of WMD terrorism."[33] The mechanisms to which the statement refers are likely the creation of the Department of Homeland Security, the National Counterterrorism Center, the National Counterproliferation Center, and the Office of the Director of National Intelligence. Moreover, the White House expressed constitutional concerns with the position.

From the perspective of executive branch flexibility, the fact that the law requires the coordinator to be confirmed by the Senate implies that the incumbent would be required to testify before Congress. While keeping Congress well informed about measures to combat nuclear terrorism is wise, the Commission on the Prevention of Weapons of Mass Destruction Proliferation and Terrorism concluded, "Senate confirmation would therefore likely compel the next President to place the Coordinator outside of the NSC [National Security Council] staff."[34] The commission recommended that should the president not want it to be Senate-confirmed position that a request be made to Congress to amend the law. The commission found that to be effective, the incumbent in any such position should be a senior-level and respected expert, be perceived as speaking for the president, and "have the budgetary authority (including a direct link to the Office of Management and Budget [OMB]) to assess funding levels, fix shortfalls, and adjust programs."[35] Michael Leiter, director of the NCTC, an agency responsible, in part, for coordinating strategic operational counterterrorism planning and integrating all instruments of national power for counterterrorism initiatives, recently stated that his relationship with the OMB is "incredibly important." He needs the assistance of OMB budget examiners so that "when they sit down with departments and agencies, we ensure that budgets and programs, now and into the future, are aligned with these [national counterterrorism] priorities."[36]

In January 2009 the Obama administration appointed Gary Samore, a former Clinton administration official, to the NSC position of special assistant to the president and White House coordinator for arms control and weapons of mass destruction, proliferation, and terrorism.[37] The NSC is the primary governmental body formally charged with integrating U.S. foreign and defense policies. NSC staff provide advice to the president, are not subject to Senate confirmation, and do not generally testify before Congress. While the new position's portfolio of issues includes nuclear terrorism, it has broader, yet related, arms control responsibilities, which may result, arguably, in a dilution of the type of focus on preventing WMD terrorism that Congress and the WMD Commission originally intended. Moreover, the position's budgetary authorities have not been made clear publicly. In the absence of direct or indirect control over budgetary execution related to WMD terrorism, effectively coordinating and directing resources to achieve national goals and objectives to prevent WMD terrorism may be problematic.

To illustrate the breadth of nuclear terrorism programs spread across the U.S. government, appendix B provides a sampling of the cabinet agencies and programs that have responsibility for some elements of nuclear terrorism. Appendix C also provides a description of the major U.S. government programs and initiatives to deter, detect, prevent, and respond to nuclear terrorism.

The agency list does not include the following entities, which have important roles to play in deterring, detecting, defeating, preventing, and responding to nuclear terrorism:

- *The U.S. Intelligence Community*—seventeen agencies and organizations, all of which to some extent, whether at the tactical or strategic level, are collecting, analyzing, or taking counterterrorism or counter WMD actions. The nature of intelligence is such that collectors and analysts will often not know the specific end goal of the inimical activity against which they are operating, so whether it is directly related to a nuclear terrorist attack or a conventional attack is almost immaterial. Their goal is to use national technical means, including but not limited to signals intelligence (SIGINT, which might provide interceptions of terrorists plotting an attack) and imagery intelligence (IMINT, which might show images of terrorist training camps), to collect intelligence that can provide insight into terrorist intentions, capabilities, and plans. Human intelligence (HUMINT) is also an incredibly valuable counterterrorism tool. The ultimate HUMINT goal is to penetrate a terrorist cell through the recruitment of a cell member or insertion of a controlled agent into the cell to inform on terrorist plots. Financial intelligence, as coordinated by the U.S. Department of the Treasury, can help stanch terrorist operations by undermining the logistical ability of the cell to move financial resources, people, information, and material necessary to implement a plot.

- *Intelligence Community centers*—the National Counterterrorism Center (NCTC) and the National Counterproliferation Center (NCPC). Both the NCTC and the NCPC were established pursuant to the Intelligence Reform and Terrorism Prevention Act (IRTPA) of 2004 (Public Law 108-458).[38] The NCTC has two primary roles. First, it serves as the primary U.S. entity for integrating and analyzing all intelligence relating to terrorism. For this function, the Director of the NCTC reports to the Director of National Intelligence. Second, the NCTC serves as the primary strategic operational counterterrorism planning entity for the U.S. government. Because this function is broader than intelligence, the Director of the NCTC reports to the president when wearing this hat. As envisioned in the IRTPA, the NCPC would have the same essential functions as the NCTC, representing an all-source analytical hub for all intelligence relating to proliferation and coordinating counterproliferation plans across the U.S. government. However, the Commission on the Intelligence Capabilities of the United States Regarding Weapons of Mass Destruction concluded in March 2005, "We doubt that it is a good idea to replicate the [NCTC] model—and the mixed reporting relationships it creates—in other substantive areas."[39] The commission recommended, as was subsequently accepted by the George W. Bush administration, a smaller NCPC body that might be as large as one hundred people to serve "as the DNI's Mission Manager for counterproliferation issues; it would not conduct analysis itself, but would instead be responsible for *coordinating* analysis and collection of nuclear, biological, and chemical weapons across the intelligence community." Unlike the NCTC, then, the NCPC performs no policy or operational coordinating functions.

NET ASSESSMENT: U.S. GOVERNMENT MACHINERY

Governmental "czars" have generally been ineffective, largely due to their unclear authorities and lack of control over budgets. As Matthew Bunn and Andrew Newman of Harvard University have recommended, while the NSC "traditionally does not implement programs or allocate budgets itself . . . when presidential priority is clear, strong NSC staff can work with the Office of Management and Budget to ensure that agencies' budgets are aligned with strategy. . . . A 'crosscut' of all budgets related to preventing nuclear terrorism [could be prepared] and put under a single [OMB] budget examiner, to ease problems of coordination."[40] Organizational fixes are not silver bullets, as agencies tend to jealously guard turf and missions. However, now that the NSC position of special assistant to the president and White House coordinator for arms control and weapons of mass destruction, proliferation, and terrorism has been established, if the incumbent is afforded the appropriate budgetary authority with and through OMB and is able to sustain high-level interest in and support for integrating all elements of national power to counter nuclear terrorism, the results could be promising. One critical function of this position will be to integrate both the supply- and demand-side policy programs and initiatives such that the sum total of their effectiveness is synergistic. There may be no realistic, near-term technical or supply-side optimal solution to prevent nuclear terrorism. However, concurrent and integrated improvements to the supply and demand sides of the nuclear terrorism threat could have a force multiplier effect such that the preventive outcome of integration is greater than any single policy's effect. Aggressively overseeing the implementation of the defense-in-depth approach to preventing nuclear terrorism is a critical function that must be addressed at the NSC level.

Legislative oversight of nuclear terrorism is a microcosm of congressional oversight of national security matters. According to the Commission to Prevent WMD Proliferation and Terrorism, "The current structure of congressional oversight of national security is a relic of the Cold War. . . . In the House, 16 committees and 40 subcommittees now assert jurisdiction over DHS. In the Senate, 14 committees and 18 subcommittees share this responsibility."[41] As two commissions did before it, the Graham-Talent WMD Commission recommended that Congress should reform its oversight both structurally and substantively to better address cross-cutting issues like nuclear terrorism. Congressional jurisdiction is painstakingly difficult to change.

Bilateral and multilateral international cooperation on measures to prevent nuclear terrorism and proliferation is essential. Nuclear security remains only as good as its weakest link; therefore, nations have a common interest in preventing nuclear terrorism anywhere. This cooperation can take the form of support for certain initiatives, such as the Proliferation Security Initiative or a multilateral nuclear fuel bank, or for bilateral initiatives, such as a commitment by the United States and Russia to fulfill their NPT obligations by pursuing strategic nuclear force reductions.

THE INTERNATIONAL NONPROLIFERATION REGIME
AND NUCLEAR TERRORISM

There are numerous international programs and initiatives designed to combat nuclear terrorism. The international nuclear nonproliferation regime is relevant to nuclear terrorism insofar as the greater the number of nuclear weapons states, de jure or de facto, the greater the targets for terrorists seeking to acquire a nuclear weapon or fissile material. However, from a nuclear terrorism perspective, the nuclear nonproliferation regime is only as good as its weakest link. There are numerous nation-states outside the international nuclear nonproliferation regime—Pakistan, for example—that could intentionally or unintentionally provide the necessary materials and know-how to a terrorist group to go nuclear. The international nonproliferation regime has undoubtedly contributed substantially to the fact that as of today no terrorist group or other nonstate actor has acquired a nuclear weapon. However, despite the numerous international initiatives to prevent nuclear terrorism, as Friedrich Steinhausler of the University of Salzburg has commented, "Regrettably, there is a pronounced lack of international coordination of related activities, generally inadequate means for strengthening physical security in financially disadvantaged countries, widespread unwillingness to adhere to an internationally accepted minimum level of physical protection, coupled with a frequent deficit of legal means to enforce compliance with security-related technical and operational requirements."[42]

The core of the nuclear nonproliferation regime is the NPT, which entered into force in 1970 and currently has 192 states as parties. There are two categories of NPT members: nuclear weapons state parties (United States, Russia, China, United Kingdom, and France) and nonnuclear weapons state parties to the treaty. India, Pakistan, Israel, and North Korea are not parties to the NPT.[43] While the NPT is not specifically designed to prevent nuclear terrorism, it is designed to cap the number of states that possess nuclear weapons, thereby limiting the states that could transfer nuclear weapons or fissile material to terrorist groups. The essence of the NPT "grand bargain" is represented by the three pillars of the treaty: nonproliferation, disarmament, and access to technologies that allow for the peaceful use of nuclear energy. With respect to nonproliferation, each nuclear weapons state party to the treaty commits not to transfer to "any recipient whatsoever nuclear weapons or other explosive devices . . . and not . . . to assist, encourage, or induce any non-nuclear weapon state to manufacture or otherwise acquire nuclear weapons or other nuclear explosive devices, or control over such weapons or explosive devices."[44] Non-nuclear weapons state parties to the treaty agree "not to receive the transfer from any transferor whatsoever of nuclear weapons . . .; not to manufacture or otherwise acquire nuclear weapons . . .; and not to seek or receive any assistance in the manufacture of nuclear weapons."[45] With respect to disarmament, "Each of the Parties to the Treaty undertakes to pursue negotiations in good faith on effective measures relating to the cessation of the nuclear arms race . . . and to nuclear disarmament."[46]

The third pillar of the NPT concerns the peaceful use of nuclear power. The NPT stipulates, "Nothing in this Treaty shall be interpreted as affecting the *inalienable right* [emphasis added] of all Parties to the Treaty to develop, research, produce, and use nuclear energy for peaceful purposes. . . . All Parties . . . have the right to participate in the fullest possible exchange of equipment, materials, and scientific and technical information for the peaceful use of nuclear energy."[47] It is this last pillar—the peaceful use of nuclear energy—that countries can exploit to develop nuclear weapons. Iran claims its substantial development and deployment of centrifuge technology used to enrich uranium is solely for peaceful nuclear energy purposes, as natural uranium's isotopic concentration of ^{235}U is less than 1 percent and it must be enriched to about "5 percent" (LEU) for nuclear power reactor fuel. As mentioned in chapter 5, however, the number "5 percent" is not in the NPT, and the same technologies used to enrich natural uranium to LEU can be used to convert LEU to HEU. Multilateral nuclear fuel banks address this challenge by allowing countries to develop peaceful nuclear power in a manner that does not represent proliferation risks. NPT compliance issues continue to represent a challenge to the nuclear nonproliferation regime.

Speaking at a June 2009 IAEA Board of Governors meeting, then director general ElBaradei stated, "Without an Additional Protocol, we can only talk about declared nuclear material. We have learned since 1991 in Iraq that if any country tries to divert nuclear material, they don't divert it from declared material, they divert through a clandestine programme."[48] In 1993 the IAEA began an effort to enhance its ability to detect undeclared nuclear activities. The result was the development of what has become known as the Additional Protocol to the basic verification agreement some NPT states have with the

IAEA. The Additional Protocol, which is voluntary, broadens the ability of the IAEA to "check for clandestine nuclear facilities by providing the agency the authority to visit any facility, declared or not, to investigate questions about or inconsistencies in a state's nuclear declarations."[49] Like other international measures, however, participation has been uneven and implementation slow. According to ElBaradei, there are substantial shortcomings in the agency's legal authority, and "of the 163 States with safeguards agreements, only 88 now have additional protocols in force—not much more than half."[50] As of March 2011, 107 nations have additional protocols in place. Iran, a country of great proliferation concern, does not have an additional protocol in force.[51]

The May 2010 NPT Review Conference will raise numerous perennial issues, including the concrete progress that nuclear weapons states are making in disarmament, measures to enhance regime compliance and detection of undeclared nuclear activities, perceptions among nonnuclear weapons states that the international community is placing increasing restrictions on the peaceful use of nuclear power, and concerns over how Iranian breakout could be a death knell for the NPT. North Korea represents another major challenge to the nuclear nonproliferation regime. Should North Korea formally and legally declare itself to be a nuclear weapons power and permanently cease all negotiations with other nations to dismantle its nuclear weapons program, the regime would be undermined. Should Iran make the political decision to become a nuclear weapons power, the regime would similarly be stressed. Yet forty years after the treaty's inception, its continued existence and the willingness of parties to review progress on each of its central pillars are a testament to the regime's success. Despite challenges, the regime has proved to be relatively flexible and durable, and has contributed to ensuring that the 1960s vision of a world of twenty to thirty nuclear powers has not come to fruition. In a demonstration of political will, which must be matched with action, President Obama has committed the United States to implementing its obligations to move toward disarmament. In April 2009 he stated, "The basic bargain of the NPT is sound: countries with nuclear weapons will move toward disarmament, countries without nuclear weapons will not acquire them, and all countries can access peaceful nuclear energy."[52]

Other international legal instruments to prevent nuclear terrorism include the following.

United Nations Security Council Resolution 1540. Passed in April 2004, United Nations Security Council Resolution 1540, acting under Article VII of the UN Charter (actions with respect to threats and breaches to peace and acts of aggression), provides that all states,

- in accordance with their national procedures, shall adopt and enforce *appropriate effective* [emphasis added] laws which prohibit any non-state actor to manufacture, acquire, possess, develop, transport, transfer, or use nuclear, chemical, or biological weapons and their means of delivery, in particular for terrorist purposes, as well as attempts to engage in any of the foregoing activities, participate in them as an accomplice, assist, or finance them [operative paragraph 2] . . .
- shall take and enforce effective measures to establish domestic controls to prevent the proliferation of nuclear, chemical, or biological weapons . . . and to this end shall develop and maintain appropriate effective: (1) measures to account for and secure such items in production, use, storage, or transport, (2) physical protection measures . . . , (3) border controls and law enforcement efforts to detect, deter, prevent, and combat, including through international cooperation when necessary, the illicit trafficking and brokering in such items, (4) national export and trans-shipment controls.[53]

Implementation progress on these measures has been relatively slow.[54] The United States continues to be the only country thus far to have submitted an implementation action plan outlining concrete actions that it will take to implement the resolution. Nevertheless, the resolution and the work of the UN 1540 Committee increase the level of awareness of nuclear terrorism, and the IAEA, through its Office of Nuclear Security, is assisting states in implementing the resolution. However, the bottom line with respect to 1540 is that it has not resulted in the development of what is arguably necessary: a set of clear and specific nuclear security standards, the implementation of which is mandatory. This is not, however, unlike many international endeavors that must continually balance international security interests with national sovereignty.

The IAEA Convention on the Physical Protection of Nuclear Material. This convention, which entered into force in 1987, was ratified by 112 member states. It is primarily designed to protect nuclear material in international transport. In 2005 state parties adopted a legally binding amendment to the convention that would require them "to protect nuclear facilities and nuclear material in peaceful domestic use, storage, and during transport." However, the amendment has yet to enter into force, as it has not been ratified by two-thirds of the 112 state parties to the convention. As Friedrich Steinhausler points out, the convention suffers from the following maladies: (1) national authorities determine levels of physical protection based on national assessments of threat, which can vary widely; (2) there is no international and legally binding minimum standard for physical security; and (3) measures taken to strengthen physical security are considered confidential and are not subject to external assessment.[55] From a terrorist perspective, not only may a group opportunistically leverage situations in which fissile material has become available (through government instability or a coup), one has to assume that fissile material acquisition efforts will be targeted against the weakest security link. One can expect that differing assessments of the nuclear terror threat and divergent security practices will be exploited by terrorists seeking to acquire fissile material.

IAEA recommendations on the physical protection of nuclear material and nuclear facilities (Information Circular [INFCIRC] 225). The IAEA, largely through its International Physical Protection Advisory Service (IPPAS), has been proactive in providing member states with information and training with respect to the physical protection of nuclear material. Information Circular 225, for example, sets out state-of-the-art measures for physical protection. According to the IAEA, "Principles of physical protection are realized through administrative and technical measures, including physical barriers. The measures for the physical protection of nuclear material in use and storage and during transport, and of nuclear facilities, presented herein are recommended for use by States as required in their physical protection systems."[56] Although INFCIRC 225 outlines "requirements" for physical protection of nuclear material against unauthorized removal and sabotage, and measures to protect material in transport, these measures remain only recommendations to member states.

The International Convention on the Suppression of Acts of Nuclear Terrorism. The convention, adopted in 2005 and entered into force in July 2007, "requires State Parties to make certain acts criminal offenses in national law, establish jurisdiction over such offenses, prosecute or extradite persons alleged to have committed the defined criminal offenses, and engage in cooperation and mutual legal assistance with respect to objectives of the Convention."[57] Along with other international legal mechanisms mentioned above, the convention is part of the legal basis for the Global Initiative to Combat Nuclear Terrorism (GI). Launched by President George W. Bush and President Vladimir Putin in July 2006, the GI seeks to

> expand and accelerate efforts that develop partnership capacity to combat nuclear terrorism on a determined and systematic basis. Together with other participating countries and interacting closely with the IAEA, we will take steps to improve participants' capabilities to: ensure accounting, control, and physical protection of nuclear material and radioactive substances, as well as security of nuclear facilities; detect and suppress illicit trafficking or other illicit activities involving such materials, especially measures to prevent their acquisition and use by terrorists; respond to and mitigate the consequences of acts of nuclear terrorism; ensure cooperation in the development of technical means to combat nuclear terrorism; ensure that law enforcement takes all possible measures to deny safe haven to terrorists seeking to acquire or use nuclear materials; and to strengthen our respective national legal frameworks to ensure the effective prosecution of, and the certainty of punishment for, terrorists and those who facilitate such acts.[58]

The GI currently counts over seventy members as partners. As of November 2008, four international GI meetings have been conducted, and an Implementation and Advisory Group (IAG) has been established to assist in coordinating the implementation of GI activities. While the GI remains a positive force for raising awareness of nuclear terrorism, for ensuring political leaders continue to have nuclear terrorism on their agendas, and in increasing information sharing and best practices on nuclear terrorism, it suffers flaws. As Friedrich Steinhausler points out, some of these flaws include (1) the activities GI partners undertake are subject to available national resources and in austere fiscal times will be subject to downward pressure, (2) the IAG is only an informal body without legal authority for enforcement, and (3) "there is no mechanism foreseen which would enable an objective assessment of the actual improvement achieved by the Initiative, provided participating nations can reach a consensus on minimum standards on physical protection standards for nuclear materials and facilities."[59]

The Nuclear Suppliers Group and the Zangger Committee. The Nuclear Suppliers Group (NSG) was established in 1975 in response to the 1974 Indian nuclear explosion, which demonstrated that nuclear technology transferred for peaceful purposes can be misused. The NSG currently has forty-five participating governments.[60] The primary purpose of the NSG is "to prevent the proliferation of nuclear weapons through export controls of nuclear and nuclear-related material, equipment, and technology, without hindering international cooperation on peaceful uses of nuclear energy."[61] The NSG maintains a list of controlled technologies (a "trigger list") that is periodically updated.[62] The NSG has also reached out to non-NSG members to create awareness of issues related to the supply of sensitive technology and to work with other international organizations, such as the aforementioned UN 1540 Committee, to help "close gaps in the nonproliferation regime that proliferation networks attempt to exploit."[63] According to the GAO, the NSG has refused, however, to adopt a proposal raised by President George W. Bush in 2004 that NSG members should refuse to sell nuclear-related technologies to countries that have not signed the NPT's Additional Protocol providing for a more rigorous IAEA inspection regime. Finally, like many other international groups, the NSG operates by consensus and depends on the cohesion of its members to be effective.

The Zangger Committee interprets NPT, Article III, paragraph 2, in an attempt to harmonize nuclear export control policies for NPT participants. Paragraph 2 includes the language: "Each State Party to the Treaty undertakes not to provide . . . equipment or material especially designed or prepared for the processing, use, or production of special fissionable material to any non-nuclear-weapon State for peaceful purposes, unless the source or special fissionable material shall be subject to the safeguards required by this Article." The Zangger Committee interprets what constitutes such equipment or material. Like the NSG, the Zangger Committee produces a trigger list that includes, among many other items, gas centrifuges used to enrich uranium.[64]

Items on the trigger list may be exported to nonnuclear weapons state parties, but such an export triggers safeguards as a condition of supply. The Zangger Committee has some challenges; it has thirty-six member states, and important nuclear suppliers such as India, Israel, North Korea, and Pakistan do not participate. Lack of broader membership can substantially undermine the organization's effectiveness. Moreover, as an informal group of nuclear supplier countries that are parties to the NPT, the committee has no legal authority.

International nonproliferation regimes are invaluable insofar as they create international norms against aberrant behavior and raise international awareness about development of measures to prevent WMD proliferation. Any international agreement or regime must continually weigh the limits of national sovereignty as it attempts to develop legally binding measures on as broad a set of members as possible. Membership is important, as single country outliers can undermine the integrity of the entire regime. The nuclear nonproliferation regime has made it more difficult for nation-states to become nuclear powers, and by extension, fewer nuclear powers have made a terrorist's task more difficult. However, terrorists are not attempting to develop full-scale nuclear programs and, as a result, have no need for much of the infrastructure and technologies controlled in the regime. Terrorists need fissile material, machine equipment, and, most important, know-how to fashion a crude nuclear device. The nuclear nonproliferation regime may be somewhat effective at controlling material and equipment, but controlling nuclear weapons knowledge may prove more difficult.

EIGHT

Concluding Thoughts

onventional wisdom would lead one to conclude that nuclear terrorism in the United States is a clear and present danger—that the threat is imminent and nearly inevitable given the inexorable diffusion of technology and the intent of some terrorist groups to inflict mass casualties on the United States. Conventional wisdom is, however, only half right—the nuclear terrorism threat is clear yet not necessarily present and not inevitable.

If one defines "clear" in terms of (1) the existence of terrorist groups that have the stated intent to acquire weapons of mass destruction, including, although not exclusively, nuclear weapons, and (2) the grave consequences of nuclear terrorism, then the threat of nuclear terrorism is clear. "Present" may be defined as the existence of terrorist groups having the financial, technical, logistical, operational, and scientific capability to (1) acquire an intact nuclear weapon, recruit an insider having the knowledge to override electronic protection codes, transport the weapon undetected across U.S. borders, and detonate it; or (2) (although not necessarily in this linear sequence) acquire the requisite amount of fissile material, develop a safe haven to house the activities of the nuclear team, recruit appropriately skilled scientists and technicians (those having tacit knowledge and experience) to build an IND without being detected, conduct a number of tests (except of the weapon itself) to have some level of confidence that the weapon would work (regardless of yield), transport the IND across numerous nation-state borders undetected (assuming the weapon is not built in the United States), and detonate the weapon at the target of choice. The nuclear terrorism supply chain is long, and there are many opportunities for U.S. and international intelligence, nuclear security, law enforcement, and border security officials to break it. The "good guys" only have to be right once to prevent nuclear terrorism. To believe that nuclear terrorism is inevitable is to believe in technical determinism. Conventional wisdom and a belief in technical determinism in the 1960s projected a world of twenty to thirty nuclear powers today. That did not happen for numerous reasons, not the least of which is conscious policy decisions followed up by national and international actions to prevent it from occurring. With sustained senior-level political leadership and determination to continue to secure vulnerable fissile material globally while concurrently eviscerating terrorist group nuclear capabilities, the same positive results can be achieved.

If the threat is clear but not present, however, the United States and the world community cannot disregard the threat. Low-probability/high-consequence events are ignored at society's peril. Prudent policy does not underestimate or overestimate an adversary's capabilities. The sophisticated terrorist groups determined to attack the United States with WMD are neither ten feet tall nor two feet tall. Nuclear threat overestimation—through the development and the public pronouncement of worst-case scenarios—can (1) undermine national security by creating and sustaining an atmosphere of national fear that can be debilitating and weaken societal resiliency; (2) lead to preventative wars based on fallible intelligence that can be costly in terms of national treasure, blood, and missed opportunities; and (3) possibly lead to mass-casualty conventional attacks by discounting an operational conservatism some terrorist groups have practiced historically. As the November 2008 terrorist attack in Mumbai, India, demonstrates, low-technology terrorist attacks remain an instrumental element of terrorist tactics. Realistic nuclear terror risk assessments should be based not solely on U.S. vulnerabilities but also on the real intentions and capabilities of terrorist adversaries. Nuclear threat underestimation risks strategic surprise with potentially grave consequences.

There is no monolithic nuclear terrorism threat. That is, one must differentiate between the threat of a fission device, which would likely be manifested through the detonation of an IND, and that of a radiological dispersion device. While each device would cause fear, an IND would likely have more far-reaching consequences, both physical and psychological. The probabilities associated with each are also dynamic, but absolute stochastic numbers should not be accorded as much credence as the underlying trends associated with the nuclear terrorism threat. One must also differentiate between a nation-state's nuclear program and a nonstate actor's clandestine efforts to develop an IND. While the former will require substantial investment in the development of a nuclear fuel cycle, the development of an IND to serve terrorist ends requires no such infrastructure. There is, however, an obvious link between nation-state nuclear weapons programs and nonstate actors; that is, the more states that possess nuclear material and the implicit know-how to develop a nuclear weapon, the greater the target set for terrorist groups. However, one should not assume that nation-states with nuclear weapons—even if there are more of them—will sell or otherwise transfer those weapons or fissile material to terrorist groups.

Given the imperfections associated with physical security regimes and personnel reliability programs, the high likelihood of asymmetrical terrorist threats extending into the future, and the continued existence of nuclear weapons in the midterm, the complete eradication of the nuclear terrorism threat is an inspirational goal. In an open society existing in a globalized world where information, technology, ideas, finances, and persons move freely and rapidly, the risk of nuclear terrorism must be actively managed on both the demand and supply side.

THE DEMAND SIDE OF NUCLEAR TERRORISM

The intent of nefarious nonstate actors, such as al Qaeda, is well known. Meetings between Pakistani nuclear scientists and al Qaeda leadership, as well as documented attempts to acquire fissile material, demonstrate a sincere effort to develop a nuclear capability. While the group may have religious justification for the use of WMD against infidels, a number of terrorist recantation books have spurred a debate (the outcome of which remains undetermined) within the jihadist enterprise over the use of indiscriminate violence. Although increasingly under stress, al Qaeda seems to be maintaining and reinforcing a safe haven within Pakistan's Federally Administered Tribal Areas, which could enhance the group's ability to plan and execute sophisticated attacks against the West. However, these facts must also be weighed against the progress that the United States and its allies have made since 9/11 in degrading the operational capability of core al Qaeda, a group whose active support and participation would be essential to the success of any nuclear terrorist plot. As NCTC director Michael Leiter concluded, "Because of a series of . . . successful endeavors, core al-Qa'ida and its ability to project threats to Western Europe and the United States is much lower than it was last year, and I think in many ways lower than it has been for quite some time. . . . Their ability to train and deploy recruits has certainly been seriously diminished over the past year."[1]

The number of terrorist groups possessing both the intent and the capability to attack the United States should not be overstated. Some terrorist groups affiliated with core al Qaeda certainly have the intention to detonate a nuclear device in the United States, but intention unmarried to capability, while worthy of monitoring and undermining, does not translate into a clear and present nuclear terrorism threat. There are no terrorist groups, to the best of current public knowledge, that possess the *combined* capability and intent to attack the United States with nuclear weapons. Absence of evidence is not, however, evidence of absence; the unknown unknowns make for sleepless policymaker nights. However, in the absence of reliable intelligence, assuming there are scores of terrorist groups with nuclear intent and capability is unwarranted as it unnecessarily inflates the threat.

Construction, delivery, and successful detonation of a nuclear device within the United States are neither exceedingly easy nor exceedingly difficult for a sophisticated terrorist group. In the supply chain of events through which a terrorist group must pass, there are numerous opportunities for the United States and its global partners to disrupt the terrorist plot by exploiting what Michael Levi refers to as Murphy's Law of Nuclear Terrorism. While the foundation of U.S. national security policy should not rest upon a terrorist group's errors in plotting a nuclear attack, U.S. policy tools should be realistically structured so as to exploit terrorist weaknesses and vulnerabilities proactively and opportunistically.

THE SUPPLY SIDE OF NUCLEAR TERRORISM

Stockpiles of fissile material today include between 1,400 and 2,000 metric tons of HEU and approximately 500 metric tons of separated plutonium. India, Pakistan, and possibly Israel and North Korea continue to produce fissile material for nuclear weapons. While progress continues to be made through programs like the Global Threat Reduction Initiative, HEU is still used in commercial applications, including as fuel for over one hundred research reactors in over forty countries around the world, and the material is protected at various levels of security. President Obama's commitment to secure all vulnerable fissile material in the world in four years is aggressive. Yet implementation will likely not be easy given numerous challenges, not the least of which may be the belief among some nations that it is their sovereign right to hold this material, however dangerous it may seem to international security. Notwithstanding United Nations Security Council Resolution 1540's call for "appropriate effective" security standards, no single set of binding international nuclear security standards exists. As a result, there are substantial differences in national nuclear security standards, derived from disparities in nuclear terrorism threat assessments and financial capabilities, among other factors. The U.S. Intelligence Community, through the Nuclear Materials Information Program, recently developed a prioritized list of the fissile material it believes is most at risk. This program, the details of which remain classified, is especially important, as the absence of a prioritized strategy could leave the most vulnerable fissile material in place.

While it is true that if there are no loose nukes, no nascent nukes, and no new nuclear states the probability for nuclear terrorism decreases substantially, prudent national security planning must assume imperfect defenses, and thus the multilayered defense-in-depth approach is an appropriate framework for combating nuclear terrorism. Yet an overemphasis on nuclear measures within this framework would fail to leverage the very real effect nonnuclear tools can have on the deterrence of, detection of, prevention of, and response to nuclear terrorism. Law enforcement and intelligence are tools that are as important as fissile material detection technologies. Building societal resilience at home by communicating clearly with the public how they should respond to a potential nuclear attack is also essential to deterrence by denial, or denying terrorists their goal of "taking down" the United States. Simply stated, there are no magic policy wands or silver bullets that will eliminate the threat of nuclear terrorism. All agencies within the U.S. government must leverage not only their individual mission-based strengths but also their international liaison relationships to combat nuclear terrorism.

Preventing future nuclear proliferation among nation-states is clearly not inconsequential in the effort to prevent nuclear terrorism. The greater the number of nuclear-armed states, the more fissile material being produced; the more fissile material and weapons components being transported, the greater their vulnerability to seizure by terrorists. This is particularly true in the volatile Middle East, where Iran, a state that has mastered uranium enrichment, may be moving in the direction of becoming a nuclear weapons state. Should Iran test a nuclear weapon, the pressure will be on the United States to extend its nuclear umbrella to Egypt and Saudi Arabia and perhaps to all of the Gulf Cooperation Council states to dissuade these nations from purchasing nuclear weapons illicitly or developing their own indigenous nuclear programs. If the "Arab Spring" revolts across the Middle East and North Africa in early 2011 result in new regimes sympathetic to or directly or indirectly supportive of al Qaeda, this could lead to the establishment of additional terrorist safe havens, an unwelcome development for forces contributing to the potential for nuclear terrorism. However, the assumption that irrational leaders will transfer their nation's "crown jewels" to terrorist groups is one that does not stand up to critical analysis.[2] While there may be some limited situations in which a desperate national leader, convinced of his own regime's demise, may transfer a nuclear weapon to a terrorist group, in the vast majority of cases national leaders would rarely jeopardize their regime's and their own survival to assist an uncontrollable terrorist group in achieving its goals. If the nuclear terrorism taboo is ever crossed, any regime harboring a nascent nuclear weapons program at odds with the international community would be wise to question the standard of evidence the target state will demand before it assesses culpability and takes (perhaps extreme) retaliatory action.

No serious analyst of nonproliferation in general, and nuclear terrorism specifically, disputes that since the Soviet Union fell the United States has made significant progress in making nuclear stockpiles and weapons more secure.[3] Notwithstanding a relatively slow start, the nonproliferation progress the United States and Russia have made is impressive, given the rapidity of the change and the amount of weapons and material that needed to be accounted for and returned to Russia from the three nonnuclear weapons states— Belarus, Kazakhstan, and Ukraine—that inherited nuclear weapons after the dissolution of the Soviet Union in 1991. Yet twenty years later, nuclear terrorism remains a clear, if not present, global threat. Only through sustained political leadership at the highest levels will the various impediments to combating nuclear terrorism—whether unilateral, bilateral, or multilateral or pertaining to secrecy, sovereignty, or complacency—be surmounted in a manner that enhances national security.

THE CONVENTIONALIST AND THE SKEPTIC

It could be argued that the distinction drawn in this book is one without a difference, that is, that both conventionalists and skeptics believe that if terrorists acquired nuclear weapons it would constitute a grave threat to U.S. national security. Yet beyond this area of agreement, there are substantial differences not only concerning nuclear terrorism threat assessment and probability but also in the optimal policy mix to combat nuclear terrorism. It may only be a question of emphasis—which policy tools each group might have a relative preference for—but there is nevertheless a difference. Notional conventionalists might believe that nuclear security can be perfect or near perfect; therefore, their recommendations focus on the supply side—lock up or clean out all nuclear material and the problem will be resolved. This preference is born out of the compelling fact that the acquisition of fissile material is the primary impediment to a terrorist acquiring nuclear capability. Conventionalists might also advocate some level of support for other layers in a multilayered defense system and for counterterrorism initiatives to address the demand side, but their focus and preference are for supply-side measures. Conventionalists might also advocate a strong declaratory policy communicating to all nation-states that should they assist terrorists in acquiring nuclear weapons in any manner they will be held fully accountable.

Alternatively, the notional skeptic might believe that all security regimes are inherently imperfect and that the acquisition of fissile material by terrorists, while alarming, does not necessarily mean a terrorist could build a crude nuclear device, deliver it to U.S. shores, and detonate it. As a result, while skeptics agree that locking up or cleaning out fissile material is a part of the solution set, they would likely believe it is only one element, and not necessarily the most important element, of the optimal policy mix. Skeptics might tend to prioritize a multilayered system of defenses against nuclear terrorism that places equal value on locking up fissile material *and* the nonnuclear means of combating nuclear terrorism, including traditional counterterrorism, intelligence, law enforcement, and homeland security measures. With respect to declaratory retaliation policy and nation-state sponsorship of nuclear terrorism, skeptics might find that the threat of military retaliation against allies Russia and Pakistan for their potential negligence in protecting nuclear weapons of fissile material lacks credibility. As a result, they might advocate a policy of more direct engagement with these states to secure weapons and fissile material rather than threatening them with (possibly unconventional) military retaliation after an IND has been detonated in the United States.

These notional distinctions in threat assessments might flow through to nuclear terrorism resource allocation decisions. In a $14 trillion economy, it could be compellingly argued that the United States can afford to allocate substantial resources to both demand- and supply-side nuclear terrorism risk reduction measures. Compared to overall defense outlays, supply-side reduction measures, such as the Cooperative Threat Reduction Program and MPC&A programs, have cost very little. According to Matthew Bunn and Andrew Newman of Harvard University, addressing supply-side issues, "Nuclear security is affordable: a level of security that could greatly reduce the risk of nuclear theft could be achieved for all nuclear stockpiles world-wide for an initial investment of roughly one percent of annual defense spending for a single year."[4] However, conventionalists and skeptics might allocate resources differently.

Conventionalists might emphasize that additional resources should be focused on supply-side risk reduction and perhaps new grand bargains through which nations are accorded positive security guarantees or other "carrots," such as a guaranteed supply of nuclear fuel in exchange for forgoing uranium enrichment. Invariably any such program is perceived as a quid pro quo of national sovereignty for international security—an exchange that continues to align and perpetuate the nuclear "haves" against the nuclear "have-nots." Yet each nation, depending on numerous internal and regional factors, will calculate how much sovereignty, if any, it may be willing to cede to an international organization for a collective security "good" such as the absence of nuclear terrorism. Creative management of these perceptions will be an important part of negotiations concerning how much additional compliance and inspection authority agencies such as the IAEA receive. Conventionalists might ask what new incentives and disincentives can curtail proliferation of nuclear technologies. What incentives and disincentives can allied nations use to convince nations possessing fissile material, but are reluctant to part with it, to give up that material? What are the most promising nuclear detection technologies that can be deployed in the next three to five years?

Skeptics might spend relatively more on demand-side risk reduction and ask what steps the United States can take to influence terrorists to believe that the detonation of a nuclear weapon is not in their self-interest. What counterterrorism strategies are most effective at undermining terrorist group nuclear capability? How should the United States best determine and then ameliorate long-term root causes of international terrorism? How can the United States effectively deter nation-states currently possessing nuclear weapons or nuclear weapons–related technologies from providing it to terrorist groups? Owing to a lack of a meaningful correlation between mass-casualty attacks and WMD use, skeptics might prefer to focus more on the demand side, that is, to engage in counterterrorism methods that are effective irrespective of the type of weapon that a sophisticated terrorist group might use to inflict mass casualties.

FINAL RECOMMENDATIONS

In the final analysis, today's policies and actions to deter, detect, prevent, and respond to nuclear terrorism must proceed along numerous and concurrent paths. On the supply side, using the Intelligence Community's Nuclear Materials Information Program as a key to securing in place or cleaning out fissile material should remain a high priority. Preventing Iran from acquiring nuclear weapons (or creatively managing the regional and global implications of such a development) and restarting negotiations with North Korea to convince it to accept nuclear disarmament are also high-priority items. Preventing Pakistan from emulating 1979 Iran should be the nation's highest priority. A radical jihadist regime with nuclear weapons is a clear and present threat to U.S. national security, yet it should also be recognized that the transition from a nonstate actor to a state actor changes the deterrence equation. Enhancing nuclear forensics, including attribution capacity and detection technologies, is another essential supply-side tool that can serve as a force multiplier in deterring nation-states from trafficking in nuclear technologies and fissile material. Working with Russia to ensure that Cooperative Threat Reduction mechanisms and practices (in place since 1991) continue to be implemented is critically important to prevent regression to an earlier and more dangerous period.

From a demand-side perspective, sophisticated terrorist groups such as al Qaeda need to have their capabilities constrained and need to be eventually destroyed using all means of national power. Al Qaeda safe havens anywhere should be actively targeted and eliminated, although not necessarily through a large U.S. military presence or solely through kinetic instruments of power. Foreign partner intelligence, law enforcement, security, and military entities, to the extent they exist, are best placed to understand terrorist group modus operandi as well as areas of greatest terrorist group vulnerability. Currently, this translates into continuing to work with Afghanistan and Pakistan, through the provision of incentives and disincentives, to ensure the al Qaeda safe havens in the region are destroyed sustainably and in a manner that is cognizant of the unstable domestic political situation in both countries. The United States must better leverage its competitive advantage, technological and information dominance, to undermine al Qaeda's sophisticated use of the Internet as a recruitment, operational, and fund-raising tool. Another high counterterrorism priority should be to support in any manner possible (while hiding the United States' hand) those schools of thought within the jihadist enterprise that have been questioning the use of indiscriminate violence that is likely to kill innocent Muslims. Counterinsurgency techniques—clear, hold, build—must be flexibly and creatively implemented, with direct and active participation by foreign partners' military, law enforcement, and security services, in order to eliminate in a sustainable manner ungoverned territories used by national and regional insurgents and by international terrorists with broader objectives.

If not already in place, elite and interdisciplinary U.S. intelligence teams with direct access to the special assistant to the president and White House coordinator for arms control and weapons of mass destruction, proliferation, and terrorism should be established to decrease the supply- and demand-side risks of nuclear terrorism. These teams could be directed against traditional hard targets and nonstate actors, as well as clandestine nuclear procurement networks. Greater and timelier international sharing of intelligence relating to nuclear security, nuclear scientists, and nuclear activity counterterrorism leads would contribute substantially to early warning of nuclear terrorism. Advances in analytic tradecraft and innovative intelligence collection methods are valuable tools that assist in the development of accurate nuclear terrorism threat assessments.

Finally, the oftentimes competing interests of sovereignty and collective international security must be creatively managed such that nuclear "haves" and "have-nots" both believe it is in their vital national security interests to prevent nuclear terrorism. All of the aforementioned initiatives will have a far higher probability of success if U.S. senior-level leadership strengthens international support for the nuclear nonproliferation regime and ensures that nuclear terrorism is not deemphasized with temporal distance from the attacks of September 11, 2001.

APPENDIX A

U.S. Policy Options to Counter Nuclear Terrorism

Regardless of one's assessment of the probability of nuclear terrorism, there are no responsible analysts who believe the probability is zero. The question then becomes, what are some of the most salient options to reduce both supply- and demand-side elements of the nuclear terrorism equation? Which options build on existing programs and increase the urgency with which these programs are implemented? There may also be certain actions that the United States or the international community should *not take* in order to decrease the risk of nuclear terrorism. There are numerous proactive measures that can be categorized as unilateral, bilateral, or multilateral that the United States and the international community can take to reduce the risk of nuclear terrorism on both the supply and demand sides. There are also "stretch goals" that are aspirational, inspirational, and long term in nature, as well as goals that are organizational and bureaucratic and could be made in the short term. However, it seems to be the case that all the relatively "low-hanging fruit"— particularly on the nuclear security side, such as highly vulnerable weapons-grade fissile material—has been harvested. Sustained high-level political support, domestically and internationally, must be encouraged to further reduce the risk of nuclear terrorism in the years ahead.

Actions taken by the permanent five members of the United Nations Security Council, which also represent the five nuclear weapons state parties to the NPT, are important with respect to the signals they send to the rest of the world about the importance of nuclear weapons. As the interim report of the Congressional Commission on the Strategic Posture of the United States finds:

> It is not clear that actions we take on our nuclear program affect the nuclear calculus of North Korea or Iran, or necessarily others, but they do affect the actions of nations whose cooperation we need to deal with North Korea and Iran, as well as other proliferation problems. In short, if the US by its actions indicates to other nations that we are moving seriously to decrease the importance and role of nuclear weapons, we increase our chance of getting the kind of cooperation we need to deal effectively with the dangers of proliferation.[1]

ASPIRATIONAL GOAL—GLOBAL NUCLEAR DISARMAMENT: THE ULTIMATE NUCLEAR TERRORISM REMEDY

One of the central issues in the nuclear terrorism debate concerns whether the threat of nuclear terrorism can be eradicated. Given the irrevocable laws of nature, fissile material does not occur naturally. On the one hand, conventionalists believe that since only a handful of nations produce fissile material, if the international community can influence these nations to protect this fissile material *perfectly*, then nuclear terrorism can be eradicated. Skeptics, on the other hand, believe that because so much fissile material currently exists globally and because all physical security regimes tend to have imperfections, the international community is likely unable to completely eradicate the global threat of nuclear terrorism. Rather, skeptics would argue, the international community must actively manage the nuclear terrorism threat.

These arguments notwithstanding, there is one certain way to eradicate the nuclear terrorism threat and that is by the global elimination of nuclear weapons.[2] Simply put, no nuclear weapons, no nuclear terrorism. This aspirational and inspirational goal was recently advocated by a series of eminent foreign policy experts, including former secretary of defense William J. Perry, former secretaries of state George P. Shultz and Henry A. Kissinger, and former senator Sam Nunn.[3] The United Kingdom's foreign secretary Margaret Beckett recently stated, "What we need is both a vision—a scenario for a world free of nuclear weapons—and action—progressive steps to reduce warhead numbers and to limit the role of nuclear weapons in security policy. These two strands are separate but they are mutually reinforcing. Both are necessary, but at the moment too weak."[4]

Numerous other foreign policy notables in the United States have expressed a preference for moving in this direction, including James A. Baker III, Zbigniew Brzezinski, Frank Carlucci, Melvin Laird, and Colin Powell. The point is that while this may be a stretch goal, it is nevertheless one worth pursuing, and there are concrete actions that can be taken today by the United States, Russia, and the international community in order to move in this direction. In the words of Shultz, Perry, Kissinger, and Nunn:

> In some respects, the goal of a world free of nuclear weapons is like the top of a very tall mountain. From the vantage point of our troubled world today, we can't even see the top of the mountain, and it is tempting and easy to say we can't get there from here. But the risks from continuing to go down the mountain or standing pat are too real to ignore. We must chart a course to higher ground where the mountaintop becomes visible.[5]

As the United States and Russia possess 95 percent of the world's nuclear warheads, they have special responsibility to lead the world toward this vision. Tempering the vision of former secretaries of state and defense is the current secretary of defense Robert Gates, who has served five U.S. presidents (Jimmy Carter, Ronald Reagan, George H. W. Bush, George W. Bush, and Barack Obama). Secretary Gates recently stated that all five presidents under whom he served wanted to eliminate nuclear weapons. However,

> all have come up against the reality that as long as others have nuclear weapons, we must maintain some level of these nuclear weapons ourselves to deter potential adversaries and to reassure over two dozen allies and partners who rely on our nuclear umbrella for their security, making it unnecessary for them to develop their own. . . . The power of the nuclear weapons and their strategic impact is a genie that cannot be put back in the bottle, at least for a very long time. While we have a long-term goal of abolishing nuclear weapons once and for all, given the world in which we live, we have to be realistic about that proposition.[6]

Following are numerous unilateral, bilateral, and multilateral methods advanced by foreign policy practitioners and academics alike toward the reduction of risk of nuclear terrorism. Some of these actions can be taken on the nuclear security side, and some can be taken on the counterterrorism side.

However, any and all initiatives taken to reduce the risk of nuclear terrorism should remain cognizant of the potential policy trade-offs between counter-proliferation and counterterrorism. Arguably, the area of greatest danger, and therefore most urgent attention, lies at the "crossroads of terrorism and proliferation—in the poorly governed areas of Pakistan."[7]

UNILATERAL

While the threat of nuclear terrorism is clearly best addressed with global solutions, as the first country to develop and the only country to ever use nuclear weapons, the United States has a special responsibility to assume a leadership role in the development and implementation of measures to combat nuclear terrorism. The following are some measures the United States could take (and in some instances is taking to an extent) unilaterally that would work toward decreasing the risk of nuclear terrorism. Taking these actions does not, of course, directly influence North Korea to disgorge its nuclear weapons or prevent Iran from engaging in nuclear weapons work. However, these seemingly intractable nuclear proliferation problems demand a united international response, and the United States may be better positioned to lead such international efforts if it is perceived as upholding its end of the nuclear nonproliferation bargain outlined in the NPT.

Conduct top to bottom review of U.S. nuclear security assistance programs. Given the fact that many of the nuclear security programs in place have been in operation for at least five years, and some for over fifteen years, it may be a propitious time to implement a top to bottom review of all global nuclear security programs. A number of studies have been conducted by outside panels established by the government, and these could serve as guideposts for a broader, high-level, NSC-led assessment of the performance of U.S. nuclear security programs and recommendations for the future.[8] How are the programs, designed in another time under different circumstances, yet with consistent purpose, performing? Do any of the programs need to be phased out? Do additional resources need to be dedicated to new programs to replace them?

Direct top to bottom review of U.S. performance in the "long war." There appears to be broad recognition in official and nonofficial channels that military power alone will not allow the United States to prevail against the forces of Islamic extremism. "Soft power" tools such as public diplomacy, winning the war of ideas, and working to support democracy where it is already occurring endogenously, among other ideas, have all been mentioned as areas where the United States has not achieved its full potential in the fight against Islamic extremism. It is not necessarily anomalous for U.S. interests (such as the free flow of oil from the Persian Gulf or the prevention of terrorist attacks in the United States) to exist in tension with U.S. values (such as the promotion of democracy and respect for human rights). Exploiting terrorist weakness by amplifying the voices of moderation within the Islamic community, understanding why recruited terrorists leave terrorist organizations and working to support the motivations for such departures, and actively targeting terrorism recruitment and propaganda efforts in the cyber realm are all among the initiatives that could be further enhanced to undermine terrorism.

Intelligence, homeland security, and law enforcement have a critical role to play in countering nuclear terrorist plots by undermining terrorist efforts in general. As Matthew Bunn and Andrew Newman recently wrote, "The best chances to stop [a nuclear terrorism plot] lie not in exotic new detection technologies, but in a broad counterterrorist effort, ranging from intelligence and other operations to target high-capability terrorist groups to addressing anti-American hatred that makes recruiting and fund-raising easier, and makes it more difficult for other governments to cooperate with the United States."[9] Similarly, the aggressive use of law enforcement and intelligence and the cooperation of U.S. intelligence and law enforcement agencies with overseas counterparts are the most valuable tools in interdicting illicit trafficking in fissile material.

Consider removal of U.S. tactical nuclear weapons from Europe. As events have demonstrated, even U.S. nuclear weapons security is not flawless. Tactical nuclear weapons are highly attractive to terrorists. While nuclear deterrence remains an important element of U.S. national security, given shifts in the U.S.-Russian relationship since 1991, the strategic and tactical arguments for such deployments must be weighed against potential costs, including potential terrorist targeting. Some have viewed the presence of tactical nuclear weapons on European soil as unnecessary given the end of the Cold War and the fact that the United Kingdom has eliminated tactical nuclear weapons from its arsenal.[10] Others have concluded that "the deployment of nuclear weapons in Europe is not a Service or regional combatant command issue—it is an *Alliance* issue. As long as NATO members rely on U.S. nuclear weapons for deterrence—and as long as they maintain their own dual-capable aircraft as part of that deterrence—no action should be taken to remove them [U.S. tactical nuclear weapons] without a thorough and deliberate process of consultation."[11] The first step in this analysis from a U.S. national interest perspective took place in the Obama administration's first Nuclear Posture Review.

Work to build societal resilience. The chorus of fear that has been propagated by some within the government, media, and academia has resulted in a populace that is fearful for its collective security. While situational awareness and an understanding of the threats facing society are welcome, the constant focus on worst-case scenarios causes the population to live in fear. Such pervasive fear undermines societal resilience, or the ability of a nation's populace to face whatever dangers terrorism or any other threat presents and to understand that how the people react to such threats determines the extent to which terrorists perceive they have achieved their goals. As the Graham-Talent Commission on WMD found, "If we show potential terrorists that we are ready as a community and as a nation—then they are less likely to believe that their attack can achieve all of its destructive goals."[12] In short, a well-informed and prepared community can contribute to the prevention of an attack through reinforcing deterrence by denial and, should a WMD event happen, through responding in a manner that does not cause mass panic. Consequence management, then, is an essential and inherently public task—a cooperative effort between government and the populace. One action recommended by the Graham-Talent Commission was that the federal government should work with a "consortium of state and local governments to develop a publicly available checklist of actions each level of government should take to prevent or ameliorate the consequences of WMD terrorism."[13] Greater public openness about the threats, statistics illustrating the likelihood of a citizen being hurt in a terrorist attack, and information on how the populace should respond to a nuclear terrorism attack would also enhance societal resilience. The move away from the erstwhile Homeland Security Advisory System to the more targeted National Threat Advisory System is a positive development in this area.

Consider ratification of the Comprehensive Test Ban Treaty. The Comprehensive Test Ban Treaty (CTBT) bans all underground nuclear tests with a maximum force equal to 150,000 tons of TNT.[14] Negotiated by the United National Conference on Disarmament, it was adopted by the United Nations General Assembly on September 10, 1996, and subsequently opened for signature on September 24, 2006, when the United States signed it. As of December 9, 2008, 180 states have signed the treaty and 148 have ratified it. The United States, for various reasons, has not ratified the treaty, yet it has continued a unilateral moratorium on nuclear testing since 1992.[15] The CTBT is an old issue in the arms control community, but it remains an important element of the nuclear nonproliferation regime.[16] All members of the NPT, by their signature and ratification, are committed to pursue negotiations relating to the cessation of the nuclear arms race and to nuclear disarmament. Ratification of the CTBT by the United States would send a strong message that the United States is living up to its NPT bargain, continues to support nuclear nonproliferation, and encourages other parties that have not ratified the treaty, including China, India, Egypt, Israel, and Iran, to do so.[17] Yet the moratorium on testing, like the issue of global nuclear disarmament, runs into the realities of international security today. As Secretary of Defense Gates recently stated, "To be blunt, there is absolutely no way we can maintain a credible deterrent and reduce the number of weapons in our stockpile without either resorting to testing our stockpile or pursuing a [nuclear weapon] modernization program."[18] Resumption of nuclear testing would clearly undermine the international nuclear nonproliferation regime by demonstrating to nuclear "have-nots" or threshold nations that nuclear weapons remain an important tool of international power.

Ensure U.S. machinery to combat nuclear terrorism is well coordinated. U.S. nuclear security programs are fairly well dispersed across the Departments of Homeland Security, Defense, State, Energy, and Justice (see appendix B). In the executive branch, beyond the dispersed nature of nuclear security programs, the Graham Commission has documented the diffused nature of policy coordination, illustrating that one agency calculated that its senior officials attend "22 PCCs [White House–National Security Council Policy Coordination Committees], sub-PCCs, interagency working groups, and interagency policy groups that hold weekly meetings; 69 [groups] that hold monthly meetings; [and] 198 [groups] that hold meetings annually, semiannually, quarterly, bimonthly, monthly, biweekly, weekly, or on an ad hoc basis."[19] Such diffused coordination undermines accountability, saps agency officials' time to do their jobs, and results in overmanagement of some issues and lack of management of other issues, according to the Graham-Talent Commission. Although a coordinator for WMD terrorism does not necessarily need to be established with the advice and consent of the U.S. Senate, the individual should be highly respected in the nonproliferation community, have ready access to the president, and have influence in the formulation and execution of nuclear security budgets across agencies, likely through the Office of Management and Budget.[20] As mentioned earlier, the Obama administration named Gary Samore, a respected nonproliferation specialist, as special assistant to the president and White House coordinator for arms control and weapons of mass destruction, proliferation, and terrorism. The budgetary authorities for this position remain unclear, but given the position's location within the NSC, any budgetary authority is likely to be exercised indirectly through the OMB.

Continue aggressive nuclear detection technology research and development. The current status of nuclear detection technology is relatively poor, especially when it comes to being able to detect even a lightly shielded amount of HEU or a crude nuclear device using HEU. Passive systems being used today and even ASP systems being contemplated for future use are not highly effective. However, there are some promising active detection technologies that may enhance the nation's ability to detect fissile material, if provided further research and development. As one layer in the multilayered detection system, aggressive research and development on promising systems, including muon beams, should be pursued. As part of a comprehensive review of U.S. nuclear strategy, consideration should be given to enhancing research and development of active detection systems.

Fund academic programs in nuclear forensics. A number of studies have documented that the pool of professionals available in the field of nuclear forensics is decreasing over time. As this field is an invaluable element of deterring state actors from transferring a nuclear weapon or fissile material to a terrorist group, developing a long-term flow of scientists into this field could prove beneficial to countering nuclear terrorism.

Continue discussion of expanded deterrence and U.S. declaratory policy. Expanding deterrence to nation-states that have nuclear weapons or fissile material to influence them not to provide such material to terrorists remains a topic of discussion. Some believe that a doctrine of negligence should be enacted whereby any nation, through the willful or unintentional provision of fissile material to a terrorist group, would be subject to military retaliation. Others believe it is unrealistic to think that the United States would retaliate militarily against Russia or Pakistan given that (1) the United States has substantial common interests with each of these nations, and leakage from either, while inexcusable, does not warrant an attack that could have severe unintended consequences, both strategically and tactically; and (2) if a terrorist nuclear weapon detonated in the United States was able to be traced back to either country, the United States' first priority would likely be to ask for assistance from that country to quickly learn if any additional weapons or material were missing, in the interest of preventing a second nuclear detonation in the United States.

BILATERAL

From a nuclear terrorism perspective, the United States' relationships with Russia and Pakistan are two of the most important bilateral relationships.[21] Although no nation is an island and nuclear terrorism may be best addressed through multilateral means, Russia and Pakistan likely represent the greatest risk of fissile material leakage. Russia has over one thousand metric tons of fissile material located at widely dispersed nuclear facilities and buildings. While much of the material has been protected through the Cooperative Threat Reduction Program, for numerous reasons, not the least of which is prohibited access to some material by Russia, some material remains less well protected. Moreover, corruption and potential compromise of insiders remain significant concerns. The U.S.-Pakistani relationship, which has to be considered in a regional context, is the other critical bilateral relationship for nuclear terrorism. As the Graham-Talent Commission noted, Pakistan lies at the nexus of terrorism and nuclear weapons. Former CIA officer Bruce Riedel stated recently, "I have said on many occasions that Pakistan is the most dangerous country in the world: International terrorism, nuclear proliferation, the threat of nuclear war, drugs, democracy deficit, and Islam all come together in an extraordinarily combustible way."[22] Pakistan is a fragile democracy possessing between sixty and one hundred nuclear warheads and has a substantial presence of terrorist groups within its borders. Its military and intelligence services, particularly elements within the ISI, have supported terrorist and insurgent groups to fight as Pakistan's proxies in Kashmir, India, and Afghanistan.

With respect to Russia, some initiatives worthy of pursuing include the following:

- The United States and Russia have renewed their commitment to strategic arms reductions,[23] Article VI of the NPT to "pursue negotiations in goodfaith on effective measures relating to the cessation of the nuclear arms race . . . and to nuclear disarmament." President Barack Obama and President Dmitri A. Medvedev expressed an interest in pursuing nuclear arms control in their first meeting at the G-20 Summit hosted by the United Kingdom in April 2009 when both leaders "agreed to work together to fulfill our obligations under Article VI of the Treaty on Non-Proliferation of Nuclear Weapons and demonstrate leadership in reducing the number of nuclear weapons in the world. . . . We agreed to pursue new and verifiable reductions in our strategic offensive arsenals in a step-by-step process beginning by replacing the Strategic Arms Reduction Treaty with a new legally binding treaty."[24] At the July 2009 U.S.-Russia Summit in Moscow, a framework for a follow-on to START was confirmed with the following limits: (1) on nuclear warheads, a range between 1,500 and 1,675 (START limit is 2,200); and (2) on strategic delivery vehicles (missiles and strategic bombers), a range between 500 and 1,100 (START limit is 1,600).[25] In December 2010 the U.S. Senate provided its advice and consent to the ratification of New START, which limits the numbers of deployed strategic nuclear warheads to no more than 1,550 each. This is a substantial foreign policy achievement.
- They should increase warning time for nuclear missile launches. According to a recent study, Russia has some 1,300 nuclear weapons on high (launch on warning or launch under attack) alert.[26] Although the United States' early warning and communications systems are more reliable and redundant than Russia's are, the United States also has missiles on high-alert status. Currently it would take the United States and Russia only thirty minutes to hit reciprocal targets with ICBMs. The prompt launch capability carries with it, according to Sam Nunn, "an increasingly unacceptable risk of an accidental, mistaken, or unauthorized launch."[27] While this may not necessarily be of direct concern from a nuclear terrorism perspective, al Qaeda would do anything in its power to serve as a catalyst for a war between great powers. The Cold War is over, but there will inevitably be tension between the United States and Russia on numerous global issues; taking missiles off rapid alert and response would increase time for decision makers to contemplate their actions, thus enhancing stability.

- The United States and Russia should continue to decrease fissile material stockpiles through, among other means, continued implementation of the Plutonium Disposition Agreement and the HEU Purchase Agreement (Megatons to Megawatts). Under the terms of the Plutonium Disposition Agreement, signed in September 2000, the United States and Russia agreed to transform 34 metric tons of plutonium each (of 50 metric tons declared excess to military needs) into a proliferation-resistant form of fissile material over twenty years. According to the U.S. Enrichment Corporation, as of December 31, 2010, Russia has recycled 412 (of a committed 500) metric tons of weapons-grade HEU into LEU for civilian fuel reactors.[28] This translates into the elimination of fissile material for over sixteen thousand warheads. Consideration should be given to the question of whether (and if so how much) additional fissile material in Russia and the United States could be categorized as being "excess to military needs."
- While substantial progress has been made in securing Russian fissile material and nuclear warhead sites, there is still more progress to be made. Rapid upgrades have been completed at 85 percent of the buildings slated to receive them, and comprehensive upgrades have been completed at 70–75 percent of all buildings in the former Soviet Union with weapons-usable material.[29] Aggressive DOE targets to complete these upgrades should be vigorously supported, politically and financially.[30]
- As the Cooperative Threat Reduction Program enters a new phase, with Russia assuming greater responsibility for updating and maintaining U.S. nuclear security equipment and facilities installed through the program, Russia will need to take on responsibility for its own nuclear security—including the dedication of resources once provided by the United States. A true nuclear partnership between the two countries must be maintained to protect the tons of fissile material housed across Russia.
- Consider the creation of bilateral nuclear forensics teams, building on the professional relationships established under the Nunn-Lugar program. Such an action could benefit the forces of deterrence, as bilateral forensics teams could leverage more information and skill sets to attribute nuclear material.
- As the United States has appointed a single person to act as a coordinator for preventing WMD terrorism, such a position in Russia (if it does not

already exist) might facilitate sustained high-level interaction akin to the Gore-Chernomyrdin Commission that functioned under former president William Clinton.[31]

With respect to Pakistan, some initiatives worth pursuing include the following:

- The United States walks a tightrope in its relations with Pakistan. It wants the country to fight terrorism aggressively and eradicate any al Qaeda safe havens in FATA or any other location within the country. However, the United States does not want to push the fragile democracy (currently also experiencing substantial economic distress) too far in the direction of cracking down against radical jihadists, given that there are pockets of Pakistanis who are sympathetic to radicalism; the United States does not want to be a catalyst for an overthrow of the existing government. Continued stress in the bilateral relationship over U.S. drone strikes against terrorist targets in Pakistan must be actively managed.

- The United States should continue to offer nuclear security training for Pakistani personnel. Personnel reliability programs are an essential element of nuclear security, as security is only as good as its weakest link. If nuclear security personnel, technicians, and managers are sympathetic to radical Islamist entities within Pakistan, insider collusion becomes more likely. Insider collusion can defeat even the best physical security measures.

- The United States should work with the government of Pakistan to help it build institutions and counterterrorism capacity that will better allow it to fight terrorism within its borders and better meet the needs of its population for security, economic opportunity, and education. This is not to state that the lack of vibrant democracy is the cause of terrorism or that democracy will quell terrorism. However, a fragile indigenous democracy will have a difficult time mustering the support it needs to aggressively target terrorism within its borders, one of the central challenges in the U.S.-Pakistani relationship. Moreover, the United States may wish to reconsider how the substantial counterterrorism aid it provides to Pakistan is allocated. What concrete results has the aid achieved in the past? How effective has U.S. aid been in preventing terrorists from using Pakistan's FATA as a continuing safe haven for operational planning? How might aid be restructured to better serve U.S. and Pakistani mutual counterterrorism interests? What trade-offs have been made by the United States in its relationship with Pakistan; has counterterrorism been favored over counterproliferation? How effective have been Pakistan's nonproliferation actions taken in the aftermath of the A. Q. Khan proliferation scandal? The Enhanced Partnership with Pakistan Act of 2009 passed by Congress in October 2009 authorizes up to $1.5 billion per year for development, economic, and democratic assistance (i.e., civilian assistance) to Pakistan for fiscal years 2010–2014. The act also requires the Department of State to conduct oversight of this assistance and to produce periodic reports.

- While it is highly likely that the United States has already done so, the development and gaming of contingency plans to ensure the security of Pakistani nuclear weapons and fissile material in the event of a governmental coup or collapse are essential tasks. While such a mission will be exceedingly difficult for numerous reasons, it would be imprudent not to plan for such a contingency.

MULTILATERAL

Move the international approach to combating nuclear terrorism from voluntary to mandatory. Graham Allison of Harvard University advocates the establishment of a new "Global Alliance against Terrorism" that would "require an unambiguous commitment to the principles of assured nuclear security. States would have to guarantee that all nuclear weapons and materials in their territories were beyond the reach of terrorists and thieves."[32] The means of securing nuclear weapons and fissile material would have to be "sufficiently transparent that leaders of all member states could reassure their own citizens that terrorists would never get a bomb from another alliance member."[33] The alliance Graham envisions would require these actions in exchange for certain benefits. Member states would have to define the security level of weapons and fissile material and assure others that these levels of security had been achieved. Members would also be required to deposit samples of nuclear materials in an international library that would "be available for use in identifying the source of any weapons or material that found its way into terrorists' hands."[34] The members would also define accountability, that is, what actions would be taken against a state that provided a weapon or fissile material to a terrorist group that then used it against another state. In return, if nuclear weapons or fissile material were stolen, members that had met the new standards in securing their materials and made their safeguards sufficiently transparent to other members would be judged less negligent.[35] In short, in exchange for doing the right thing, these countries could be assured that they would be unlikely targets for retaliatory action. Nonmember states would automatically face more suspicion. Moreover, according to Allison, "members of the alliance would also undertake to clarify the consequences of knowingly allowing nuclear material to fall into terrorist hands. Those consequences would not necessarily involve military retaliation; alternatives such as exacting financial reparations would certainly be explored and might prove more realistic. Consequences would also be different for different violators, since threatening nuclear retaliation against Russia would not be credible."[36]

More policy options follow that have themes related to providing the international community with additional authority to aggressively police international nuclear security. However, in order for any nation-state to forgo some element of national sovereignty—to commit to binding and enforceable nuclear safeguards, for example—it must find it in its self-interest to do so. A reasonable question is, can the appropriate set of incentives and disincentives be put in place to convince sovereign states to make such a decision?

Consider a revision to Article IV of the NPT—no "nascent nukes."[37] While a relatively radical option, the next NPT Review Conference could be used to pursue the option of opening the NPT for amendment. The risk, of course, is that once the treaty is opened the "grand bargain" could also be undermined. Article IV of the NPT provides all member states with the "inalienable right" to acquire nuclear power for peaceful purposes. As mentioned throughout this book, if a nation builds a nuclear infrastructure for the development of peaceful nuclear power generation, including the ability to enrich uranium and reprocess spent fuel, it has surmounted a major impediment to the development of nuclear weapons. If the rationale for the establishment of nuclear power generation is energy security, the international community (if it is committed to nuclear nonproliferation) must establish a means of providing nuclear fuel to nations interested in civilian nuclear power generation so they do not need to develop it indigenously. Such a fuel bank was established by the IAEA in December 2010. How it will be implemented in practice is an open question as its operating principles are market based. If a state's supply arrangements are disrupted, they would have access to the nuclear fuel reserve under impartial IAEA control. A potential future quid pro quo could be that in exchange for forgoing uranium enrichment and spent fuel reprocessing and putting an Additional Protocol into force, a reliable supply of nuclear fuel would be provided at market prices. Importantly, forgoing uranium enrichment does not necessarily mean a nation no longer has the right, under the NPT, to participate in scientific exchanges in pursuit of nuclear power.

Renew the commitment to pursue negotiations relating to nuclear disarmament. This is part of the grand bargain enshrined in the NPT: The nuclear "haves" are committed to pursue negotiations toward nuclear disarmament. While unilateral measures taken pursuant to agreements not ratified by parliaments can be successful in decreasing the number of warheads, they are reversible and not subject to verification. Strategic arms reduction treaties such as New START with viable verification regimes and transparency go a long way toward enhancing the credibility of nuclear weapons states as they seek to strengthen the nuclear nonproliferation regime. The 2000 NPT Review Conference produced a thirteen-step document on nuclear disarmament, which included, among other recommendations, the negotiation of a treaty banning the production of fissile material and ratification of the Comprehensive Test Ban Treaty.[38] Some have suggested the nuclear "haves" have not made substantial progress toward implementing these thirteen steps, thereby sending a message to the nuclear "have-nots" that nuclear weapons remain important instruments of international power.[39] In July 2009 Presidents Obama and Medvedev made numerous strategic arms control and nuclear security commitments that, if implemented, will demonstrate that the United States and Russia are meeting their NPT obligations.[40]

Secure and reduce existing nuclear stockpiles. As documented by the IPFM, substantial stocks of fissile material remain protected at various levels of security across the world. The Nuclear Materials Information Program sponsored by the U.S. Department of Energy is developing a list of the most vulnerable sources of HEU and plutonium. A new organization, the World Institute of Nuclear Security (WINS), cosponsored by the Nuclear Threat Initiative (as financially supported by the Peter G. Peterson Foundation), the Institute for Nuclear Materials Management, and the U.S. Department of Energy, will work through the professionals responsible for on-the-ground security and "will collect the world's best security practices for dealing with nuclear facilities and materials and share that with their peers worldwide. These security professionals are in the best position to know where the vulnerabilities are, how to improve security, and how to ensure that improvements are implemented quickly and effectively."[41] WINS will not duplicate the essential activities of the IAEA; rather, it is focused on nuclear operators as key personnel who, through cooperation among themselves and with the IAEA, can help implement a global nuclear security regime.

Develop a multinational global database of nuclear materials to support nuclear forensics. Having a reliable and accurate nuclear forensics program can contribute to nuclear terrorism deterrence by providing a disincentive to transfer fissile material or nuclear weapons to a terrorist group. However, according to a number of studies, there is little international sharing of materials databases.[42] The primary limitation is the sensitivity of the data, but great benefits in terms of time and accuracy could result from sharing, under appropriate circumstances.

Leverage United Nations Security Council Resolution 1540 as a tool to develop a set of globally recognized, accepted, transparent, and binding nuclear security standards. Currently, although the IAEA provides training on nuclear safeguards, there is no single set of globally accepted and binding international nuclear safeguards. United Nations Security Council Resolution 1540, passed on April 28, 2004, calls for

> all states, in accordance with their national procedures, [to] adopt and enforce *appropriate effective* [emphasis added] laws which prohibit any non-State actors to manufacture, acquire, possess, develop, transport, transfer, or use nuclear, chemical, or biological weapons and their means of delivery, in particular for terrorist purposes. . . . All states should develop and maintain *appropriate effective* [emphasis added] measures to account for and secure such items in production, use, storage, or transport. . . . All states should develop and maintain *appropriate effective* [emphasis added] physical protection measures; . . . border controls and law enforcement efforts to detect, deter, prevent, and combat . . . illicit trafficking in such items . . . [and] national export and trans-shipment controls over such items.[43]

Perhaps out of respect for national sovereignty, however, "appropriate effective" has not been defined. While this may be understandable with respect to enforcement of national export control laws, for example, with respect to security of fissile material and nuclear weapons, a set of consistent and transparent best practices standards could be promulgated, even if enforcement remained the responsibility of national authorities.

It has been recommended that a gold standard be developed similar to that which protects the over four thousand metric tons of gold bullion stored at Fort Knox in Kentucky. However, there are significant differences between gold stored at Fort Knox and fissile material. For example, while fissile material is fairly mobile (as a result of its use and production in the civilian nuclear power–generating process), very little gold is brought into or taken out of Fort Knox. Also, not all countries have the resources that the United States does to implement the terms of Resolution 1540. These facts notwithstanding, a consistent standard, perhaps based on nuclear security best practices as determined by the IAEA and supported by WINS, could go far toward having a single performance benchmark against which national programs could be rated for nuclear security performance. Although 1540 applies even to nations that do not have civilian or military nuclear programs (they could still be used as transit points in illicit trafficking networks, for example), for those nations that do possess fissile material and cannot or will not protect it to the agreed-upon international standard, some argue the fissile material should be removed. This is, of course, a highly contentious issue, as it involves the question of national sovereignty versus international security. If, for example, a nation with a research reactor using HEU has not (1) allowed the reactor to be converted to burn LEU or other nonweapons-grade fuel, (2) taken action to protect HEU to the aforementioned gold standard even with offered international assistance, or (3) responded to incentives to minimize any negative employment effects associated with decommissioning an HEU-fueled research reactor, what recourse does the international community have? At what point, if any, do the common interests of international security trump a nation's desire to maintain fissile material, even if that material is not protected to some exacting international standard? If the issue in nonperformance was one of unwillingness to secure the material as opposed to an inability that could be remedied with international assistance, how would the international community enforce the appropriate effective security standards?

Strengthen the IAEA and put teeth in its verification regime. According to ElBaradei, the nuclear verification regime—the inspection and oversight mission of the IAEA—needs to be strengthened along four parallel tracks: "adequate legal authority, state-of-the-art technology, timely access to all relevant information, and sufficient human and financial resources."[44] As mentioned in chapter 7, only 107 of 163 parties to the NPT with safeguards agreements have an Additional Protocol in force. According to ElBaradei, "The Agency's verification efforts cannot be fully effective until the additional protocol becomes the universal standard."[45] ElBaradei commissioned an Eminent Persons Study to examine the work of the agency and make recommendations about its future. One of the commission's recommendations was: "In order to address the threat of nuclear terrorism, the Commission urges Member States to negotiate *binding* agreements—not voluntary, as at present—to set effective global nuclear security standards and give the agency the resources and authority to help ensure they are implemented."[46]

Consider the negotiation of a Fissile Material Cutoff Treaty.[47] The idea behind such a treaty is to ban the further production of fissile material for military purposes. As it stands currently, India, Pakistan, and possibly Israel and North Korea are producing fissile material for nuclear weapons purposes.[48] According to David Albright and Paul Brannan of the Institute for Science and International Security, given Pakistan's increasing capabilities in plutonium production and India's capacity to match that production, "the United States should make it a key priority to convince Pakistan to join in the negotiation of a universal, verified Fissile Material Cutoff Treaty, which would ban the production of plutonium and high-enriched uranium for nuclear explosives."[49] Negotiation of such a treaty was endorsed by the United Nations General Assembly without dissenting vote in 1993. For numerous reasons, negotiations on the treaty have never begun.[50] Like most arms control or disarmament treaties, effective verification mechanisms are one reason some countries oppose such a treaty. However, from a nuclear terrorism perspective, the less fissile material produced, the fewer the targets for terrorists to acquire it. It is recognized that nuclear terrorism cannot be considered in isolation from larger national nuclear force posture issues. In April 2009 President Obama pledged to "seek a new treaty that verifiably ends the production of fissile material intended for use in nuclear weapons."[51]

Work to ensure that North Korea disables its nuclear program and that Iran be prevented from an NPT breakout—"no new nukes." While it is not necessarily axiomatic that the current de facto nuclear power North Korea or a future nuclear-armed Iran would provide a weapon or fissile material to a terrorist group, precluding this potential through disarming both countries is in the best interest of international security. It is estimated that North Korea has developed an arsenal of around eight to ten bombs, while Iran has enriched enough uranium to allow it, some have estimated, to develop enough HEU (with extensive further enrichment and nuclear weapons design) for a nuclear weapon.

APPENDIX B

*Core U.S. Government Nuclear Terrorism
Programs and Initiatives*[1]

	DOD	DOE-NNSA	DOJ-FBI	DOS	DHS
DOD	Global Nuclear Lockdown Program				Global nuclear detection architecture
DOE-NNSA	Cooperative Threat Reduction: –Nuclear weapons storage security (Russia) –Nuclear weapons transportation security (Russia) WMD Proliferation Prevention	Global Threat Reduction Initiative International Nuclear Materials Protection and Cooperation International Nonproliferation Export Control and border monitoring Second Line of Defense: Core Nonproliferation and International Security		Global Initiative to Combat Nuclear Terrorism Global Threat Reduction Initiative	Global nuclear detection architecture
DOJ-FBI			WMD Directorate–Legal Attaché: –Liaison with DHS, DOD, DOE, DOS, Intelligence Community		
DOS		HEU Purchase Agreement (Megatons to Megawatts) Global Initiatives for Proliferation Prevention		Proliferation Security Initiative Nonproliferation of WMD Expertise Export Control and Related Border Security Assistance	Global nuclear detection architecture
DHS		Second Line of Defense: Megaports Initiative			Global nuclear detection architecture: –Domestic Nuclear Detection Office –Secure Cities Initiative –Container Security Initiative

APPENDIX C

Summary of Core U.S. Government Programs to Prevent Nuclear Terrorism

DEPARTMENT OF DEFENSE

Cooperative Threat Reduction. The Department of Defense manages the Cooperative Threat Reduction Program, which provides Russia, Ukraine, Belarus, and Kazakhstan with assistance in transporting, storing, and dismantling nuclear, chemical, and biological weapons. U.S. assistance has helped these nations eliminate delivery systems for nuclear weapons under the START I Treaty, secure weapons storage areas, construct a storage facility for nuclear materials removed from weapons, construct a destruction facility for chemical weapons, and secure biological weapons materials.[1]

One new program requested in the fiscal year 2011 budget is the Global Nuclear Lockdown Program, a $75 million request that is designed to supplement CTR program goals. The only new element of this request is to support Global Centers of Excellence (largely outside Russia) to share nuclear security best practices.[2]

STATE DEPARTMENT

Nonproliferation of WMD Expertise. This program is overseen by the Department of State and manages international science and technology centers in Moscow, Russia, and in Kiev, Ukraine. The purpose of these centers is to provide research grants to nuclear-related scientists and engineers to prevent them from selling their knowledge to states or nonstate actors that want to develop nuclear weapons.

Export Control and Related Border Assistance. Through this program, the Department of State facilitates training provided to foreign law enforcement and border security personnel with respect to the establishment and enforcement of export control programs designed to ensure that fissile material and nuclear-related technologies are not illicitly exported.

Proliferation Security Initiative. The Proliferation Security Initiative (PSI) is a global effort that aims to stop trafficking of WMD, their delivery systems, and related materials to and from states and nonstate actors of proliferation concern. The PSI is an innovative and proactive approach to preventing proliferation that relies on voluntary actions by states that are consistent with national legal authorities and relevant international laws and frameworks. PSI participants use existing authorities, national and international, to put an end to WMD-related trafficking and take steps to strengthen those authorities as necessary.

Global Initiative to Combat Nuclear Terrorism. Presidents George W. Bush and Vladimir Putin launched the Global Initiative to Combat Nuclear Terrorism on July 15, 2006, in St. Petersburg, Russia, to expand and accelerate the development of partnership capabilities to prevent, detect, and respond to the global threat of nuclear terrorism. The Global Initiative's goals are to (1) bring together experience and expertise from the nonproliferation, counterproliferation, and counterterrorism disciplines; (2) integrate collective capabilities and resources to strengthen the overall global architecture to combat nuclear terrorism; and (3) provide the opportunity for nations to share information and expertise in a legally nonbinding environment. The initiative currently has seventy-five partners, including all members of the European Union, according to the State Department.[3]

DEPARTMENT OF ENERGY

The National Nuclear Security Administration has numerous nuclear nonproliferation programs, a description for most of which can be found at its website. A global map of defense nuclear security programs is also located there.[4] What follows is a brief description of the major programs.

International Nuclear Materials Protection and Cooperation (INMP&C).[5] The program prevents nuclear terrorism by working in Russia and other regions of concern to (1) secure and eliminate vulnerable nuclear weapons and weapons-usable material and (2) install equipment at international crossing points and megaports to prevent and detect the illicit transfer of nuclear material. Within the INMP&C program, seven subprograms each make unique contributions. An agreement on nuclear security cooperation was reached between Presidents George W. Bush and Vladimir Putin during their February 2005 Bratislava Summit. This agreement includes, for the first time, a comprehensive joint action plan for cooperation on security upgrades of Russian nuclear facilities at Rosatom and Ministry of Defense sites and cooperation in the areas of nuclear regulatory development, sustainability, secure transportation, MPC&A expertise training, and protective force equipment. According to William H. Tobey, former deputy administrator for defense nuclear non-proliferation of the Department of Energy–National Nuclear Security Administration, the Bratislava Initiative was completed on time, which "finishes the work of securing nuclear weapons and nuclear weapons material in Russia. The Department of Energy worked at 123 sites in Russia, and the Defense Department worked at 25 sites. So between the two agencies, almost 150 weapon sites in Russia have been secured because of bilateral cooperation between the United States and Russia."[6] Yet much fissile material in Russia, particularly at research reactor sites, was beyond the purview of these programs.

Global Initiatives for Proliferation Prevention (GIPP). This program redirects displaced scientists and technical personnel with WMD "know-how" into sustained, nonmilitary employment. GIPP achieves this by engaging experts with WMD expertise in alternate technical, highly specialized research aimed at commercializing indigenous technologies. These activities take place primarily within the former Soviet Union, where GIPP will remain focused in FY 2009, with additional activities in Libya and Iraq.[7]

Nuclear Cities Initiative (NCI). According to the Department of Energy, the NCI enhances U.S. and global security by supporting weapons complex reduction in Russian nuclear cities. The NCI accomplishes this by removing functions and equipment from the weapons complex, reducing its physical footprint, and creating sustainable, alternative nonweapons work within a functioning city economy.

Global Threat Reduction Initiative. Established May 26, 2004, the GTRI is an extension and expansion of the more narrowly tailored Reduced Enrichment for Research and Test Reactors (RERTR) program, which was established in 1978. According to the Department of Energy, the reactor conversion rate for the RERTR era was 1.5 conversions per year, which has now increased to 5 conversions per year.[8] The goals are to convert, remove, and detect. First, the GTRI is to convert nuclear research reactors from the use of HEU to

LEU. Second, the program is to remove or dispose of excessive WMD-usable nuclear and radiological materials. The third goal is to protect at-risk WMD-usable nuclear and radiological materials from theft and sabotage.

International Nonproliferation Export Control. The International Nonproliferation Export Control Program (INECP) works internationally to strengthen national systems of export control, focusing efforts in countries and regions of proliferation concern. The INECP has three primary components, including export control training, the Commodity Identification Training (CIT) program, and the Cooperative Border Security Program (CBSP). The INECP works with governments and industry to build the necessary export control infrastructure to manage WMD-related controlled exports. Besides established and emerging suppliers, the CIT program also works with high-traffic trans-shipment and transit countries with geographic proximity to suppliers with inadequate controls. The goal of the CIT program is to improve the ability of these countries to control WMD-related and dual-use technology consistent with international requirements. The CBSP enhances border security through technical cooperative solutions, such as explosive detection portals installed at key border points. INECP activities are coordinated closely with the State Department–led Export Control and Related Border Security Assistance initiatives.

Second Line of Defense: Core. The Second Line of Defense: Core program deploys radiation detection equipment, training, and technical support at strategic transit and border crossings and at air and sea trans-shipment hubs in Russia and in other countries, including the former Soviet Union and Eastern Europe, to provide these governments with the technical means to detect, deter, and interdict illicit trafficking of nuclear and other radioactive materials.

Second Line of Defense: Megaports Initiative. This program is pursuing cooperation with international partners to equip key seaports (megaports) with radiation detection equipment and to provide training to appropriate law enforcement officials in order to provide them with the technical means to deter and interdict illicit trafficking in nuclear and other radioactive materials in the global maritime system.

Nuclear Materials Information Program. The essence of this classified program coordination by the National Nuclear Security Administration is to prioritize all vulnerable nuclear material around the world in order to render it safe through removal or securing it in place.

APPENDIX D

Abbreviations

AAAS	American Academy for the Advancement of Science
ASP	Advanced Spectroscopic Portal
CBRN	chemical, biological, radiological, or nuclear
CBSP	Cooperative Border Security Program
C-CMRF	CBRN Consequence Management Response Force
CIA	Central Intelligence Agency
CIT	Commodity Identification Training
CNN	Cable News Network
CTBT	Comprehensive Test Ban Treaty
DCI	director of Central Intelligence
DHS	Department of Homeland Security
DNDO	Domestic Nuclear Detection Office
DNI	director of National Intelligence
DOD	Department of Defense
DOE	Department of Energy
DSTO	Database on Nuclear Smuggling, Theft, and Orphan Radioactive Sources
EMP	electromagnetic pulse
FATA	Federally Administered Tribal Areas
FBI	Federal Bureau of Investigation
FI	Forecasting International
FY	fiscal year
GAO	Government Accountability Office

GI	Global Initiative to Combat Nuclear Terrorism
GIPP	Global Initiatives for Proliferation Prevention
GNEP	Global Nuclear Energy Partnership
GSPC	Salafist Group for Call and Combat
GTRI	Global Threat Reduction Initiative
HEU	high-enriched uranium
HUMINT	human intelligence
IAEA	International Atomic Energy Agency
IAG	Implementation and Advisory Group
ICBM	intercontinental ballistic missile
IMINT	imagery intelligence
IND	improvised nuclear device
INECP	International Nonproliferation Export Control Program
INFCIRC	Information Circular
INMP&C	International Nuclear Materials Protection and Control
IPFM	International Panel on Fissile Materials
IPPAS	International Physical Protection Advisory Service
IRTPA	Intelligence Reform and Terrorism Prevention Act
ISI	Pakistani Inter-Services Intelligence
ITDB	Illicit Trafficking Database
JTOT	Joint Technical Operations Team
LEU	low-enriched uranium
LTTE	Liberation Tamil Tigers Eelam
MIPT	Memorial Institute for the Prevention of Terrorism
MPC&A	material protection, control, and accounting
NATO	North Atlantic Treaty Organization
NCA	National Command Authority
NCI	Nuclear Cities Initiative
NCPC	National Counterproliferation Center
NCTC	National Counterterrorism Center
NEST	Nuclear Emergency Search Team
NIE	National Intelligence Estimate
NIF	National Islamic Front
NMIP	Nuclear Materials Information Program
NNSA	National Nuclear Security Administration
NPT	Nuclear Nonproliferation Treaty

NRC	Nuclear Regulatory Commission
NRDC	Natural Resources Defense Council
NSC	National Security Council
NSG	Nuclear Suppliers Group
NTI	Nuclear Threat Initiative
OMB	Office of Management and Budget
OTA	Office of Technology Assessment
PAEC	Pakistan Atomic Energy Commission
PAL	permissive action link
PCC	Policy Coordination Committee
PSA	Partnership for a Secure America
PSI	Proliferation Security Initiative
PVT-RPM	polyvinyl toluene radiation portal monitors
RDD	radiological dispersion device
RERTR	Reduced Enrichment for Research and Test Reactors
SFC	Strategic Forces Command
SIGINT	signals intelligence
SPD	Strategic Plans Division
START	Strategic Arms Reduction Treaty
UTN	Umma Tameer-E-Nau
VACIS	Vehicle and Cargo Inspection Systems
WINS	World Institute of Nuclear Security
WMD	weapon of mass destruction

EPILOGUE

The death of al Qaeda leader Osama bin Laden at the hands of U.S. Special Forces is a major counterterrorism victory for the United States and the world. While his operational role may have been somewhat constrained in recent years, bin Laden nevertheless retained the role of the senior unifying leader of the movement known as the Base. Al Qaeda has proven relatively adept at replacing operational leaders, yet replacing bin Laden may be impossible. His charismatic and dynamic leadership and propagation of jihadist ideology was unique. Although his death certainly does not signal the end of Islamic extremism, centrifugal forces within al Qaeda itself may prove more difficult to contain given the absence of the leader to which all al Qaeda recruits pledged loyalty. Increasingly marginalized within the Ummah and in the Middle East and North Africa, where nonviolent, democracy-embracing revolutions achieved what al Qaeda could not, the death of bin Laden is another major strategic blow to the group and its ideology. Bin Laden's cult of personality was a tangible and powerful force driving the organization and the ideology it spawned.

The impact of bin Laden's death on the nuclear terrorism threat remains to be seen. A spectacular al Qaeda nuclear terrorism attack anywhere in the world would substantially enhance the group's continued global relevance. It could also be compellingly argued, however, that without a strong motivational and operational leader at the helm of core al Qaeda, the capability and catalyst for organizing sophisticated WMD attacks has been substantially degraded. As STRATFOR Global Intelligence analyst Scott Stewart argues, "The good news is that as one moves down the jihadist pyramid, from core al Qaeda to the regional franchises to the grassroots, the level of terrorist tradecraft these individual possess diminishes and the threat is not as severe."[1] This is not to say that al Qaeda and its affiliates will disavow all WMD terrorism, yet there may well be more of a focus on an increased attack tempo as part of a retaliatory effort to demonstrate that al Qaeda remains relevant. At least in the near term that may mean more attacks by al Qaeda affiliates (and potentially "lone wolves") against hard or soft targets within the United States or overseas using means that are readily available. In short, operational conservatism may trump the intent—long driven by core al Qaeda—to focus on catastrophic WMD attacks that could bring the United States to the point of capitulation. Should operational conservatism become dominant practice, while the overall level of terrorism activity (including conventional attacks capable of causing mass casualties) internationally and domestically will likely increase, the aggregate threat of nuclear terrorism in the United States may decrease. Although there is no place for complacency in continuing efforts to reduce the supply and demand sides of the nuclear terrorism equation, the death of Osama bin Laden may have the net effect of increasing the nuclear terrorism margin of safety.

NOTES

Chapter 1. Introduction

1. As will be further explained below, for the purposes of this book nuclear terrorism is defined as the detonation of a nuclear weapon stolen, purchased, or otherwise received from one of nine de facto nuclear weapons states or an improvised nuclear fission device (constructed with illicitly received fissile material and fabricated into a HEU "gun-type" or "implosion-type" nuclear weapon) by a terrorist group. Gun-type nuclear weapons are simpler than implosion-type weapons in design and construction. For that reason, most analysts consider it more likely that a terrorist nuclear device will be gun-type. For a brief explanation of these two types of nuclear weapons, see the International Panel on Fissile Materials (IPFM), http://www.fissilematerials.org/ipfm/pages_us_en/fissile/fissile/fissile.php. While there are also numerous definitions of terrorism, this book uses the definition in U.S. Code, Title 18, Section 2331, which stipulates that terrorism involves "violent acts . . . that are a violation of criminal laws of the United States . . . and appear to be intended to (i) intimidate or coerce a civilian population, (ii) influence the policy of a government by intimidation or coercion, or (iii) affect the conduct of a government by mass destruction, assassination, or kidnapping." Terrorism expert Brian Michael Jenkins defines terrorism as "a calculated campaign of violence intended to create an atmosphere of fear and alarm, which, in turn, causes people to exaggerate the strength of terrorists." Moreover, any reference to weapons of mass destruction (WMD) herein refers to chemical, biological, radiological, or nuclear (CBRN) weapons. While chemical, biological, and radiological weapons are WMD, nuclear weapons are the most damaging of WMD from a physical and psychological perspective. A biological agent could conceivably cause more deaths than a nuclear weapon by infecting people across a broad geographic range. For more on how WMD are defined, see W. Seth Carus, *Defining Weapons of Mass Destruction* (Washington, DC: National Defense University Press, January 2006).

2. It should be noted that while the probability of a successful nuclear attack can be assessed in a vacuum, a real-world understanding of terrorist risk acceptance

profiles might enhance the efficacy of any such effort. There is an interaction between a terrorist group's acceptance of some level of risk of failure and the overall success of any nuclear terrorism attempt. Numerous experts have offered their assessments of the probability of a nuclear attack within the United States in the next decade. Some of these include: former secretary of defense William J. Perry and Harvard professor Graham Allison—better than 50 percent; Senator Richard Lugar's (June 2005) *Survey on Proliferation Threats and Response*—20 percent (median response—nuclear explosion anywhere in the world; 79 percent of Lugar's survey respondents also believed if there was a nuclear attack in the next ten years, a terrorist group as opposed to a government would be responsible); and Matthew Bunn, associate professor of public policy, Harvard University—29 percent (see "A Mathematical Model of the Risk of Nuclear Terrorism," *The Annals of the American Academy of Political and Social Science* 607 [September 2006]). Although Warren Buffett, chairman of Berkshire Hathaway Corporation and a consummate assessor of risk, has weighed in on this issue, his statements may have been misinterpreted. His bottom-line analysis is that the reported probability of WMD attacks "can't be meaningful. . . . I would not regard any specific number as being meaningful. I would regard the importance of reducing the probability as terribly meaningful." See Carl Bialik, "Pondering the Chances of a Nuclear Attack," *Wall Street Journal*, July 7, 2005.

3.   See remarks of former CIA director Michael Hayden before the Los Angeles World Affairs Council, September 16, 2008, https://www.cia.gov/news-information /speeches-testimony/directors-remarks-at-lawac.html. From an intelligence perspective, intent is indeed all that is necessary to warrant attention and resources; terrorist group WMD capability must be carefully monitored and blocked using all tools of national power. From a national policymaking perspective, however, it is known that groups like al Qaeda have conventional capabilities that can also cause mass destruction, thus making the appropriate national focus the decimation of the group itself, not necessarily the conventional or unconventional tools that the group may use. A dual-pronged strategy attacking both the supply and demand sides of nuclear terrorism is likely to be most effective.

4.   See Nassim Nicholas Taleb, *The Black Swan: The Impact of the Highly Improbable* (New York: Random House, 2007), xvii–xviii.

5.   While the focus in this book is on a terrorist nuclear detonation in the United States, it is recognized that such an attack anywhere in the world would, by crossing the nuclear threshold, cause substantial psychological angst among the U.S. polity and leadership and serve as a catalyst for concerted and comprehensive global action on the issue.

6.   Throughout this book the terms "fissile material" and "special nuclear material" are used interchangeably. Special nuclear material is defined in the Atomic Energy Act (U.S. Code, Title 42, Section 2014) and includes plutonium and uranium enriched in the isotope 233 or 235. HEU is uranium that has been enriched to the point that the isotopic composition of ^{235}U is 20 percent or greater. While uranium with a concentration of 20 percent or more ^{235}U is said to be weapons usable, weapons-grade HEU tends to have a concentration of 85 percent or more ^{235}U. Natural uranium is composed of approximately 0.72 percent ^{235}U and, therefore, must be enriched using various scientific processes. Reactor-grade or low-enriched uranium (LEU) is generally 3–4 percent ^{235}U. Both HEU and LEU are currently used as fuel for nuclear power reactors. Little Boy, the gun-type

nuclear weapon dropped on Hiroshima in 1945, used about sixty-five kilograms of 80 percent enriched HEU. Plutonium, meanwhile, does not occur naturally; it is produced as a result of reprocessing spent nuclear fuel. All grades of plutonium can be used for nuclear weapons. However, plutonium is far more difficult to handle than uranium. Weapons-grade plutonium is 93 percent plutonium-239. See U.S. Department of Energy, *Nonproliferation and Arms Control Assessment of Weapons-Usable Fissile Material Storage and Excess Plutonium Disposition Alternatives* (Washington, DC, January 1997). The International Atomic Energy Agency (IAEA) refers to these materials as "special fissionable material." For IAEA definitions, see "Statute of the IAEA," Article XX, http://www.iaea.org/About/statute_text.html#A1.20.

The amount of fissile material necessary to build a nuclear weapon depends on many factors, including the type and design of the weapon, the skill level of the technicians building the weapon, and the quality and enrichment of the fissile material. It has been estimated that terrorists would need approximately fifty kilograms (94 percent ^{235}U, 6 percent ^{238}U metal with a density of 18.7 g/cc) of HEU for a gun-type nuclear weapon not using a reflector. Weapons designs incorporating a reflector or using higher-density fissile material would require less, perhaps as little as twenty-five kilograms of weapons-grade (greater than 85 percent ^{235}U) HEU. The amount of plutonium required is far smaller, but given that plutonium is one of the most difficult elements to handle and manipulate, there is a sense among analysts that any terrorist IND is more likely to use HEU than plutonium. See J. Carson Mark, Theodore Taylor, Eugene Eyster, William Maraman, and Jacob Wechsler, "Can Terrorists Build Nuclear Weapons?," in *Preventing Nuclear Terrorism*, ed. Paul Leventhal and Yonah Alexander (Lexington, MA: Lexington Books, 1987). See also IPFM, http://www.fissilematerials.org/ipfm/pages_us_en/fissile/fissile/fissile.php. According to the Department of Energy (DOE), about four kilograms of plutonium are enough hypothetically to make one nuclear explosive device. The DOE also estimates that about three times that amount (twelve kilograms) of HEU would be necessary. See U.S. Department of Energy, *Drawing Back the Curtain of Secrecy: Restricted Data Declassification Decisions 1946–Present (RDD-5)* (Washington, DC, January 1, 1999). Another estimate of the amount of HEU required determined that "the amount required to obtain a one-kiloton explosion would be *substantially less* [emphasis added] than the amount of [80 percent enriched] HEU used in Little Boy [about sixty-five kilograms]." See Thomas B. Cochran and Matthew G. McKinzie, "Detecting Nuclear Smuggling," *Scientific American*, March 24, 2008. While smaller quantities of plutonium-239 could be used in constructing an implosion-type device, such a device is generally considered far more sophisticated and difficult to assemble than a gun-type device. It is more likely a terrorist IND will be gun-type and not necessarily include a reflector. As a result, quantities of fissile material required are likely to be in the forty- to fifty-kilogram range.

7. Allison stated a policy preference of "Three Nos"—no loose nukes (weapons or fissile material), no nascent nukes (no new uranium enrichment or spent fuel reprocessing plants), and no new nuclear weapons states. See Graham Allison, *Nuclear Terrorism: The Ultimate Preventable Catastrophe* (New York: Times Books, 2004), 141.

8. See Michael Levi, "Stopping Nuclear Terrorism: The Dangerous Allure of a Perfect Defense," *Foreign Affairs*, January–February 2008.

9. See Sam Nunn, "The Race between Cooperation and Catastrophe: Reducing the Global Nuclear Threat," *The Annals of the American Academy of Political and Social Science* 607 (September 2006): 49.

10. Nobel Prize–winning economist Thomas Schelling once stated: "I imply nothing derogatory or demeaning about strategic nuclear forces by emphasizing the traditional expectation that their primary use is to deter or to intimidate, and thereby to influence behavior, through the threat of enormous civilian damage. . . . It is worth remembering that on the only one occasion of the hostile use of nuclear weapons, they were used in a fashion that has to be considered 'terrorist.'" See Thomas C. Schelling, "Thinking about Nuclear Terrorism," *International Security* 6, no. 4 (Spring 1982): 67.

11. See Charles B. Curtis, president of the Nuclear Threat Initiative, "Preventing Nuclear Terrorism: Our Highest Priority—Isn't," speech before the National Defense University, May 21, 2008.

12. See William Dunlop and Harold Smith, "Who Did It? Using International Forensics to Detect and Deter Nuclear Terrorism," *Arms Control Today*, October 2006. Alternatively, a terrorist group may smuggle small amounts of HEU into the country and attempt to construct an improvised nuclear device within the United States to avoid the risks of detection when transporting an assembled or nearly assembled weapon across U.S. borders. See Peter D. Zimmerman and Jeffrey zG. Lewis, "The Bomb in the Backyard," *Foreign Policy*, November–December 2006. Even given the reported lack of a highly effective means of detecting shielded HEU being smuggled across U.S. borders, terrorists will likely not have excess fissile material and would need approximately fifty kilograms (94 percent ^{235}U, 6 percent ^{238}U metal with a density of 18.7 g/cc) for an IND. Shipping HEU into the United States still entails a degree of risk for failure that terrorists may or may not be willing to accept for this operation.

13. The ability of the United States to detect fissile material being smuggled into the country will be addressed in chapter 7.

14. See Rensselaer W. Lee III, *Smuggling Armageddon: The Nuclear Black Market in the Former Soviet Union and Europe* (New York: St. Martin's, 1998). See also Matthew Bunn, Anthony Wier, and Josh Friedman, "The Demand for Black Market Fissile Material" (Washington, DC: Nuclear Threat Initiative, 2005), http://www.nti.org/e_research/cnwm/threat/demand.asp; Center for Strategic and International Studies Task Force, *The Nuclear Black Market* (Washington, DC: Center for Strategic and International Studies, 1996); and David Albright, *Peddling Peril: How the Secret Nuclear Trade Arms America's Enemies* (New York: Free Press, 2010).

15. See Richard Falkenrath, "Confronting Nuclear, Biological, and Chemical Terrorism," *Survival* 40, no. 3 (Autumn 1998).

16. See Charles D. Ferguson and William C. Potter, with Amy Sands, Leonard Spector, and Fred Wehling, *The Four Faces of Nuclear Terrorism* (New York: Routledge, 2005). The 1986 accident at Chernobyl was exceptional for numerous reasons, not the least of which was that the reactor did not have a containment structure. All U.S. nuclear reactors have containment structures. This does not necessarily mean they are immune to terrorist attacks or that containment structures can withstand large-scale aircraft attacks of the type perpetrated on September 11, 2001. The Chernobyl accident resulted in 131 dead, 1,800 excess thyroid cancers, and the forced relocation of over 100,000 people across Europe. See Ibid., 233–35.

17. See Brian Michael Jenkins, "Will Terrorists Go Nuclear?," testimony given before the Committee on Energy and Diminishing Materials of the California State Assembly, November 19, 1975. In 1975, eighteen years before the 1993 attack on the World Trade Center in New York City, Jenkins also presciently predicted that the center would be a potential target of large-scale terrorism.

18. See Brian Michael Jenkins, *Will Terrorists Go Nuclear?* (Amherst, NY: Prometheus Books, 2008), 26.

19. Ibid., 376–77.

20. See remarks of Brian Michael Jenkins to a RAND congressional briefing, Rayburn House Office Building, September 8, 2008.

21. See U.S. Congress, Office of Technology Assessment, *The Effects of Nuclear War* (Washington, DC, May 1979).

22. See Stephen M. Younger, former head of nuclear weapons research and development at Los Alamos National Laboratory, *Endangered Species: How We Can Avoid Mass Destruction and Build a Lasting Peace* (New York: Harper, 2007), 95.

23. See Allison, *Nuclear Terrorism*, 4–5.

24. This is just one of many potential nuclear attack scenarios. If a terrorist group acquires a nuclear weapon, it might not be willing to assume the risk of shipping the weapon to the United States via commercial ship transport. Terrorists know that many major U.S. and international harbors are equipped with technology that may detect the device into which they have invested much time, resources, and energy; therefore, they may ship a weapon via other means, such as by private ship or commercial or private aircraft. Moreover, some have posited that terrorists might consider shipping fissile material into the United States for ultimate nuclear weapons construction within the United States. This scenario has many limitations, but it would negate the necessity of shipping a fully or nearly assembled weapon into the United States. The Port of Long Beach was, incidentally, the port through which ABC News in 2003 smuggled a lead-lined steel pipe containing a 6.8-kilogram (15-pound) cylinder of depleted uranium in a shipping container that originated in Jakarta, Indonesia. While depleted uranium and HEU do not have identical signatures, scientists consulting with ABC News concluded that "even lightly shielded with lead and steel, depleted and highly enriched uranium have similarly weak radiation signals." See Cochran and McKinzie, "Detecting Nuclear Smuggling."

25. See Roger C. Molander, RAND Corporation, "Perspectives on the Threat of Nuclear Terrorism," testimony before the Senate Committee on Homeland Security and Governmental Affairs, April 15, 2008. See also Charles Meade and Roger C. Molander, *Considering the Effects of a Catastrophic Terrorist Attack* (RAND, 2006) and Lynn E. Davis, Tom LaTourrette, David E. Mosher, Lois M. Davis, and David R. Howell, *Individual Preparedness and Response to Chemical, Radiological, Nuclear, and Biological Attacks* (RAND, 2003).

26. See Michael A. Levi, *Deterring State Sponsorship of Nuclear Terrorism*, Special Report 39 (New York: Council on Foreign Relations, September 2008).

27. See John Mueller, "Six Rather Unusual Propositions about Terrorism," *Terrorism and Political Violence* 17 (Autumn 2005): 491.

28. See Falkenrath, "Confronting Nuclear, Biological, and Chemical Terrorism," 48–50.

29. Ibid.

30. See Senate Committee on Homeland Security and Governmental Affairs, *Nuclear Terrorism: Providing Medical Care and Meeting Basic Needs in the Aftermath— the Federal Response*, 110th Cong. (2008).

31. Falkenrath, "Confronting Nuclear, Biological, and Chemical Terrorism," 48–50.

32. See testimony of Charles E. Allen, former undersecretary of intelligence, U.S. Department of Homeland Security, and Rolf Mowatt-Larssen, former director of the Office of Intelligence and Counterintelligence, U.S. Department of Energy, before the Senate Committee on Homeland Security and Governmental Affairs, April 2, 2008. For an understanding of U.S. policy with respect to Pakistan and the FATA, see testimony of the Honorable John D. Negroponte, former deputy secretary of state, before the Senate Foreign Relations Committee, May 20, 2008, http://foreign.senate.gov/hearings/2008/hrg080520pp.html.

33. Terrorism analyst Marc Sageman is less concerned with al Qaeda Central or the core al Qaeda leadership currently based in the mountainous regions between Afghanistan and Pakistan. He is more concerned with loose-knit cells of Western-born Muslims or Muslim immigrants studying and working in the West, that is, groups that may receive motivation and inspiration from al Qaeda Central but not necessarily direct tasking, training, or support from al Qaeda leadership. See Marc Sageman, *Leaderless Jihad: Terror Networks in the Twenty-First Century* (Philadelphia: University of Pennsylvania Press, 2008). For a rebuttal of this perspective, see Bruce Hoffman, "The Myth of Grass Roots Terrorism: Why Usama bin Laden Still Matters," *Foreign Affairs*, May–June 2008.

34. See National Intelligence Council, "Key Judgments," in *The Terrorist Threat to the U.S. Homeland* (Washington, DC, July 2007). See also Philip Mudd, "Evaluating the Al-Qa-ida Threat to the U.S. Homeland," *CTC Sentinel*, August 2010.

35. Statement of Suleiman Abu Ghaith, press spokesman for Osama bin Laden, nine months after the terrorist attacks of 9/11. As quoted in Allison, *Nuclear Terrorism*, 12.

36. See Bruce Hoffman, *Inside Terrorism*, rev. ed. (New York: Columbia University Press, 2006). See also Daniel Benjamin and Steven Simon, *The Age of Sacred Terror* (New York: Random House, 2002); and Jessica Stern, *Terror in the Name of God: Why Religious Militants Kill* (New York: Harper Collins, 2003).

37. Currently, under the terms of the Nuclear Nonproliferation Treaty (NPT), the cornerstone of the international nuclear nonproliferation regime, there are five nuclear weapons states. These states are the United States, the Russian Federation, the People's Republic of China, the United Kingdom, and France. Non-NPT nuclear weapons states include Israel, India, Pakistan, and the Democratic People's Republic of Korea (North Korea). While India, Pakistan, and Israel have not signed the NPT, North Korea did sign the NPT but subsequently withdrew in 2003. See Joseph Cirincione, *Bomb Scare: The History and Future of Nuclear Weapons* (New York: Columbia University Press, 2007). For an assessment of the North Korean nuclear program, see Mary Beth Nikitin, "North Korea's Second Nuclear Test: Implications of U.N. Security Council Resolution 1874," CRS Report for Congress (Washington, DC, April 15, 2010); and Larry A. Niksch, "North Korea's Nuclear Weapons Development and Diplomacy," CRS Report for Congress (Washington, DC, March 30, 2009), http://assets.opencrs.com/rpts/RL33590_20080121.pdf.

38. See IPFM, *Global Fissile Material Report, 2007*, www.fissilematerials.org.

39. See Matthew Bunn, *Securing the Bomb 2010: Securing All Nuclear Materials in Four Years* (Cambridge, MA, and Washington, DC: Project on Managing the Atom, Harvard University, and Nuclear Threat Initiative, April 2010) for an overview of the current status of the security of nuclear weapons and materials globally. See also Matthew Bunn, "The Risk of Nuclear Terrorism and the Next Steps to Reduce the Danger," testimony before the Senate Committee on Homeland Security and Governmental Affairs, April 2, 2008.

40. See Jenkins, *Will Terrorists Go Nuclear?*
41. "State-to-state nuclear threat" is meant to connote the traditional threat faced by the United States from the nuclear-armed Soviet Union. Some would argue that the Soviet nuclear threat to the United States was not "terrorist," as the Soviet Union was not a terrorist group. However, as mentioned in note 10, Nobel Prize–winner Thomas Schelling believes that the only time nuclear weapons were used, they were used in a terrorist manner.
42. Originally from Leo Szilard, "Atomic Bombs and the Postwar Position of the United States in the World," memorandum for President Franklin D. Roosevelt, March 1945. Quoted in Richard Falkenrath et al., *America's Achilles' Heel: Nuclear, Biological, and Chemical Terrorism and Covert Attack* (Cambridge, MA: MIT Press, 1998), xxi.
43. CIA, Directorate of Intelligence, Office of Political Research, *Managing Nuclear Proliferation: The Politics of Limited Choice* (Washington, DC, December 1975), 29. See Micah Zenko, "Intelligence Estimates of Nuclear Terrorism," *The Annals of the American Academy of Political and Social Science* 607 (September 2006).
44. As will be expanded on below, explicit knowledge is knowledge one can acquire from simply reading source material, but tacit or implicit knowledge can only be achieved through experience. It is one thing to read, for example, about how to form HEU or plutonium into appropriate subcritical forms for explosion and quite another to have the skill sets to actually accomplish this and other necessary tasks successfully.
45. See Chaim Braun and Christopher F. Chyba, "Proliferation Rings—New Challenges to the Nuclear Nonproliferation Regime," *International Security* 29, no. 2 (Fall 2004).
46. See Scott D. Sagan, "Why Do States Build Nuclear Weapons? Three Models in Search of a Bomb," *International Security* 21, no. 3 (1996–97): 54–86. Sagan posits three models: a "security model" under which states acquire nuclear weapons to increase national security from foreign threats, a "domestic politics model" that envisions nuclear weapons as political tools used to advance parochial domestic and bureaucratic interests, and a "norms model" under which nuclear weapons decisions are made because weapons acquisition or restraint provides an important normative symbol of a state's modernity and identity. Nonstate actors may seek to acquire nuclear weapons so they can approximate the power of a nation-state and, depending on the nonstate actor, realize what may be apocalyptic goals.
47. See Robert S. Norris and Hans M. Kristensen, "Pakistan's Nuclear Forces, 2007," *Bulletin of Atomic Scientists* 63, no. 3 (May–June 2007): 71. See also Steven R. David, "The Nightmare Scenario: Why You Should Worry about Pakistan's Nukes," *Foreign Policy*, May 2009.
48. Speech of IAEA director general Mohamed ElBaradei at the Beijing International Ministerial Conference on Nuclear Energy in the Twenty-First Century, Beijing, China, April 20, 2009. According to the IAEA, since February 2007 Iran has manufactured at least 3,606 kilograms of LEU (in the form of uranium hexafluoride [UF_6]), which may be sufficient to enrich enough HEU for one nuclear bomb. Moreover, the IAEA has verified Iran has produced 25.1 kilograms of UF_6 enriched to 19.7 percent. This does not necessarily mean, however, that Iran has the technology and capability to build and detonate a nuclear weapon. See IAEA, *Implementation of the NPT Safeguards Agreement and relevant provisions of Secu-*

rity Council Resolutions in the Islamic Republic of Iran (Vienna, Austria, February 25, 2011).

49. In a June 26, 2008, hearing before the Senate Homeland Security and Governmental Affairs Committee, *Nuclear Terrorism: Providing Medical Care and Meeting Basic Needs in the Aftermath—the Federal Response*, three senior federal officials were asked to rate their agencies' readiness for a nuclear attack. On a scale of 1 to 10, with 10 being best, the ratings were as follows: (a) Federal Emergency Management Agency 7, (b) Health and Human Services 5–6, and (c) Department of Defense 5. An Arlington County, Virginia, fire department official rated his locality a 4–5 range. See "Feds, Local, Differ about How Prepared U.S. Is to Respond to a Nuclear Attack," *CQ Homeland Security*, June 26, 2008.
50. See "Plutonium: An Element at Odds with Itself," *Los Alamos Science* 200, no. 26 (2000).
51. See Simen A. Ellingsen, "Safeguards against Nuclear Terrorism: HEU vs. Plutonium," *Defense and Security Analysis* 24, no. 2 (June 1, 2008): 143.

Chapter 2. The Terrorist Pathway to a Nuclear Weapon Detonation
1. As quoted from Zenko, "Intelligence Estimates of Nuclear Terrorism," 90.
2. If it is a direct and willing transfer—whether a gift or purchase—it is likely that one condition of the terrorist acquisition is the provision of the codes or other measures necessary to actually detonate the device. If a theft of an intact nuclear weapon is successful and the terrorist group cannot overcome the security measures on the weapon, should they exist, one terrorist strategy might be to harvest the fissile material from the weapon and use the HEU or plutonium in the group's own crude device. However, the terrorists would also confront certain technical difficulties here, as many nuclear weapons have devices that will render the weapon inoperable should tampering be detected.
3. This presumes the target country is the United States. However, there are situations in which an international border need not be crossed with fissile material. For example, if Chechen terrorists acquired fissile material from a Russian facility and constructed a crude nuclear device for detonation in Moscow, they would not have to cross any international borders.
4. If a nuclear weapon is acquired, it may be directly transported to the target destination. However, if the weapon is not operational due to various safety features, it may be transported to a safe haven while safety feature information is acquired from an insider.
5. This scenario assumes terrorists have determined that the risks of smuggling in weapons components, particularly highly valuable and relatively scarce fissile material, outweigh the potential benefits. Terrorists may also determine there is no need to smuggle a nuclear weapon once it is armed and simply detonate it in place, and then claim they have more such weapons.
6. See Michael Levi, *On Nuclear Terrorism* (Cambridge, MA: Harvard University Press, 2007), 8. It should also be pointed out, however, that while all terrorists may not necessarily be "ten feet tall," Murphy's Law could operate against the United States. As William C. Potter of the Monterey Institute of International Studies points out, "As we adjust our sights to deal with less-than-10-foot terrorists, we should not discount the possibility that poorly conceived and implemented U.S. foreign policy can serve as a terrorist growth hormone." See William C. Potter, "Book Review: Using Murphy's Law against Nuclear Terrorists," *Arms Control Today*, April 2008.

7.   Levi, *On Nuclear Terrorism*, 140–41.
8.   One nuclear terrorism path that is oftentimes not mentioned is if a terrorist group evolves into a political force and thus acquires legitimacy. Of course, if this occurs the group may not necessarily remain a terrorist group per se, and the shift from nonstate actor to nation-state substantially changes the deterrence equation. The group or political entity would now have a "return address," would have national assets that could be targeted, and, therefore, would be more susceptible to traditional deterrence (by punishment). For scenarios under which terrorists have transitioned to political leaders, see Marvin J. Cetron and Owen Davies, *55 Trends Now Shaping the Future of Terrorism* (Newtown, CT: Forecasting International, February 2008), 7–9, http://www.carlisle.army.mil/proteus/docs/55-terror.pdf.
9.   See Peter Bergen, "Commentary: WMD Terrorism Fears Are Overblown," CNN, December 8, 2008, http://articles.cnn.com/2008-12-05/politics/bergen.wmd_1_nuclear-weapons-chemical-weapons-mass-destruction?_s=PM:POLITICS.
10. There is an inherent assumption in all nonproliferation and counterproliferation interest groups that all nuclear proliferation among nation-states is negative and, therefore, must be stopped. Some academics have questioned this fundamental assumption, concluding that it is not axiomatic that measured and slow nuclear proliferation will cause grave damage to international security. Kenneth N. Waltz, professor of political science at Columbia University, argues, "Countries have to take care of their own security. If countries feel insecure and believe that nuclear weapons would make them more secure, America's policy of opposing the spread of nuclear weapons will not prevail. . . . The measured spread of nuclear weapons does not run against our interests and can increase the security of some states at a price they can afford. . . . New nuclear states will feel the constraints that present nuclear states have experienced. New nuclear states will be more concerned for their safety and more mindful of dangers than some of the old ones have been. The likelihood of war decreases as deterrent and defensive capabilities increase. Nuclear weapons make wars hard to start. These statements hold for small as for big nuclear powers. Because they do, the gradual spread of nuclear weapons is more to be welcomed than feared." See Scott D. Sagan and Kenneth N. Waltz, *The Spread of Nuclear Weapons: A Debate Renewed* (New York: Norton, 2003), 43–45. According to Steven R. David, political scientist at Johns Hopkins University, Waltz's arguments hold true in the context of India and Pakistan. David concluded that "so long as both countries possess nuclear weapons, of course, the possibility of nuclear war exists, but its likelihood remains low. There is evidence that their possession of nuclear weapons prevented India and Pakistan from going to full-scale conventional war, as they had done so often in the past when both countries lacked nuclear arms." See Steven R. David, *Catastrophic Consequences: Civil Wars and American Interests* (Baltimore, MD: Johns Hopkins University Press, 2008), 54.
11. See Younger, *Endangered Species*, 24.
12. Bergen, "Commentary: WMD Terrorism Fears Are Overblown."
13. North Korea is a signatory of the Nonproliferation Treaty but withdrew from the treaty on January 10, 2003. It subsequently tested its first nuclear device in October 2006. North Korea has participated intermittently in six-party talks (with China, the United States, Japan, South Korea, and Russia) aimed at dismantling its nuclear weapons program. North Korea pulled out of the talks in April 2009

in response to a rebuke from the United Nations for the launch of a long-range missile. North Korea is not a member of the Missile Technology Control Regime, an "informal and voluntary association of countries which share the goals of non-proliferation of unmanned delivery systems capable of delivering weapons of mass destruction, and which seek to coordinate national export licensing efforts aimed at preventing their proliferation." See http://www.mtcr.info/english/index.html. On May 25, 2009, North Korea conducted a second nuclear test that, according to the director of national intelligence, had an explosive yield of "approximately a few kilotons." The United Nations Security Council condemned the nuclear test and imposed additional sanctions to seize certain military goods shipped out of North Korea, among other measures. The United Nations did not provide any new international authority for national military forces to be used to inspect North Korean ships. See United Nations Security Council Resolution 1874 (2009).

Israel attacked the Syrian nuclear reactor at Al Kibar, Syria, on September 6, 2007. Following months of official silence, the U.S. government confirmed on April 24, 2008, that the "Syrians constructed this reactor for the production of plutonium with the assistance of North Korea." The U.S. Intelligence Community judged that North Korea assisted in the construction of the reactor because (1) the technology in the Syrian reactor was much like that used by North Korea (a gas-cooled, graphite-moderated reactor similar to that which exists in Yongbyon, North Korea), (2) nuclear-related North Koreans were involved in a project in Syria in the vicinity of Al Kibar, and (3) there was evidence of North Korean cargo being transferred, most likely to the reactor site, in 2006. See Office of the Director of National Intelligence, "Background Briefing with Senior U.S. Officials on Syria's Covert Nuclear Reactor and North Korea's Involvement" (Washington, DC, April 24, 2008), http://dni.gov/interviews/20080424_interview.pdf.

Regarding North Korea's insurance fraud, see Blaine Harden, "Global Insurance Fraud by North Korea Outlined: Government Has Collected Millions of Dollars on Large, Suspicious Claims," *Washington Post*, June 18, 2009. For an assessment of the history of North Korea's nuclear program, see Joel S. Witt, Daniel Poneman, and Robert L. Gallucci, *Going Critical: The First North Korean Nuclear Crisis* (Washington, DC: Brookings Institution, April 2004).

14. For an assessment of Iranian ballistic missile programs, see Steven A. Hildreth, "Iran's Ballistic Missile Programs: An Overview," CRS Report for Congress (Washington, DC, February 4, 2009). For information on Iran's nuclear program, see Senate Foreign Relations Committee, *Iran: Where We Are Today*, S. Prt. 111-19 (Washington, DC, May 4, 2009). See also David Albright and Jacqueline Shire with Paul Brannan and Andrea Scheel, *Nuclear Iran: Not Inevitable* (Washington, DC: Institute for Science and International Security, January 21, 2009). See also Paul K. Kerr, "Iran's Nuclear Program: Status," CRS Report for Congress (Washington, DC, June 23, 2008). For the status of Iran's negotiations with the International Atomic Energy Agency, see IAEA, *Implementation of the NPT Safeguards Agreement*. According to the IAEA, Iran currently has approximately 3,606 kilograms of LEU hexafluoride. For an assessment of U.S.-Iranian nuclear interactions, see William Burr, "A Brief History of U.S.-Iranian Nuclear Negotiations," *Bulletin of Atomic Scientists* 65, no. 1 (January 2009). For an Intelligence Community assessment of Iran's nuclear program, see National Intelligence Council, *Iran: Nuclear Intentions and Capabilities*, National Intelligence Estimate (Washington, DC, November 2007).

15. For background on Pakistan's nuclear forces, see Norris and Kristensen, "Pakistan's Nuclear Forces, 2007," 71–74. Pakistan continues to update its nuclear weapons facilities and programs. See the Institute for Science and International Security, http://isis-online.org/publications/southasia/index.html.

16. See Douglas Franz and Catherine Collins, *The Man from Pakistan: The True Story of the World's Most Dangerous Nuclear Smuggler* (New York: Twelve Publishing, 2008); Gordon Corera, *Shopping for Bombs: Nuclear Proliferation, Global Insecurity, and the Rise and Fall of the AQ Khan Network* (New York: Oxford University Press, 2006); Douglas Franz, *The Nuclear Jihadist: The True Story of the Man Who Sold the World's Most Dangerous Secrets . . . And How We Could Have Stopped Him* (New York: Twelve Publishing, 2007); and Adrian Levy and Catherine Scott-Clark, *Deception: Pakistan, the United States, and the Secret Trade in Nuclear Weapons* (New York: Walker Publishing, 2007) for fairly comprehensive coverage of the Khan network.

17. See Levi, *Deterring State Sponsorship of Nuclear Terrorism*, 21–23.

18. David E. Sanger and Thom Shanker, "U.S. Debates Deterrence for Nuclear Terrorism," *New York Times*, May 8, 2007. See also Joseph Biden, "CSI Nukes," *Wall Street Journal*, June 4, 2007.

19. While such an illicit transfer may be perceived by Western policymakers as being irrational, given their unique national goals, adversarial nations may find it risky yet nevertheless worth the risk. "Mirror-imaging," or projecting Western-style thought processes onto an adversary, can yield strategic surprises. Understanding an adversary's culture, means of processing information, and decision-making style is essential to projecting how it might act under various scenarios.

20. See *National Strategy to Combat Weapons of Mass Destruction*, December 2002, 3.

21. See Daniel Byman, "Do Counterproliferation and Counterterrorism Go Together?," *Political Science Quarterly* 122, no. 1 (2007): 33.

22. See STRATFOR Global Intelligence, "Debunking Myths about Nuclear Weapons and Terrorism" (Austin, TX, May 29, 2009), http://www.stratfor.com/analysis/20090528_debunking_myths_about_nuclear_weapons_and_terrorism.

23. See Jenkins, *Will Terrorists Go Nuclear?*, 143.

24. Ayman al-Zawahiri, al Qaeda's second in command, drafted a letter to Abu Mus'ab al-Zarqawi (now deceased), loosely known as the leader of al Qaeda in Iraq, warning Zarqawi that his violent action in Iraq might alienate the Iraqi people and thus run the risk of "repeating the mistake of the Taliban, who restricted participation on governance to students and people of Qandahar alone. . . . Therefore, I stress to you . . . the need to direct the political action equally with the military action." Letter from Ayman al-Zawahiri to Abu Mus'ab al-Zarqawi, July 9, 2005, http://ctc.usma.edu/harmony/pdf/CTC-Zawahiri-Letter-10-05.pdf.

25. See William J. Perry, "Proliferation on the Peninsula: Five North Korean Nuclear Crises," *The Annals of the American Academy of Political and Social Science* 607 (September 2006): 85.

26. See U.S. Intelligence Community, "Acquisition of Technology Relating to Weapons of Mass Destruction and Advanced Conventional Munitions, 1 January to 31 December 2005," http://www.fas.org/irp/threat/wmd-acq2005.pdf.

27. See "U.S. Officials Worry about North Korean Proliferation," *Global Security Newswire*, May 28, 2009. Former U.S. National Security Adviser general James Jones reportedly stated that while a worst-case scenario is the North Korean development of a viable nuclear weapon and delivery system, "the imminent threat

is the proliferation of that type of technology to other countries and potentially to terrorist organizations and non-state actors." With respect to North Korea, Siegfried Hecker, metallurgist and emeritus director of the Los Alamos National Laboratory, stated, "We cannot dismiss that the [forty to fifty kilograms of plutonium that he assessed North Korea separated] . . . may be exported to terrorist groups. This is most likely to occur when North Korea perceives the existence of the regime or its nation as terminally threatened." Siegfried Hecker, "Toward a Comprehensive Safeguards System: Keeping Fissile Materials out of Terrorists' Hands," *The Annals of the American Academy of Political and Social Science* 607 (September 2006): 130.

28. For an assessment of the intelligence maladies associated with the NIE, see Commission on the Intelligence Capabilities of the United States Regarding Weapons of Mass Destruction, "Report to the President of the United States" (Washington, DC, March 31, 2005), particularly chapter 1, http://www.gpoaccess.gov /wmd/pdf/full_wmd_report.pdf. See also "Iraq's Continuing Programs for Weapons of Mass Destruction," unclassified excerpts from the October 2002 National Intelligence Estimate, http://www.globalsecurity.org/intell/library /reports/2002/nie_iraq_october2002.htm. As postwar evidence has clearly determined, Iraq did not possess nuclear weapons.

29. See Andrei Kokoshin, "A Nuclear Response to Nuclear Terror: Reflections of Nuclear Preemption," *The Annals of the American Academy of Political and Social Science* 607 (September 2006): 60.

30. See Mark E. Bleck and Paul R. Souder, *PAL Control of Theater Nuclear Weapons,* Sandia National Laboratory Report (Albuquerque, NM, March 1984), http:// www.cs.columbia.edu/~smb/nsam-160/pal.html#SF87.

31. See Charles D. Ferguson, *Preventing Catastrophic Nuclear Terrorism,* Special Report 11 (New York: Council on Foreign Relations, March 2006).

32. As will be expanded upon in chapter 5, this includes how states resolve the "always/never" dilemma, or how to ensure that nuclear weapons are "always" available to strike or counterstrike but "never" used in an unauthorized manner.

33. See Byman, "Do Counterproliferation and Counterterrorism Go Together?," 36.

34. See Robert S. Litwak, *Regime Change: U.S. Strategy through the Prism of 9/11* (Washington, DC: Woodrow Wilson Center Press and Johns Hopkins University Press, 2007), 293.

35. Paul Williams, author of *The Al-Qaeda Connection: International Terrorism, Organized Crime, and the Coming Apocalypse* (Amherst, NY: Prometheus Books, 2005), has claimed that al Qaeda has purchased suitcase nuclear weapons from the Russians and has hired former Spetsnaz and KGB operatives to provide maintenance for the weapons (without which the weapons would not likely work). The credibility of this claim is open to question. While unclassified sources cannot refute the claim with certainty, the fact that none of these weapons have been used by al Qaeda or Chechen terrorists within Russia provides some degree of confidence that the weapons, which did exist, have not been acquired by terrorists. See Nikolai Sokov, "Suitcase Nukes: Permanently Lost Luggage" (Monterey, CA: James L. Martin Center for Nonproliferation Studies, February 13, 2004), http://cns.miis.edu/stories/040213.htm. Also see Robin M. Frost, *Nuclear Terrorism after 9/11* (London: Routledge, 2005), 21–22.

36. As quoted in Allison, *Nuclear Terrorism,* 45.

37. See Sokov, "Suitcase Nukes: Permanently Lost Luggage."

38. The Davey Crockett carried the W54 warhead, which has a yield of 0.01 kilotons, or 10 tons of TNT, approximately two to four times as powerful as the ammonium nitrate bomb used in the attack against the Alfred P. Murrah Federal Building in April 1995. Launched from a recoilless rifle, the Davy Crockett had a range of about 1.5–2.5 miles. For more information on the Davy Crockett, see Brookings Institution, http://www.brookings.edu/projects/archive/nucweapons/davyc.aspx. Also see Sokov, "Suitcase Nukes: Permanently Lost Luggage."
39. See "Russian Roulette: A Report on the Safety and Security of Russia's Nuclear Arsenal," PBS, 1999, http://www.pbs.org/wgbh/pages/frontline/shows/russia/.
40. See Nikolai Sokov, "'Suitcase Nukes': A Reassessment" (Monterey, CA: James L. Martin Center for Nonproliferation Studies, September 23, 2002), http://cns.miis.edu/stories/020923.htm.
41. See Sokov, "Suitcase Nukes: Permanently Lost Luggage."
42. This does not mean that al Qaeda would not opportunistically seize a chance to execute another "spectacular" attack that would demonstrate its continued relevance and power in the aftermath of 9/11. While a spectacular attack could involve a radiological dispersion device, it could also be another mass-casualty attack using conventional weapons. For thoughts on operational conservatism, see Craig Whitlock, "Homemade, Cheap and Dangerous," *Washington Post*, July 5, 2007. While not discounting al Qaeda's intent to acquire and use WMD, the article points out that a thirty-nine-page memo recovered from an al Qaeda laptop found in Pakistan in 2004 advised terrorists to "make use of that which is available at your disposal and . . . bend it to suit your needs, [improvise] rather than waste valuable time becoming despondent over that which is not within your reach." The author of the memo, Dhiren Barot, a British citizen, said he developed the philosophy by "observing senior planners at al-Qa'ida training camps."
43. See Robert Gates, "Nuclear Weapons and Deterrence in the 21st Century," speech before the Carnegie Endowment for International Peace, October 28, 2008, http://carnegieendowment.org/events/index.cfm?fa=eventDetail&id=1202&&prog=zgp,zru& proj=znpp,zusr.
44. Bunn, *Securing the Bomb 2010.*
45. See Matthew Bunn and Anthony Wier, "Securing Nuclear Warheads and Materials: Converting Research Reactors" (Washington, DC: Nuclear Threat Initiative, 2004), 1, www.nti.org/e_research/cnwm/securing/convert/asp. The twenty-ton estimate includes fresh, in-core, and irradiated HEU. In many cases the irradiated HEU also poses a proliferation and terrorism threat because at many research reactors the fuel was only lightly irradiated, has been cooling for many years, and is in fuel elements of modest size, meaning that the fuel elements are no longer sufficiently radioactive to be self-protecting against theft.

Chapter 3. Fissile Material Compromise—Notification and Detection
1. See William C. Potter and Elena Sokova, "Illicit Nuclear Trafficking in the NIS: What's New? What's True?," *Nonproliferation Review* 9, no. 2 (Summer 2002): 116.
2. See Lyudmila Zaitseva and Kevin Hand, "Nuclear Smuggling Chains," *American Behavioral Scientist* 46, no. 6 (February 2003): 840. See also Lee, *Smuggling Armageddon.* Lee's central recommendations for stanching the illicit transfer of nuclear materials include (1) ensuring enhanced cooperation and training amongst nontechnical counterproliferation assets, such as intelligence, police, and law enforcement services; and (2) addressing one of the root causes of such

transfers—the economic imperative that both criminals and more sophisticated nuclear managers may feel to supply such materials to real or perceived buyers. Volatile oil prices have clearly had an impact on Russian economic development, yet the effect such volatility has on Russian budget outlays for nuclear security is unclear. See World Bank, *Russian Economic Report*, no. 16 (Washington, DC, June 2008).

3. See Lawrence Scott Sheets, "A Smuggler's Story," *Atlantic*, April 2008, www.theatlantic.com/doc/print/200804/uranium-smuggling.

4. See Lyudmila Zaitseva, "Illicit Trafficking in Radioactive Materials," in *Nuclear Black Markets: Pakistan, A.Q. Khan and the Rise of Proliferation Networks—a Net Assessment* (London: International Institute for Strategic Studies, 2007), 121.

5. Red mercury is an unknown substance that many early suppliers of alleged nuclear material pedaled to unsuspecting and naive buyers in numerous hoax schemes. The few samples seized by police were identified as mercury oxide, mercuric iodide, or mercury mixed with red dye. See ibid., 122. According to terrorism expert Brian Michael Jenkins, "We are still in doubt about whether red mercury . . . actually exists as anything more than a scientist's theory, a con man's scam, and a scary story—impossible to confirm, impossible to kill." See Jenkins, *Will Terrorists Go Nuclear?*, 169.

6. Other entities within the U.S. government, including those within the intelligence community and the DHS's Domestic Nuclear Detection Office (DNDO), also maintain their own proprietary databases. The international criminal police organization (INTERPOL) and the IAEA, with financial support from the U.S. Department of Energy, also track illicit nuclear materials trafficking through Project Geiger. See http://www.interpol.int/public/nuclearterrorism/default.asp.

7. See "Statute of the IAEA," Article II, http://www.iaea.org/About/statute_text .html#A1.2.

8. As of September 2010, 111 countries and organizations are members of the ITDB. See IAEA, "Illicit Trafficking Database, http://www.ns.iaea.org/security/itdb.asp.

9. See Zaitseva, "Illicit Trafficking in Radioactive Materials," 120.

10. See Rolf Mowatt-Larssen, former director of the DOE Office of Intelligence and Counterintelligence, *Preventing Nuclear Terrorism: A Global Intelligence Imperative*, Policy Watch 1151 (Washington, DC: Washington Institute for Near East Policy, April 30, 2009).

11. See IAEA, "Illicit Trafficking Database."

12. IAEA, *Full Report: 2005 Nuclear Trafficking Statistics*. See also Lyudmila Zaitseva and Friedrich Steinhausler, "Illicit Trafficking of Nuclear and Other Radioactive Material: The 'Net' Security Threat," *International Journal of Nuclear Law* 1, no. 2 (2006).

13. See IAEA, *ITDB Factsheet for 2006*, table 1 (Vienna, Austria, 2007), http://www.iaea.org/NewsCenter/News/2006/traffickingstats2005.html. This total does not include the 18.5 kilograms of HEU of unknown enrichment that Russian authorities were reportedly able to prevent from being compromised in 1998 in the Chelyabinsk region of Russia, because it was never confirmed by the Russian Federation to the IAEA.

14. A zero tolerance for illicit transfer of fissile material is appropriate. This presupposes, however, that there is a known and accurate baseline for how much HEU and plutonium were produced in the first place, a presumption that many view as unrealistic. However, fissile material is without doubt a strategic commodity not

unlike oil. Supply of the former must be closely controlled and supply of the latter must be ensured to protect U.S. and global national security.

15. See Victor Yerastov, "Minatom Has All Conditions for Providing Safety and Security of Nuclear Material," *Yaderny Kontrol Digest* 5, no. 1 (Winter 2000), http://www.pircenter.org/english/ncdigest/index.htm. See also Secretary of Energy Advisory Board, *A Report Card on the Department of Energy's Nonproliferation Programs with Russia* (Washington, DC: U.S. Department of Energy, January 10, 2001), 7.

16. See Zaitseva, "Illicit Trafficking in Radioactive Materials,"126.

17. See Government Accountability Office (GAO), *Nuclear Nonproliferation: Progress Made in Improving Nuclear Security at Russian Nuclear Sites, but Long-Term Sustainability of U.S.-Funded Security Upgrades Is Uncertain,* GAO-07-404 (Washington, DC, February 2007).

18. Given the uncertainties associated with global supply of narcotics, there is a dearth of reliable statistics on global interdiction rates, that is, the amount of narcotics interdicted globally expressed as a percentage of total global narcotics production. However, according to one expert, an estimate of a 10 percent interdiction rate has been used historically to reflect the amount of narcotics successfully taken out of illicit trafficking into the United States.

19. See Brian Michael Jenkins, "Unconquerable Nation: Knowing Our Enemy, Strengthening Ourselves" (Santa Monica, CA: Rand, 2006), 81.

20. See *The Final Report of the National Commission on Terrorist Attacks upon the United States,* July 2004. See also Matthew Levitt and Michael Jacobson, *The Money Trail: Finding, Following, and Freezing Terrorist Finances,* Policy Focus 89 (Washington, DC: Washington Institute for Near East Policy, November 2008).

21. See Louise I. Shelley, "Trafficking in Nuclear Materials: Criminals and Terrorists," *Global Crime* 7, nos. 3–4 (August–November 2006): 555.

22. See William Langewiesche, *The Atomic Bazaar: The Rise of the Nuclear Poor* (New York: Farrar, Straus and Giroux, 2007).

23. Ibid. It has also been alleged that the slow security guard response to the breach at the Pelindaba nuclear research facility in South Africa may have been related to insider collusion. See "Pelindaba: Finding Anton Gerber," *60 Minutes,* December 4, 2008, http://www.cbsnews.com/stories/2008/12/04/60minutes/main4647778.shtml.

24. See Sara Daly, John Parachini, and William Rosenau, *Aum Shinrikyo, Al-Qa'ida, and the Kinshasa Reactor: Implications of Three Case Studies for Combating Nuclear Terrorism* (Santa Monica, CA: Rand, 2005), ix.

25. See Lee, *Smuggling Armageddon.*

26. See Bunn, *Securing the Bomb 2010.*

27. White House press briefing, April 13, 2010.

28. Dr. ElBaradei's term at the IAEA ended November 30, 2009. He was replaced by Mr. Yukiya Amano, a Japanese Foreign Ministry official. For Dr. ElBaradei's comments on safety and security, see the statement of IAEA director general Mohamed ElBaradei to the Sixty-Third Regular Session of the United Nations General Assembly, October 28, 2008. Individual nations possessing fissile material develop their own state systems of accountancy and control. At the request of a nation, the IAEA provides substantial technical assistance in the form of its National Security Series publications. These publications are available at http://www-ns.iaea.org/security/nuclear_security_series.htm. The IAEA also has de-

veloped two nuclear security plans and, upon request, has worked with IAEA member states to assist them in developing nuclear security measures.

29. See Friedrich Steinhausler, "What It Takes to Become a Nuclear Terrorist," *American Behavioral Scientist* 46, no. 6 (February 2003): 790.

30. According to Friedrich Steinhausler, professor of physics and biophysics at the University of Salzburg, Austria, "The only legally binding international requirements obligate the adherence to The Convention of the Physical Protection of Nuclear Material while the nuclear material is in international transport. There is no such obligation while the material is in domestic use, storage, and transit." Article 17, paragraph 2, of the convention provides that "any dispute of this charter which cannot be settled in the manner prescribed in paragraph 1 shall, at the request of any party to such dispute, be submitted to arbitration or referred to the International Court of Justice for decision. Where a dispute is submitted to arbitration, if, within six months from the date of the request, the parties to the dispute are unable to agree on the organization of the arbitration, a party may request the President of the International Court of Justice or the Secretary-General of the United Nations to appoint one or more arbitrators. In case of conflicting requests by the parties to the dispute, the request to the Secretary-General of the United Nations shall have priority." Even this legally binding language is weak, given that parties to the convention are also allowed to declare that their nations are not bound by these terms. See IAEA, *The Convention of the Physical Protection of Nuclear Material*, Information Circular (INFCIRC)/274/Rev.1 (Vienna, Austria, May 1980), http://www.iaea.org/Publications/Documents/Infcircs/Others/inf274rl.shtml.

31. See statement of IAEA director general Mohamed ElBaradei, October 28, 2008.

32. An Additional Protocol to a country's existing safeguards agreement provides the IAEA with enhanced authority to conduct more intrusive inspections to detect undeclared nuclear activity. As of December 2010, there were 104 states with an Additional Protocol in force. For statistics on NPT members with Additional Protocols in force see http://www.iaea.org/OurWork/SV/Safeguards/sg_protocol.html.

33. As mentioned in chapter 2, North Korea initially was a member of the NPT but subsequently withdrew from it, the only country to do so, in 2003. Six-party talks designed to denuclearize the Korean Peninsula are currently in suspension given North Korea's long-range missile test in April 2009 and its May 2009 nuclear test.

34. See IAEA, *Implementation of the NPT Safeguards Agreement*, February 25, 2011.

35. Technology also plays an important role with respect to nuclear terrorism deterrence, as will be discussed later. Nuclear forensics and attribution technologies are essential elements of extended deterrence.

36. See National Research Council, Committee on Science and Technology for Countering Terrorism, *Making the Nation Safer: The Role of Science and Technology in Countering Terrorism* (Washington, DC: National Academies Press, 2002), 55.

37. For an assessment of the ways to expand and strengthen the Department of Defense Cooperative Threat Reduction Program, see National Academy of Sciences, *Global Security Engagement: A New Model for Cooperative Threat Reduction* (Washington, DC: National Academies Press, 2009). See also Kenneth N. Luongo, "Loose Nukes in New Neighborhoods: The Next Generation of Proliferation Prevention," *Arms Control Today*, May 2009.

38. See David Albright and Paul Brannan, *The Al Kibar Reactor: Extraordinary Camouflage, Troubling Implications* (Washington, DC: Institute for Science and

International Security, May 12, 2008), http://isis-online.org/publications/syria
/index.html.

39. See statement of IAEA director general Mohamed ElBaradei, October 28, 2008.
This finding may be all the more salient given that, according to David Albright
of the Institute for Science and International Security, Mohamed ElBaradei stated in the wake of the Israeli bombing of the Syrian reactor at Al Kibar, "Our
experts who have carefully analyzed the satellite imagery say it is unlikely that
this building was a nuclear facility." A subsequent U.S. Intelligence Community
briefing on April 24, 2008, provided substantial support for the argument that
the facility was indeed a nuclear reactor with similarities to a North Korean gas-
graphite reactor design. See Albright and Brannan, *The Al Kibar Reactor*, 2.
Rolf Mowatt-Larssen, former director of intelligence and counterintelligence at
the Department of Energy, has proposed that the IAEA develop its own intelligence unit. Mowatt-Larssen reportedly stated this is necessary in order to "overcome bureaucratic and security impediments to finding a way via the IAEA or
another [multilateral] way to greatly expand how nations work together to find
loose nukes." See Mark Heinrich, "IAEA May Need Intelligence Arm against
Atom Terror," Reuters, April 1, 2009, http://uk.reuters.com/article/idUK-
TRE53058O20090401. For a variety of reasons, such a unit appears unlikely to
be developed soon. See Elaine M. Grossman, "Boost in IAEA Intelligence Capability Looks Unlikely in Near-Term," *Global Security Newswire*, June 22, 2009.

40. See statement of Rolf Mowatt-Larssen before the Homeland Security and Governmental Affairs Committee, U.S. Senate, April 2, 2008.

41. See John Despres, "Intelligence and the Prevention of Nuclear Terrorism," in
Leventhal and Alexander, *Preventing Nuclear Terrorism*.

42. For information on the FBI's Legal Attaché program, see FBI, http://www.fbi
.gov/contact/legat/legat.htm. See also Thomas V. Fuentes, assistant director,
Office of International Operations, Federal Bureau of Investigation, statement
before the Subcommittee on Border, Maritime, and Global Counterterrorism of
the House Homeland Security Committee, October 4, 2007.

43. See George Tenet and Bill Harlow, *At the Center of the Storm: My Years at the
CIA* (New York: HarperCollins, 2007), 276.

44. Mowatt-Larssen, *Preventing Nuclear Terrorism*.

45. See remarks by former national security adviser Stephen J. Hadley at the Proliferation Security Initiative Fifth Anniversary Senior-Level Meeting, May 28, 2008,
http://www.whitehouse.gov/news/releases/2008/05/print/20080528-3.
html. Secretary of Defense Robert Gates stated these exact words in a speech
before the Carnegie Endowment for International Peace on October 28, 2008.
See Gates, "Nuclear Weapons and Deterrence in the 21st Century."

46. See Levi, *Deterring State Sponsorship of Nuclear Terrorism*, 13–14.

47. Shielding dampens the emissions of gamma rays, neutrons, and other particles
from fissile material, making it more difficult to detect them. It is easier to shield
HEU than plutonium, and readily available materials can be used for shielding
purposes.

48. The DNDO was established in 2005 pursuant to National Security Presidential Directive-43/Homeland Security Presidential Directive-14 to "coordinate
efforts of Federal, State, and local partners to strengthen national nuclear and
radiological detection capabilities, to address the threat of nuclear terrorism." See
Vayl S. Oxford, director of the DNDO, "Nuclear Terrorism Prevention: Status

Report of the Federal Government's Assessment of New Radiation Detection Monitors," statement before the House Committee on Energy and Commerce, Subcommittee on Oversight and Investigations, September 18, 2007.

49. See Domestic Nuclear Detection Office, Department of Homeland Security, *Congressional Justification FY2009*, DNDO R&DO-2. As quoted in Dana A. Shea, "The Global Nuclear Detection Architecture," CRS Report for Congress (Washington, DC, September 23, 2008).

50. See GAO, *Nuclear Detection: Domestic Nuclear Detection Office Should Improve Planning to Better Address Gaps and Vulnerabilities*, GAO-09-257 (Washington, DC, January 2009).

51. For an assessment of nuclear detection technologies, see Jonathan Medalia, "Detection of Nuclear Weapons and Materials: Science, Technologies and Observations," CRS Report for Congress (Washington, DC, November 6, 2008), http://www.fas.org/sgp/crs/nuke/R40154.pdf.

52. While the systems may be effective at detecting radiation, they "often cannot distinguish between benign sources, such as cat litter, and material that can be used in weapons." See Robert O'Harrow Jr., "Radiation Detector Plan Falls Short, Audit Shows," *Washington Post*, September 4, 2008.

53. See Gene Aloise, "Combating Nuclear Smuggling: DHS Needs to Consider Full Costs and Complete All Tests Prior to Making a Decision on Whether to Purchase Advanced Portal Monitors," statement before the Committee on Homeland Security and Governmental Affairs, U.S. Senate, September 25, 2008.

54. See GAO, *Combating Nuclear Smuggling: DHS's Phase 3 Test Report on Advanced Portal Monitors Does Not Fully Disclose the Limitations of the Test Results*, GAO-08-979 (Washington, DC, September 2008).

55. See GAO, *Combating Nuclear Smuggling: Lessons from DHS Testing of Advanced Radiation Detection Portal Monitors*, GAO-09-804T (Washington, DC, June 25, 2009). See also GAO, *Combating Nuclear Smuggling: DHS Has Made Some Progress, but Not Yet Completed a Strategic Plan for Its Global Nuclear Detection Efforts or Closed Identified Gaps*, GAO 10-883T (Washington, DC, June 30, 2010). In December 2010, DNDO delivered it long-awaited strategic plan on global nuclear detection architecture to Congress. See Martin Matishak, "Homeland Security Delivers Nuclear Detection Plan to Capitol Hill," *Global Security Newswire*, January 5, 2011.

56. See Cochran and McKinzie, "Detecting Nuclear Smuggling."

57. See Matthew Bunn and Andrew Newman, *Preventing Nuclear Terrorism: An Agenda for the Next President* (Cambridge, MA, and Washington, DC: Harvard University Press and Nuclear Threat Initiative, November 2008).

58. See Simon Labov and Garret Jernigan, "Foundation to Improve Passive Detection Systems" (Washington, DC: National Nuclear Security Administration, 2003), http://rdc.llnl.gov/rdp/foundation.html.

59. While standoff platforms can aim a beam from a distance (for example, from an aircraft to a ship), the beam would still need to get close enough to the ship to detect radiation emissions from the radiological source.

60. Interview with Dr. Peter Nanos, former director of Los Alamos National Laboratory, currently affiliated with the U.S. Department of Defense, Defense Threat Reduction Agency, and the Johns Hopkins University Applied Physics Laboratory, June 27, 2008. Others have offered alternative time frames. See Defense Science Board, *Report of the Defense Science Board Task Force of Preventing and*

Defending against Clandestine Nuclear Attack (Washington, DC: Department of Defense, June 2004), http://www.ciaonet.org/wps/dod61/dod61.pdf.

61. See the third Richard Nixon–John Kennedy presidential debate, October 13, 1960, http://www.wagingpeace.org/articles/2003/11/17_carnegie_jfk-nuclear.htm.

62. See Seth Jones, "Defeating Terrorist Groups," testimony before the House Armed Services Committee, Subcommittee on Terrorism, Unconventional Threats and Capabilities, September 18, 2008.

Chapter 4. The Nuclear Terrorism Threat Spectrum—Demand

1. See *World at Risk: The Report of the Commission on the Prevention of WMD Proliferation and Terrorism* (New York: Vintage Books, December 2008).

2. See remarks by President Barack Obama, Hradcany Square, Prague, Czech Republic, April 5, 2009, http://www.whitehouse.gov/the_press_office/Remarks-By-President-Barack-Obama-In-Prague-As-Delivered/.

3. See Harris Interactive, "The War on Terror: What Is It? Who Are Our Enemies and How Likely Are Different Types of Terrorist Attacks in the United States?" (New York, June 22, 2007), http://www.harrisinteractive.com/harris_poll/index.asp?PID=776. Derivatively quoted from Jenkins, *Will Terrorists Go Nuclear?*, 293.

4. See Norman J. Rabkin, director of national security preparedness issues, National Security and International Affairs Division, GAO, "Combating Terrorism: Issues in Managing Counterterrorist Programs," testimony before the Subcommittee on Oversight, Investigations, and Emergency Management, Committee on Transportation and Infrastructure, U.S. House of Representatives, April 6, 2000. Further, Bernard Brodie, RAND military strategist and former professor of political science at the University of California–Los Angeles, wrote: "The defense community of the United States is inhabited by peoples of wide range of skills and of considerable imagination. All sorts of notions and proposals are churned out, and often presented for consideration with the prefatory words 'It is conceivable that . . . ' Such words establish their own truth, for the fact that someone has conceived of whatever proposition follows is enough to establish that it is conceivable. Whether it is worth a second thought, however, is another matter. It should undergo a good deal of thought before one begins to spend money on it." See Bernard Brodie, "Development of Nuclear Strategy," *International Security* 2 (Spring 1978): 83. As quoted in John Mueller, "The Atomic Terrorist: Assessing the Likelihood" (Columbus: Ohio State University Press, January 1, 2008), http://polisci.osu.edu/faculty/jmueller/APSACHGO.PDF.

5. Jenkins, *Will Terrorists Go Nuclear?*, 209.

6. Ibid., 210–11.

7. While Arkin would clearly be considered a skeptic for purposes of this study, his thoughts are included here only to illustrate the point that there are those who question conventional wisdom and American public perception about the relatively high probability of a nuclear terrorist attack against the United States. See William Arkin, "The Continuing Misuses of Fear," *Bulletin of Atomic Scientists* 62, no. 5 (September–October 2006).

8. See Daniel Byman, *The Five Front War: The Better Way to Fight Global Jihad* (Hoboken, NJ: John Wiley and Sons, 2008), 135.

9. It is recognized that public statements of terrorist leaders can also constitute disinformation campaigns and can be targeted at disparate domestic and interna-

tional audiences. However, such public statements should be assessed in a historical context and not necessarily discounted.

10. See testimony statement of Charles E. Allen, April 2, 2008.

11. For further exploration of this line of thinking, see "How Likely Is a Nuclear Attack on the United States?," an online discussion between Michael Levi of the Council on Foreign Relations and Professor Graham Allison of Harvard University, April 20, 2007, http://www.cfr.org/publication/13097/how_likely_is_a_nuclear_terrorist_attack_on_the_united_states.html.

12. See Ron Suskind, *The One Percent Doctrine: Deep Inside America's Pursuit of Its Enemies Since 9/11* (New York: Simon & Schuster, 2006), 62. Rolf Mowatt-Larssen, former director of the Department of Energy's Office of Intelligence and Counterintelligence, seems to support this 1 percent solution, arguing that "even a minute chance that terrorists might have that ability [to pull off a nuclear attack] changes the equation dramatically." See Mowatt-Larssen, *Preventing Nuclear Terrorism*.

13. For the dangers associated with worst-case scenario planning, see Suskind, *The One Percent Doctrine*.

14. See Robert W. Hahn and Cass R. Sunstein, "The Precautionary Principle as Basis for Decision Making," *Economists' Voice* 2, no. 2, article 8 (2005): 1. See also Philipp Bobbitt, *Terror and Consent: The Wars for the Twenty-First Century* (New York: Alfred A. Knopf, 2008), 476–77.

15. See Michael Krepon, "The Mushroom Cloud That Wasn't," *Foreign Affairs*, May–June 2009.

16. See Byman, *The Five Front War*, 131–33. For the Leif Wenar quote, see Mueller, "Six Rather Unusual Propositions about Terrorism," 487. For an alternative hypothesis, see Sherry Horowitz, "It May Be Best to Assume the Worst," *Security Management*, January 2009. The author bases this assessment on the writings of Paul Willen, an economist with the Federal Reserve Bank in Boston who drew analogies between the subprime crisis and homeland security.

17. None of the panelists chosen by the Senate committee came from a "skeptic" school of thought.

18. See Rolf Mowatt-Larssen, "The Strategic Threat of Nuclear Terrorism," remarks at the Washington Institute for Near East Policy, June 16, 2008. While it may be true that, as former DNI John Negroponte testified, "nearly 40 terrorist organizations, insurgencies, or cults have used, possessed, or expressed an interest in chemical, biological, radiological, or nuclear agents or weapons," the only terrorist organization to directly threaten the homeland, according to the Intelligence Community, is al Qaeda. See John Negroponte, "Annual Threat Assessment of the DNI," testimony before the Senate Armed Services Committee, February 28, 2006.

19. See Glenn Carle, "Overstating Our Fears," *Washington Post*, July 13, 2008.

20. See John Mueller, *Overblown: How Politicians and the Terrorism Industry Inflate National Security Threats, and Why We Believe Them* (New York: Free Press, 2006), 13.

21. See Fareed Zakaria, "The Only Thing We Have to Fear. . . ," *Newsweek*, May 24, 2008.

22. See Simon Fraser University, Human Security Report Project, *Human Security Brief 2007* (Vancouver, Canada, 2007), 8–20, http://www.humansecuritybrief.info/. A central tenet of this argument is that Iraq is in a civil war, an assertion some would question.

23. See Raphael F. Perl, "International Terrorism: Threat, Policy and Response," CRS Report for Congress (Washington, DC, January 3, 2007), 6, http://www .fas.org/sgp/crs/terror/RL33600.pdf.

24. Testimony of Secretary Janet Napolitano before the United States House of Representatives Committee on Homeland Security, "Understanding the Homeland Threat Landscape—Considerations for the 112th Congress," February 9, 2011.

25. See National Intelligence Council, "Key Judgments," July 2007.

26. DCI Tenet is infamous for prewar (Iraq 2003) statements and advice to the president about weapons of mass destruction in Iraq that were ultimately proven incorrect and based on poor analytical tradecraft and sources of questionable reliability and validity. See Commission on the Intelligence Capabilities of the United States Regarding Weapons of Mass Destruction, "Report to the President," 7–11. With respect to intelligence on Iraq's WMD programs, the commission found "the Community's Iraq assessment was crippled by its inability to collect meaningful intelligence on Iraq's nuclear, biological, and chemical weapons programs. . . . Lacking good intelligence, analysts and collectors fell back on old assumptions and inferences drawn from Iraq's past behavior and intentions." With respect to human intelligence, the commission found "intelligence officials within the CIA failed to convey to policymakers new information casting serious doubt on the reliability of a human intelligence source known as 'Curveball.' . . . In this instance, once again, the Intelligence Community failed to give policymakers a full understanding of the frailties of the intelligence on which they were relying." Intelligence remains by its very nature fallible. Reaching conclusions with the highest degrees of certainty is relatively rare. While al Qaeda is not Iraq, similar intelligence maladies must be guarded against.

27. See Lewis A. Dunn, *Can Al-Qaeda Be Deterred from Using Nuclear Weapons?* (Washington, DC: National Defense University Press, July 2005), 2.

28. See Chris McIntosh and Ian Storey, "Between Acquisition and Use: Examining the Improbability of Nuclear Terrorism," January 29, 2008, http://totalwonkerr .com/1584/nuclear-terrorism-not-gonna-happen.

29. Ibid.

30. Ibid.

31. Ibid.

32. Ibid.

33. Ibid.

34. Ibid.

35. Ibid.

36. See Dunn, *Can Al-Qaeda Be Deterred from Using Nuclear Weapons?*

37. See Hamid Mir interview with Osama bin Laden, "Usama Claims He Has Nukes: If U.S. Uses N-Arms, It Will Get Same Response," *Dawn: The Internet Edition*, November 10, 2001, http://www.dawn.com/2001/11/10/top1.htm.

38. Ibid.

39. See Jenkins, *Will Terrorists Go Nuclear?*, 251–55.

40. See Dunn, *Can Al-Qaeda Be Deterred from Using Nuclear Weapons?*

41. In the United States, Bruce E. Ivins, a scientist at a Department of Defense laboratory, allegedly was behind a series of anthrax attacks that targeted politicians and journalists. The attacks created panic and led to the deaths of five persons. According to terrorism analyst Peter Bergen, Ivins "was one of the leading biological weapons researchers in the United States. Even this brilliant scientist could

only 'weaponize' anthrax to the point that it killed a handful of people. Imagine how difficult it would be for the average terrorist, or even above-average terrorist, to replicate such efforts." See Bergen, "Commentary: WMD Terrorism Fears Are Overblown."

The case of Aum Shinrikyo is only the most prominent of four cases. Three other cases, including the Rajneeshee religious cult (United States 1984), the Liberation Tamil Tigers Eelam (LTTE) of Sri Lanka (Sri Lanka 1990), and al Qaeda's Iraqi affiliate (Iraq 2006–2007), have involved a very limited tactical use of chemical agents as weapons. In the case of the Rajneeshee, the group attempted to influence a local election by poisoning the local population. The Rajneeshee spread the bacteria *Salmonella typhimurium* over ten salad bars at local restaurants. The intent of the attack was not to kill large numbers of people but to decrease voter participation. There were 751 persons injured, yet no fatalities. The attack was not immediately recognized as being deliberate. See J. V. Parachini, "Comparing Motives and Outcomes of Mass Casualty Terrorism Involving Conventional and Unconventional Weapons," *Studies in Conflict and Terrorism* 24, no. 5 (March 2001): 390–91. The (now defeated) LTTE struck an isolated Sri Lankan armed forces facility with chlorine gas. According to terrorism expert Bruce Hoffman, the chlorine gas attack was part of a broader assault on the facility and did not result in any fatalities, although sixty soldiers were hospitalized for gas exposure. See Hoffman, *Inside Terrorism*. In the Iraqi case, al Qaeda's Iraqi affiliate laced several of its bombs with chlorine. "Those attacks sickened hundreds of Iraqis, but victims who died in assaults did so more from the blast of the bombs than because of inhaling chlorine. Al-Qa'ida stopped using chlorine in its bombs in Iraq more than a year ago." See Bergen, "Commentary: WMD Terrorism Fears Are Overblown."

42. See Hoffman, *Inside Terrorism*, 119.
43. See Daly, Parachini, and Rosenau, *Aum Shinrikyo, Al-Qa'ida, and the Kinshasa Reactor*, 6. Derivatively cited from Daniel Metraux, *Aum Shinrikyo and Japanese Youth* (Lanham, MD: University Press of America, 1999), 30–36.
44. See Daly, Parachini, and Rosenau, *Aum Shinrikyo, Al-Qa'ida, and the Kinshasa Reactor*, 13.
45. See D. W. Brackett, *Holy Terror: Armageddon in Tokyo* (New York: Weatherhill, 1996). See also Robert Jay Lifton, *Destroying the World to Save It: Aum Shinrikyo, Apocalyptic Violence, and the New Global Terrorism* (New York: MacMillan, 2000).
46. See Daly, Parachini, and Rosenau, *Aum Shinrikyo, Al-Qa'ida, and the Kinshasa Reactor*, 18.
47. Ibid.
48. Asahara was arrested in 1996 and was subsequently tried and convicted. He was sentenced to death in 2004 and is currently awaiting execution. See Holly Fletcher, *Aum Shinrikyo (Japan, Cultists, Aleph, Aum Supreme Truth)* (New York and Washington, DC: Council on Foreign Relations, May 28, 2008), http://www .cfr.org/publication/9238/#2.
49. Ibid.
50. See Gary Ackerman and William C. Potter, "Catastrophic Nuclear Terrorism: A Preventable Peril," in *Global Catastrophic Risks*, ed. Nick Bostrom and Milan M. Cirkovic (Oxford: Oxford University Press, 2008), 410. Governmental collapse is, of course, one of the primary concerns in Pakistan, where al Qaeda currently has a substantial presence.

51. See Brian Michael Jenkins et al., *Terrorism: What's Coming—the Mutating Threat* (Oklahoma City: Memorial Institute for the Prevention of Terrorism, 2007), 13. It should be noted that in 1975 Jenkins assessed that "terrorists want a lot of people watching, not a lot of people dead." The period during which this was written, however, falls within what terrorism expert David Rapoport refers to as the "third wave" of terrorism, a time during the 1970s when religion was a part of terrorism but not the driving force behind it. See David C. Rapoport, "The Fourth Wave: September 11 in the History of Terrorism," *Current History*, December 2001. With the benefit of time, former NSC staffers Steven Simon and Daniel Benjamin have noted that the "new trend" is waged by religious militants "who want a lot of people watching *and* a lot of people dead." See Steven Simon and Daniel Benjamin, "America and the New Terrorism," *Survival* 42, no. 1 (Spring 2000): 59.

52. The results were: (1) Rajneeshee 1984 (0 fatalities, 751 casualties); (2) LTTE 1990 (0 fatalities, 63 casualties); (3) World Trade Center 1993 (6 fatalities, 1,000+ casualties); (4) Aum 1995 (13 fatalities, 1,000 casualties); (5) Oklahoma City bombing (168 fatalities, 1,000+ casualties); and (6) Africa embassy bombings (224 fatalities, 5,000 casualties). See Parachini, "Comparing Motives and Outcomes of Mass Casualty Terrorism," 389–401.

53. Ibid.

54. See Gavin Cameron, "WMD Terrorism in the United States: The Threat and Possible Countermeasures," *Nonproliferation Review* 7, no. 1 (Spring 2000): 165.

55. Terrorism expert Peter Bergen has recommended an Office of Metrics be established within the Office of the Director of National Intelligence to "monitor public opinion, democracy-promotion, nation-building, and terrorism metrics." According to Bergen, this would help the United States understand whether it is making progress as it fights terrorism. See testimony of Peter Bergen, Schwartz Senior Fellow—New America Foundation, before the House Permanent Select Committee on Intelligence, April 9, 2008.

56. See Jenkins, "Will Terrorists Go Nuclear?"

57. See Jenkins, *Will Terrorists Go Nuclear?*, 241.

58. See Stephen E. Flynn, "America the Resilient: Defying Terrorism and Mitigating Natural Disasters," *Foreign Affairs*, March–April 2008.

59. See Tenet and Harlow, *At the Center of the Storm*, 279. The implication is that the detonation of a nuclear weapon would destroy the U.S. economy. While a crude nuclear detonation would no doubt cause substantial disruption and costs to the U.S. and global economies, if not followed by successive nuclear attacks, it is highly unlikely that a single nuclear weapon could destroy a resilient $14 trillion economy.

60. See Ackerman and Potter, "Catastrophic Nuclear Terrorism," 408.

61. See Jenkins, *Will Terrorists Go Nuclear?*, 191.

62. See Lawrence Wright, "The Rebellion Within: An Al-Qa'ida Mastermind Questions Terrorism," *New Yorker*, June 2, 2008.

63. In early March 2008, Zawahiri published *The Exoneration: A Treatise Exonerating the Community of the Pen and the Sword from the Debilitating Accusation of Fatigue and Weakness* to respond to the criticism of his former mentor, Dr. Fadl. See Federation of American Scientists, www.fas.org/irp/eprint/zawahiri.pdf.

64. See Ackerman and Potter, "Catastrophic Nuclear Terrorism," 406–11. The authors cite the experiences of groups such as Avenging Israel's Blood. See E.

Sprinzak and I. Zertal, "Avenging Israel's Blood," in *Toxic Terror: Assessing Terrorist Use of Chemical and Biological Weapons*, ed. J. Tucker (Cambridge, MA: MIT Press, 2000), 17–42.

65. Ackerman and Potter, "Catastrophic Nuclear Terrorism," 409.
66. See Stern, *Terror in the Name of God*, 281–82.
67. See Hoffman, *Inside Terrorism*.
68. See Ackerman and Potter, "Catastrophic Nuclear Terrorism," 410.
69. See Rohan Gunaratna, *Inside Al Qaeda: Global Network of Terror* (New York: Columbia University Press, 2002), 92–93.
70. Ibid.
71. Ibid.
72. There is a wide body of literature that covers the Islamic version of matters apocalyptic. At the most generic level, Americans, possibly represented by the people of Ad mentioned twenty-four times in the Koran, are immoral, corrupt, and either controlled by or in control of the "Zionist entity" Israel. American presidents or other personages, possibly national political leaders, are often referred to as Dajjal (the Muslim Antichrist). Dajjal can be portrayed as a "demon-like being who appears from the east, conquering the whole Muslim world, putting many to the sword and all to the test." There are some linkages between Christian apocalyptic views, such as the Book of Revelation, and Muslim apocalyptic beliefs. According to David Cook, an expert on Muslim apocalyptic, Muslim apocalyptic beliefs tend to include a healthy dose of anti-Semitism linking the people of Ad to the Jews of the Zionist entity. Muslim apocalyptic portrays the world as we currently know it ending via massive tidal waves, fires, floods, or nuclear explosions destroying the United States and its Zionist and European allies. New York City is often singled out in Muslim apocalyptic literature as having a particularly pernicious influence on the world due to the high concentration of Jewish people who reside there. David Cook outlines the potential dangers associated with this school of thought: "[Muslim apocalyptic] still has the power to give hope to an otherwise hopeless group of people. . . . This fantasy provides a hopeful future in which the world will finally be righted. Islam will be generally accepted, rule will once again be in the hands of rightful caliph, and the technology which should have been Muslim will be returned to this reconstituted Muslim empire. . . . There is an unbelievable level of arrogance in the Muslim apocalyptic writers' renditions of the end-times, and their hypocrisy in saying that the U.S. alone is guilty of it is quite startling." See David Cook, "America, the Second Ad: Prophecies about the Downfall of the United States," www.mille.org/scholarship/papers/ADAM .html. For more information on Muslim apocalyptic, see David Cook, *Contemporary Muslim Apocalyptic Literature* (Syracuse, NY: Syracuse University Press, 2005). See also Jean-Pierre Filiu, *The Rise of Apocalyptic Islam: Causes and Implications*, Policy Watch 1427 (Washington, DC: Washington Institute for Near East Policy, November 13, 2008). Mr. Filiu stated, "As the majority of its readership does not interpret apocalypticism literally, the genre's rise does not represent an immediate political threat. Instead, apocalyptic literature is a coping mechanism for day-to-day frustration. It helps 'compensate' for the current economic and social crises by associating them with the foretold decline of Islam before the end of days. Without motivating the reader to any particular action, it promises retribution against the perceived evildoers and a post-apocalyptic recompense: the rise of Islam, justice, and peace."

73. Gunaratna, *Inside Al Qaeda*.
74. Ibid. As much as al Qaeda advocates restoration of the Caliphate, its goals are more practical—to eliminate apostate regimes in the Middle East and infidel regimes anywhere in the world allied or associated with the United States or what al Qaeda refers to as the "Zionist entity."
75. See Tom Gjelten, "Evaluating al-Qaida's Nuclear Strategy," *All Things Considered*, National Public Radio, August 12, 2008.
76. See Jenkins, *Will Terrorists Go Nuclear?*, 97.
77. See Dan Stober, "No Experience Necessary," *Bulletin of Atomic Scientists* 59, no. 2 (March–April 2003).
78. Ibid.
79. Skeptics might argue that such conditions gave the Nth Country group a distinct advantage over a terrorist group attempting the same task.
80. Stober, "No Experience Necessary."
81. Ibid.
82. See John A. McPhee, *The Curve of Binding Energy* (New York: Farrar, Straus and Giroux, 1973), 8.
83. Ibid. See also Stober, "No Experience Necessary."
84. See U.S. Congress, Office of Technology Assessment, *Nuclear Proliferation and Safeguards*, NTIS order PB-275843 (Washington, DC, June 1977), 17.
85. See Zimmerman and Lewis, "The Bomb in the Backyard." The irresistible option argument is also consistent with a group such as al Qaeda's desire to have each successive spectacular attack be more grand and impactful than previous attacks. Al Qaeda reportedly canceled a gas (hydrogen cyanide) attack in New York in 2003 because its leadership did not believe such an attack would be perceived as sufficiently more catastrophic than 9/11. See Suskind, *The One Percent Doctrine*, 194. Yet the irresistible option argument is undermined by a number of factors, including (1) while it may be irresistible from an intent standpoint, from a capabilities perspective the continued degrading of core al-Qa'ida lessens its ability to conduct complex attacks and (2) a preference for operational conservatism (that is, a failed nuclear attack would likely be perceived by terrorists as failure in the eyes of God). A less grandiose and conventional attack using reliable and available explosives might also allow the terrorists to achieve their goals.
86. See Luis W. Alvarez, *Adventures of a Physicist* (New York: Basic Books, 1987), 125.
87. See *The Final Report of the National Commission on Terrorist Attacks upon the United States*, 380.
88. See David Samuels, "Atomic John," *New Yorker*, December 15, 2008.
89. Formula quantity is defined as strategic special nuclear material in any combination in a quantity of 5,000 grams: 5 kilograms or more computed by the formula grams = (grams contained ^{235}U) + 2.5 (grams ^{233}U + grams plutonium). Formula quantity for ^{235}U, then, would be 5 kilograms. Carson Mark et al. believe that as much as 52 kilograms of ^{235}U metal enriched to 94 percent would be necessary. In the presence of an effective reflector, as little as 25 kilograms of weapons-grade HEU might prove sufficient. Alternatively, if uranium oxide powder enriched to 94 percent were used, approximately 110 kilograms would be necessary. See Mark et al., "Can Terrorists Build Nuclear Weapons?"
90. These "tricks of the trade" have been referred to by analysts as explicit versus tacit knowledge. Sonia Ben Ouagrham-Gormley, a senior staff member at the James Martin Center for Nonproliferation Studies of the Monterey Institute of

International Studies and adjunct professor at Johns Hopkins University's School of Advanced International Studies, concludes, "Specialized knowledge, however, is difficult to come by. Knowledge can be divided generally into two categories: explicit knowledge (information or instructions that can be formulated in words, symbols, formulas, or diagrams and can be easily transferred) and tacit knowledge (unarticulated, personally held knowledge or skills that a scientist or technician acquires and transfers through a practical, hands-on process and direct interaction with other scientists). Explicit information such as designs and instructions cannot be efficiently used in the absence of the related tacit knowledge." See Sonia Ben Ouagrham-Gormley, "Nuclear Terrorism's Fatal Assumptions," *Bulletin of Atomic Scientists* (Web edition), October 23, 2007, http://www.thebulletin .org/web-edition/op-eds/nuclear-terrorisms-fatal-assumptions.

91. See Younger, *Endangered Species*, 86–95.
92. See Schelling, "Thinking about Nuclear Terrorism," 61–77.
93. Other analysts have taken issue with Steinhausler's statement that terrorists would need access to advanced equipment, stating that such equipment is not necessary. "To see this it is only necessary to reflect upon what was available in 1945 when the first nuclear weapons were designed and assembled." See Anna M. Pluta and Peter D. Zimmerman, "Nuclear Terrorism: A Disheartening Dissent," *Survival* 48, no. 2 (Summer 2006): 55–70.
94. See Steinhausler, "What It Takes to Become a Nuclear Terrorist," 782–95.
95. See Karl-Heinz Kamp, "An Overrated Nightmare," *Bulletin of Atomic Scientists* 52, no. 4 (July–August 1996).
96. See Christoph Wirz and Emmanuel Egger, "Use of Nuclear and Radiological Weapons by Terrorists?," *International Review of the Red Cross* 87, no. 859 (September 2005): 497–510.
97. See Jenkins, *Will Terrorists Go Nuclear?*, 154.
98. See Mark et al., "Can Terrorists Build Nuclear Weapons?"
99. See David Albright, Kathryn Beuhler, and Holly Higgins, "Bin Laden and the Bomb," *Bulletin of Atomic Scientists* 58, no. 1 (January–February 2002): 24.
100. See David Albright, "Al-Qaeda's Nuclear Program: Through the Window of Seized Documents," in *Policy Forum Online*, Special Forum 47 (San Francisco: Nautilus Institute, November 6, 2002).
101. A small sampling of these includes the following: the Advisory Panel to Assess Domestic Response Capabilities for Terrorism Involving Weapons of Mass Destruction (the Gilmore Commission), chartered in 1998. The panel produced five reports, which are accessible at http://www.rand.org/nsrd/terrpanel/. Another report, *Countering the Changing Threat of International Terrorism* (the Bremer Commission), was published in June 2000 and is available at http://www.fas .org/irp/threat/commission.html. Another commission is the post-9/11 National Commission on Terrorist Attacks upon the United States, the final report of which is available at www.9-11commission.gov/report/911Report.pdf. See also the Commission on the Intelligence Capabilities of the United States Regarding Weapons of Mass Destruction (the Robb-Silberman Commission); its report is available at www.wmd.gov. One additional commission, established pursuant to the implementing recommendations of the 9/11 Commission Act (Public Law 110-53), is the Commission on the Prevention of Weapons of Mass Destruction Proliferation and Terrorism. This latest commission released its report in December 2008; it is available at www.preventwmd.gov.

102. See National Intelligence Council, *Global Trends 2025: A Transformed World* (Washington, DC, November 2008), 69.

103. Ibid.

104. According to the Pew Global Attitudes Project, the share of Muslims who found suicide bombing a justified means of defending Islam fell throughout the period from 2002 to 2008. In Lebanon, 74 percent of Muslims considered suicide bombing as justified in 2002, but that percentage tumbled to 32 percent in 2008. Pakistani support for suicide bombing plunged from 33 percent to 5 percent. While al Qaeda leader Osama bin Laden inspired substantial confidence in a few predominately Muslim countries in 2003, his popularity plummeted in recent years. Confidence among Jordanian Muslims has dropped from 56 percent in 2003 to 19 percent in 2008; a mere 2 percent of Muslims in Lebanon and 3 percent in Turkey said in 2008 that they were confident bin Laden would do the right thing in world affairs. See Pew Global Attitudes Project, *Global Public Opinion in the Bush Years* (Washington, DC: Pew Research Center, December 18, 2008), http://pewglobal.org/reports/display.php?ReportID=263.

105. See Jenkins, *Will Terrorists Go Nuclear?*, 107.

106. See Dennis C. Blair, director of National Intelligence, testimony before the Senate Armed Services Committee, February 2, 2010.

107. See the James Martin Center for Nonproliferation Studies at the Monterey Institute of International Studies, Weapons of Mass Destruction Terrorism Research Program, http://cns.miis.edu/cns/projects/wmdtrp/index.htm. See also Albright, "Al Qaeda's Nuclear Program"; Sammy Salama and Lydia Hansell, "Does Intent Equal Capability? Al-Qaeda and Weapons of Mass Destruction," *Nonproliferation Review* 12, no. 3 (November 2005); Tenet and Harlow, *At the Center of the Storm*; Michael Scheuer, *Through Our Enemies' Eyes: Osama bin Laden, Radical Islam, and the Future of America* (Washington, DC: Potomac Books, 2006), among others. Another set of congressionally mandated reports of some utility here concern the issue of foreign countries' acquisition during the preceding six months of dual-use and other technology useful for the development or production of weapons of mass destruction (including nuclear weapons, chemical weapons, and biological weapons) and advanced conventional munitions. Unclassified versions of these reports are published and provided to congressional leadership and the intelligence committees pursuant to section 721 of the FY 1997 Intelligence Authorization Act. The reports are available from the Office of the Director of National Intelligence's website, www.dni.gov.

108. "Core" or "central" al Qaeda refers to the centralized leadership of al Qaeda— its top inspirational and operational leaders. Terrorism expert Bruce Hoffman defines this group as the remnants of the pre-9/11 al Qaeda organization. "Although its core leadership includes some of the familiar, established commanders of the past, there are a number of new players who have advanced through the ranks as a result of the death or capture of key al-Qa'ida senior-level managers such as Abu Atef, KSM [Khalid Sheikh Mohammed], Hambali, Abu Faraj al-Libi, and Abu Hamza Rabia. . . . This category comes closest to the al-Qa'ida operational template or model evident in the 1998 East Africa embassy bombings and 9/11 attacks. Such high-value, 'spectacular' attacks are entrusted only to al-Qa'ida's professional cadre: the most dedicated, committed, and absolutely reliable element of the movement." See testimony of Bruce Hoffman before the House Armed Services Committee, Subcommittee on Terrorism, Unconventional Threats and Capabilities, February 14, 2007.

109. See remarks by Mr. Edward Gistaro, former national intelligence officer for transnational threats, Washington Institute for Near East Policy, August 12, 2008.
110. Testimony of Peter Bergen, April 9, 2008.
111. Ibid.
112. Ibid.
113. Ibid. The tactics of winning or losing are important. Indeed, the definitions of winning and losing continue to be debated. However, in a recent RAND study of how terrorist groups end, it was found that 73 percent of religious-based terrorist groups are defeated through the use of local police and intelligence services. Another 11 percent ended because they joined the political process, and the remaining 16 percent ended because of military force. See Jones, "Defeating Terrorist Groups." RAND examined 648 terrorist groups that existed between 1968 and 2006 for its studies. See also Audrey Kurth Cronin, "How al-Qaida Ends: The Decline and Demise of Terrorist Groups," *International Security* 31, no. 1 (Summer 2006): 7–48. See also Michael Jacobson, "Why Terrorists Quit: Gaining from al-Qa'ida's Losses," *CTC Sentinel* 1, no. 8 (July 2008). The CTC is West Point's Combating Terrorism Center. Jacobson concludes, "The stories of [terrorist group] 'drop-outs' are of more than academic interest. . . . Counterterrorism officials have spent a great deal of effort trying to understand the process of radicalization, but strikingly little work has been done on the flip side of the coin: the factors that can turn a would-be fanatical killer into a somewhat chastened citizen." See also Washington Institute for Near East Policy, *Rewriting the Narrative: An Integrated Strategy for Counterradicalization* (Washington, DC, 2009).
114. See Peter Bergen, "Confronting al-Qaeda: Understanding the Threat in Afghanistan and Beyond," testimony before the Senate Foreign Relations Committee, October 7, 2009.
115. See public opinion surveys conducted by Terror Free Tomorrow, http://www.terrorfreetomorrow.org/template.php?section=PL.
116. See National Intelligence Council, *Global Trends 2025*, 69.
117. Ibid.
118. See testimony of Peter Bergen, April 9, 2008.
119. Ibid.
120. National Intelligence Council, *Global Trends 2025*, 69.
121. Testimony of Bruce Hoffman, February 14, 2007.
122. Remarks by the Honorable Michael E. Leiter, director of the National Counterterrorism Center, Aspen Institute, Washington, DC, April 9, 2009.
123. Sageman, *Leaderless Jihad*, 127.
124. See Matte Eilstrup-Sangiovanni and Calvert Jones, "Assessing the Dangers of Illicit Networks: Why al-Qaida May Be Less Threatening Than Many Think," *International Security* 33, no. 2 (Fall 2008): 7–10.
125. See testimony of Peter Bergen, April 9, 2008.
126. The earliest public documentation that Osama bin Laden and al Qaeda were attempting to acquire nuclear weapons dates to February 2001, when bin Laden was on trial, in absentia, for the 1998 bombing of U.S. embassies in Kenya and Tanzania. During this trial, Jamal Ahmad al-Fadl described how, as far back as late 1993, while in the Sudan, he had helped al Qaeda attempt to acquire fissile material. For courtroom transcripts concerning the three days of al-Fadl's testimony, see http://cns.miis.edu/pubs/reports/binladen.htm. For bin Laden's

comments, see Rahimullah Yusufzai, "The World's Most Wanted Terrorist: An Interview with Osama bin Laden," ABC News, http://www.islamistwatch.org /blogger/localstories/05-06-03/ABCInterview.html#. See also Scheuer, *Through Our Enemies' Eyes*, 72.

127. See Tenet and Harlow, *At the Center of the Storm*, 269.
128. Nasir bin Hamd al-Fahd, *A Treatise of the Legal Status of Using Weapons of Mass Destruction against Infidels*, May 2003, 9, www.carnegieendowment.org/static/ npp/fatwa.pdf.
129. Ibid., 22.
130. See testimony of Charles E. Allen, April 2, 2008.
131. See Albright, "Al Qaeda's Nuclear Program." See also Albright, *Peddling Peril*.
132. In January 2009 it was reported that al Qaeda in the Islamic Maghreb (Morocco, Algeria, and Tunisia) experienced an accident in attempting to weaponize either chemical or biological agents. While the credibility of this information is questionable, if true it might indicate that al Qaeda's WMD knowledge has not improved significantly. At a minimum, if true it also demonstrates continued WMD intent. See Eli Lake, "Al-Qaeda Bungles Arms Experiment," *Washington Times*, January 19, 2009.
133. See Stefan Leader, "Usama bin Laden and the Terrorist Search for WMD," *Jane's Intelligence Review* 11, no. 6 (June 1999). According to a RAND study, "Usama's buyers weren't physicists, and the people selling to him were trying to rip him off." See Daly, Parachina, and Rosenau, *Aum Shinrikyo, Al-Qa'ida, and the Kinshasa Reactor*, 33.
134. See Gunaratna, *Inside Al Qaeda*, 11.
135. See Albright, Beuhler, and Higgins, "Bin Laden and the Bomb," 23.
136. See Tenet and Harlow, *At the Center of the Storm*, 262.
137. See Kamran Khan and Molly Moore, "2 Nuclear Experts Briefed Bin Laden, Pakistanis Say," *Washington Post*, December 12, 2001.
138. Ibid.
139. See Tenet and Harlow, *At the Center of the Storm*, 262.
140. Ibid., 264.
141. See Khan and Moore, "2 Nuclear Experts Briefed Bin Laden."
142. Tenet and Harlow, *At the Center of the Storm*, 268.
143. See David Sanger, Douglas Frantz, and James Risen, "A Nation Challenged: Intelligence—Nuclear Experts in Pakistan May Have Links to Al-Qa'ida," *New York Times*, December 9, 2001.
144. See U.S. Intelligence Community, "Acquisition of Technology Relating to Weapons of Mass Destruction and Advanced Conventional Munitions, 1 January through 30 June 2001," http://www.fas.org/irp/threat/bian_jan_2002.htm.
145. See Albright, "Al Qaeda's Nuclear Program."
146. Ibid.
147. See Commission on the Intelligence Capabilities of the United States Regarding Weapons of Mass Destruction, "Report to the President," 267.
148. See David E. Sanger, "A Pakistani Assassin's Long Reach," *New York Times*, January 9, 2011.
149. See Nicholas D. Kristof, "An American Hiroshima," *New York Times*, August 11, 2004. The term as related to al Qaeda originates with Hamid Mir, the Pakistani journalist (see note 37) who has claimed that al Qaeda has smuggled nuclear weapons into the United States through Mexico and will use them to ignite an

American Hiroshima. The basis for this claim, according to Mir, is his interviews with al Qaeda representatives.

150. See John Rollins, "2008–2009 Presidential Transition: National Security Considerations and Options," CRS Report for Congress (Washington, DC, April 21, 2008), http://opencrs.com/document/RL34456.

151. See Cetron and Davies, 55 *Trends Now Shaping the Future of Terrorism*.

152. Ibid., 8.

153. Michael Leiter, "Looming Challenges in the War on Terror," remarks at the Washington Institute for Near East Policy, February 13, 2008.

154. The Pakistani government oftentimes publicly condemns the U.S. drone attacks, as they have been responsible for the killing of civilians, yet reportedly in private it supports such attacks on Taliban camps. The continued use of drone attacks by the United States in Pakistan in late 2010–early 2011 has been a source of serious tension in U.S.-Pakistan relations. For a critical assessment of U.S. drone attacks, see David Kilcullen and Andrew McDonald Exum, "Death from Above, Outrage down Below," *New York Times*, May 17, 2009. See also Liam Stack, "Fresh Drone Attacks in Pakistan Reignite Debate," *Christian Science Monitor*, July 8, 2009. Others have argued with certain public acknowledgments by the Obama administration that the drone strikes are consistent with U.S. counterterrorism policies. See Stuart Gottlieb, "Obama's Drone-Strike Counterterrorism Policy," *Foreign Policy: The Argument*, April 7, 2009, http://experts.foreignpolicy.com /posts/2009/04/07/obama_s_drone_strike_counterterrorism_policy.

155. See Leiter, "Looming Challenges in the War on Terror."

Chapter 5. The Nuclear Terrorism Threat Spectrum—Supply

1. See Dr. Mohamed ElBaradei, "Preventing Nuclear Catastrophe: Where Do We Go from Here?," statement at the International Conference on the Prevention of Nuclear Catastrophe, Luxembourg, May 24, 2007.

2. See U.S. Department of Defense, *Quadrennial Defense Review Report* (Washington, DC, February 6, 2006), 32.

3. Matthew Bunn and Andrew Newman of Harvard University suggest the establishment of interagency "tiger teams" to develop approaches to overcome the obstacles to gaining cooperation for nuclear security upgrades or removal of nuclear materials in many key countries. See Bunn and Newman, *Preventing Nuclear Terrorism*, 12.

4. Updates for this material can be found in IPFM, *Global Fissile Material Report— Balance the Books: Production and Stocks, 2010*, www.fissilematerials.org.

5. See Ole Reistad and Styrkaar Hustveit, "HEU Fuel Cycle Inventories and Progress of Global Minimization," *The Nonproliferation Review* 15, no. 2 (July 2008): 266–87. Appendix 2 provides a list of operational, shut-down, and converted HEU-fueled research reactors.

6. See Senate Foreign Relations Committee, *Chain Reaction: Avoiding a Nuclear Arms Race in the Middle East*, S. Prt. 110-34 (Washington, DC, February 2008). The Final Report of the Congressional Commission on the Strategic Posture of the United States, released May 6, 2009, found "it appears that we are at a 'tipping point' in proliferation. If Iran and North Korea proceed unchecked to build nuclear arsenals, there is a serious possibility of a cascade of proliferation following." Report available at http://www.usip.org/programs/initiatives /congressional-commission-the-strategic-posture-the-united-states.

7. See statement of Rolf Mowatt-Larssen, director of the Office of Intelligence and Counterintelligence, U.S. Department of Energy, before the Senate Homeland Security and Governmental Affairs Committee, April 2, 2008.

8. See National Nuclear Security Administration, "NNSA Announces Removal of All Highly Enriched Uranium (HEU) from Serbia," December 22, 2010.

9. See IPFM, *Global Fissile Material Report, 2010*. See also Alexander Glaser and Zia Mian, "Fissile Material Stocks and Production, 2008," *Bulletin of Atomic Scientists* 65, no. 1 (January–February 2009).

10. For numbers of U.S. and Russian warheads, see the Nuclear Notebook series published in the *Bulletin of Atomic Scientists*. The Nuclear Notebook is prepared by Robert S. Norris of the Natural Resources Defense Council and Hans M. Kristensen of the Federation of American Scientists. For Russia, see "Russian Nuclear Forces, 2008," *Bulletin of Atomic Scientists* 64, no. 2 (May–June 2008); for the United States, see "U.S. Nuclear Forces, 2009," *Bulletin of Atomic Scientists* 65, no. 2 (March–April 2009). New START will limit the number of deployed Russian and U.S. strategic nuclear warheads to 1,550 each. See Amy Woolf, *The New START Treaty: Central Limits and Key Provisions*, a CRS Report for Congress (Washington, DC, June 18, 2010).

11. See U.S. Department of Energy, *Plutonium: The First Fifty Years—United States Plutonium Production, Acquisition, and Utilization from 1944 to 1994* (Washington, DC, February 1996), http://www.osti.gov/bridge/product.biblio.jsp?query_id=3&page=0&osti_id=219368.

12. See Hecker, "Toward a Comprehensive Safeguards System," 123.

13. According to Hecker, the "missing" approximately 12,000 kilograms were explained as follows: 3,400 kilograms expended in wartime and tests, 2,800 kilograms declared as inventory differences, 3,400 kilograms as waste (normal operating losses), 1,200 kilograms as fission and transmutation, 400 kilograms as decay and other removals, 100 kilograms in U.S. civilian industry, 700 kilograms exported to foreign countries, and a 100-kilogram rounding difference, along with classified transactions. "Inventory differences," also referred to as "material unaccounted for," are defined as differences between the quantities of material in accounting records and the quantities determined to be in physical inventories. See ibid.

14. See Cirincione, *Bomb Scare*, 92.

15. Hecker, "Toward a Comprehensive Safeguards System," 123.

16. Ibid., 125.

17. See Norris and Kristensen, "Pakistan's Nuclear Forces, 2007," 71. Pakistan's first warheads used the implosion design but used HEU instead of plutonium. According to the Natural Resources Defense Council, these first warheads used approximately fifteen to twenty kilograms per warhead. Estimates of the number of Pakistan's nuclear warheads range as high as one hundred.

18. David Albright and Paul Brannan, *Update on Khushab Plutonium Reactor Construction Projects in Pakistan* (Washington, DC: Institute for Science and International Security, April 23, 2009).

19. See David E. Sanger and William J. Broad, "Officials Fear Bomb Design Went to Others," *New York Times*, June 16, 2008. "In recent months . . . officials have begun to confirm that they found the electronic design for a bomb itself among the material seized from some of Dr. Khan's lieutenants, a Swiss family, the Tinners." Two nuclear weapons' designs were found within the Khan network. The first was discovered when Libya renounced nuclear weapons in 2003 and turned

over documents to U.S., British, and IAEA officials. "The first design was for an unwieldy but effective Chinese design from the mid-1960s that Libya acknowledged obtaining from the Khan network." The newly discovered design, however, was for a miniaturized warhead that might fit atop some of the most widely available ballistic missiles. While a terrorist group is unlikely to deliver a weapon via ballistic missile, a smaller design could facilitate smuggling. Moreover, reportedly, this new advanced design was found in electronic format, which could have made its sharing with a broad range of buyers relatively simple.

20. See "Pakistan: Instability Raises Nuclear Safety Concerns," *Oxford Analytica*, August 31, 2007.
21. See "Khan: Musharraf in on North Korean Nuke Deal," Associated Press, July 4, 2008, http://www.cbsnews.com/stories/2008/07/04/world/printable 4234534.shtml. A book, *Goodbye Shahzadi* by Shyman Bhatia, a journalist who was close to former prime minister Benazir Bhutto, claims that on a state visit to North Korea, Bhutto smuggled in critical data on uranium enrichment to help facilitate a missile deal with North Korea. Proliferation expert David Albright of the Institute for Science and International Security said the assertion "makes sense"; there were signs of "funny procurements" in the late 1980s by North Korea that suggested a nascent effort to assemble a uranium enrichment project. See Glenn Kessler, "Bhutto Dealt Nuclear Secrets to North Korea, Book Says," *Washington Post*, June 1, 2008. The United States has not been provided direct access to Dr. Khan.
22. See "The Next 5 Big Nuclear Stories: A Conversation with Mark Hibbs," with Matthew Bunn and Joseph Cirincione, Carnegie Endowment for International Peace, International Proliferation Conference, June 26, 2007, transcript by Federal News Service.
23. See Allison, *Nuclear Terrorism*, 37.
24. See Mark Mazzetti and Eric Schmitt, "CIA Outlines Pakistan Links with Militants," *New York Times*, July 30, 2008. Afghanistan charged that the ISI was complicit in the suicide bombing of the Indian Embassy in Kabul, Afghanistan.
25. See Zahid Hussain, "Taliban Move Closer to Islamabad," *Wall Street Journal*, April 23, 2009.
26. Thom Shanker and David E. Sanger, "Pakistan Is Rapidly Adding Nuclear Arms, U.S. Says," *New York Times*, May 18, 2009.
27. See K. Alan Kronstadt, "Addressing the U.S.-Pakistan Strategic Relationship," testimony before the Senate Committee of Homeland Security and Governmental Affairs, June 12, 2008. See also statement of DNI Mike McConnell before the House Permanent Select Committee on Intelligence, February 7, 2008.
28. See Thomas Donnelly, "Bad Options, or How I Stopped Worrying and Learned to Live with Loose Nukes," in *Pakistan's Nuclear Future: Worries Beyond War*, ed. Henry D. Sokolski (Washington, DC: Nonproliferation Education Center, 2008), 351, http://www.npec-web.org/Frameset.asp?PageType=Books&Book ID=141059615.
29. For updates on Pakistani-U.S. relations, see K. Alan Kronstadt, "Pakistan-U.S. Relations," CRS Report for Congress (Washington, DC, February 6, 2009).
30. For an assessment of how civil unrest in Pakistan may affect the security of Pakistan's nuclear weapons, see Steven R. David, *Catastrophic Risks: Civil Wars and American Interests* (Baltimore, MD: Johns Hopkins University Press, 2008).
31. See David E. Sanger, "Strife in Pakistan Raises U.S. Doubts over Nuclear Arms," *New York Times*, May 4, 2009.

32. See "Pakistan in Crisis: Interview with Benazir Bhutto," CNN, November 5, 2007.

33. See "Pakistan Rejects Nuke Weapon Fears," CNN, January 9, 2008, http://www.cnn.com/2008/WORLD/asiapcf/01/09/pakistan.nuclear/index.html. The Pakistani Foreign Ministry responded that ElBaradei's remarks "ignore the fact that the strategic assets of Pakistan are fully secure under multilayered safeguards and controls exercised by the National Command Authority."

34. See J. Michael McConnell, director of National Intelligence, testimony before the Senate Armed Services Committee, February 27, 2008. For more on the security of Pakistan's nuclear weapons, see Paul K. Kerr and Mary Beth Nikitin, *Pakistan's Nuclear Weapons: Proliferation and Security Issues*, a CRS Report for Congress (Washington, DC, December 7, 2010).

35. In August 2001 Pakistani scientists Sultan Bashiruddin Mahmood and Adbul Majeed, met with Osama bin Laden and al Qaeda's second in command, Ayman-al-Zawahiri, in Kabul, Afghanistan, to discuss nuclear, chemical, and biological weapons. See Khan and Moore, "2 Nuclear Experts Briefed Bin Laden." According to Pakistani authorities, while these scientists were involved in uranium enrichment and plutonium production, neither had experience in the construction of a nuclear weapon. Notwithstanding this claim, the question needs to be asked—how much does U.S. intelligence know about the nuclear scientists who are experts in constructing a nuclear weapon in Pakistan or any other de facto nuclear nation? Does the United States know their identities? Is the international community able to tag and track their travels and interactions? Intelligence is an essential tool in the effort to prevent nuclear terrorism.

36. See Dr. Stephen P. Cohen, "The U.S.-Pakistan Strategic Relationship and Nuclear Safety/Security," testimony before the Senate Committee on Homeland Security and Governmental Affairs, June 12, 2008. Pakistan has had a particularly close relationship with Saudi Arabia.

37. Peter D. Feaver, "Command and Control in Emerging Nuclear Nations," *International Security* 17, no. 3 (Winter 1992–93): 160–87.

38. For an analysis of strategic stability between India and Pakistan, see Zachary Davis, ed., *The India-Pakistan Military Standoff: Crisis and Escalation in South Asia* (New York: Palgrave Macmillan, 2011).

39. David, *Catastrophic Consequences*. See also Scott D. Sagan, "Indian and Pakistani Nuclear Weapons," in Sagan and Waltz, *The Spread of Nuclear Weapons*, 103. For an assessment of how Pakistan and India narrowly averted a nuclear exchange in 2001–2002, see Zachary S. Davis, ed., *The India-Pakistan Military Standoff: Crisis and Escalation in South Asia* (New York: Palgrave Macmillan, 2011).

40. See Pamela Constable, "Pakistan's Plans for New Fight Stir Concern," *Washington Post*, June 24, 2009. Secretary of State Hilary Clinton, testifying before the House Foreign Affairs Committee in April 2009, stated that the "Pakistani government is basically abdicating to the Taliban and to the extremists." See Glenn Kessler, "Clinton: Pakistani Government Abdicating to 'Extremist' Forces," *Washington Post*, April 23, 2009.

41. See Peter Lavoy, *Pakistan's Nuclear Posture: Security and Survivability*, Nonproliferation Policy Education Center, http://www.googlesyndicatedsearch .com/u/NPEC?q=Lavoy+and+Pakistan+Nuclear+Postures&domains=npec-web.org&sitesearch=npec-web.org.

42. See Naeem Salik, *Minimum Deterrence and India-Pakistan Nuclear Dialogue: Case Study on Pakistan*, South Asia Security Project Case Study 1/2006 (Como, Italy: Landau Network—Centro Volta, March 2006), 10, http://www.centrovolta

.it/landau/2006/01/01/CaseStudyMinimumDeterrenceAndIndiaPakistan
NuclearDialogue.aspx. See also Kerr and Nikitin, *Pakistan's Nuclear Weapons,*
2010.

43. Salik, *Minimum Deterrence and India-Pakistan Nuclear Dialogue,* 11, quoting
Abdul Sattar, Agha Shahi, and Zulfiqar Ali Khan, "Securing the Peace," *News
International,* October 5, 1991.

44. See Farah Zhara, "Pakistan's Road to a Minimum Nuclear Deterrent," *Arms
Control Today,* July–August 1999.

45. David, *Catastrophic Consequences.*

46. See Paul Kerr and Mary Beth Nikitin, *Pakistan's Nuclear Weapons: Proliferation and Security Issues,* CRS Report for Congress (Washington, DC, January
14, 2008). See also Mahmud Ali Durrani, "Pakistan's Strategic Thinking and
the Role of Nuclear Weapons," Occasional Paper 37 (Albuquerque, NM: Cooperative Monitoring Center, July 2004), www.cmc.sandia.gov/cmc-papers
/sand2004-3375p.pdf.

47. See Kerr and Nikitin, *Pakistan's Nuclear Weapons,* 2008, 5.

48. See Robin Walker, "Pakistan's Evolution as a Nuclear Weapons State: Lt. Gen.
Khalid Kidwai's CCC Address," *Strategic Insights,* November 1, 2006, http://
www.nps.edu/academics/centers/ccc/news/kidwaiNov06.html.

49. Molly Moore and Kamran Khan, "Pakistan Moves Nuclear Weapons: Musharraf
Says Arsenal Now Secure," *Washington Post,* November 11, 2001.

50. See Cohen, "The U.S.-Pakistan Strategic Relationship and Nuclear Safety/
Security."

51. See Pervez Hoodbhoy, "A State of Denial," *International Herald Tribune,* January 16, 2008. Hoodbhoy does not believe, however, that Pakistan is going to
descend into civil war or that its nuclear weapons will go astray in the next five
years. See Pervez Hoodbhoy, "Whither Pakistan? A Five-Year Forecast," *Bulletin
of Atomic Scientists* (Web edition), June 3, 2009, http://www.thebulletin.org
/web-edition/features/whither-pakistan-five-year-forecast.

52. See Tenet and Harlow, *At the Center of the Storm,* 266.

53. For an assessment of the Pakistani-U.S. relationship, see Kronstadt, "Pakistan-
U.S. Relations." See also Council on Foreign Relations, *U.S.-Pakistan Relations,*
http://www.cfr.org/publication/15260/. See also Stephen Cohen, "The Nation
and the State of Pakistan," *Washington Quarterly,* Summer 2002; and Stephen
Cohen, "The Jihadist Threat to Pakistan," *Washington Quarterly,* Summer 2003.

54. See Cohen, "The U.S.-Pakistan Strategic Relationship and Nuclear Safety/
Security."

55. See K. Alan Kronstadt, *Pakistan: Key Current Issues and Developments,* a CRS
Report for Congress (Washington, DC, June 1, 2010). See also Cohen, "The
U.S.-Pakistan Strategic Relationship and Nuclear Safety/Security," summary.
For an assessment of how the aid has been administered, see GAO, *Combating
Terrorism: Increased Oversight and Accountability Needed over Pakistan Reim-
bursement Claims for Coalition Support Funds,* GAO-08-06 (Washington, DC,
June 2008), http://searching.gao.gov/query.html?charset=iso-8859-1&ql
=&rf=4&qt=Pakistan.

56. See Kronstadt, "Pakistan-U.S. Relations."

57. See Robert Birsel and Arshad Mohammed, "U.S. Gives Pakistan Aid for Those
Fleeing Swat Valley," Reuters, May 19, 2009. For one description of the broader
U.S. assistance relationship, see Senate Foreign Relations Committee, S. 962, the
Enhanced Partnership with Pakistan Act of 2009, S. Report 111-33 (Washing-

ton, DC, June 23, 2009). S. 962 passed the Senate in June 2009 and has been submitted to the House.

58. Shanker and Sanger, "Pakistan Is Rapidly Adding Nuclear Arms."

59. See IAEA, *Treaty on the Non-Proliferation of Nuclear Weapons*, INFCIRC/140 (Vienna, Austria, April 22, 1970), 2.

60. See David Albright, *Securing Pakistan's Nuclear Weapons Complex* (Muscatine, IA: Stanley Foundation, October 2001), http://www.isis-online.org/publications /terrorism/stanleypaper.html.

61. The discussion of whether and to what extent the United States should help emerging nuclear weapons powers with nuclear assistance goes back decades. The arguments balance legal concerns as enshrined in U.S. law (Atomic Energy Act of 1946, as amended) and international law (the Nuclear Nonproliferation Treaty of 1968) against concerns that not providing such technologies could also undermine national security. For an assessment of the history of these arguments, see Richard H. Ullman, "The Covert French Connection," *Foreign Policy*, Summer 1989.

62. This widely dispersed nature of Pakistan's nuclear weapons was confirmed by Secretary of State Hilary Clinton in testimony before the House Foreign Affairs Committee on April 23, 2009. Secretary Clinton reportedly stated, "Why are we so concerned about this [the expansion of Pakistan Taliban]? One of the reasons is nuclear weapons. We spend a lot of time worrying about Iran. Pakistan already has them, and they are widely dispersed in the country—they are not at a central location." See "Clinton Worried by Possible Extremist Access to Pakistani Nukes," *Global Security Newswire*, April 24, 2009.

63. See Moore and Khan, "Pakistan Moves Nuclear Weapons."

64. See David E. Sanger and William J. Broad, "U.S. Secretly Aids Pakistan in Guarding Nuclear Arms," *New York Times*, November 18, 2007.

65. Ibid.

66. See Sanger, "Strife in Pakistan Raises U.S. Doubts."

67. Bryan Bender, "Pakistan, U.S. in Talks on Nuclear Security: Aim to Keep Technology away from Terrorists; Uranium May Be Shipped to America for Disposal," *Boston Globe*, May 5, 2009.

68. See Walker, "Pakistan's Evolution as a Nuclear Weapons State." See also Kenneth N. Luongo and Brig. Gen. (Ret.) Naeem Salik, "Building Confidence in Pakistan's Nuclear Security," *Arms Control Today*, December 2007. Dr. Stephen P. Cohen, an expert on Pakistan, suggested that China may have provided Pakistan with technology to secure and control its nuclear weapons. See Cohen, "The U.S.-Pakistan Strategic Relationship and Nuclear Safety/Security," 2.

69. See Sharon Otterman and Jayshree Bajoria, "Backgrounder: Controls on Pakistan's Nuclear Technology" (New York and Washington, DC: Council on Foreign Relations, February 20, 2008). See also Sanger, "A Pakistani Assassin's Long Reach."

70. See David E. Sanger, "A Pakistani Assassin's Long Reach."

71. See Sanger and Broad, "U.S. Secretly Aids Pakistan."

72. Senate Foreign Relations Committee, *The Nomination of Dr. Condoleezza Rice to Be Secretary of State*, 109th Cong. (2005). As quoted in Kerr and Nikitin, *Pakistan's Nuclear Weapons*, 2008.

73. See Donnelly, "Bad Options," for one arbitrary scenario outlining the difficulties associated with a U.S. military intervention to secure Pakistani nuclear weapons and fissile material.

74. See David E. Sanger, "Obama's Worst Pakistan Nightmare," *New York Times Magazine Preview*, January 11, 2009.
75. See "Pakistan: Nuke Security Fool-Proof," CNN, January 26, 2008, http://cnn.com/2008/WORLD/asiapcf/01/26/musharraf.nuclear/index.html.
76. Secretary of Defense Robert Gates reportedly told *New York Times* reporter David E. Sanger that "there is no human vetting system that is entirely reliable," pointing out that lie detector and other screening techniques that CIA employees regularly undergo have, at times, failed to identify spies. See Sanger, "Obama's Worst Pakistan Nightmare."
77. See Luongo and Salik, "Building Confidence in Pakistan's Nuclear Security." See also Kerr and Nikitin, *Pakistan's Nuclear Weapons*, 2010.
78. Andrew Marshall, "Loose Nukes in Pakistan: How Real Is the Risk?," Reuters, May 14, 2009.
79. See Sanger, "Obama's Worst Pakistan Nightmare."
80. For an assessment of the inherent limitation of intelligence, see Richard K. Betts, "The New Politics of Intelligence: Will Reforms Work This Time?," *Foreign Affairs*, May–June 2004. See also Roberta Wohlstetter, *Pearl Harbor: Warning and Decision* (Palo Alto, CA: Stanford University Press, 1962); Mark Lowenthal, "The Real Intelligence Failure: Spineless Spies," *Washington Post*, May 25, 2008.
81. See Byman, "Do Counterproliferation and Counterterrorism Go Together?," 44.
82. See Cohen, "The U.S.-Pakistan Strategic Relationship and Nuclear Safety/Security."
83. For a text of the U.S.-India Agreement for Peaceful Nuclear Cooperation (123 Agreement), see U.S. Department of State, http://web.archive.org/web/20080709111810/http://www.state.gov/r/pa/prs/ps/2007/aug/90050.htm. For analysis of the costs and benefits of the agreement, see Esther Pan and Jayshree Bajoria, "The U.S.-India Nuclear Deal" (New York and Washington, DC: Council on Foreign Relations, July 21, 2008), http://www.cfr.org/publication/9663/. See also Paul Kerr, "U.S. Nuclear Cooperation with India: Issues for Congress," CRS Report for Congress (Washington, DC, April 23, 2008), http://opencrs.com/document/RL33016/2008-04-23%2000:00:00.
84. See Asif Mehmood, "Pakistan Wants India-Style Nuclear Deal with the U.S.," *The Nation*, July 25, 2008, http://www.nation.com.pk/pakistan-news-newspaper-daily-englishonline/Politics/25-Jul-2008/Pakistan-wants-Indiastyle-nuclear-deal-with-US.
85. Russia seems to be demonstrating revanchist behavior, as it violated international norms and laws by invading sovereign Georgia, a former member of the Soviet Union sitting on its southern border, in August 2008. According to Strobe Talbott, former deputy secretary of state, "A question that looms large in the wake of the past week is whether Russian policy has changed with regard to the permanence of borders." See Strobe Talbott, "Russia's Ominous New Doctrine," *Washington Post*, August 15, 2008. Terrorist expert Brian Michael Jenkins warns that "given American concerns about nuclear proliferation and the possibility of nuclear terrorism, tying U.S.-Russian cooperation in the nuclear domain with the current Russia-Georgia quarrel may amount to shooting ourselves in the foot in a misguided attempt to punish Russia." See Brian Michael Jenkins, "Georgia Dispute Derails Bid to Stop Nuclear Terrorism," *Providence Journal*, October 6, 2008. The "reset" of U.S.-Russian relations initiated by the Obama administration, while not ignoring these concerns, seems to have ameliorated them. The reset has yielded tangible progress—the passage of New START—which will not,

in and of itself, prevent nuclear terrorism but demonstrates to the world that Russia and the United States are meeting their obligations under the NPT. Such cooperation among major nuclear powers can flow through into cooperation in other nuclear nonproliferation endeavors, although this is not always the case.

86. For an up-to-date scorecard on the accomplishments of the Cooperative Threat Reduction Program, see *The Nunn-Lugar Scorecard: Destroying Weapons and Materials of Mass Destruction through Cooperation*, http://lugar.senate.gov/nunn-lugar/scorecard.html. Also see Defense Threat Reduction Agency, *Fact Sheet—Cooperative Threat Reduction*, http://www.dtra.mil/newsservices/fact_sheets/index.cfm. For a comprehensive overview of the Cooperative Threat Reduction program, see Amy F. Woolf, "Nonproliferation and Threat Reduction Assistance: U.S. Programs in the Former Soviet Union," CRS Report for Congress (Washington, DC, January 3, 2008), http://opencrs.com/document/RL31957/.

87. See William Langewiesche, "How to Get a Nuclear Bomb," *Atlantic Monthly*, December 2006, 10–11.

88. The panel caveats that the information for Russia is "highly uncertain" (plus or minus three hundred metric tons), as Russia does not provide official data on fissile material. See IPFM, *Global Fissile Material Report, 2010*, 10–11.

89. See Norris and Kristensen, "Russian Nuclear Forces, 2008," 71.

90. See Hans Kristensen, "Russian Tactical Nuclear Weapons," Federation of American Scientists Strategic Security Blog, March 25, 2009, http://www.fas.org/blog/ssp/2009/03/russia-2.php#more-1019. Kristensen and Robert Norris estimate that total Russian tactical nuclear weapons (army, air—mission defense, navy, air force) number approximately 5,390. By comparison, U.S. tactical nuclear weapons number approximately 500 (200 of which are stationed in Europe). As the United States and Russia begin the process of negotiating a follow-on to START I, balance in tactical nuclear weapons may become an issue of contention. See Philip P. Pan, "Key Item for Obama, Medvedev: New Arms Talks," *Washington Post*, April 1, 2009.

91. According to Hans Kristensen of the Federation of American Scientists, the United States currently has between 150 and 240 tactical nuclear weapons stationed in five countries and six military bases across Europe. During the height of the Cold War, the number of U.S. tactical nuclear weapons in Europe ranged from 1,000 to 7,000. See Hans Kristensen, "U.S. Nuclear Weapons Withdrawn from the United Kingdom," Federation of American Scientists Strategic Security Blog, June 26, 2008, http://www.fas.org/blog/ssp/2008/06/us-nuclear-weapons-withdrawn-from-the-united-kingdom.php. For an assessment of U.S. nuclear weapons security, see Maj. Gen. Polly A. Peyer, *Air Force Blue Ribbon Review of Nuclear Weapons Policies and Procedures*, February 8, 2008, http://www.fas.org/blog/ssp/2008/06/usaf-report-%e2%80%9cmost%e2%80%9d-nuclear-weapon-sites-in-europe-do-not-meet-us-security-requirements.php. This report was ordered by Secretary of Defense Robert Gates after two recent incidents indicating lax security over U.S. nuclear weapons and nuclear weapons components. Also see William Potter and Nikolai Sokov, "Tactical Nuclear Weapons: The Nature of the Problem" (Monterey, CA: James Martin Center for Nonproliferation Studies, January 2001); Alistar Millar, "The Pressing Need for Tactical Nuclear Control," *Arms Control Today*, May 2002.

92. See National Intelligence Council, *Annual Report to Congress on the Safety and Security of Russian Nuclear Facilities and Military Forces* (Washington, DC, February 2002), http://www.fas/org/irp/nic/icarussiansecurity.htm.

93. See Langewiesche, *The Atomic Bazaar*, 30.
94. Ibid., 51.
95. See National Intelligence Council, *Annual Report to Congress*, February 2002.
96. See National Intelligence Council, *Annual Report to Congress on the Safety and Security of Russian Nuclear Facilities and Military Forces* (Washington, DC, December 2004), www.dni.gov/nic/PDF_GIF_otherprod/russiannuke04.pdf.
97. See National Intelligence Council, "Key Points," in *Annual Report to Congress on the Safety and Security of Russian Nuclear Facilities and Military Forces* (Washington, DC, April 2006), http://www.fas.org/irp/nic/russia0406.html.
98. National Intelligence Council, "Key Points," April 2006.
99. See National Intelligence Council, *Annual Report to Congress*, December 2004, 6.
100. See National Counterterrorism Center, Worldwide Incidents Tracking System, http://wits.nctc.gov/ViewIncident.do?incidentId=6466.
101. See Ellen Barry, "Deadly Blast Comes at Sensitive Time for Russia," *New York Times,* January 24, 2011.
102. See Walter Lacqueur, *The New Terrorism: Fanaticism and the Arms of Mass Destruction* (New York: Oxford University Press, 1999), 73.
103. See Jenkins, *Will Terrorists Go Nuclear?*, 83–84.
104. See GAO, *Nuclear Nonproliferation*.
105. See Anthony Wier and Matthew Bunn, "Funding for U.S. Efforts to Improve Controls over Nuclear Weapons, Materials, and Expertise Overseas: Recent Developments and Trends," paper, Project on Managing the Atom, Belfer Center for Science and International Affairs, February 2007. For an update through Fiscal Year 2011, see Michelle Marchesano, "Funding Analysis of FY11 International WMD Programs: National Nuclear Security Administration and Department of Defense," Partnership for Global Security, Policy Update, January 2011.
106. See Secretary of Energy Advisory Board, *A Report Card*. More recently, Public Law 110-53, Subtitle E, Section 1851, established the Commission on the Prevention of Weapons of Mass Destruction Proliferation and Terrorism. The commission updated the report card in an appendix. For members of the commission, see http://speaker.house.gov/newsroom/pressreleases?id=0666. The commission provided its report to the president and Congress on December 4, 2008; it can be accessed at www.preventwmd.org.
107. Report of the Commission on the Prevention of Weapons of Mass Destruction Proliferation and Terrorism, iv.
108. Ibid.
109. There are two basic types of security upgrades: rapid and comprehensive. Rapid upgrades include such activities as "bricking up windows in buildings where nuclear material is stored; installing strengthened doors, locks, and nuclear container seals; establishing controlled access areas around nuclear material; and implementing procedures that require the presence of two people when nuclear material is handled." Rapid upgrades are easily implemented and result in immediate, though limited, security improvements. Comprehensive upgrades include "electronic sensors, motion detectors, and close circuit television systems to detect intruders; central alarm stations, where guards can monitor cameras and alarms; and computerized nuclear material accounting systems." See GAO, *Nuclear Nonproliferation: Comprehensive U.S. Planning and Better Foreign Cooperation Needed to Secure Vulnerable Nuclear Materials Worldwide*, December 2010, GAO-11-227, 4.

110. See Bunn, *Securing the Bomb 2010*, figure 3.1, Progress in Nuclear Security Upgrade in Russia and Other Eurasian States, 33.

111. Matthew Bunn, *Securing the Bomb 2008* (Cambridge, MA, and Washington, DC: Project on Managing the Atom, Harvard University, and Nuclear Threat Initiative, November 2008), 14. It should be noted, however, that Russia's newfound wealth is relatively fragile; it is directly related to commodity, specifically oil and natural gas, prices. As the prices of oil and natural gas fluctuate, so too will a significant source of Russia national wealth, the effects of which are uncertain for nuclear security.

112. See Nikolai Sokov, "CNS Analysis of the Russian Government's White Paper on WMD Nonproliferation" (Monterey, CA: James Martin Center for Nonproliferation Studies, July 25, 2006), www.cns.miis.edu/ pubs/week/060726.htm.

113. Ibid.

114. See GAO, *Nuclear Nonproliferation*, December 2010.

115. See the Bob Stump National Defense Authorization Act for Fiscal Year 2003, Public Law 107-314, Section 3156(b)(1), codified at U.S. Code, Title 50, Section 2343.

116. See Langewiesche, *The Atomic Bazaar*, 44–45.

117. See GAO, *Nuclear Nonproliferation*, 26.

118. See Julian Borger, "Nuclear Bomb Material Found for Sale on Georgia Black Market," *The Guardian*, November 7, 2010, http://www.guardian.co.uk/world /2010/nov/07/nuclear-material-black-market-georgia. The concern is that the amount smuggled is just a sample of a larger amount of available weapons-grade HEU.

119. Presidents Barack Obama and Dmitri Medvedev, meeting in London at the G-20 Summit on April 1, 2009, proposed a new strategic arms reduction agreement be negotiated by the end of 2009. In an April 5, 2009, speech in Prague, President Obama also offered a number of other initiatives designed to prevent nuclear terrorism, including ratification of the Comprehensive Test Ban Treaty, the negotiation of a treaty to ban the production of fissile material, strengthening the NPT, the establishment of an international nuclear fuel bank, and a new international effort to secure all vulnerable nuclear material around the world within four years. See remarks by President Barack Obama, April 5, 2009. The U.S. Senate provided its advice and consent to New START in December 2010.

120. See remarks by President Obama at the New Economic School Graduation, Moscow, Russia, July 7, 2009, http://www.whitehouse.gov/the_press_office /REMARKS-BY-THE-PRESIDENT-AT-THE-NEW-ECONOMIC-SCHOOL-GRADUATION/.

121. The terms of the Joint Understanding include a reduction in the level of allowable warheads from 2,200 under START to a range of 1,500–1,675, and a reduction of the allowable number of delivery vehicles (missiles and strategic bombers) from a START level of 1,600 to a range of 500–1,100. See White House, *The Joint Understanding for the START Follow-on Treaty*, July 6, 2009, http://www .whitehouse.gov/the_press_office/FACT-SHEET-The-Joint-Understanding-for-the-START-Follow-on-Treaty.

122. See U.S. Intelligence Community, "Acquisition of Technology Relating to Weapons of Mass Destruction and Advanced Conventional Munitions, 1 January through 31 December 2006," http://www.fas.org/irp/threat/wmd-acq2006.pdf.

123. See Office of the Director of National Intelligence, News Release 23-09, June 15, 2009. In response to the North Korean nuclear test of May 25, 2009, on June

12, 2009, the United Nations Security Council passed Resolution 1874, which, inter alia, condemned the nuclear test and called upon all states to "inspect, in accordance with their national authorities and legislation, and consistent with international law, all cargo to and from the DPRK in their territory, including seaports and airports, if the State concerned has information that provides reasonable grounds to believe the cargo contains" arms and related material. See United Nations Security Council Resolution 1874 (2009).

124. See Nuclear Threat Initiative, "North Korea Nuclear Profile," http://www.nti .org/ e_research/profiles/NK/Nuclear/index_157.html.

125. Ibid.

126. For an assessment of the six-party talks, see Niksch, "North Korea's Nuclear Weapons Development and Diplomacy."

127. See U.S. Department of State, Joint Statement of the Fourth Round of the Six-Party Talks, September 19, 2005.

128. See Niksch, "North Korea's Nuclear Weapons Development and Diplomacy," summary.

129. The "action-for-action" principle was embodied in the September 2005 Six-Party Joint Statement, which implied no benefits would be provided to North Korea until the six parties were satisfied that the country had verifiably reached the milestones outlined in the statement. See Christopher R. Hill, assistant secretary of state for East Asian and Pacific affairs, "North Korea Six-Party Talks and Implementation Activities," testimony before the Senate Committee on Armed Services, July 31, 2008.

130. Ibid.

131. See Blaine Harden, "North Korea Plans to Resume Processing of Nuclear Fuel," *Washington Post*, September 25, 2008.

132. See John R. Bolton, "Bush's North Korea Surrender Will Have Lasting Consequences," *Wall Street Journal*, October 13, 2008.

133. See Sanger and Shanker, "U.S. Debates Deterrence for Nuclear Terrorism."

134. During the Cuban Missile Crisis of 1962, fearful that the Soviet Union might transfer nuclear weapons to Cuban leader Fidel Castro, President John F. Kennedy issued the following unambiguous warning to Soviet leader Nikita Krushchev: "It shall be the policy of this government to regard any nuclear missile launched from Cuba against any nation in the Western Hemisphere as an attack by the Soviet Union on the United States requiring a full retaliatory response against the Soviet Union." Khrushchev understood this meant full-scale nuclear war. See Graham Allison, "How to Keep the Bomb from Terrorists," *Newsweek*, March 23, 2009.

135. On April 5, 2009, North Korea launched what it claimed was a space launch vehicle or a ballistic missile to place a communications satellite into space. The launch constituted a violation of United Nations Security Council Resolution 1716 (2006), which demanded that North Korea not launch any ballistic missiles, and was condemned by the Security Council on April 13, 2009. On April 14, 2009, North Korea informed the IAEA that it was "immediately ceasing all cooperation with the IAEA. . . . The inspectors have also been asked to leave the DPRK at the earliest possible time." Six-party talks remain stalled as of mid-July 2009. On May 25, 2009, North Korea conducted a second nuclear weapon test. South Korea subsequently became an official member of the Proliferation Security Initiative, an international counterproliferation arrangement to inspect cargo ships for illicit transfer of controlled technologies. North Korea then abrogated

the 1953 armistice and stated that any seizure or inspection of a North Korean vessel (as envisioned by United Nations Security Council Resolution 1874 [June 12, 2009]) would be interpreted by North Korea an act of war. See Mark E. Manyin, *North Korea: Back on the Terrorism List?* CRS Report for Congress (Washington, DC, June 29, 2010). In November 2010, North Korea revealed to a visiting American nuclear scientist a sophisticated uranium enrichment plant. Dr. Siegfried S. Hecker, former director of the Los Alamos National Laboratory, traveled to North Korea and visited the facility at the invitation of North Korea and reportedly commented that he was "stunned" by the sophistication of the new plant, including its ultramodern control room. See David E. Sanger, "North Koreans Reveal New Plant for Nuclear Use," *New York Times,* November 20, 2010. See also Siegfried S. Hecker, "What I Found in North Korea: Pyongyang's Plutonium Is No Longer the Only Concern," *Foreign Affairs,* December 9, 2010.

136. See IAEA, *Implementation of the NPT Safeguards Agreement.*
137. See David Albright, Jacqueline Shire, and Paul Brannan, *IAEA Report on Iran: Enriched Uranium Output Steady; Centrifuge Numbers Expected to Increase Dramatically; Arak Reactor Verification Blocked* (Washington, DC: Institute for Science and International Security, November 19, 2008). See also "Iran Approaching Nuclear-Weapons Decision, CIA Chief Says," *Global Security Newswire,* January 16, 2009.
138. See IAEA, *Implementation of the NPT Safeguards Agreement.* Some experts have stated that in order to further enrich the LEU, "Iran would have to reconfigure its centrifuges and do a couple months of additional processing." See William J. Broad and David E. Sanger, "Iran Said to Have Nuclear Fuel for One Weapon," *New York Times,* November 20, 2008.
139. For an assessment of Iranian military procurement networks, see David Albright, Paul Brannan, and Andrea Scheel, *Iranian Entities' Illicit Military Procurement Networks* (Washington, DC: Institute for Science and International Security, January 12, 2009). Original source: United States District Court, Southern District of Florida, *United States vs. Ali AkbarYahya, F. N. Yaghmaei General Trading et al., Superseding Indictment,* Case no. 08-20222-CR-LENARD(s), September 11, 2008.
140. See Paul K. Kerr, John Rollins, and Catherine A. Theohary, *The Stuxnet Computer Worm: Harbinger of an Emerging Warfare Capability,* a CRS Report for Congress (Washington, DC, December 9, 2010).
141. See David Albright, Paul Brannan, and Christina Walrond, *Did Stuxnet Take Out 1,000 Centrifuges at the Natanz Enrichment Plant?* (Washington, DC: Institute for Science and International Security, December 22, 2010).
142. See National Intelligence Council, "Key Judgments," in *Iran: Nuclear Intentions and Capabilities.* A new NIE on Iran was published but not publicly released in early 2011. The 2011 NIE reportedly concluded that Iran had resumed research on key components for a nuclear weapon. See Greg Miller and Joby Warrick, "U.S. report finds debate in Iran on building nuclear bomb," *Washington Post,* February 19, 2011. For another view, see EastWest Institute, *Iran's Nuclear and Missile Potential: A Joint Threat Assessment by U.S. and Russian Technical Experts* (New York, May 2009), http://www.ewi.info/announcements/news/.
143. This NIE was highly contentious as it undermined international efforts to levy additional sanctions against the Iranian regime for its alleged nuclear weapons development activities. See Paul J. Kerr, "Iran's Nuclear Program: Tehran's Com-

pliance with International Obligations," CRS Report for Congress (Washington, DC, December 4, 2008).

144. See statement of IAEA director general Mohamed ElBaradei, October 28, 2008. The "alleged studies" to which ElBaradei refers are studies the agency became aware of that indicate that Iran may be pursuing a nuclear weapons program.

145. Statement of IAEA director general Mohamed ElBaradei, October 28, 2008. According to ElBaradei, "One implication of a nuclear renaissance is the spread of nuclear material to many more countries. This naturally increases the risk that nuclear material could be diverted to make nuclear weapons. *It is worth noting that countries that master uranium enrichment and plutonium separation become de facto nuclear weapons capable states. This means they have the ability to develop nuclear weapons in a very short time if they walked out of the Non-Proliferation Treaty, or managed to do so in a clandestine manner* [emphasis added]."

146. See William J. Broad, "A Tantalizing Look at Iran's Nuclear Program," *New York Times*, April 29, 2008.

147. Thomas Erdbink, "Iran Claims to Install Newer, Faster Centrifuges," *New York Times*, April 9, 2008.

148. See Albright, Shire, and Brannan, *IAEA Report on Iran*.

149. See Steven Erlanger, "Talks on Iran's Nuclear Program Close with No Progress," *New York Times*, January 22, 2011.

150. See Daniel Byman, "Iran, Terrorism, and Weapons of Mass Destruction," *Studies in Conflict and Terrorism* 31 (March 2008): 179.

151. Ibid.

152. Sheera Frenkel, "Israel Stands Ready to Bomb Iran's Nuclear Sites," *The Times* (London), April 18, 2009. While Israel may take such a move unilaterally, given the importance of Iran it is highly likely that it would consult, notify, or seek assistance (or at least acquiescence) of the U.S. government for such a provocative act. For contrasting assessments of the wisdom of preemptively striking Iran's nuclear weapons establishment, see John Bolton, "Time for an Israeli Strike?," *Washington Post*, July 2, 2009; and Greg Thielmann, "Preventive Military Action: The Worst Ways to Deal with Iran's Nuclear Program," Threat Assessment Brief (Washington, DC: Arms Control Association, June 18, 2009).

153. See William J. Broad, John Markoff, and David E. Sanger, "Israeli Test on Worm Called Crucial in Iran Nuclear Delay," *New York Times*, January 16, 2011.

154. The Iranian election held in June 2009 continues to be contested by opposition leaders. Government forces fired on Iranians protesting the election results, causing some to argue that the regime may have fatally wounded itself (perhaps over the long term) and radical Islam. See Joshua Muravchik, "For Radical Islam, the End Begins," *Washington Post*, June 28, 2009. For an opposing view—that is, that the Iranian regime will likely retain its power, at least over the short term—see Fareed Zakaria, "No Velvet Revolution for Iran," *Washington Post*, June 29, 2009.

155. For an assessment of North Korea's illicit activities, see Raphael Perl and Dick K. Nanto, "North Korean Crime for Profit Activities," CRS Report for Congress (Washington, DC, February 16, 2007), http://assets.opencrs.com/rpts/RL 33885_20070216.pdf.

156. See U.S. Department of State, *Country Report on Terrorism 2007* (Washington, DC, April 2008), chapter 3.

157. See Jean-Jacques Rousseau, *The Social Contract* (New York: Penguin, 1968), 50.

158. See Ellingsen, "Safeguards against Nuclear Terrorism," 131. According to Ellingsen, if neutrons approach each other too slowly, neutrons from spontaneous fission in one lump (one of the two subcritical pieces of fissile material) would start inducing fission on the other and vice versa, commencing the explosion before the two pieces were properly in place. The more rapid spontaneous fission activity of plutonium makes it very difficult to fire the two subcritical elements together fast enough, thus necessitating more advanced "implosion-type" nuclear weapons designs.

159. See Matthew Bunn, *Securing the Bomb 2007* (Cambridge, MA, and Washington, DC: Project on Managing the Atom, Harvard University, and Nuclear Threat Initiative, September 2007), 13–15.

160. See International Project on Fissile Materials, "The Global Distribution of Civilian High Enriched Uranium," http://www.fissilematerials.org/ipfm/pages_us _en/visual/visual/visual.php.

161. See Zia Mian and Alexander Glaser, "A Frightening Nuclear Legacy," *Bulletin of Atomic Scientists* 64, no. 4 (September–October 2008).

162. Ibid., 14.

163. Pelindaba is derived from the words *pelile*, meaning "finished," and *indaba*, meaning "discussion." The Pelindaba Nuclear Research Center includes a Safari-1 research reactor, a hot cell complex, a waste disposal site, and conversion and fuel fabrication facilities. For further discussion of these facilities, see GlobalSecurity. org, *Pelindaba Nuclear Research Center*, www.globalsecurity.org/wmd/world /rsa/pelindaba.htm. Also see "Pelindaba: Finding Anton Gerber," *60 Minutes*.

164. See Scott Pelley, *Nuke Facility Raid an Inside Job?*, CBS News, November 23, 2008, http://www.cbsnews.com/stories/2008/11/20/60minutes/main 4621623.shtml.

165. See Micah Zenko, "A Nuclear Site Is Breached: South African Attack Should Sound Alarms," *Washington Post*, December 20, 2007.

166. See IAEA, "IAEA Experts Complete Visit to Pelindaba Nuclear Facility in South Africa," IAEA press release, January 25, 2008.

167. These questions and others were raised by Matthew Bunn in "Expanding Nuclear Energy, Preventing Nuclear Terrorism," presentation to Energy and Security Seminar, Harvard University, Kennedy School of Government, March 13, 2008.

168. According to the IPFM, the reason for this broad range is uncertainty about the Russian stockpile; Russia does not provide information about the amount of HEU it has produced. David Albright of the Institute for Science and International Security estimates the amount of HEU stockpiles to be at 1,900 metric tons. However, if one subtracts the 337 metric tons that Russia has down-blended through the Megatons to Megawatts Initiative that amount falls to 1,563 tons. See Institute for Science and International Security, *Global Stockpiles of Nuclear Explosive Material* (Washington, DC, July 12, 2005 [revised September 7, 2005]). The Megatons to Megawatts Initiative between the United States and Russia was initiated in 1994 and has the purpose of down-blending 500 metric tons of Russian HEU to LEU to be purchased by the United States for use as fuel in U.S. nuclear power reactors. According to the U.S. Enrichment Corporation (a private entity acting on behalf of the U.S. government), as of December 31, 2010, approximately 412 metric tons of Russian HEU, or enough to make 16,494 nuclear warheads, has been down-blended to LEU. According to the corporation, by 2013 when the program is completed, 500 metric tons of Russian HEU, or enough to make 20,000 nuclear warheads, will have been recycled

into "enough material to produce fuel to power the United States for about two years." See www.USEC.com/megatonstomegawatts.htm.

169. See IPFM, *Global Fissile Material Report, 2007*, 11.

170. Ibid., 12.

171. See United Nations Security Council Resolution 1540 (2004), http://www .un.org/Docs/sc/unsc_resolutions04.html. At the G-20 Summit hosted by the United Kingdom in April 2009, Presidents Barack Obama and Dmitri A. Medvedev provided in a joint statement: "To strengthen nonproliferation efforts, we also declare our intent to give new impetus to implementation of U.N. Security Council Resolution 1540 on preventing non-state actors from obtaining WMD-related materials and technologies."

172. See Anya Loukianova and Cristina Hansell, "Leveraging U.S. Policy for a Global Commitment to HEU Elimination," *Nonproliferation Review* 15, no. 2 (July 1, 2008), for a discussion of the history of the United States' HEU elimination programs and their relation to global commitments to the same end.

173. See Wisconsin Project on Nuclear Arms Control, "Theft of Nuclear Material: Reducing the Risk—an Interview with William H. Tobey" (Washington, DC, January 2009).

174. U.S. Department of Energy, "Global Threat Reduction Initiative: Overview," April 2008, as requested by the author and provided by the DOE.

175. See Bunn, *Securing the Bomb 2010*, table ES-1, Global Nuclear Security Today, viii.

176. See Bunn, "Expanding Nuclear Energy, Preventing Nuclear Terrorism." According to a DOE study, *Highly Enriched Uranium (HEU): Striking a Balance— a Historical Report on the United States Highly Enriched Uranium Production, Acquisition, and Utilization Activities from 1945 through September 30, 1996*, DOE stocks of HEU "transferred to foreign countries and classified transactions" total 32.2 tons. According to NRC data, about 11.7 tons of HEU were exported for research reactor fuel and had not been returned as of 1996. See David Albright, William Walker, and Fran Berkout, *Plutonium and Highly Enriched Uranium, 1996: World Inventories, Capabilities, and Policies* (New York: Oxford University Press, 1997), 252. See also Steven Aftergood and Frank N. von Hippel, "The U.S. Highly Enriched Uranium Declaration: Transparency Deferred but Not Denied," *Nonproliferation Review* 14, no. 1 (March 2007).

177. See Alexander Glaser and Frank N. von Hippel, "Global Cleanout: Reducing the Threat of HEU-Fueled Nuclear Terrorism" (Washington, DC: Arms Control Association, January–February 2006), www.armscontroo.org/node/1969.

178. Ibid.

179. See William C. Potter, "Nuclear Terrorism and the Global Politics of Civilian HEU Elimination," *Nonproliferation Review* 15, no. 2 (2008).

180. See Loukianova and Hansell, "Leveraging U.S. Policy," 175–76.

181. See Mary Beth Nikitin et al., "Managing the Nuclear Fuel Cycle: Policy Implications of Expanding Global Access to Nuclear Power," CRS Report for Congress (Washington, DC, January 30, 2008), summary.

182. See statement of IAEA director general Mohamed ElBaradei, October 28, 2008.

183. See IAEA, *Energy, Electricity, and Nuclear Power Estimates for the Period up to 2030* (Vienna, Austria, 2007), figure 1, 14, http://www.iaea.org/OurWork/ST /NE/Pess/RDS1.shtml.

184. For an assessment of the potential difficulties these nations may have developing the necessary nuclear infrastructure, see James M. Action and Wyn Q. Bowen, "Nurturing Nuclear Neophytes," *Bulletin of Atomic Scientists* 64, no. 4 (September–

October 2008). See also U.S.-UAE Agreement for Peaceful Nuclear Cooperation (123 Agreement) for information concerning the legal framework for the "United States to engage in civil nuclear cooperation with the UAE under agreed nonproliferation conditions and controls."

185. See Peter Crail and Jessica Lasky-Fink, "Middle Eastern States Seeking Nuclear Power" (Washington, DC: Arms Control Association, May 2008), www.arms control.org/node/2993.

186. See Joby Warrick, "Spread of Nuclear Capability Is Feared: Global Interest May Presage a New Arms Race," *Washington Post*, May 12, 2008.

187. Ibid.

188. Ibid.

189. See IAEA, *Treaty on the Non-Proliferation of Nuclear Weapons*, Article IV.

190. See remarks of Patricia A. McNerney, principal deputy assistant secretary, international security and nonproliferation, at the Conference on Global Perspectives of the Proliferation Landscape: An Assessment of Tools and Policy Problems, Naval Postgraduate School, Monterey, California, June 10, 2008.

191. Ibid.

192. See IAEA, *In Focus: Revisiting the Nuclear Fuel Cycle—Multilateral Approaches to Nuclear Fuel-Cycles in Historical Context*, http://www.iaea.org/NewsCenter /Focus/FuelCycle/key_events.shtml.

193. See IAEA, "Nuclear Threat Initiative Commits $50 Million to Create IAEA Nuclear Fuel Bank," press release, September 19, 2006.

194. Ibid.

195. See IAEA, "Fuel Bank Initiative Receives Critical EU Support" (Vienna, Austria, December 10, 2008), http://www.iaea.org/NewsCenter/News/2008/fuel_ Bank.html.

196. See Nuclear Threat Initiative, "NTI in Action: Creating and International Fuel Bank," www.nit.org/b_aboutnti/b7_fuel_bank.html.

197. See U.S. Department of Energy, Office of Nuclear Energy, Office of Fuel Cycle Management, *Global Nuclear Energy Partnership Strategic Plan*, GNEP-167312, Re.0 (Washington, DC, January 2007), 1–10.

198. See Mark Holt, "Advanced Nuclear Power and Fuel Cycle Technologies: Outlook and Policy Options," CRS Report for Congress (Washington, DC, July 11, 2008).

199. See letter to the Honorable Byron L. Dorgan, chair, Subcommittee on Energy and Water Development, Senate Appropriations Committee, and the Honorable Pete V. Domenici, ranking member, Subcommittee on Energy and Water Development, Senate Appropriations Committee, from a list of over forty nonproliferation, security, and environmental experts (hereafter referred to as the Dorgan /Domenici letter). Letter dated October 31, 2007, www.ucsusa.org/assets /documents/global_security/Community-letter-GNEP-Congress_Final.pdf.

200. See David Shropshire et al., "Advanced Fuel Cycle Economic Sensitivity Analysis," INL/EXT-06-11947 (Idaho Falls: Idaho National Laboratory, December 2006), http://www.osti.gov/bridge/purl.cover.jsp;jsessionid=5C9BF1F1F77D FE270D2B354B1CB581E6?purl=/911885-0TDlYO/.

201. See Dorgan and Domenici letter, 2.

202. See Keystone Center, *Nuclear Power Fact-Finding* (Keystone, CO, June 2007), http://keystone.org/files/about/publications/FinalReport_NuclearFactFinding6_2007.pdf.

203. It is estimated that the construction of a new nuclear power reactor today requires a multibillion-dollar capital outlay. One of the last nuclear power plants

built in the United States is the Diablo Canyon plant in California, constructed in 1988 at a cost of $5.5 billion. Plants with lesser generating capacity may cost less. See "Company News: Rate Plan Approved at Diablo Canyon Unit," *New York Times*, December 12, 1988, http://query.nytimes.com/gst/fullpage.html ?res=940DE7DC1638F933A15751C1A96E948260. See Mian and Glaser, "A Frightening Nuclear Legacy."

204. See remarks by President Barack Obama, April 5, 2009.
205. See Andrew Newman and Matthew Bunn, *Funding for U.S. Efforts to Improve Controls over Nuclear Weapons, Materials, and Expertise Overseas: A 2009 Update* (Cambridge, MA: Belfer Center for Science and International Affairs, June 2009).
206. See Partnership for Global Security, "WMD Security Funding Is Inadequate to Meet Obama Administration Goals," press release, April 2, 2009, www.partnership forglobalsecurity.org. For additional ideas on how to advance WMD security, see Luongo, "Loose Nukes in New Neighborhoods."
207. See Kenneth Luongo, "Lame Duck Hobbles Nuclear Terrorism Fight," Partnership for Global Security Press Release, January 4, 2011.
208. See David Kay, "What's Missing from the Iran Debate: Building a Security Framework for a Nuclear Tehran," *Washington Post*, September 8, 2008.
209. See Josh White, "Nuclear Parts Sent to Taiwan in Error," *Washington Post*, March 26, 2008.
210. See Michael Hoffman, "B-52 Mistakenly Flies with Nukes Aboard," *Air Force Times*, September 10, 2007. Air Force Instruction (AFI) 21-204, updated May 28, 2008, *Nuclear Weapons Maintenance Procedures*, implements Air Force Policy Directive 21-2, *Munitions*. AFI 21-204 "provides guidance and procedures for the maintenance, personnel certification, the logistics movements of, and accountability procedures for nuclear weapons." AFI 21-204 is available at www .fas.org/irp/doddir/usaf/afi21-204.pdf.
211. Another eight generals have reportedly been disciplined as a result of these two incidents. See Ann Scott Tyson, "8 Generals Disciplined after Misstep on Warheads," *Washington Post*, September 25, 2008.
212. See Lolita C. Baldor, "Gates: Air Force May Consolidate Nuclear Control," Associated Press, September 13, 2008. See also Ann Scott Tyson, "Unified Nuclear Command Urged," *Washington Post*, September 13, 2008.
213. See Megan Scully, "Air Force Beginning to Shape New Command," *Government Executive*, November 12, 2008.
214. See FAS Strategic Security Blog, http://www.fas.org/blog/ssp/2008/06/us-nuclear-weapons-withdrawn-from-the-united-kingdom.php. For reasons mentioned above, tactical nuclear weapons are particularly attractive to terrorists.
215. See Peyer, *Air Force Blue Ribbon Review*.
216. See Lawrence Korb, "U.S. Air Force's Indifference toward Nuclear Weapons," *Bulletin of Atomic Scientists* (Web edition), June 17, 2008, http://www.the bulletin.org/web-edition/op-eds/the-us-air-forces-indifference-toward-nuclear -weapons.

Chapter 6. Nuclear Terrorism, Deterrence, and Attribution
1. See U.S. Strategic Command, *Essentials of Post-Cold War Deterrence—1995*, http://nautilus.org/archives/nukestrat/USA/Advisory/essentials95.PDF.
2. Ibid.

3.   Ibid.
4.   Ibid.
5.   See *The National Security Strategy of the United States of America*, February 2002, 15.
6.   See *The National Strategy for Combating Terrorism*, September 2006, 14.
7.   See White House, "President Bush Visits National University of Singapore," November 16, 2006, http://www.whitehouse.gov/news/releases/2006/11 /20061116-1.html.
8.   See remarks by National Security Adviser Stephen J. Hadley, May 28, 2008. Also see Gates, "Nuclear Weapons and Deterrence in the 21st Century."
9.   See David Wood, "Analysts Say U.S. Still Lacks Attack Deterrence: 9/11 Anniversary," *Baltimore Sun*, September 11, 2008.
10. Ibid.
11. Ibid.
12. See U.S. Department of Defense, *National Defense Strategy* (Washington, DC, June 2008), 13.
13. See Wood, "Analysts Say U.S. Still Lacks Attack Deterrence." In terms of "wiping them out now," it was disclosed that since 2004 the United States has been operating under a secret executive order "to carry out nearly a dozen previously undisclosed attacks against al-Qa'ida and other militants in Syria, Pakistan, and elsewhere," according to senior military officials. See Eric Schmitt and Mark Mazzetti, "Secret Order Lets U.S. Raid al-Qa'ida in Many Countries," *New York Times*, November 10, 2008.
14. See Eric Schmitt and Thom Shanker, "U.S. Adapts Cold-War Idea to Fight Terrorists," *New York Times*, March 18, 2008.
15. Ibid.
16. See Leiter, "Looming Challenges in the War on Terror."
17. See Brad Roberts, *Deterrence and WMD Terrorism: Calibrating Its Potential Contributions to Risk Reduction* (Alexandria, VA: Institute for Defense Analyses, June 2007), ES-1.
18. See Paul K. Davis and Brian Michael Jenkins, *Deterrence and Influence in Counterterrorism: A Component in the War on al-Qa'ida* (Santa Monica, CA: RAND, 2002).
19. See Daniel Whiteneck, "Deterring Terrorists: Thoughts on a Framework," *Washington Quarterly*, Summer 2005; Roberts, *Deterrence and WMD Terrorism*; Dunn, *Can Al Qaeda Be Deterred from Using Nuclear Weapons?*; Caitlyn Talmadge, "Deterring a Nuclear 9/11," *Washington Quarterly*, Spring 2007.
20. See Shmitt and Shanker, "U.S. Adapts Cold-War Idea."
21. See Bruce Hoffman, "The Use of the Internet by Islamic Extremists," testimony prepared for the House Permanent Select Committee on Intelligence, May 4, 2006, http://www.au.af.mil/au/awc/awcgate/congress/hoffman_testimony 4may06.pdf. Hoffman stated, "To date, at least, the United States has not effectively contested the critical, virtual battleground that the Internet has become to terrorists and their sympathizers and supporters worldwide."
22. See also Jacobson, "Why Terrorists Quit." For an assessment of internal dissent within terrorist groups and how that might be exploited, see Assaf Moghadam and Brian Fishman, eds., *Self-Inflicted Wounds: Debates and Divisions within al-Qa'ida and Its Periphery*, Harmony Project, Combating Terrorism at West Point, December 16, 2010.
23. For a recent assessment of terrorist financing and recommendations to disrupt it, see Levitt and Jacobson, *The Money Trail*.

24. See Davis and Jenkins, *Deterrence and Influence in Counterterrorism*, xiv. See also Flynn, "America the Resilient."
25. See Robert L. Gallucci, "Averting Nuclear Catastrophe: Contemplating Extreme Responses to U.S. Vulnerability," *The Annals of the American Academy of Political and Social Science* 607 (September 2006).
26. See Anders Corr, "Deterrence of Nuclear Terror: A Negligence Doctrine," *Nonproliferation Review* 12, no. 1 (March 2005). See also "The Incentive Gap: Reassessing U.S. Policies to Secure Nuclear Arsenals Worldwide," *Harvard Law Review* 121 (May 2008): 1864.
27. See Graham Allison, "Nuclear Deterrence in the Age of Nuclear Terrorism," *Technology Review* 111, no. 6 (November–December 2008): 68.
28. For a less pessimistic assessment of the security of Pakistan's nuclear weapons, see Hoodbhoy, "Whither Pakistan?" Hoodbhoy states, "Pakistan's 'urban Taliban' rather than illiterate tribal fighters pose a nuclear risk. There are indeed more than a few scientists and engineers in the nuclear establishment with extreme religious views."
29. Ibid. Apocalyptic terrorist groups hope to serve as a catalyst for just such an "end of times" situation, triggering a global nuclear war that cleanses the world of what they perceive as evil.
30. See Levi, *Deterring State Sponsorship of Nuclear Terrorism*, 12–13.
31. See Gallucci, "Averting Nuclear Catastrophe."
32. Russian cooperation has, for example, been essential to implement elements of the Global Threat Reduction Initiative, including repatriating Soviet-origin HEU fuel at research reactors around the world. Such cooperation would undoubtedly be jeopardized by any U.S. military retaliation against Russia for the inadvertent leakage of fissile material to terrorist groups.
33. See Levi, *Deterring State Sponsorship of Nuclear Terrorism*, 15.
34. Dr. Carter is currently serving as the undersecretary of defense for acquisition, technology, and logistics. See Sanger and Shanker, "U.S. Debates Deterrence for Nuclear Terrorism."
35. See Perry, "Proliferation on the Peninsula." In June 2006 William Perry and Ashton Carter stated, "If North Korea persists in [long-range ballistic missile] launch preparations, the United States should immediately make clear its intention to strike and destroy the North Korean Taepodong missile before it can be launched." See Ashton B. Carter and William J. Perry, "If Necessary, Strike and Destroy," *Washington Post*, June 22, 2006. Such a launch occurred in April 2009. Neither the United States nor any other international power deemed it necessary and prudent to preemptively attack the rocket.
36. See Levi, *Deterring State Sponsorship of Nuclear Terrorism*, 16.
37. However, the May 2009 North Korean nuclear tests may have crossed a threshold in terms of regional responses. In the aftermath of the test, South Korea joined the PSI and suggested the United States reaffirm its nuclear umbrella in writing. See Kiho Yi, "The North Korean Nuclear Test: The South Korean Reaction," *Bulletin of Atomic Scientists* (Web edition), June 5, 2009, http://www.thebulletin.org/web-edition/features/the-north-korean-nuclear-test-the-south-korean-reaction. Japan also questioned whether the U.S. nuclear umbrella is enough to keep the country safe and expressed a renewed interest in ballistic missile defense. See Masako Toki, "The North Korean Nuclear Test: The Japanese Reaction," *Bulletin of Atomic Scientists* (Web edition), May 27, 2009, http://www.thebulletin.org/web-edition/features/the-north-korean-nuclear-

test-the-japanese-reaction. China rebuked North Korea but may be more reluctant than most regional parties to advocate harsh new sanctions. See Hui Zhang, "The North Korean Nuclear Test: The Chinese Reaction," *Bulletin of Atomic Scientists* (Web edition), June 2, 2009, http://www.thebulletin.org/web-edition/features/the-north-korean-nuclear-test-the-chinese-reaction.

38. See Michael May et al., *Nuclear Forensics: Role, State of the Art, and Program Needs* (Washington, DC: American Association for the Advancement of Science, 2008), http://iis-db.stanford.edu/pubs/22126/APS_AAAS_2008.pdf.
39. One challenge with respect to nuclear forensics and North Korea is that the reactor type used in North Korea, a gas-graphite 5-MW(e), is fairly common, so the signatures that result from its reactor operation may not necessarily be easily distinguishable from others.
40. May et al., *Nuclear Forensics.*
41. There are two types of signatures: (1) empirical signatures discovered through the systematic analysis of nuclear and radiological materials and (2) predictive signatures developed from modeling, based on chemistry and physics of the nuclear fuel cycle and weapons manufacture.
42. See Royal Society, *Detecting Nuclear and Radiological Materials* (London, March 2008), http://royalsociety.org/document.asp?tip=1&id=7482.
43. See Sanger and Shanker, "U.S. Debates Deterrence for Nuclear Terrorism."
44. See Dunlop and Smith, "Who Did It?" The authors also posit that "the experiences of the Cooperative Threat Reduction program . . . suggest that access to Russian nuclear weapons data will be extremely difficult to acquire."
45. See May et al., *Nuclear Forensics*, ii.
46. Some of these initiatives have been mentioned in the Nuclear Forensics and Attribution Act (H.R. 2632), which provides the "sense of the Congress that the President should pursue bilateral and multilateral agreements to establish . . . an international framework for determining the source of any confiscated nuclear or radiological material or weapon . . . ; develop protocols for the data exchange and dissemination of sensitive information relating to nuclear or radiological materials and samples." This legislation was passed by the House of Representatives in the 110th Congress but was not taken up by the Senate. During the 111th Congress, H.R. 730 was passed into law, becoming Public Law 111-140 as signed by President Barack Obama on February 16, 2010. The legislation establishes, among other measures, a National Technical Nuclear Forensics Center within the DHS's Domestic Nuclear Detection Office and a National Nuclear Forensics Expertise Development Program. The law authorizes that the secretary (of DHS) ". . . may enter into a contractual relationship with an institution of higher education under which the amounts provided for a scholarship . . . for tuition, fees, and other authorized expenses are paid directly to the institution. . . ."
47. See Biden, "CSI Nukes."
48. Ibid.
49. See Dunlop and Smith, "Who Did It?"
50. Ibid.
51. See May et al., *Nuclear Forensics.*
52. Ibid.

Chapter 7. U.S. and International Strategies and Initiatives to Prevent Nuclear Terrorism
1. See statement from Dr. Matthew Bunn, coprincipal investigator, Project on Managing the Atom, Harvard University, before the Commission on the Prevention

of Weapons of Mass Destruction Proliferation and Terrorism, New York City, September 10, 2008.

2. Many of the nuclear terrorism initiatives in which the United States is involved are international—some were proposed bilaterally by the United States and Russia (such as the Global Initiative to Combat Nuclear Terrorism)—and were designed to involve the international community.

3. See Defense Science Board, *Report of the Defense Science Board Task Force*, 33.

4. Levi, *On Nuclear Terrorism*, 143.

5. *National Strategy to Combat Weapons of Mass Destruction*, December 2002, 2. In April 2011, the White House submitted legislation to Congress to ratify an amendment to the Convention on the Physical Protection of Nuclear Material and the International Convention for the Suppression of Acts of Nuclear Terrorism. The goal of the legislation is to update U.S. Criminal Code to strengthen the ability to investigate and prosecute acts of nuclear terrorism.

6. At the G-20 Summit hosted by the United Kingdom in April 2009, President Barack Obama and President Dmitri A. Medvedev provided in a joint statement: "We also support international negotiations for a verifiable treaty to end the production of fissile materials for nuclear weapons." In late May 2009 the United Nations Conference on Disarmament approved a working group to negotiate a treaty banning the production of fissile material for nuclear weapons. See Walter Pincus, "UN Hopes to Ban New Fissionable Material, Space-Based Weapons," *Washington Post*, June 2, 2009.

7. See remarks by National Security Adviser Stephen J. Hadley, May 28, 2008.

8. Ibid.

9. Ibid., 3. Preemptive attacks rely on infallible or nearly infallible intelligence. One of the most important foreign policy issues the Obama administration faces is the potential for Iran to develop nuclear weapons. As President Obama has stated that a nuclear-armed Iran is "unacceptable," does that commit the administration to a preemptive military strike against Iranian nuclear facilities should diplomacy fail? And given that Iran learned from Israel's preemptive strikes against Iraq (Osiraq reactor in 1981) and Syria (Al Kibar reactor in 2007), questions have to be asked about how effective a bombing campaign would be against a potentially hardened, underground, and dispersed Iranian nuclear program. If Israel preemptively bombed Iranian nuclear facilities, would Iran react as passively as Syria did in 2007? For contrasting assessments of the wisdom of preemptively attacking Iran's nuclear complex, see Bolton, "Time for an Israeli Strike?"; and Thielmann, "Preventive Military Action." As has been proven, there are measures beyond kinetic attacks that can delay a nuclear program, such as sanctions (openly engaged in) and cyber attacks (sometimes overt, sometimes covert). For an assessment of the latter, see Broad, Markoff, and Sanger, "Israeli Test on Worm."

10. For a history and compelling explanation of NEST functions, see Jeffrey T. Richelson, *Defusing Armageddon: Inside NEST, America's Secret Nuclear Bomb Squad* (New York: Norton, 2009). See also Mahlon E. Gates, "The Nuclear Emergence Response Team," in Leventhal and Alexander, *Preventing Nuclear Terrorism*.

11. See Joint Technical Operations Team, U.S. Department of Energy, National Nuclear Security Administration, http://www.nnsa.energy.gov/emergency_ops/1716.htm.

12. See Ashton B. Carter, Michael May, and William J. Perry, "The Day After: Action Following a Nuclear Blast in a U.S. City," *Washington Quarterly*, Autumn 2007.

13. See "Consequence Management Response Force to Join Army Northern Command," U.S. Army News Service, September 15, 2008.

14. See Spencer S. Hsu and Ann Scott Tyson, "Pentagon to Detail Troops to Bolster Domestic Security," *Washington Post*, December 1, 2008.

15. Ibid.

16. When it might be appropriate to shut down a clandestine nuclear weapons procurement network is an open question. Oftentimes, from an intelligence perspective, once a new node of a network (or a new hub) is discovered, it might be appropriate not to shut it down immediately as there may be valuable intelligence to collect about the group's activities and members. However, like intelligence collected against a terrorist cell, if the group is about to go operational and its activities are irreversible and consequential, it is prudent to stop the activity before operational activity commences. Given vagaries of intelligence, it may not necessarily be clear when the group is about to go operational, and thus the decision to shut it down can be highly subjective.

17. *National Strategy to Combat Weapons of Mass Destruction*, December 2002, 6.

18. See statement of Rolf Mowatt-Larssen before the Homeland Security and Governmental Affairs Committee, U.S. Senate, April 2, 2008.

19. See Commission on the Intelligence Capabilities of the United States Regarding Weapons of Mass Destruction, "Report to the President." See also *Report on the U.S. Intelligence Community's Prewar Intelligence Assessments of Iraq*, July 7, 2004. For an overview of the intelligence discipline, see Mark Lowenthal, *Intelligence: From Secrets to Policy* (Washington, DC: CQ Press, 2005).

20. For more information on intelligence analysis maladies, see Commission on the Intelligence Capabilities of the United States Regarding Weapons of Mass Destruction, "Report to the President," chapter 8.

21. See Levi, *On Nuclear Terrorism*, 144.

22. Ibid.

23. See *National Strategy to Combat Weapons of Mass Destruction*, December 2002, 6.

24. See Ashton B. Carter and Robert G. Joseph, "Strengthening Our Strategy against WMD," *Boston Globe*, August 14, 2008. See also Curtis, "Preventing Nuclear Terrorism."

25. See 9/11 Public Discourse Project, *Report on the Status of 9/11 Commission Recommendations, Part III: Foreign Policy, Public Diplomacy and Nonproliferation*, November 14, 2005. The 9/11 Commission said, in part, "Our report shows that al-Qa'ida has tried to acquire or make weapons of mass destruction for at least the last ten years. There is no doubt the United States would be a prime target. Preventing the proliferation of these weapons warrants a maximum effort— by strengthening counterproliferation efforts, expanding the Proliferation Security Initiative, and supporting the Cooperative Threat Reduction Program." See *The Final Report of the National Commission on Terrorist Attacks upon the United States*, July 2004, 381. Cochairmen of the 9/11 Commission Thomas Kean and Lee Hamilton advised the Obama administration in transition, in the form of a *Washington Post* op-ed, "The highest priority for the Obama presidency must be securing nuclear weapons and materials to prevent them from falling into dangerous hands. . . . If terrorists cannot gain access to weapons-grade material, they cannot build a nuclear device. Achieving this goal will require close cooperation and trade-offs with not only Russia but dozens of countries, but we can imagine no threat more dire." See Thomas H. Kean and Lee H. Hamilton, "Job One:

First Things First, Mr. President-elect—Some Thoughts on What Obama's Top Priority Should Be," *Washington Post*, November 9, 2008.

26. For more recent information on this topic, see Luongo, "Loose Nukes in New Neighborhoods."

27. See Brian. D. Finlay, *Nuclear Terrorism: U.S. Policies to Reduce the Threat of Nuclear Terror* (Washington, DC: Partnership for a Secure America, September 2008), http://www.psaonline.org/downloads/NUCLEAR%20report%208-28-08.pdf.

28. See GAO, *Nuclear Nonproliferation*, December 2010. See also GAO, *Combating Nuclear Smuggling: Efforts to Deploy Radiation Detection Equipment in the United States and in Other Countries*, GAO-05-840T (Washington, DC, June 21, 2005). See also Defense Science Board, *Report of the Defense Science Board Task Force*; and Defense Science Board, *Protecting the Homeland: Report of the Defense Science Board 2000 Summer Study, Executive Summary, Volume I* (Washington, DC: Department of Defense, February 2001).

29. See *World at Risk*, 82.

30. See Finlay, *Nuclear Terrorism*.

31. See Public Law 110-53, Title XVIII, Subtitle D, Section 1814(b)(3), codified at 50 U.S.C. 2931.

32. See Public Law 110-53, Title XVIII, Subtitle D.

33. See Executive Office of the President, Office of Management and Budget, Statement of Administration Policy, "H.R. 1—Implementing the 9/11 Commission Recommendations Act of 2007," January 9, 2007.

34. *World at Risk*, 85.

35. Ibid.

36. Remarks and questions and answers by the director of the National Counterterrorism Center, Mr. Michael E. Leiter, American Bar Association—Standing Committee on Law and National Security, Washington, DC, May 6, 2009.

37. "Gary Samore: WMD Czar," *Foreign Policy: The Cable*, January 23, 2009, http://thecable.foreignpolicy.com/posts/2009/01/23/gary_samore_wmd_czar.

38. Public Law 108-458, Title I. Available at http://www.gpoaccess.gov/serialset/creports/pdf/108-796/titlei_reform_intel.pdf.

39. The Commission on the Intelligence Capabilities of the United States Regarding Weapons of Mass Destruction, "Report to the President," 328.

40. Bunn and Newman, *Preventing Nuclear Terrorism*, 8. With respect to alignment of strategy and resources, see Cindy Williams and Gordon Adams, *Strengthening Statecraft and Security: Reforming U.S. Planning and Resource Allocation* (Cambridge, MA: MIT Security Studies Program, June 2008), 45–56. For a breakdown of U.S. nuclear security spending, see Stephen I. Schwartz and Deepti Choubey, *Nuclear Security Spending: Assessing Costs, Examining Priorities* (Washington, DC: Carnegie Endowment for International Peace, January 2009). According to Schwartz and Choubey, appropriations for nuclear threat reduction in FY 2008 amounted to $5.165 billion, or approximately 10 percent of the total U.S. nuclear weapons–related appropriations (excluding classified programs).

41. See *World at Risk*, 89.

42. See Friedrich Steinhausler, "Legal Instruments to Prevent Nuclear WMD Use by Non-State Actors," *Strategic Insights*, December 2008.

43. North Korea is a signatory of the NPT but subsequently withdrew from the treaty on January 10, 2003. It tested a nuclear device in October 2006 and again in May 2009.

44. See IAEA, *Treaty on the Non-Proliferation of Nuclear Weapons*, Article I.

45. Ibid., Article II.
46. Ibid., Article VI.
47. Ibid., Article IV.
48. See Mohamed ElBaradei, "Intervention on Non-Proliferation Issues," statement at IAEA Board of Governors, June 15, 2009.
49. Ibid.
50. Ibid.
51. Iran signed an Additional Protocol in 2003 yet ceased adherence to it in September 2005. The United States has signed an Additional Protocol to its existing safeguards agreement with the IAEA. The protocol has been in force since January 6, 2009.
52. See remarks by President Barack Obama, April 5, 2009.
53. See United Nations Security Council Resolution 1540 (2004), http://daccessdds.un.org/doc/UNDOC/GEN/N04/328/43/PDF/N0432843.pdf?Open Element.
54. See United Nations Security Council, *Report of the Committee Established Pursuant to Security Council Resolution 1540 (2004)*, S/2008/493, http://daccessdds.un.org/doc/UNDOC/GEN/N08/409/78/PDF/N0840978.pdf?Open Element.
55. See Steinhausler, "Legal Instruments to Prevent Nuclear WMD Use."
56. See IAEA, *The Physical Protection of Nuclear Material and Facilities*, INFCIRC/225/Rev. 4 (Corrected), http://www.iaea.org/Publications/Documents/Infcircs/1999/infcirc225r4c/rev4_content.html.
57. See David M. Fidler, "International Convention on the Suppression of Acts of Nuclear Terrorism Enters into Force," *American Society of International Law Insights* 11, no. 18 (July 5, 2007).
58. See Joint Statement by George Bush and Vladimir Putin on the Global Initiative to Combat Terrorism, July 16, 2006.
59. See Steinhausler, "Legal Instruments to Prevent Nuclear WMD Use."
60. For a list of these nations, see Nuclear Suppliers Group, http://www.nuclearsuppliersgroup.org/member.htm.
61. See GAO, *Nonproliferation: U.S. Efforts to Combat Nuclear Networks Need Better Data on Proliferation Risks and Program Results*, GAO-08-21 (Washington, DC, October 2007), 9.
62. These lists are compiled in IAEA, INFCIRC/254, Part 1, and INFCIRC/254, Part 2. Available at http://www.nuclearsuppliersgroup.org/Leng/05-pubblic.htm.
63. See GAO, *Nonproliferation*, 10.
64. This list is published by the IAEA in INFCIRC/209, as amended, which could be located at http://www.zanggercommittee.org/Zangger/Publications/default.htm.

Chapter 8. Concluding Thoughts
1. Remarks by the Honorable Michael E. Leiter, April 9, 2009.
2. See STRATFOR Global Intelligence, ."Debunking Myths about Nuclear Weapons and Terrorism."
3. For updated assessments on this progress, see *The Nunn-Lugar Scorecard*, available at http://lugar.senate.gov/nunnlugar/scorecard.html. See also White House, *Fact Sheet: Defending against Weapons of Mass Destruction Terrorism*, December 2008, http://www.whitehouse.gov/news/releases/2008/12/20081203-4.html#; and U.S. Department of Energy, National Nuclear Security Administra-

tion, *NNSA: Working to Prevent Nuclear Terrorism* (Washington, DC, December 2008), http://www.nnsa.energy.gov/news/982.htm.

4. See Bunn and Newman, *Preventing Nuclear Terrorism*. See also Newman and Bunn, *Funding for U.S. Efforts.*

Appendix A. U.S. Policy Options to Counter Nuclear Terrorism

1. See Congressional Commission on the Strategic Posture of the United States (facilitated by the U.S. Institute of Peace), *America's Strategic Posture: The Final Report,* Washington, DC, 2009, http://www.usip.org/strategic-posture-commission/view-the-report.

2. See George Perkovich, *Abolishing Nuclear Weapons: Why the United States Should Lead* (Washington, DC: Carnegie Endowment for International Peace, October 2008).

3. George P. Shultz, William J. Perry, Henry A. Kissinger, and Sam Nunn, "Toward a Nuclear-Free World," *Wall Street Journal,* January 15, 2008.

4. Ibid. Other international groups, including Global Zero, an organization set to initiate an effort to rid the world of nuclear weapons within twenty-five years, are strong advocates for global nuclear disarmament. According to some arms control advocates, Global Zero's approach differs from past attempts to get to zero; it is encouraging direct talks between global leaders and it is not advocating what past efforts have—a step-by-step approach that some argue is too slow. See "Statesmen to Promote Global Nuclear Disarmament," *Global Security News-wire,* December 8, 2008, http://gsn.nti.org/gsn/nw_20081208_6843.php. See also Philip Taubman, "Learning Not to Love the Bomb," *New York Times,* February 19, 2009.

5. Shultz et al., "Toward a Nuclear-Free World."

6. See Gates, "Nuclear Weapons and Deterrence in the 21st Century."

7. See Bob Graham et al., "Executive Summary, Letter of Transmittal," in *World at Risk.*

8. See Secretary of Energy Advisory Board, *A Report Card.* See also Bob Graham et al., "Review of Implementation of the Baker-Cutler Report," in *World at Risk,* 113–21.

9. See Bunn and Newman, *Preventing Nuclear Terrorism.*

10. The United Kingdom has maintained, however, that some of its strategic Trident missiles had a "sub-strategic" mission. See Kristensen, "Russian Tactical Nuclear Weapons."

11. See U.S. Department of Defense, *Report of the Secretary of Defense Task Force on DOD Nuclear Weapons Management, Phase II: Review of the DOD Nuclear Mission* (Washington, DC, December 2008), v.

12. See Bob Graham et al., "The Role of the Citizen," in *World at Risk,* 108.

13. Ibid., 109.

14. For an assessment of the technical ability to monitor nuclear explosions, see Paul G. Richards and Won-Young Kim, "Monitoring Nuclear Explosions," *Scientific American,* March 2009, 70–77. The authors conclude, "Detecting a test of a nuclear weapon has become so effective and reliable that no nation could expect to get away with secretly exploding a device having military significance."

15. For an explanation of some of these reasons, see Jonathan Medalia, "Comprehensive Nuclear-Test Ban Treaty: Background and Current Developments," CRS Report for Congress (Washington, DC, May 28, 2008), http://www.carnegieendowment.org/static/npp/reports/RL33548.pdf.

16. At the G-20 Summit hosted by the United Kingdom in April 2009, President Barack Obama and President Dmitri A. Medvedev provided in a joint statement: "As a key measure of nonproliferation and disarmament, we underscored the importance of the entering into force of the Comprehensive Nuclear Test Ban Treaty." These commitments were also made in the U.S.-Russian Summit held in Moscow, Russia, in July 2009.

17. See Elaine M. Grossman, "Strategic Posture Panel Reveals Split over Nuclear Test Pact Ratification," *Global Security Newswire*, May 7, 2009. The commission to which the article refers is the Congressional Commission on the Strategic Posture of the United States, chaired by former secretary of defense William Perry. Dr. Perry reportedly stated, "I do support ratifying the CTBT. I think that the national security interests of the United States are best served by ratifying it. . . . About half of [the commission's] members disagree with ratification of the CTBT."

18. See Gates, "Nuclear Weapons and Deterrence in the 21st Century."

19. See Graham et al., "The Role of the Citizen," 84.

20. Ibid. The commission recommended, "The next Congress should amend Public Law 110-53 to eliminate the requirement to establish an Office of the United States Coordinator for Prevention of Weapons of Mass Destruction Proliferation and Terrorism, while retaining the mandate to appoint a senior presidential advisor with the responsibilities of the Coordinator."

21. The U.S.-North Korean and U.S.-Iranian relationships are no less important but are perhaps better addressed multilaterally.

22. See "A Nightmare We Cannot Afford in the 21st Century," an interview with former CIA case officer Bruce Riedel, *Der Spiegel*, December 8, 2008, http://www.spiegel.de/international/world/0,1518,595148,00.html.

23. For a summary of strategic arms control options, see Amy Woolf, specialist in nuclear weapons policy, "Strategic Arms Control After START: Issues and Options," CRS Report for Congress (Washington, DC, April 3, 2009). Three recent unclassified studies have addressed the United States' strategic posture, including (1) the Congressional Commission on the Strategic Posture of the United States, *America's Strategic Posture*; (2) the Council on Foreign Relations, *U.S. Nuclear Weapons Policy*, April 2009, http://www.cfr.org/publication/19226/; and (3) the Federation of American Scientists and the Natural Resources Defense Council, *From Counterforce to Minimal Deterrence: A New Nuclear Policy on the Path Toward Eliminating Nuclear Weapons*, Occasional Paper no. 7, April 2009, www.fas.org/programs/ssp/nukes/doctrine/targeting.pdf.

24. See Helene Cooper and Peter Baker, "Seeking New Start, U.S. and Russia Press New Arms Talks," *New York Times*, April 1, 2009. See also remarks by President Barack Obama, April 5, 2009.

25. See White House, *The Joint Understanding for the START Follow-on Treaty*.

26. See Federation of American Scientists, Natural Resources Defense Council, and Union of Concerned Scientists, *Toward True Security: Ten Steps the Next President Should Take to Transform U.S. Nuclear Weapons Policy* (Cambridge, MA, February 2008), 5.

27. See testimony of former U.S. senator Sam Nunn before the Commission on the Prevention of Weapons of Mass Destruction Proliferation and Terrorism, New York City, September 10, 2008.

28. See U.S. Enrichment Corporation (USEC) Megatons to Megawatts Program, www.usec.com/megatonstomegawatts.htm. By comparison, the United States

declared 198 metric tons of weapons-grade material as excess to its military needs and has disposed of approximately 50 metric tons. See IPFM, *Global Fissile Material Report, 2007.*

29. See Bunn, *Securing the Bomb 2010.* See also, GAO, *Nuclear Nonproliferation,* December 2010.

30. Financially, Bunn and Newman of Harvard University have advocated that President Obama "seek an appropriation in the range of $500 million, to be available until expended, that can be spent flexibly on high-priority actions to reduce the risk of nuclear theft." See Bunn and Newman, *Preventing Nuclear Terrorism,* 12. For a 2009 update, see Andrew Newman and Matthew Bunn, *Funding for U.S. Efforts to Improve Controls over Nuclear Weapons, Materials, and Expertise Overseas.*

31. This commission, cochaired by former U.S. vice president Albert Gore and former Russian prime minister Viktor Chernomyrdin, was created by President Clinton and President Yeltsin after their April 1993 summit meeting in Vancouver. The commission's original mandate was to support cooperation in the areas of space, energy, and high technology. The commission's mandate expanded its scope to include four additional areas of U.S.-Russian cooperation: business development, defense conversion, the environment, and health.

32. See Allison, "Nuclear Deterrence in the Age of Nuclear Terrorism," 68.

33. Ibid.

34. Ibid.

35. Ibid.

36. Ibid.

37. See G. John Ikenberry and Anne-Marie Slaughter, *Forging a World of Liberty under Law: U.S. National Security in the 21st Century* (Princeton, NJ: Princeton University, September 27, 2006). See also George Perkovich et al., *Universal Compliance: A Strategy for Nuclear Security* (Washington, DC: Carnegie Endowment for International Peace, June 2007). See also Allison, *Nuclear Terrorism.*

38. For the thirteen steps, see Arms Control Association, *2000 NPT Review Conference Final Document* (Washington, DC, June 2000), http://www.armscontrol.org/act/2000_06/docjun.

39. See Lawrence Scheinman, "Disarmament: Have the Five Nuclear Powers Done Enough?," *Arms Control Today,* January–February 2005, http://www.armscontrol.org/act/2005_01-02/Scheinman.

40. See White House, http://www.whitehouse.gov/search/?keywords=nuclear%20security.

41. See Nuclear Threat Initiative, "World Institute for Nuclear Security (WINS) Is Launched in Vienna; New Organization Will Strengthen Security for Nuclear Materials" (Washington, DC, September 29, 2008). The organization has the support of the IAEA and will work closely with it in Vienna.

42. See Royal Society, *Detecting Nuclear and Radiological Materials.* See also May et al., *Nuclear Forensics.*

43. See United Nations Security Council Resolution 1540 (2004), http://www.un.org/Docs/sc/ unsc_resolutions04.html.

44. See statement of IAEA director general Mohamed ElBaradei, October 28, 2008.

45. See ElBaradei, "Putting Teeth in the Nuclear Non-Proliferation and Disarmament Regime."

46. See statement of IAEA director general Mohamed ElBaradei, October 28, 2008.

47. The United Nations Conference on Disarmament voted in May 2009 to begin negotiations on a Fissile Material Cutoff Treaty. The original United Nations

General Assembly consensus resolution calling for the negotiation of such a treaty was passed in December 1993. In March 1995 the Conference on Disarmament established an ad hoc committee with a mandate to negotiate such a treaty. See Nuclear Threat Initiative, *Fissile Material Cut-off Treaty*, http://www.nti.org /db/china/fmctorg.htm.

48. See IPFM, *Global Fissile Material Report, 2008: Scope and Verification of a Fissile Material (Cutoff) Treaty*, www.fissilematerials.org.
49. Albright and Brannan, *Update on Khushab Plutonium Reactor.*
50. For information on this proposed treaty, see IPFM, *Global Fissile Material Report, 2008.*
51. See remarks by President Barack Obama, April 5, 2009.

Appendix B. Core U.S. Government Nuclear Terrorism Programs and Initiatives

1. It is recognized that this depiction only contains a limited set of the U.S. government's programs, initiatives, and organizations working on nuclear terrorism. As documented throughout this book, the U.S. Intelligence Community—specifically the National Counterterrorism Center, the National Counterproliferation Center, and mission managers for Iran and North Korea, to mention a few—has an important role to play in the prevention of nuclear terrorism. Moreover, the White House established the position of coordinator for arms control and weapons of mass destruction, proliferation, and terrorism to serve as the focal point for U.S. initiatives in this area. Nonproliferation professional Gary Samore has assumed this position, located within the NSC, in the Obama administration.

Appendix C. Summary of Core U.S. Government Programs to Prevent Nuclear Terrorism

1. See Woolf, "Nonproliferation and Threat Reduction Assistance."
2. See Kenneth Luongo, "Deconstructing U.S. Funding for Nuclear Materials Security," *Bulletin of Atomic Scientists*, April 8, 2010.
3. See U.S. Department of State, "The Global Initiative to Combat Nuclear Terrorism," http://www.state.gov/t/isn/c18406.htm.
4. For the National Nuclear Security Administration's program descriptions, see http://nnsa.energy.gov/aboutus/ourprograms/nonproliferation. For the global map of defense nuclear security programs, see http://nnsa.energy.gov/sites /default/files/nnsa/inlinefiles/DNN_Nonproliferation_Global_Map_0710.pdf.
5. For FY 2009, the Defense Nuclear Nonproliferation budget request of the Department of Energy is $1.247 billion, of which $430 million (35 percent of the total) is for international material protection, control, and accounting. A total of $220 million (18 percent of the total) is requested for the Global Threat Reduction Initiative. See U.S. Department of Energy, *FY 2009 Congressional Budget Request, National Nuclear Security Administration* (Washington, DC, February 2008).
6. See Wisconsin Project on Nuclear Arms Control, "Theft of Nuclear Material."
7. See speech by William Tobey, deputy administrator of the NNSA, to the U.S. Industry Coalition Annual Meeting, March 7, 2007.
8. See U.S. Department of Energy, National Nuclear Security Administration, Office of Global Threat Reduction, *Strategic Plan: Reducing Nuclear and Radiological Threats Worldwide* (Washington, DC, January 2007), 7.

Epilogue

1. See Scott Stewart, "Bin Laden's Death and the Implications for Jihadism," STRATFOR Global Intelligence, May 3, 2011, http://www.stratfor.com/weekly /20110502-bin-ladens-death-and-implications-jihadism.

SELECTED BIBLIOGRAPHY

Ackerman, Gary, and Jeremy Tamsett, eds. *Jihadists and Weapons of Mass Destruction.* Boca Raton, FL: CRC Press, 2009.

Allison, Graham, ed. *Confronting the Specter of Nuclear Terrorism.* Thousand Oaks, CA: Sage, 2006.

———. *Nuclear Terrorism: The Ultimate Preventable Catastrophe.* New York: Times Books, 2004.

Alvarez, Luis A. *Adventures of a Physicist.* New York: Basic Books, 1987.

Benjamin, Daniel, and Steven Simon. *The Age of Sacred Terror.* New York: Random House, 2002.

Bergen, Peter. *The Osama bin Laden I Know.* New York: The Free Press, 2006.

Bobbitt, Philip. *Terror and Consent: The Wars for the Twenty-First Century.* New York: Alfred A. Knopf, 2008.

Bostrom, Nick, and Milan M. Cirkovic. *Global Catastrophic Risks.* Oxford: Oxford University Press, 2008.

Bunn, Matthew. *Securing the Bomb 2007.* Cambridge, MA, and Washington, DC: Project on Managing the Atom, Harvard University, and Nuclear Threat Initiative, September 2007.

———. *Securing the Bomb 2008.* Cambridge, MA, and Washington, DC: Project on Managing the Atom, Harvard University, and Nuclear Threat Initiative, November 2008.

———. *Securing the Bomb 2010: Securing All Nuclear Materials in Four Years.* Cambridge, MA, and Washington, DC: Project on Managing the Atom, Harvard University, and Nuclear Threat Initiative, April 2010.

Byman, Daniel. *The Five Front War: The Better Way to Fight Global Jihad.* Hoboken, NJ: John Wiley and Sons, 2008.

Cirincione, Joseph. *Bomb Scare: The History and Future of Nuclear Weapons.* New York: Columbia University Press, 2007.

Clarke, Richard A. *Against All Enemies: Inside America's War on Terror.* New York: The Free Press, 2004.

————, ed. *Defeating the Jihadists: A Blueprint for Action.* New York: The Century Foundation, 2004.

————. *Your Government Failed You: Breaking the Cycle of National Security Disasters.* New York: Harper, 2008.

Cook, David. *Contemporary Muslim Apocalyptic Literature.* Syracuse, NY: Syracuse University Press, 2005.

David, Steven R. *Catastrophic Consequences: Civil Wars and American Interests.* Baltimore, MD: Johns Hopkins University Press, 2008.

Falkenrath, Richard A., Robert D. Newman, and Bradley A. Thayer. *America's Achilles' Heel: Nuclear, Biological, and Chemical Terrorism and Covert Attack.* Cambridge, MA: MIT Press, 1998.

Ferguson, Charles D., and William C. Potter. *The Four Faces of Nuclear Terrorism.* With Amy Sands, Leonard Spector, and Fred Wehling. New York: Routledge, 2005.

Frost, Robin M. *Nuclear Terrorism after 9/11.* London: Routledge, 2005.

Gunaratna, Rohan. *Inside Al Qaeda: Global Network of Terror.* New York: Columbia University Press, 2002.

Hoffman, Bruce. *Inside Terrorism.* Rev. ed. New York: Columbia University Press, 2006.

Howard, Russell D., and James J. F. Forest. *Weapons of Mass Destruction and Terrorism.* New York: McGraw-Hill, 2008.

Jenkins, Brian Michael. *Will Terrorists Go Nuclear?* Amherst, NY: Prometheus Books, 2008.

Langewiesche, William. *The Atomic Bazaar: The Rise of the Nuclear Poor.* New York: Farrar, Straus and Giroux, 2007.

Laqueur, Walter. *The New Terrorism: Fanaticism and the Arms of Mass Destruction.* Oxford: Oxford University Press, 1999.

Larsen, Randall J. *Our Own Worst Enemy: Asking the Right Questions about Security to Protect You, Your Family, and America.* New York: Grand Central Publishing, 2007.

Lee, Rensselaer W., III. *Smuggling Armageddon: The Nuclear Black Market in the Former Soviet Union and Europe.* New York: St. Martin's, 1998.

Leventhal, Paul, and Yonah Alexander, eds. *Nuclear Terrorism: Defining the Threat.* Washington, DC: Pergamon-Brassey's, 1986.

————. *Preventing Nuclear Terrorism.* Washington, DC: Lexington Books, 1987.

Levi, Michael. *Deterring State Sponsorship of Nuclear Terrorism.* Special Report 39. New York: Council on Foreign Relations, 2008.

————. *On Nuclear Terrorism.* Cambridge, MA: Harvard University Press, 2007.

Levy, Adrian, and Catherine Scott-Clark. *Deception: Pakistan, the United States, and the Secret Trade in Nuclear Weapons.* New York: Walker Publishing, 2007.

Litwak, Robert S. *Regime Change: U.S. Strategy through the Prism of 9/11.* Washington, DC: Woodrow Wilson Center Press and Johns Hopkins University Press, 2007.

————. *Rogue States and U.S. Foreign Policy: Containment after the Cold War.* Washington, DC: Woodrow Wilson Center Press and Johns Hopkins University Press, 2000.

McPhee, John A. *The Curve of Binding Energy.* New York: Farrar, Straus and Giroux, 1973.

Mueller, John. *Overblown: How Politicians and the Terrorism Industry Inflate National Security Threats, and Why We Believe Them*. New York: The Free Press, 2006.

National Research Council, Committee on Science and Technology for Countering Terrorism. *Making the Nation Safer: The Role of Science and Technology in Countering Terrorism*. Washington, DC: National Academies Press, 2002.

Perkovich, George, et al. *Universal Compliance: A Strategy for Nuclear Security*. Washington, DC: Carnegie Endowment for International Peace, 2007.

Post, Jerrold M. *The Mind of the Terrorist: The Psychology of Terrorism from the IRA to Al-Qaeda*. New York: MacMillan, 2007.

Richelson, Jeffrey T. *Defusing Armageddon: Inside NEST, America's Secret Nuclear Bomb Squad*. New York: Norton, 2009.

Sagan, Scott D., and Kenneth N. Waltz. *The Spread of Nuclear Weapons: A Debate Renewed*. New York: Norton, 2003.

Sageman, Mark. *Leaderless Jihad: Terror Networks in the Twenty-First Century*. Philadelphia: University of Pennsylvania Press, 2008.

Scheuer, Michael. *Through Our Enemy's Eyes: Osama bin Laden, Radical Islam, and the Future of America*. Washington, DC: Potomac Books, 2006.

Serber, Robert. *The Los Alamos Primer: The First Lectures on How to Build an Atomic Bomb*. Berkeley: University of California Press, 1992.

Stern, Jessica. *Terror in the Name of God: Why Religious Militants Kill*. New York: Harper Collins, 2003.

Taleb, Nassim Nicholas. *The Black Swan: The Impact of the Highly Improbable*. New York: Random House, 2007.

Tenet, George, and Bill Harlow. *At the Center of the Storm: My Years at the CIA*. New York: HarperCollins, 2007.

Weissman, Steve, and Herbert Krosney. *The Islamic Bomb: The Nuclear Threat to Israel and the Middle East*. New York: Times Books, 1981.

Williams, Paul L. *The Al Qaeda Connection: International Terrorism, Organized Crime, and the Coming Apocalypse*. Amherst, NY: Prometheus Books, 2005.

Younger, Stephen M. *Endangered Species: How We Can Avoid Mass Destruction and Build a Lasting Peace*. New York: Harper, 2007.

INDEX

Note: Page numbers followed by *f* or *t* indicate figures or tables. Page numbers followed by n or nn indicate notes.